D1606507

PERSUASION

SAGE ANNUAL REVIEWS OF COMMUNICATION RESEARCH

Other Books in this Series:

Volume 8

SAGE ANNUAL REVIEWS OF COMMUNICATION RESEARCH

Persuasion:
New Directions
in
Theory and Research

MICHAEL E. ROLOFF

and

GERALD R. MILLER

Editors

SAGE Publications   Beverly Hills   London

For information address:

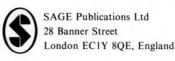

SAGE Publications, Inc.
275 South Beverly Drive
Beverly Hills, California 90212

SAGE Publications Ltd
28 Banner Street
London EC1Y 8QE, England

Printed in the United States of America

Library of Congress Cataloging in Publication Data
Main entry under title:

Persuasion: new directions in theory and research.

  (Sage annual reviews of communication research ; v. 8)
  Includes bibliographies.
  1. Persuasion. I. Roloff, Michael E. II. Miller,
Gerald R.
BF637.P4P43   153.8'52   79-21202
ISBN 0-8039-1213-7
ISBN 0-8039-1214-5 pbk.

FIRST PRINTING

079779

CONTENTS

FOREWORD

Michael E. Roloff and Gerald R. Miller

A COMMON NOTION about the genesis of any academic endeavor is that ideas burst forth from the heads of scholars after extended contemplation about issues. Generally, such intense concentration is thought to take place in staid environments such as libraries and doctoral seminars. The origins of this project add a new twist to this notion. Sometimes ideas have their beginnings in unplanned exchanges at such raucous, casual events as cocktail parties!

The first editor happened to be engaged in conversation with a visiting professor who serves on the editorial boards of several communication journals. After the mandatory gossip about mutual acquaintances, the conversation turned to current research. The discussion was lively until Roloff mentioned the results of a recently completed "persuasion study," at which point the visitor evinced a marked decrease in interest. This impression was confirmed when the visitor said, "You may have some difficulty finding a publishing outlet. Reviewers are not responding well to 'persuasion studies' anymore." Because of the festive nature of the occasion, depression arising from the comment was momentary. Still, the comment prompted an investigation. After examining recent volumes of communication journals and talking to colleagues, a consensus emerged: for some reason(s), the number of "persuasion studies" published in the 1970s has declined.

At this point, we began to speculate on the causes of this apparent dearth of interest in "persuasion research." Miller had coauthored an article suggesting some factors which may have led to the present state of affairs (Miller and Burgoon, 1978). We felt the factors accurately assessed the problem but did not constitute sufficient justification for reduced interest. To us, diminished interest in persuasion seemed lamentable for three reasons.

First, persuasion remains a critical process for our entire society. An examination of current events establishes persuasion as a vital human activity: (1) an American president is attempting to persuade citizens that they will no longer be able to use energy in the way they have become accustomed; (2) oil companies are attempting to persuade the American public that their profits are not excessive; and (3) the OPEC nations are hiring a public relations firm to persuade the peoples of the world that OPEC is not the cause of oil shortages. On this issue alone various groups are expending a great deal of money and, ironically, energy in persuasion.

Second, persuasion remains an important area for study. While some communication researchers may have become disenchanted with the area, most programs continue to teach persuasion both in a variety of other courses as well as a separate course itself. Enrollment in these courses remains high, attesting to the interest of many students in the persuasion process.

Third, persuasion seems to underlie many of the other research areas in communication. You may have noticed the quotation marks enclosing the phrases "persuasion studies" and "persuasion research." As Miller and Burgoon (1978) have noted, these terms bring to mind a restricted research area, one that typically involves the attempt of one person to change the attitudes of many people in an experimental setting. While this description accurately portrays much activity commonly labeled "persuasion research," it ignores the fact that persuasion is involved in other topic areas as well. Certainly, research concerning bargaining and negotiation, advertising, and family interaction to name just a few is concerned with the ways people influence each other. This is true despite the fact that it is not usually included under the label "persuasion research."

Instead of academic hand-wringing, we chose to create a volume to represent continuing communicative and psychological interest in persuasion and to suggest new directions for persuasion research.

The book can be divided into two broad sections: conceptual issues and contextual issues. The first six chapters represent issues in persuasion that transcend situations. Miller provides conceptual distinctions which describe the behavioral outcomes of persuasion, thus providing a framework for examining persuasive effects on overt behavior instead of attitudes alone.

Roloff also seeks to expand theory and research on persuasion. Just as Miller's chapter is concerned with probing the behavioral effects of persuasion, Roloff advocates moving more vigorously into areas of human behavior where the persuader and persuadee are not self-aware.

Whereas Roloff provides insight into the factors affecting self-awareness in the persuasion process, Perloff and Brock deal with the cognitive responses that occur during persuasive transactions. Their chapter provides important insights into factors that influence counterarguing against persuasive messages as well as cognitive factors that may enhance the persistence of persuasion.

Cronkhite and Liska examine one of the traditional areas of persuasion research: reactions to the source of a persuasive message. Moving beyond traditional conceptualizations of source credibility, they provide a model relying on attribution processes to predict reactions to persuasive sources.

Burgoon and Bettinghaus describe several message factors known to influence the persuasion process. They include analyses of new approaches to persuasive effects and source selection of persuasive messages.

The last conceptual chapter deals with a largely ignored but important area of persuasive effects: nonmessage factors that facilitate persuasion. Bostrom reviews studies dealing with the influence of a variety of drugs and the presence of others on stimulation of the central nervous system and subsequent effects on persuasion.

While the first six chapters consider general models that apply to persuasion in numerous situations, the last five examine persuasion as it functions in specific contexts. Littlejohn (1978) has underscored the importance of contextual analyses of communication. In terms of persuasion, the contextual approach emphasizes the necessity of adapting general principles to specific situations. Indeed, theoretical diversity across various contexts is readily apparent.

Bettinghaus (1973) has argued that our understanding of persuasion would be enhanced by examining interactive persuasive situations, for attempts to persuade are usually reciprocal. The first two contextual chapters deal with contexts characterized by mutual influence attempts.

Berger examines persuasion as it operates in family interaction. Within the family context, social exchange principles become important as individuals barter for relational rewards than others has important implications for the study of power within the family.

Tedeschi and Rosenfeld also focus on reciprocal influence. Their analysis of bargaining stresses the importance of communicating information, both as a facilitator and inhibitor of bargaining outcomes.

Fontes and Bundens examine one of the more complex contexts in which persuasion occurs, the legal setting. The audiences to be influenced change at various points in the legal process and the tactics are modified to adapt to these individual audiences.

Chestnut reviews a recent theoretical formulation describing persuasion aimed at consumers. His analysis includes both cognitive and noncognitive factors that influence consumer decisions.

Atkin considers the role of persuasion in the political process. His discussion of persuasion in the mass setting focuses on voter behavior and how it is influenced by the media. Atkin suggests various theoretical models that should be used to examine important facets of political persuasion.

The reader will quickly note the diversity of the article found in this volume. This diversity of content reflects the diversity of the phenomenon under scrutiny. The volume draws its strength from the differing theories of persuasion and the differing contexts in which persuasion occurs.

Contributors to a volume such as this one are often placed in a conflict situation. On the one hand, they hope their efforts adequately describe the extant state of persuasion theory and research; on the other, they hope the volume will spur increased interest in the area so that the research described will become incomplete. We believe the chapters in this volume comprise thorough and heuristic analyses of current work in persuasion. Their strength will ultimately be measured by the time it takes to move beyond them.

REFERENCES

BETTINGHAUS, E.P. (1973). Persuasive communication. 2nd edition. New York: Holt, Rinehart and Winston.

LITTLEJOHN, S. (1978). Theories of human communication. Columbus: Charles Merrill.

MILLER, G.R. and BURGOON M. (1978). "Persuasion research: Review and commentary." In B.D. Ruben (ed.), Communication yearbook 2. New Brunswick, N.J.: Transaction Books, 29-48.

Chapter 1

ON BEING PERSUADED
Some Basic Distinctions

Gerald R. Miller

A VOLUME DEALING with the process of persuasion should profit from a tentative answer to the question: What does it mean to be *persuaded*? The well-advised qualifier "tentative" underscores two limitations of the analysis offered in this chapter. First, as with most complex definitional issues, the author has no illusions that his answer will satisfy every reader—or, for that matter, any reader. After all, a lively debate has raged for centuries over the defining characteristics of the term "persuasion," and it would be the heighth of naiveté or arrogance to assume that this brief analysis will lay to rest all outstanding definitional controversies. Second, at a more modest level, this chapter certainly does not address all the questions raised in succeeding chapters of this volume. The authors of these chapters have attacked numerous theoretical and applied issues of persuasion from various vantage points; to subsume all the nuances of their remarks about the persuasive process is a formidable, if not impossible, task far exceeding the capabilities of this writer.

Notwithstanding these disclaimers, this chapter can assist readers in making sense out of many of the issues explored later by providing a general frame of reference for viewing the process of persuasion. Stated differently, the chapter seeks to establish broad definitional boundaries for

arase "being persuaded." Furthermore, in the process of staking out
e boundaries, certain persistent issues will inevitably be identified,
issues that heavily influence some of the positions taken in other chapters.
Thus, this chapter anticipates rather than resolves subsequent scholarly
debates.

BEING PERSUADED: THE CENTRAL ELEMENTS

Persuasive attempts fall short of blatant coercion: persuasion, as typically conceived of, is not *directly* coercive. Coercion takes the form of guns
or economic sanctions, while persuasion relies on the power of verbal and
nonverbal symbols. Frequently, of course, coercive acts are preceded by
persuasive messages; seldom is a child's allowance suspended or an armed
attack launched on a neighboring state without a period of message
exchanges. These messages are aimed at persuading the child to study
harder at school or at persuading the neighboring state to relinquish claim
to a parcel of disputed territory. If persuasion proves inadequate to the
task at hand, economic or military force may be employed to achieve the
desired compliance.

From these examples, it follows that much persuasive discourse is
indirectly coercive; that is, the persuasive effectiveness of messages often
depends heavily on the credibility of threats and promises proffered by the
communicator. If the child perceives that the threatening parent is, for
some reason or another, unlikely to suspend the child's allowance, the
parent's persuasive messages will have minimum impact on the child's
study habits. Similarly, threats of armed attacks by nations with powerful
defense establishments usually cause potential adversaries to take persuasive appeals quite seriously, while the same threats uttered by countries of
limited military might are likely to be greeted with scorn or amusement.
One can only speculate how the ensuing 1962 scenario might have differed
had the government of Haiti, rather than the United States, called on the
Soviet Union to dismantle its missiles in Cuba under threat of naval
blockade and possible attack on the missile sites themselves.

Some students of persuasion have found it distasteful to ponder the
indirectly coercive dimension of many persuasive exchanges, perhaps
because the notion of *means control*—Kelman's (1961) term for describing
a situation where the influence agent, or persuader, is successful because of
his or her ability to dispense rewards or punishments—conflicts with the
way persuasion ought to function in a democratic society. Simons
(1974:174-175) captures the crux of this ideological opposition well:

Although persuasion is often characterized as a weak sister in relation to its relatives within the influence family—note such expressions as "talk is cheap," "talk rather than substance," and "mere rhetoric"—it is nevertheless regarded by many as a more ethical method of influencing others. One generally shuns the coercive label like the plague, takes pains to deny that he is bribing others when he offers them inducements, and represents himself as a persuader—if possible, as someone using "rational persuasion." Persuasion is especially valued as an instrument of democracy. . . . Officials of government proudly proclaim that ours is indeed a system run by persuasion. . . . Inducements and constraints are said to have no place in ideally democratic forms of government; they are the coinage of the realm of corrupt governments or of totalitarian regimes.

Simons goes on to argue convincingly that in the rough-and-tumble world of everyday social conflict, as distinct from the polite confines of drawing-room controversy, coercive potential determines the relative impact of most persuasive messages.

The prevalence of indirectly coercive elements in many persuasive transactions can also be detected by examining the symbolic weapons readily available to would-be persuaders. Marwell and Schmitt (1967) have generated a list of 16 strategies which can be used to gain compliance from others. Several of these strategies—among them *promise, threat,* or *aversive stimulation*—clearly derive their effectiveness from the persuader's ability to dispense rewards or mete out punishments to the intended persuadee(s). More subtlely dependent upon coercive pressure are strategies stressing the harmful social consequences of failure to comply with message recommendations, as well as strategies underscoring the social rewards resulting from compliance—such as *moral appeal, altruism, esteem positive,* or *esteem negative.* To be sure, many people would hesitate to equate blackballing with blackjacking. Nevertheless, in a society where the pervasive importance of "being respected," "being popular," and "being 'in'" extends to matters so trivial as the name tag one sports on a pair of denim jeans, it would be a mistake to underestimate the coercive potential of social approval and disapproval, a fact readily grasped by those who create the country's daily diet of media advertisements and commercials.

The preceding discussion has alluded to a second defining characteristic of the phrase "being persuaded": persuasion relies upon symbolic transactions. Though a Mafia hireling in a Hollywood production may remark menacingly, "It looks like you need a little persuading," as he starts to work over a stubborn merchant who has refused to purchase mob protection, the scholarly endeavors of persuasion researchers—and, for that matter, the ordinary language usages of the term "persuasion"—have consistently centered on the manipulation of symbols. In the domain of verbal utterances, this distinction fosters little ambiguity, since language is inherently symbolic. When Chairman Brezhnev recently appealed for Senate ratification of the SALT II treaty by linking its adoption with "divine" approval, most observers probably would have agreed that he was embarked on a persuasive campaign, albeit one employing symbolic weapons not usually found in communist arsenals. In the nonverbal realm, however, the distinction does not emerge as crisply, and there is often room for disagreement as to whether a particular nonverbal act is or is not symbolic. When Chairman Khruschev banged his shoe on a U.N. table during his 1959 visit to the United States, some observers might have interpreted his behavior as symbolic and reflecting persuasive intent, but others might have interpreted it as nothing more than a manifestation of poor manners by an uncouth visitor. Granted, the latter interpretation also involved a symbolic inference, but not one directly linked to conscious persuasive intent.

In view of the ambiguous status of some nonverbal behaviors, the utility of restricting the term "persuasion" to symbolic transactions may seem questionable. Unfortunately, the conceptual alternative is even more troublesome, for it would permit any act which sought to modify another's behavior to qualify as an instance of persuasion. Rather than falling prey to the unmanageable generality fostered by such definitional permissiveness and allowing the persuasive process to be conceived of so broadly that it embraces almost every instance of social behavior, it seems wiser to struggle with occasional uncertainty. In most instances, language is an integral aspect of the persuasive transaction, with nonverbal behavior coming into play as an instrument for reinforcing the meaning and/or credibility of verbal messages. Since the goal of this chapter is to identify the central definitional elements of the phrase "being persuaded" rather than to fix its precise outer boundaries, imposition of a symbolic criterion is consistent with the prevailing theoretical and empirical concerns of persuasion scholars.

Upon agreeing that individuals are persuaded by symbolic means, the question can be raised as to whether certain types of symbolic strategies should be viewed as typifying the persuasion process, with others being exempted. More specifically, some writers (such as Rowell, 1932a, 1932b; Woolbert, 1917) have explored the wisdom of distinguishing between convincing and persuading—the so-called *conviction/persuasion duality*. This duality holds that persuasion relies primarily on symbolic strategies which trigger the emotions of intended persuadees, while conviction is accomplished primarily by using strategies rooted in logical proof and which appeal to persuadees' reason and intellect. Stated in evaluative terms, conviction derives its force from people's rationality, while persuasion caters to their irrationality.

While this distinction has unquestionably influenced some of the research carried out by contemporary persuasion researchers—for example, studies comparing the relative persuasiveness of logical and emotional appeals, such as those conducted by Hartmann (1936), Matthews, (1947), and Weiss (1960)—its utility seems dubious at best. Attempts to crisply conceptualize and operationalize distinctions between logical and emotional appeals have been fraught with difficulty (Becker, 1963). As a result of prior learning, almost all ordinary language is laden with emotional overtones. Even the appeal to "be logical" itself carries strong normative force; indeed, Bettinghaus (1973:157-158) found that messages containing cues stressing the importance of logical thought were highly persuasive even though the arguments presented were themselves illogical. Faced with these considerations, it seems more useful to conceive of persuasive discourse as an amalgam of logic and emotion, while at the same time granting that particular messages may differ in the relative amount of each element. Furthermore, the motivation for distinguishing between conviction and persuasion rests largely on value concerns for the way influence ought to be accomplished: influence resulting from rational, reasoned messages is ethically preferable to influence resulting from appeals to the emotions—appeals that in the eyes of some writers (for example, Diggs, 1964; Nilsen, 1966) "short circuit" the reasoning processes. Though questions regarding the relative moral acceptability of various means and ends of persuasion are of vital import to all citizens of a democratic society (including persuasion researchers), conceptual distinctions that make for sound ethical analysis may sometimes make for unsound scientific practice. The conviction/persuasion duality strikes the author as such a conceptual animal. People are seldom, if ever, persuaded by "pure" logic or "pure" emotion; indeed, as the previous comments suggest, it is doubtful that these "pure" cases exist in humanity's workaday persuasive commerce.

Thus, the phrase "being persuaded" applies to *situations where behavior has been modified by symbolic transactions (messages) which are sometimes, but not always, linked with coercive force (indirectly coercive) and which appeal to the reason and emotions of the person(s) being persuaded.* This definition still suffers from lack of specificity concerning the kinds of behavioral modification that can result from persuasive communication. Let us next turn our attention to this problem.

BEING PERSUADED: THREE BEHAVIORAL OUTCOMES

In popular parlance, "being persuaded" is equated with instances of behavioral conversion; that is, individuals are persuaded when they have been induced to abandon one set of behaviors and to adopt another. Thus, the assertion, "I am going to try to persuade Gerry to quit smoking," translates into the following situation: (1) Gerry is presently engaged in smoking behaviors; and, (2) I want to induce him to stop these behaviors and begin to perform nonsmoking behaviors. On the surface, the phrase "nonsmoking behaviors" may seem nonsensical, but as any reformed smoker will attest, the transition from smoking to not smoking involves acquisition of a whole new set of behavioral alternatives ranging from substituting gum or mints for cigarettes to sitting in the nonsmoking rather than the smoking sections of restaurants. Indeed, the success of attempts to persuade people to stop smoking may often hinge on inducing them to adopt certain of these new behaviors.

Despite the tendency to equate persuasion with behavioral conversion, it seems useful to distinguish between three different behavioral outcomes commonly served by the persuasion process. Though some overlapping must be granted (the three outcomes are not always mutually exclusive) the utility of the distinction rests on the fact that the outcome sought sometimes affects the relative importance of variables contained in the persuasive equation, as well as the probable ease or difficulty with which persuaders may hope to accomplish their goals.

BEING PERSUADED AS A RESPONSE-SHAPING PROCESS

Frequently, individuals possess no clearly established pattern of responses to specific environmental stimuli. In such instances, persuasion takes the form of shaping and conditioning particular response patterns to these stimuli. Such persuasive undertakings are particularly relevant when dealing with persons who have limited prior learning histories, or with situations where radically new and novel stimuli have been introduced into the environment.

Though it may be fallacious to assert that the mind of a small child is a *tabula rasa*, it is indisputable that children initially lack a response repertory for dealing with most social, political, economic, and ethical matters. Much of what is commonly referred to as *socialization* consists of persuading the child to respond consistently (shaping responses) to stimuli associated with these matters. Thus, at a relatively early age the child can be observed responding as a "good" Catholic (Lutheran, Presbyterian, Unitarian-Universalist, atheist, etc.) should respond, expressing rudimentary opinions about political candidates or programs, and manifesting a relatively consistent code of conduct and ethics in dealing with others. In these instances, parents, teachers, ministers, peers, and others collectively shape and condition the responses the child performs.

It should be emphasized that all instances of response-shaping are not commonly thought of as instances of being persuaded. This distinction, while admittedly nebulous and slippery, implies that persuasion is a species of the genus commonly labeled *learning*. For instance, it would sound strange to speak of children *being persuaded* to tie their shoes correctly; typically, we assert that they have *learned* to tie their shoes. On the other hand, should children refuse to attempt shoe-tieing behaviors, rebel against feeding themselves, and neglect to pick up clothing or toys, they are likely to be bombarded with messages by parents and teachers aimed at shaping these behaviors. If such messages produce the desired effect, the communicators are likely to claim they have persuaded the children to become more self-reliant or independent; if not, they will probably lament the failure of their persuasive mission and devise other strategies for coping with the problem. In short, the behaviors associated with "being persuaded" are usually directly linked with more abstract attitudes and values which are prized by society or some significant segment of it; or as Doob (1947) phrases it, responses considered socially significant by the individual's society.

As indicated earlier, response-shaping is not limited to small children. When the first nuclear device exploded over Hiroshima in 1945, humanity witnessed the advent of a radically new energy source whose effects were so awesome they could scarcely be compared with anything preceding them. Before that August day, no one, save perhaps a few sophisticated physicists and technologists, had acquired patterns of responding to such concepts as *nuclear warfare* or *nuclear power,* since these concepts were literally unheard of by most persons. That considerable response-shaping has occurred in the interim from 1945 to 1980 is attested to by the currently raging controversy regarding the wisdom of developing nuclear power sources: members of the Clamshell Alliance have been persuaded that the dangers of nuclear power far outweigh its potential benefits, while officials of the Nuclear Regulatory Agency have been convinced that the contributions of nuclear energy can be realized without serious attendant risks for humankind.

It must be granted, of course, that such instances of response-shaping are often confounded by elements of people's prior learning histories. While citizens of 1945 had acquired no established patterns of responding to the concept *nuclear warfare,* most of them had developed response repertoires vis-à-vis the concept *warfare.* For those who already viewed warfare as ethically and politically irresponsible, nuclear weapons were yet a further argument for the abolition of armed conflict, a powerful new persuasive weapon in their pacific arsenal. Conversely, those who sought to defend the continued utility of war as an instrument of national policy were forced to reevaluate their strategic doctrines; post-World War II *Realpolitik,* as embodied in the messages of spokespersons like Henry Kissinger, spawned doctrinal concepts such as *limited war* and *strategic deterrence.* (As an aside, these concepts have not seemed to carry the same persuasive force as earlier ones: people who were motivated to enthusiastic efforts by the battle cry for "unconditional surrender" in World War II grew quickly disenchanted with the "limited war/limited objectives" rhetoric of the Korean and Vietnam conflicts.)

In the case of the concept *nuclear power,* the confounding influences of prior learning, while more subtle, are nevertheless present. Arguing for greater concern with values rather than attitudes in studying persuasion, Rokeach (1968, 1973) has contended that

> a person has as many values as he has learned beliefs concerning desirable modes of conduct and end-states of existence, and as many attitudes as direct or indirect encounters he has had with specific objects and situations. It is thus estimated that values number in the dozens, whereas attitudes number in the thousands [1973: 18].

Applying Rokeach's contention to this example, it follows that while individuals may have no established response patterns for the stimulus "nuclear power"—to use his terminology, they may have no present attitude about the issue—they are likely to have well-developed response repertories for such terminal values (Rokeach, 1973) as *family security* and *a comfortable life.* Inevitably, messages seeking to persuade these persons to adopt a particular response stance regarding nuclear power will be linked to these values. Thus, an anti-nuclear power spokesperson may assert, "The existence of nuclear power plants, such as Three Mile Island, poses a threat to the safety of your family," while an advocate of increased development of nuclear power facilities may contend, "Only by expanded use of nuclear power can you hope to retain the many comforts and conveniences you now enjoy." In both cases, success in shaping the responses of the intended persuadee hinges upon the linkage of these responses to strongly held values; that is, the public will be persuaded to the extent it perceives that maintenance of an important value, or values, mandates adoption of a particular set of responses regarding the issue of nuclear power.

In spite of the limitations and complications outlined above, it remains useful to conceive of response-shaping and conditioning as one behavioral

manifestation of "being persuaded." Traditionally, the persuasion literature has characterized this process as "attitude formation," reserving the
term "attitude change" for attempts to replace one set of established
behaviors with another. From a pragmatic vantage point, messages seeking
to shape and condition responses may have a higher likelihood of success
than communications aiming at converting established behavioral patterns;
in addition, the two goals may imply the use of differing persuasive
strategies. Moreover, from a scientific perspective, the two outcomes may
suggest different theoretical and empirical literatures; for example, learning theories thus far have been most frequently and profitably employed
in the arena of response-shaping and conditioning. Thus, for persuasive
practitioner and researcher alike, the distinction possesses potential utility.

BEING PERSUADED AS A RESPONSE-REINFORCING PROCESS

> Rather than aiming at changes in attitudes and behaviors, much
> persuasive communication seeks to reinforce currently held convic-
> tions and to make them more resistant to change. Most Sunday
> sermons serve this function, as do keynote speeches at political
> conventions and presidential addresses at meetings of scholarly soci-
> eties. In such cases, emphasis is on making the persuadees more
> devout Methodists, more active Democrats, or more committed
> psychologists, not on converting them to Unitarianism, the Socialist
> Workers Party, or romance languages [Miller and Burgoon, 1973:5].

The position espoused in the preceding quotation is certainly not
earth-shaking, even though the popular tendency to view persuasion as a
tool for bringing about conversion may cause people to overlook, or
shortchange, this important behavioral outcome. The response-reinforcing
function underscores the fact that "being persuaded" is seldom, if ever, a
one-message proposition; instead, people are constantly *in the process of*
being persuaded. If an individual clings to an attitude (and the behaviors
associated with it) more strongly after exposure to a communication, then
persuasion has occurred as surely as if the individual had shifted from one
set of responses to another. Moreover, those beliefs and behaviors most
resistant to change are likely to be grounded in a long history of con-
firming messages, along with other positive reinforcers. One current theory
of attitude formation and change holds that the strength of people's
attitudes depends entirely on the number of incoming messages about the
attitude issue they have processed (Saltiel and Woelfel, 1975).

There are strong grounds for believing that much persuasive communication in our society serves a response-reinforcing function. Although
students of persuasion disagree about the extent to which the selective

exposure principle (Festinger, 1957) dictates message choices (Freedman and Sears, 1965; Sears and Freedman, 1967), few, if any, would question people's affinity for supportive information (McGuire, 1969). Such an affinity, in turn, suggests that under conditions of voluntary exposure, the majority of individuals' persuasive transactions will involve messages that reinforce their existing response repertories. This possibility is further supported by early mass media research documenting the reinforcement function served by the media (e.g., Katz and Lazarsfeld, 1955).

If people do, in fact, relish hearing what they already believe, it may seem that the response-reinforcing function of persuasion is so simple as to require little concern. Distortion of information is not as likely to occur, and the initial credibility of the communicator should have less impact than in cases when persuasive intent centers on response-shaping or behavioral change—though even in the case of response reinforcement the work of Osgood and his associates (Osgood and Tannenbaum, 1955; Osgood et al., 1957) indicates that extremely low credibility may inhibit persuasive impact. Logical fallacies and evidential shortcomings are likely to be overlooked, while phenomena such as counterarguing (Brandt, 1976; Festinger and Maccoby, 1964; Osterhouse and Brock, 1970) will be largely absent. Unquestionably, message recipients are set to be persuaded; hence, would-be persuaders are assured of optimal conditions for plying their communicative wares.

Nevertheless, there are at least three good reasons for not losing sight of the response-reinforcing dimension of "being persuaded." For the practicing communicator, this dimension underscores the importance of keeping old persuasive friends as well as making new ones. In the heat of a political campaign or a fund-raising drive, it may be tempting to center efforts on potential converts at the expense of ignoring those whose prevailing response tendencies already coincide with the intent of the political candidate or the fund raiser. Such a mistake can easily yield low vote counts or depleted treasuries. Turning to the interpersonal sphere, close relationships may be damaged, or even terminated, because the parties take each other for granted—in the terminology employed here, fail to send persuasive messages aimed at reinforcing mutually held positive attitudes and mutually performed positive behaviors. In short, failure to recognize that being persuaded is an ongoing process requiring periodic message attention can harm one's political aspirations, pocketbook, or romantic relationship.

The need for continued reinforcement of acquired responses also constitutes one possible explanation for the emphemerality of many persuasion research outcomes. The typical persuasion study involves a single message, presented to recipients under controlled laboratory conditions, with a measure of attitude or behavior change taken immediately afterward. On numerous occasions researchers have observed immediate changes, only to discover that they have vanished when later follow-up measures are taken. Although a number of substantive and procedural reasons can be offered for the fleeting impact of the persuasive stimulus, one obvious explanation rests in the likelihood that the behaviors engendered by the message received no further reinforcement after the recipients departed from the research setting. Thus, the response-reinforcing dimension of being persuaded has implications for the way persuasion researchers design and interpret their studies.

Perhaps most important, however, is the fact that all response reinforcing strategies and schedules are not destined to be equally effective. Research using cultural truisms (McGuire, 1964, 1969) has demonstrated the low resistance to change which results when behaviors and attitudes rest on a history of nearly 100 percent positive reinforcement; apparently, too much exclusively behavior-congruent information is not a good thing. Though studies such as those of McGuire and Burgoon and his associates (1973, 1974) have been characterized as dealing with the problem of *inducing resistance to persuasion,* the conceptualization that has been offered here views this label as a misnomer. Research dealing with the response-reinforcing function of persuasion is research on *how* to persuade, albeit in a different sense than the popular usage implies, a position that has also recently been espoused by other writers (Burgoon et al., 1978). Including response reinforcement as one of the three behavioral outcomes subsumed under the phrase "being persuaded" not only calls attention to the continued need for research concerning the workings of the reinforcing process, but it results in a tidier conceptualization than has previously existed.

BEING PERSUADED AS A RESPONSE-CHANGING PROCESS

As has been repeatedly noted, "being persuaded" is most typically thought of as a response-changing process: smokers are persuaded to become nonsmokers; automobile drivers are persuaded to walk or use public transportation; Christians are persuaded to become Moslems, and so on. Popular usage equates *being persuaded* with *being changed.* Moreover, definitions of persuasion found in most texts emphasize the notion of changing responses (Bettinghaus, 1973; Cronkhite, 1969), and even when other terms such as "modify" (Brembeck and Howell, 1952) or "influence" (Scheidel, 1967) are used, the lion's share of the text is devoted to analysis of persuasion as a response-changing process.

s view of persuasion is, of course, consistent with the ideological tenets of democratic societies. Problems of social and political change are problems of persuasion; the public must be induced to change present attitudes and behaviors to comport with the realities of new situations. The current energy crisis provides a convenient illustration of the process at work. Eschewing more coercive steps such as rationing, those charged with managing America's energy resources have bombarded the public with messages urging behavioral changes calculated to conserve these resources: dialing down thermostats, driving at slower speeds (a message buttressed by the coercive power of speeding laws), and voluntarily sharing rides—to mention but a few. Naturally, patience and faith in persuasion are not boundless (indeed, by the time this chapter appears in print, gasoline rationing may be a reality); nevertheless, the democratic ethic strongly mandates that attempts to change behavior symbolically should precede more coercive remedies.

If one departs from the realm of public policy issues to conceive also of persuasion as a process involving modification of people's relational behaviors, a step recently urged by this writer (Miller and Burgoon, 1978), the same change-centered orientation is readily apparent. For instance, the continuing popularity of Dale Carnegie-type courses rests primarily on the following claim: our instruction will motivate you to change your manner of self-presentation (that is, to alter established patterns of social behavior); this change, in turn, will cause others to change dramatically their patterns of responding to you (that is, others will be persuaded by your changed behavior to relate to you in different ways). Similarly, the popularity of Zimbardo's (1977) shyness volume and the spate of books and courses that deal with assertiveness training attest to the pervasiveness of people's attempts to alter their ongoing social behaviors and, concomitantly, to persuade others to respond differently to them. Although these processes are typically treated under such rubrics as *interpersonal communication* and *interpersonal relations,* the conceptualization outlined here argues that they should be counted as instances of the response-changing dimension of "being persuaded."

The largely unchallenged hegemony of the response-changing conception of persuasion obviates the need for further discussion. Most prior research in persuasion deals with behavioral change; at best, it treats response-shaping and response reinforcement indirectly. What remains in order to complete this analysis of the phrase "being persuaded" is a brief consideration of the way persuasive effects have typically been characterized.

WHAT IS SHAPED, REINFORCED, OR CHANGED

Although such terms as "response" and "behavior" have been employed herein to refer to the effects of persuasive communications, the concept "attitude" has also been mentioned on several occasions. Its emergence is not surprising, for concern with attitude formation and change has consistently guided the efforts of persuasion researchers ever since Allport (1935) confidently proclaimed *attitude* to be the single most important concept in social psychology. Notwithstanding widespread faith in the utility of the attitude construct, certain of its conceptual aspects pose knotty problems for students of persuasion. If "being persuaded" is to be considered synonymous with "shaping, reinforcing, and changing attitudes," these problems eventually must be resolved.

In persuasion research, an attitude is an *intervening variable*; that is, it is an internal mediator that intrudes between presentation of a particular overt stimulus and observation of a particular overt response (Fishbein and Ajzen, 1975; Triandis, 1971). Oskamp (1977:7) captures the crux of the matter, stating: "In social science, the term [attitude] has come to mean 'a posture of the mind,' rather than of the body."

Given its conceptual status, all statements about the construct *attitude* (or *attitude formation* or *attitude change*) are, of necessity, inferential; no means exist for directly observing or measuring an attitude. If someone asserts, "Roloff has a positive attitude about research," it means that the speaker has probably observed one or more of the following behaviors: Roloff proclaiming the importance of research, Roloff gathering data, Roloff writing research reports, Roloff foregoing a recreational outing to analyze data at the computer center, Roloff investing substantial sums of money in journals containing research reports, and so on. What the person has *not* observed is Roloff's *attitude* toward research; instead, his "positive attitude" is an inference (in the terminology of one currently popular theoretical position, an *attribution*) based on observation of Roloff's research-related behaviors.

Although this point is patently obvious, its implications have often escaped persuasion researchers. Nowhere has the mischief perpetrated by this oversight been more evident than in the countless pages written about the misleadingly labeled *attitude-behavior* problem (Liska, 1975). The crux of this problem lies in the minimal relationship often observed between verbal indicators of an attitude (that is, paper-and-pencil "attitude" scales) and other attitudinally related behavior. While the issue centers on lack of correlation between two behavioral measures, persuasion researchers have fallen into the trap of reifying the paper-and-pencil verbal reports traditionally used as inferential measures of the attitude construct.

Despite any rational justification for doing so, persuasion researchers have continued to equate responses to these scales with the intervening variable of attitude and to speak of other responses as behavior—hence, the roots of the so-called *attitude-behavior* problem [Miller, in press:5].

Pointing out this basic conceptual confusion in no way suggests that the minimal relationships observed between verbal attitude reports and other attitudinally related behaviors are unimportant to persuasion researchers. Since they are both convenient to administer and lend themselves to a variety of statistical operations, paper-and-pencil verbal reports have been, and are likely to continue to be, widely used to measure persuasive effects. Any useful, reasonably fully developed theory of persuasion must seek to identify the conditions that determine when verbal reports will be correlated with other types of attitudinal behavior. Still, the continuing emphasis on attitude as the primary dependent variable, along with the prevailing tendency to view verbal reports *as* attitudes, may have done more to hinder this search than to help it.

Most writers also posit that attitudes are motivational, or drive-producing (Allport, 1935; Doob, 1947; Oskamp, 1977). Whether current methods of attitude measurement tap this drive-producing dimension is open to serious question. The motivational force of an attitude stems from the strength or intensity with which it is held. Most widely used attitude scales measure only the magnitude of the attitude's deviation from zero; in other words, the degree of positiveness or negativeness respondents assign to their positions. If pressed, many persuasion researchers would probably argue that extremely deviating responses—for example, *plus three* or *minus three* responses on a seven-interval, semantic differential-type scale—reflect more strongly held attitudes than responses falling closer to the scale's midpoint. *There is no necessary relationship between the position of one's attitude about an issue and the strength with which the attitude is held: position and intensity may be viewed usefully as two relatively independent dimensions.* Undoubtedly, people frequently have middling plus three or minus three attitudes; they may, for example, say that killing harp seals is "very good" or "very bad," yet not feel strongly about the issue. Conversely, less sharply polarized viewpoints sometimes may be held with great intensity; after weighing the matter thoroughly, an individual may conclude that killing harp seals is "slightly good" or "slightly bad," and at the same time feel quite strongly about the issue. It should be noted that the drive-producing potential of the attitude is one potentially important determinant of the extent to which verbal responses will correlate with other attitudinally consistent behaviors: if a respondent consistently says that killing harp seals is "very bad," but if the issue is relatively un-involving, that person will be unlikely to engage in more demanding, higher-threshold responses (Campbell, 1963) such as giving money to naturalist organizations that oppose harp seal harvests, circulating anti-harp seal harvest petitions, or journeying to the scene of the harvest to demonstrate against it. On the other hand, if the issue is very involving and the drive-producing potential of the attitude is therefore high, these related behaviors are more likely to occur.

In some preliminary work, several of us (Miller, 1967; Peretz, 1974) have sought to index the drive-producing potential of attitudinal stimuli by measuring the vigor of the respondent's behavior (Brown, 1961). Rather than marking responses to attitudinal stimuli on paper, respondents press the appropriate button and the vigor of the button press is recorded. Since respondents experiencing high drive states are expected to behave more vigorously, the magnitude of the button press is assumed to be directly related to the attitude's intensity. Though findings have been mixed, as well as confounded with numerous technical problems encount-ered in developing the instrumentation, some encouraging results have been obtained. In one study, Michigan State University football players responded quite vigorously to highly involving items dealing with the abolition of football scholarships and the presumed academic inferiority of athletes, while at the same time responding less vigorously (yet as posi-tively or negatively) to items judged on an a priori basis to be less involving.

If using attitude as a primary behavioral indicant of "being persuaded" poses perplexing problems, what can be done to remedy the situation? One approach lies in retaining the construct while at the same time seeking to refine it and to add to its utility by building more comprehensive models of attitude change (Fishbein and Ajzen, 1975). A second pos-sibility involves replacing attitude with some other intervening construct, such as value (Rokeach, 1968, 1973). Finally, persuasion researchers can abandon their reliance on mediating processes and focus exclusively on behavioristic analyses of persuasive effects. Although this latter possibility has received limited attention, a recent controversial paper (Larson and Sanders, 1975) has questioned the utility of predispositional, mediating constructs and has suggested that the function of persuasion might be viewed more fruitfully as the appropriate alignment of *behavior* in various social situations.

Regardless of the direction a researcher's preferences may point, it remains clear that "being persuaded" is a process grounded in behavioral data. No matter if the goal is shaping, reinforcing, or changing responses, both practical and scientific success hinge on careful observation and measurement of persuasive impact. Perhaps inferences to intervening variables, such as attitudes and values, will eventually prove indispensable to theoretical success, but these constructs are not essential ingredients of the conceptual analysis of "being persuaded" that has been offered in this chapter.

REFERENCES

ALLPORT, G.W. (1935). "Attitudes." In C.M. Murchison (ed.), Handbook of social psychology. Worcester, MA: Clark University Press.

BECKER, S. L. (1963). "Research on logical and emotional proof." Southern Speech Journal, 28:198-207.

BETTINGHAUS, E.P. (1973). Persuasive communication. New York: Holt, Rinehart and Winston.

BRANDT, D.R. (1976). "Listener propensity to counterargue, distraction, and resistance to persuasion." Presented at the convention of the International Communication Association, Portland, Oregon.

BREMBECK, W.L., and HOWELL, W.A. (1952). Persuasion. Englewood Cliffs, NJ: Prentice-Hall.

BROWN, J.S. (1961). The motivation of behavior. New York: McGraw-Hill.

BURGOON, M., and CHASE, L.J. (1973). "The effects of differential linguistic patterns in messages attempting to induce resistance to persuasion." Speech Monographs, 40:1-7.

BURGOON, M., and KING, L.B. (1974). "The mediation of resistance to persuasion strategies by language variables and active-passive participation." Human Communication Research, 1:30-41.

BURGOON, M., COHEN, M., MILLER, M.D., and MONTGOMERY, C.L. (1978). "An empirical test of a model of resistance to persuasion." Human Communication Research, 5:27-39.

CAMPBELL, D.T. (1963). "Social attitudes and other acquired behavioral dispositions." In S. Koch (ed.), Psychology: A study of a science (vol. 6). New York: McGraw-Hill.

CRONKHITE, G.L. (1969). Persuasion: Speech and behavioral change. Indianapolis: Bobbs-Merrill.

DIGGS, B.J. (1964). "Persuasion and ethics." Quarterly Journal of Speech, 50: 359-373.

DOOB, L.W. (1947). "The behavior of attitudes." Psychological Review, 54:135-156.

FESTINGER, L. (1957). A theory of cognitive dissonance. Evanston, IL: Row, Peterson.

FESTINGER, L., and MACCOBY, N. (1964). "On resistance to persuasive communications." Journal of Abnormal and Social Psychology, 68:359-366.

FISHBEIN, M., and AJZEN, I. (1975). Belief, attitude, intention and behavior: An introduction to theory and research. Reading, MA: Addison-Wesley.

FREEDMAN, J.L., and SEARS, D.O. (1965). "Selective exposure." In L. Berkowitz (ed.), Advances in experimental social psychology (vol. 2). New York: Academic Press.

HARTMANN, G.W. (1936). "A field experiment on the comparative effectiveness of 'emotional' and 'rational' political leaflets in determining election results." Journal of Abnormal and Social Psychology, 31:99-114.

KATZ, E., and LAZARSFELD, P.F. (1955). Personal influence. New York: Free Press.

KELMAN, H.C. (1961). "Processes of opinion change." Public Opinion Quarterly, 25:57-78.

LARSON, C., and SANDERS, R. (1975). "Faith, mystery, and data: An analysis of 'scientific' studies of persuasion." Quarterly Journal of Speech, 61:178-194.

LISKA, A.E. (1975). The consistency controversy: Readings on the impact of attitude on behavior. Cambridge, MA: Schenkman.

MCGUIRE, W.J. (1964). "Inducing resistance to persuasion: Some contemporary approaches." In L. Berkowitz (ed.), Advances in experimental social psychology (vol. 1). New York: Academic Press.

——— (1969). "The nature of attitudes and attitude change." In G. Lindzey and E. Aronson (eds.), Handbook of social psychology (vol. 3). Reading, MA: Addison-Wesley.

MARWELL, G., and SCHMITT, D.R. (1967). "Dimensions of compliance-gaining behavior: An empirical analysis." Sociometry, 30:350-364.

MATTHEWS, J. (1947). "The effect of loaded language on audience comprehension of speeches." Speech Monographs, 14:176-187.

MILLER, G.R. (1967). "A crucial problem in attitude research." Quarterly Journal of Speech, 53:235-240.

——— (in press). "Afterword." In D.P. Cushman and R. McPhee (eds.), Message-attitude-behavior relationship: Theory, methodology and application. New York: Academic Press.

——— and BURGOON, M. (1973). New techniques of persuasion. New York: Harper & Row.

——— (1978). "Persuasion research: Review and commentary." In B.D. Ruben (ed.), Communication yearbook 2. New Brunswick, NJ: Transaction Books.

NILSEN, T.R. (1966). Ethics of speech communication. Indianapolis: Bobbs-Merrill.

OSGOOD, C.E., and TANNENBAUM, P.H. (1955). "The principle of congruity in the prediction of attitude change." Psychological Review, 62:42-55.

OSGOOD, C.E., SUCI, G.J., and TANNENBAUM, P.H. (1957). The measurement of meaning. Urbana: University of Illinois Press.

OSKAMP, S. (1977). Attitudes and opinions. Englewood Cliffs, NJ: Prentice-Hall.

OSTERHOUSE, R.A., and BROCK, T.C. (1970). "Distraction increases yielding to propaganda by inhibiting counter-arguing." Journal of Personality and Social Psychology, 15:344-358.

PERETZ, M.D. (1974). "Studies on the measurement of attitude intensity." Unpublished masters thesis, Michigan State University.

ROKEACH, M. (1968). Beliefs, attitudes, and values. San Francisco: Jossey-Bass.

——— (1973). The nature of human values. New York: Free Press.

ROWELL, E.Z. (1932a). "Prolegomena to argumentation: Part I." Quarterly Journal of Speech, 18:1-13.

——— (1932b). "Prolegomena to argumentation: Part II." Quarterly Journal of Speech, 18:224-248.

SALTIEL, J., and WOELFEL, J. (1975). "Inertia in cognitive processes: The role of accumulated information in attitude change." Human Communication Research, 1:333-344.

SEARS, D.O., and FREEDMAN, J.L. (1967). "Selective exposure to information: A critical review." Public Opinion Quarterly, 31:194-213.

SCHEIDEL, T.M. (1967). Persuasive speaking. Glencoe, IL: Scott, Foresman.

SIMONS, H.W. (1974). "The carrot and stick as handmaidens of persuasion in conflict situations." In G.R. Miller and H.W. Simons (eds.), Perspectives on communication in social conflict. Englewood Cliffs, NJ: Prentice-Hall.

TRIANDIS, H.C. (1971). Attitude and attitude change. New York: John Wiley.

WEISS, W. (1960). "Emotional arousal and attitude change." Psychological Reports, 6:267-280.

WOOLBERT, C.H. (1917). "Conviction and persuasion: Some considerations of theory." Quarterly Journal of Speech, 3:249-264.

ZIMBARDO, P.G. (1977). Shyness: What it is and what to do about it. Reading, MA: Addison-Wesley.

Chapter 2

SELF-AWARENESS AND THE PERSUASION PROCESS
Do We Really *Know* What We're Doing?

Michael E. Roloff

It is our less conscious thoughts and our less conscious actions which mainly mould our lives and the lives of those who spring from us.

Samuel Butler

A man of action, forced into a state of thought, is unhappy until he can get out of it.

John Galsworthy

Much psychological research relies on a theoretical model that depicts the individual as one who is cognitively aware most of the time, and who consciously, constantly, and systematically applies "rules" to incoming information about the environment in order to formulate interpretations and courses of action.

Ellen Langer

The preceding quotations suggest different conceptions of the relationship between human thought and action. The first two, drawn from literature, suggest that conscious activity is relatively unimportant in determining action or is something that people attempt to avoid. The third citation,

AUTHOR'S NOTE: The author acknowledges with appreciation the assistance of Charles R. Berger for his literature review direction, Gerald R. Miller for his insightful taken from a review of consciousness in attribution processes, suggests that most psychologists consider consciousness an important part of human activity. While Langer's conclusion refers to attribution processes, it is equally applicable to persuasion.

The notions of consciousness, awareness, and thought pervade definitions of persuasion, descriptions of the persuasion process, and theories used to predict persuasive effects. In definitions of persuasion, the conscious intent of a persuader is either explicitly or implicitly assumed. For example, Bettinghaus (1973:10) defines persuasion as "a conscious attempt by one individual to change the attitudes, beliefs or the behavior of another individual or group of individuals through the transmission of some message." This representative definition indicates that persuasion is assumed to involve conscious intent on the part of the persuader to affect the receiver of a persuasive message. Indeed, one might also expect that this conscious attempt to persuade involves a selection of a strategy perceived to be most effective and the control of message and environmental variables so as to maximize the likelihood that the strategy will be effective. It is not surprising, therefore, that conceptualizations of the selection of compliance-gaining techniques or power strategies focus on the persuader's perception of the likelihood that a given strategy will provide the greatest returns (Tedeschi et al., 1972).

Not only is the persuader assumed to be consciously active in the persuasion process, but so is the receiver of a persuasive message. Bettinghaus (1973:30) writes: "Perception of a persuasive message is not a passive process. The receiver is as active in the receiving process as is the source in the transmitting process. The attitudes and beliefs of the receiver mediate the way in which the message will be received and responded to."

The theories commonly used to predict persuasive effects are even more explicit in their assumptions of the conscious activity of the receiver of a persuasive message. Tedeschi et al. (1971:685) describe the common assumptions of four consistency theories: balance, congruity, psycho-logic and cognitive dissonance. "These theories have in common the treatment of the individual as an internally active processor of information who sorts through and modifies a multitude of cognitive elements in an attempt to achieve some type of cognitive coherence."

Even theories relying on mathematical formulations of persuasion processes implicitly assume the conscious control of behavior. Fishbein and

comments on an early draft of this chapter, Mary Ralston and Irene Klotz for their ability to transform my unorthodox scrawl into a coherent typed form, and Karen M. Roloff for her stylistic revisions of the final draft. Also, Erika Britt Roloff, age 2, provided necessary diversion because she, like all of us, produces much behavior without awareness!

Ajzen (1975) argue that persons' behavioral intentions can be predicted by a weighted combination of their attitude toward a behavior and their perceptions of significant other expectations (subjective norm). In addition, the behavioral intentions are assumed to predict actual behavior under most conditions.

In providing a behavioral alternative to cognitive theories, Bem (1972) implies some degree of cognitive processing. In some cases, individuals are assumed to be aware of their own internal states, while in other situations they must consciously reflect upon external cues to determine their inner states.

While this review of a substantial body of literature is brief, the citations are representative of the trends in the study of persuasion. Both persuader and persuadee are assumed to be conscious and aware of their attitudes, beliefs, and behaviors during the persuasion process. Consequently, research and theory have attempted to model the persuasion process as though both the persuader and persuadee are rationally controlling their behavior.

It is not my purpose to discredit these approaches; these conceptualizations have provided students of persuasion with a thorough knowledge of certain aspects of the persuasion process. However, this chapter will argue that the focus on the thoughtful control of behavior only describes part of the process. Those parts of the persuasion process that are not controlled by the conscious reflection on our beliefs, attitudes, and behaviors have largely been ignored. In support of this contention, this chapter will be divided into three sections: (1) the psychology of self-awareness; (2) the role of self-awareness in source attempts to persuade; and (3) the role of self-awareness in persuasive effects. Each section will present theory and research to suggest new directions for the study of the persuation process.

THE PSYCHOLOGY OF SELF-AWARENESS

Just as the positions described in the preceding section represent a point on a continuum which suggests that people are generally aware of themselves, a contrasting position at the other end of the continuum might argue that people are not aware of themselves but are controlled by the environment, unconscious drives, or some mystical or physical entity. The position suggested here avoids either extreme by arguing that individuals vary in their degree of self-awareness and subsequently are not *always* reflective of their attitudes, beliefs, or previous behaviors prior to and during a specific action. Many psychologists suggest that differences in self-awareness may be attributed to three factors: processual differences, individual differences, and situational differences.

PROCESSUAL DIFFERENCES IN SELF-AWARENESS

Some theorists have suggested that people have only limited access to information about—and, consequently, control—of their mental activities and behaviors. Nisbett and Wilson (1977a) reviewed a number of experiments that cast doubts upon the ability of individuals to report accurately a variety of their cognitive processes. Their analysis of the literature produced three conclusions:

1. People often cannot report accurately on the effects of particular stimuli on higher order, inference-based responses. . . .

2. When reporting on the effects of stimuli, people may not interrogate a memory of the cognitive processes that operated on the stimulus. Instead, they may base their reports on implicit, apriori theories about the causal connection between stimulus and response. . . .

3. Subjective reports about higher mental processes are sometimes correct, but even the instances of correct report are not due to direct introspective awareness. Instead, they are due to the incidentally correct employment of apriori causal theories [Nisbett and Wilson, 1977a:233].

In other words, when subjects are asked about how they reached a decision or if a stimulus had an effect on their cognitive processes, their answer has less to do with their actual awareness of the process than with their judgment about whether the process might reasonably operate in a manner suggested by the question. If the description of the process provided by the individual accurately chronicles what occurred, it is primarily due to the correctness of their application of an apriori theory rather than actual awareness of the process.

Most important to persuasion, Nisbett and Wilson cite several instances (for example, Goethals and Reckman, 1973) where subjects experienced attitude changes according to questionnaire responses, but reported that no change occurred. Furthermore, subjects did not accurately recall their precommunication attitudes. Interestingly, personal correspondence from Zimbardo and Aronson to Nisbett and Wilson indicated that subjects in their dissonance experiments did not report going through cognitive experiences similar to dissonance arousal or reduction. Thus, while people in persuasion situations may change in a manner consistent with our theoretical perspectives, their self-reports about the change processes are at variance with our observations of them in the situation.

Argyle (1969, 1975) developed a model that extends the notion of self-awareness to social behavior. His social skills model assumes that a person's social behavior can be described by five elements: (1) the goals of a skilled performance; (2) the selective perception of cues; (3) central translation processes; (4) motor responses; and (5) feedback and corrective action. The first element suggests that actors have certain goals they are aware of which include changing beliefs, attitudes, and behaviors. The second element concerns individuals' monitoring of the other persons in the interactions as well as the individuals' own behaviors. Argyle argues that some behaviors, such as nonverbal communication, operate below a person's level of awareness. The third element assumes that people take whatever information they have perceived and translate it into a plan of action. The translation process may be conscious or, in some cases, may become automatic. Assuming that a plan has been formulated, Argyle suggests that overt behavior follows. These motor responses are organized into a hierarchical system in which the lower-level units are automatic and habitual while the higher levels are under cognitive control. Finally, individuals assess feedback about the success or failure of their plans and, again, individuals may not be conscious of their reaction to the feedback.

INDIVIDUAL DIFFERENCES IN SELF-AWARENESS

While there appears to be certain processes that most people are unaware of, there are individual differences that may influence our awareness of the remaining processes. Two individual difference variables have been found to influence self-awareness: self-consciousness and self-monitoring. Fenigstein et al (1975) argue that people vary in their degree of self-consciousness. Some tend to focus on thoughts, feelings, and behavior much of the time and consequently spend a great deal of time making decisions or plans concerning themselves. Other individuals tend to spend virtually no time reflecting on their own motives or how they appear to others. A 23-item scale was developed to identify people of varying degrees of self-consciousness. The responses of 452 men and women were factor analyzed with three factors emerging. The first factor, labeled *private self-conscious,* was concerned with attending to one's inner thoughts and feelings. The second factor, termed *public self-consciousness,* reflected a general awareness of the self as a social object. *Social anxiety,* the third factor, was defined by discomfort in the presence of others. Public self-consciousness was moderately correlated with private self-consciousness (.23) and social anxiety (.21). The correlation between private self-consciousness and social anxiety was negligible (.11).

Since the time of original report, a variety of factors have been related to self-consciousness. Two studies have focused on other personality characteristics that might be correlated with self-consciousness. Carver and Glass (1976) found that public self-consciousness was significantly correlated with IQ, activity level, and sociability. Social anxiety was negatively correlated with IQ, activity level, and sociability. Private self-consciousness was uncorrelated with any of the personality scales employed; however, it was significantly correlated with public self-consciousness. Turner et al. (1978) examined the relationship between self-consciousness and another set of personality characteristics across six samples. Private self-consciousness was positively correlated with scales measuring internal processes such as thoughtfulness, imagery, emotionality, and self-monitoring. Public self-consciousness was positively correlated with thoughtfulness, femininity, test anxiety, and self-monitoring while negatively correlated with masculinity. Both public and private self-consciousness were negatively correlated with self-esteem. Social anxiety was negatively correlated with social desirability, masculinity, sociability, and self-monitoring while positively correlated with femininity and emotionality. All of the subscale correlations were significant (private/public anxiety: .31; private/social anxiety: .14; public/social anxiety: .21).

Besides describing the related personality characteristics of people who are self-conscious, research has also focused on how people describe themselves and their inner states. Turner (1978b) predicted that high private self-conscious people would be more self-aware and therefore describe themselves in greater detail than low private self-conscious people. Indeed, he found that high private self-conscious individuals generated a significantly bigger list of self-descriptors than those of low private self-conscious individuals. In a similar study, Turner (1978c) found a positive correlation between social anxiety and the amount of time it took subjects to attribute socially desirable and undesirable traits to themselves. Furthermore, private self-consciousness was negatively correlated with response time only for socially undesirable traits. Scheier and Carver (1977) investigated the effect of self-consciousness and self-descriptions of emotional state. In one experiment, subjects were exposed to either positive slides (nudes) or negative slides (atrocity victims) and were asked to describe their reactions to each. As predicted, a significant self-consciousness by slide interaction was found, such that persons high in private self-consciousness were more extreme in their reactions to the slides than low private self-conscious participants. High privates evaluated the positive slides as being more pleasant and the negative slides as being more negative than low privates. In a second experiment, Scheier and Carver (1977) put subjects through a mood induction procedure which made them feel elated or depressed. High private self-conscious subjects reported feeling more elated or depressed than low private self-conscious subjects.

Not only does self-consciousness appear to be related with the ability to report internal states, it is also related to the consistency between persons' self-reports and actual behaviors. Turner and Peterson (1977) had subjects characterize their typical and maximal levels of anger and elation and sometime later enact their responses to typical or maximal anger or elation situations. As predicted, the correlations between self-reports and actual behaviors were significantly higher for low public self-conscious subjects than high public self-conscious subjects. Because of their greater awareness of self-related information, high private self-conscious subjects were expected to give more accurate self-reports than low private self-conscious subjects. However, the results were mixed; the correlations between self-report of anger and actual behavior were larger for high privates than for low privates but were in the opposite direction for elation.

In a similar analysis, Turner (1978a) investigated the correlation in an interaction between self-reports of typical and maximal dominance and actual typical and maximal dominance. As expected, higher correlations between self-report and behavior were found for high private self-conscious subjects who were also low in public self-consciousness. The lowest correlations were found for subjects who were both low in private self-consciousness and high in public self-consciousness. These individuals rarely reflected about themselves and were likely to shape their behavior to conform to the expectations of others.

Scheier et al. (1978) asked subjects to fill out a self-report of aggressiveness and several weeks later put them into an experiment in which they were to shock another person. As predicted, the correlation between self-report of aggressiveness and shocking was higher for high private self-conscious subjects than for low private self-conscious subjects.

One study focused on how self-consciousness affects a person's reactions to others. Fenigstein (1979) found that high public self-conscious individuals were significantly less attracted to a group which rejected them and were less likely to continue affiliating with that group than people low in public self-consciousness.

Turner (1977) looked at the relationship between self-consciousness and anticipatory attitude change, a study directly relevant to persuasion. Several studies have found that subjects change their attitudes in the direction of a persuader's announced position without hearing the communication itself (Hass and Mann, 1976; Cialdini et al., 1973). Turner predicted that, because of their greater concern about how they are viewed by others, high public self-conscious subjects should be more likely to change their attitude to be consistent with the persuader's prior to receiving the message. A similar argument was advanced for social anxiety. The results of the study indicated that subjects high in social anxiety were significantly more likely to change their attitudes in anticipation of receiving a persuasive message than subjects low in social anxiety. The means for public self-consciousness were in the predicted direction, although not significantly different from each other.

These findings suggest that people high in private self-consciousness may be more aware of their own beliefs, attitudes, and behaviors during the persuasion process than people low in private self-consciousness. Interestingly, people high in public self-consciousness and social anxiety may be more sensitive to the demands of others within the persuasion process. As such, they may attend more to others than to their own internal states.

A second individual difference variable that affects self-awareness is self-monitoring. Snyder (1974) described self-monitors as persons who observe and control their self-presentation and expressive behavior. He described the goals of the self-monitor as follows: (1) to communicate accurately one's true emotional state by means of an intensified expressive presentation; (2) to communicate accurately an arbitrary emotional state which need not be congruent with actual emotional experience; (3) to conceal adaptively an inappropriate emotional state and appear unresponsive and unexpressive; (4) to conceal adaptively an inappropriate emotional state and appear to be experiencing an appropriate one; and (5) to appear to be experiencing some emotion when actually experiencing nothing and a nonresponse is inappropriate. In addition, Snyder argues that high self-monitors tend to be acutely sensitive to situational cues that indicate the appropriateness of a given expression or behavior. In order to identify high and low self-monitors, a 25-item scale was developed which was found to be negatively correlated with social desirability and the MMPI Psychopathic Deviate Scale.

In the Snyder (1974) study, peers reported that high self-monitors were good at learning socially appropriate behaviors in new situations, exercising self-control of emotional expression, and effectively creating the impressions they wanted. Theatrical actors scored higher in self-monitoring than did university students. High self-monitors who were required arbitrarily to present a given emotion to judges were found to be more accurate in their presentation than low self-monitors. There was a nonsignificant tendency for high self-monitor judges to be better at judging emotions than low self-monitor judges. Finally, high self-monitors were significantly more likely to consult normative responses to attitudinal questions than low self-monitors.

Current research on self-monitoring can be categorized into three broad areas. First, some research is investigating the way in which self-monitors view themselves and others. Jones and Baumeister (1976) examined the reactions of high and low self-monitors to ingratiators. Subjects viewed a videotape of two people interacting after having been told that the behavior of one of the two had been motivated by the promise of a monetary reward if that person was able to gain the other's respect. During the interaction, the ingratiator was either agreeable with the other person in the interaction or autonomous. High self-monitors tended to have negative reactions to the individual who shaped his or her behavior in order to maximize rewards, whereas they tended to like the individual who resisted such temptation. High self-monitors felt that the individual who was motivated by money to agree was significantly less candid than the individual who was promised money but still indicated some differences of opinion. Low self-monitors tended to like a person who was agreeable regardless of motive. High self-monitors were more affected by fore-warning them of the motives of the ingratiator prior to observing the interaction. High self-monitors perceived that the naive subject in the videotaped interaction probably behaved differently than they would have in the same interaction. Interestingly, high self-monitors expected that the naive subject in the videotaped interaction probably behaved as would a low self-monitor and low self-monitors expected that the receiver would behave as would a high self-monitor. Berscheid et al. (1976) found that low self-monitors, when compared with low self-monitors, recalled more information about a person whom they anticipated dating, were more confident in rating the traits of the person, liked the person more, and rated the person more positively. Geizer et al. (1977) exposed subjects to videotapes of "To Tell the Truth" and found that high self-monitors were better able than low self-monitors to predict the participant who was truthful.

One study looked at the way self-monitors attribute responsibility to themselves. Arkin et al. (1979) found that high self-monitors tended to adjust their self-attributions according to situational cues in a manner different from low self-monitors. High self-monitors tend to attribute more personal responsibility to themselves when they have been successful than when they have been unsuccessful in a task, particularly when their behavior was likely to be examined by others. Low self-monitors tend to attribute more personal responsibility when they have failed, particularly when their behavior will not be observed by others. No significant differences were found for low self-monitors when they were examined by others regardless of success or failure. While the results for high self-monitors were explainable from their increased concern for situational cues, the results for low self-monitors are not as easily explained. The authors report that the finding may be related to the multidimensional nature of the self-monitoring scale. A factor analysis revealed a social anxiety dimension in the self-monitoring scale similar to the social anxiety dimension in the self-consciousness scale. Low self-monitors tended to agree with the items making up the social anxiety dimension. Arkin et al. argued that since low self-monitors seek to avoid attention, they avoid not only blame resulting from failure but also praise for success.

The second area of research is concerned with the expressive control of self-monitors. Lippa (1976) examined the ability of self-monitors to role-play introversion and extroversion. In general, high self-monitors were perceived as more extroverted and outgoing than low self-monitors. Across three trials, high self-monitors demonstrated larger differences in role-played introversion and extroversion than did low self-monitors. The assessed extroversion of the role-players was significantly correlated with judged extroversion. In both the introversion and extoversion trials, the correlations between assessed and judged extroversion were higher for high self-monitors than low self-monitors. Thus, even though high self-monitors tended to change their behavior to conform to the role-playing requirements to a greater extent than low self-monitors, their true level of extroversion tended to lead through to a greater extent.

Ickes and Barnes (1977) examined the communication between high and low self-monitors. Dyads composed of a high self-monitor and a low self-monitor experienced more periods of silence than did dyads composed of people similar in their level of self-monitoring. These silences produced self-reported feelings of self-consciousness, particularly for high self-monitors. High self-monitors reported feeling more self-conscious communicating with a low self-monitor than with a high self-monitor and perceived that this self-consciousness was also felt by their low self-monitor partner. Low self-monitors in the mixed dyads perceived themselves and their partners as being relatively un-self-conscious. Furthermore, self-monitoring seem to be related to sex role behavior. Because people high in self-monitoring are concerned with the social appropriateness of their behavior, they may be more inclined to behave according to sex roles. Ickes and Barnes found that high self-monitoring females used a larger total number of expressive gestures and devoted significantly more time to expressive gestures, while, on the other hand, high self-monitoring males used fewer expressive gestures and devoted less time to expressive gestures. In terms of communication styles, high self-monitors were more likely to initiate conversation and initiated a greater number of conversational sequences. Both high and low self-monitors perceived that high self-monitors had a greater need to talk. High self-monitors were perceived by low self-moni-

tors as having more directive and high self-monitors perceived both themselves and their partners as having been guided by each others' behaviors
more than low self-monitors.

Brothen (1977) examined the use of manipulative strategies by high
and low self-monitors. Subjects were asked to manipulate another's liking
for them by using adjectives that were positive or negative to describe the
other. High self-monitors were found to be more likely to use a gain/loss
strategy to create a negative affect with the other.

The third broad area of research utilizing self-monitoring is concerned
with conformity, attitude/behavior relationships, and attitude change.
Snyder and Monson (1975) examined the tendency of self-monitoring
individuals to conform to group judgments. In the first study reported,
subjects were put into a situation in which conformity pressures would
arise (risky shift). In one condition, subjects were told that their decisions
would be evaluated by an audience (public condition) and in another
condition, subjects made their decisions only in the presence of the rest of
the group (private condition). As expected, high self-monitors were significantly more likely to conform to the group opinion in the private condition than in the public condition. Also, as predicted, low self-monitors did
not vary their conformity significantly across the two conditions. In the
second study, subjects indicated how likely they would be to engage in a
variety of behaviors in hypothetical situations. As expected, high self-
monitors reported more situational variation for themselves than did low
self-monitors. Furthermore, high self-monitors reported more situational
variation for themselves than an acquaintance in a similar situation,
whereas low self-monitors reported less situational variation for themselves
than for an acquaintance.

Rarick et al. (1976) found that high self-monitors reported more
situational variation in conformity than low self-monitors. Subjects
responded to 12 hypothetical situations, seven of which were dyadic and
five which were group in nature. In each case, subjects were led to believe
that they were in the minority. As predicted, high self-monitors con-
formed more than low self-monitors in group situations, and the two did
not differ in conformity in the dyadic situations.

Snyder and Swann (1976) found that attitude toward affirmative
action was significantly correlated with verdicts in a hypothetical affirmative action suit for low self-monitors (.42) but not for high self-monitors
(.03). Snyder and Tanke (1976) report two studies examining persuasion
and self-monitoring. Subjects were placed into groups which wrote counterattitudinal essays under conditions of minimal or maximal freedom of
choice. As predicted, the effect of counterattitudinal advocacy was influenced by both choice and self-monitoring. Overall, participants assigned to

the choice condition changed their attitude more toward agreement with the essays than those in the no-choice condition; but the influence of choice was most pronounced for low self-monitors and not at all for moderate self-monitors or high self-monitors. In the second study, subjects were given greater latitude as to whether they would write a counterattitudinal or proattitudinal essay concerning affirmative action. When correlating the final self-reported attitudes with judged attitude expressed in the counterattitudinal essays, significantly greater correlations were found for low self-monitors (.65, p < .02) than for high self-monitors (-.04, n.s.). Similarly, in the proattitudinal essays, the correlation between attitude and judged essay positions was significantly greater for low self-monitors (.99 p < .001) than for high self-monitors (.73, p < .03). When examining attitude change in the counterattitudinal conditions, low self-monitors showed a greater shift in attitude than high self-monitors, although the difference was not significant. However, an examination of the percentage of low self-monitors who shifted their attitude toward the message (83.3%) was significantly greater than the same percentage of high self-monitors (45.5%).

SITUATIONAL DIFFERENCES IN SELF-AWARENESS

Instead of arguing that people differ in self-awareness based upon processual or individual differences, other theorists argue that people are differentially self-aware depending upon the situation. Indeed, Smith and Miller (1978) suggested that the conclusions reached by Nisbett and Wilson (1977a) are overstated. Instead, Smith and Miller argue that people are aware of higher order mental processes in certain situations. When persons encounter a situation that is novel or challenging, they tend to be aware of the mental processes. If a routine situation is encountered, responses may be automatic and beyond our awareness.

Duval and Wicklund (1972) argue that people are conscious of their environment but tend to focus their attention on specific aspects of their environment. Because people cannot attend to more than one set of cues at a time, they tend to fluctuate between two states: objective self-awareness and subjective self-awareness. The former state is characterized by the conscious focus of individuals on their own personal history, body, or any other personal aspect. The latter state is described as a feeling of control over and being at one with the environment. Consistent with this notion, Duval and Ritz (1971) report that subjects focusing on their image in a mirror while performing a task tended to attribute greater control of their behavior to the external environment than subjects who performed the task without the mirror being present.

Each of the states can be produced through situational factors. Duval and Wicklund suggest that as a general principle, any situation that reminds individuals of their status as objects in the world will create objective self-awareness. Research has verified predictions for behavior derived from the objective state using audio tapes (Wicklund and Duval, 1971), videotapes (Duval and Wicklund, 1972), mirrors (Buss and Scheier, 1976), the presence of others (Scheier et al., 1974), and concentrating on a sound attributed to one's heartbeat (Fenigstein and Carver, 1978). Any setting that focuses attention away from self to the external environment should create subjective self-awareness. While many of the manipulations creating subjective self-awareness have involved reducing the objective state (for example, no mirror or no audience conditions), Duval and Wicklund (1972) report creating the subjective state by having subjects concentrate on a task.

As indicated, the objective state creates a focus on self. Geller and Shaver (1975) found that subjects who concentrate on a mirror and a videotape recording of themselves took longer to describe the color of self-relevant words in the Stroop Color-Word Test. No such delay was observed for neutral words or when the subjects were not in the presence of the mirror or camera. Fenigstein and Carver (1978) obtained similar findings by having subjects focus on a sound attributed to their heartbeats.

Ickes et al. (1977) discovered that when subjects were videotaped during their responses to a "who am I" questionnaire, they tended to list more words describing self and their responses tended to be more individuated. In addition, low self-monitors made more individuated responses in the high objective state than in the low objective state; the responses of high self-monitors were unaffected by the camera.

Carver and Scheier (1978) observed that the presence of a mirror or audience tended to increase the use of self-focus sentence completions. The mirror tended to increase self-focus sentence completions moreso for low private self-conscious people than for high private self-conscious people.

Scheier and Carver (1977) found that male subjects reported they were significantly more attracted to slides of nude females when they made the reports in the presence of a mirror. Furthermore, subjects put through a mood induction procedure reported feeling significantly more elated or depressed when the procedure was conducted in the presence of a mirror.

Gibbons et al. (1979) report that people in the objective state were less influenced by a placebo effect. They tended to be more aware of their internal states and subsequently reported being less aroused by the placebo.

This self-focus also affects the attribution process. Wicklund and Duval (1971) report three experiments in which subjects attributed less self-blame for failure when engaging in a task (subjective self-awareness) than when not focusing on a task. Buss and Scheier (1976) discovered that objective self-awareness, induced through the presence of a mirror, produced a greater number of self-attributions for the outcomes of a behavior than without a mirror, although the difference was not significant. Interestingly, private self-consciousness also affected self-attribution such that high private self-conscious individuals made significantly more self-attributions than low private self-conscious individuals. Fenigstein and Carver (1978) found that subjects who concentrated on a sound allegedly produced by their own heartbeats made more self-attributions for hypothetical outcomes than did subjects exposed to the same sound but told the sound was caused by an extraneous source. Arkin and Duval (1975) report that the objective state influenced the attribution of individuals depending upon whether they were actors in a situation or merely observers. When a videotape camera was not operating, actors attributed more causality to the situation than the observers; when videotaping, actors attributed less causality to the situation than did the observers. Under conditions of a stable environment, the absence of a camera prompted actors to attribute more causality to the situation than when the camera was operating. In the same condition, the absence of a camera caused observers to attribute less causality to the situation than when the camera was present. Blanche (1975) produced a similar finding even when sensory information was limited by blindfolding subjects during the experiment. Federoff and Harvey (1976) observed that the presence of a camera produced greater self-attributions for positive outcomes of a behavior relative to negative outcomes. Furthermore, the camera produced greater attributions to another person when positive outcomes were expected but negative outcomes actually occurred.

This greater self-awareness as a result of the objective state was originally hypothesized to be threatening to the individual. Objective self-awareness was thought to increase the likelihood that individuals would become aware of discrepancies between their real and ideal selves. As a result, it was hypothesized that people would avoid the objective state. When placed into the objective state, it was predicted that persons would either attempt to remove themselves from the situation or reduce the perceived discrepancy between the real and ideal self.

Consistent with their theorizing, Duval et al. (1972) found that subjects tended to avoid objective self-awareness when they were made aware of a large discrepancy between ideal and real self. Scheier and Wicklund (cited in Wicklund, 1975b) discovered that subjects reported higher ideal self standards when in the objective state than in a lessened state of objective self-awareness. This increased ideal ranking was made even though the subject had been given a bogus lower real score by the experimenter resulting in an even larger discrepancy between ideal and real self.

However, the relationship between objective self-awareness and self-evaluation has not always been found aversive. Ickes et al. (1973) observed that subjects who listened to recordings of their own voices while filling out self-esteem items manifested lower self-esteem than subjects who listened to recordings of others' voices. However, they also found that the impact on self-esteem was strongest on the initial items and reduced with subsequent self-evaluations. In other words, the impact of objective self-awareness may be adapted to. In addition, when subjects were given positive feedback about themselves, objective self-awareness increased self-esteem. Similarly, Davis and Brock (1975) discovered that when subjects received positive feedback about themselves, the objective state resulted in an increase in the use of first person pronouns; when subjects received negative feedback there was a significant reduction in the use of first person pronouns. Gibbons and Wicklund (1976) reported that subjects who received positive feedback showed a higher preference for listening to their own voices than those receiving negative feedback. Fenigstein (1979) observed female subjects in interviews in which they received positive or negative feedback. The presence of the mirror increased the negative evaluation of the interview when negative feedback was provided and increased the positive evaluation of the interview when positive feedback was given. The kind of feedback seemed to generalize not only to a similar evaluation of self but also of the situation.

Besides feedback, other limitations have been found. Lefcourt et al. (1975) found that people believing in internal locus of control demonstrated a greater incidence of nonverbal adapters (anxiety reactions) in the objective state than those believing in external locus of control. In addition, Ferris and Wicklund (cited in Wicklund, 1975b) demonstrated that the negative impact of the objective state on the ideal-real self discrepancy can be reduced by providing a distraction which directs the focus away from self. Consequently, Wicklund (1975b) modified the theory to state that objective self-awareness will prompt self-examination and, as a result, persons may become very critical or very favorable toward themselves.

Recently, Hull and Levy (1979) suggested another reformulation of the objective state; they argue that self-criticism and self-attribution are not typical of the objective state but are by-products produced by factors in the situation. Rather, they suggest self-awareness is "a heightened sensitivity to particular forms of available information: specifically the self-relevant contingencies associated with present activity and self-definitional qualities of information feedback (p. 257)." In support of their revision, they report that people high in self-consciousness tended to recall their encoding of words moreso when they were relevant to some aspect of self. Further, objectively self-aware subjects interacting with male and female experimenters made more negative self-descriptions in the presence of a male. However, this only occurred when subjects were told that the self-descriptions would be available to the experimenters. Interestingly, females described themselves as more feminine in the presence of a male experimenter than in the presence of a female experimenter, regardless of the condition. Subjects in another experiment attributed more self-responsibility for hypothetical outcomes when objectively self-aware and they believed that others would be aware of their attributions. When they believed that their self-attributions would be anonymous, the pattern was reversed: subjects attributed more self-responsibility in the low self-aware condition than in the objective state.

The objective state has also been studied with regard to its impact on behavior. Scheier et al. (1974) report male subjects were significantly less likely to engage in physical aggression toward a woman in the presence of a mirror or an audience, but only when a significant amount of eye contact occurred between the audience and the aggressor. Carver (1974) found when female subjects were given messages indicating the appropriateness of physical aggression, the objective state significantly increased their use of physical aggression. Carver (1975) observed that subjects' attitudes toward using physical aggression were significantly related to their actual use of physical aggression only under conditions of objective self-awareness. When no mirror was present, highly punitive attitudes did not produce physical aggression in any greater frequency than low punitive attitudes. Rule et al. (1975) discovered that in the presence of a mirror subjects used physical aggression in a learning experiment to a greater extent when they were told it was helpful to learning as opposed to being told that physical aggression inhibited learning. Scheier (1976) reports subjects who had been angered tended to aggress more against their antagonist when observing their reflection in a mirror. When angered, people high in private self-consciousness aggressed more than did people low in private self-consciousness. Private self-consciousness and self-awareness did not interact.

Liebling et al. (1974) investigated the relationship between objective self-awareness and cigarette smoking. After finding people in their sample expressing a belief that they smoked more cigarettes than they felt they should, their smoking behavior was observed while listening to music either in front of a mirror or without a mirror. The results indicated that the incidence of many cigarette smoking behaviors (number of puffs, flicking and holding time) actually increased in front of the morror. It should be noted, however, that the interpretation of this study is under considerable debate (see Wicklund, 1975a; Liebling et al., 1975). It was possible that objective self-awareness was reduced by having subjects listen to the music, thereby distracting them from negative self-evaluation concerning cigarette smoking.

Pryor et al. (1977) examined the effect of objective self-awareness on the relationship between self-report and actual behavior. Subjects who completed questionnaires concerning their own sociability in front of a mirror tended to provide more accurate accounts of their sociability than those without a mirror. In a second experiment, they found that the presence of a mirror produced smaller discrepancies between reported and actual SAT scores. In a third experiment, the presence of a mirror produced a higher correlation between self-report of interest in a task and the proportion of the task finished.

Gibbons (1978) found that the presence of a mirror tended to increase the consistency between attitudes toward erotica and reactions to pictures of nudes and pornographic literature.

Wicklund and Ickes (1972) studied the effect of objective self-awareness on decision-making. Subjects in a choice situation of varying difficulty tended to request more information prior to making the choice under conditions of high objective self-awareness. Mayer et al. (1975) found that subjects shown their images on a TV monitor immediately before making a decision tended to exhibit less willingness to change their decision than did subjects not shown their image.

Diener and Wallbom (1976) report that subjects given an exam with a specific time limit were significantly more likely to cheat when their attention was focused away from self than when put into the objective state. However, Vallacher and Solodky (1979) observed that subjects placed in front of a mirror and listening to tapes of their voices tended to cheat more when performing a task in which success was due to ability rather than luck. No such effect was found when the objective state was absent.

Diener and Srull (1979) observed that objectively self-aware subjects tended to reinforce themselves in a task moreso when they surpassed a standard set by others than by themselves. When a mirror was not present, they tended to reward themselves more for surpassing their own standards rather than the standards of others.

Research has also been conducted to examine the effect of objective self-awareness on task performance. Wicklund and Duval (1971) discovered that subjects tended to increase their rate of performance in the presence of a mirror. Liebling and Shaver (1973) observed that the presence of a mirror facilitated performance only under conditions of low evaluation, but the reverse was true under conditions of high evaluation. Innes and Young (1975) obtained inconsistent findings when using both an audience and a mirror in conjunction with high and low evaluation to predict task performance. Contrary to the findings of Liebling and Shaver, the highest rate of performance was in that condition in which the subjects were under high evaluation and in the presence of a mirror. Furthermore, the worst performance occurred when both an audience and a mirror were present. Innes and Young interpreted their results as suggesting that only in the latter condition did anxiety reach the point where it was disruptive to performance. An analysis indicated this condition produced the greatest anxiety, and within this condition, anxiety was positively correlated with error rate and negatively correlated with time taken to complete the task. Brockner (1979) investigated the effects of objective self-awareness on the task performance of high and low self-esteem individuals. The presence of a mirror tended to adversely affect the task performance of low self-esteem subjects but did not affect medium or high self-esteem individuals. Brockner also found that high self-consciousness (all three subscales collapsed into one) produced more errors than low self-consciousness. High self-conscious individuals did particularly worse than low self-conscious subjects in the presence of a mirror. When examining the separate subscales of self-consciousness, high social anxiety subjects performed worse than subjects low in social anxiety. This was particularly evident when the instructions for the task prompted self-attention.

Thus, the objective state tends to make people more aware of their internal states, including discrepancies between ideal and real self, emotions, and attitudes. This state increases the accuracy of self-reports and prompts greater consistency between attitudes and behavior. Interestingly, the objective state seems to increase a person's sensitivity to feedback from others. As a result of greater self-awareness in the objective state, we might expect that the objective state would influence both the source and receiver of a persuasive message. Indeed, some limited research supports this notion.

Duval and Wicklund (1972) analyzed the notion of communication sets. They argue that individuals who are involved with presenting a communication are subjectively self-aware until they pause or contemplate their remarks. When preparing for communication, persons are objectively self-aware, but when presenting the communication, they shift to subjective self-awareness. Persons who receive a communication and anticipate sending information provided by the communication to others will be more objectively self-aware and will focus on the correctness and consistency of the material. Davis and Wicklund (1972) provided subjects with a set of internally contradictory traits about another person. Subjects were asked to write an essay about the person under three conditions: (1) writing the essay in the presence of a camera that recorded their essay writing; (2) writing the essay in anticipation of reading their essay to a small audience; and (3) writing their essay with no mention of an audience and without a camera (control group). As expected, subjects who anticipated reading their essays to an audience wrote significantly more integrated essays than subjects in the control group. The camera condition produced essays that were more integrated than the control group but the difference only approached statistical significance. The camera and anticipated delivery conditions did not differ significantly in the integrativeness of the essays. Thus, the objective state increased greater concern for the quality of the presentation.

Duval and Wicklund suggest the objective state may also influence the presentation of a communication as well as the preparation. They suggest that a behavior may become automatic as a result of practice. One might expect that a person who has communicated a message many times may be able to transmit it without as much self-awareness as when the message was initially presented. The objective state might influence the presentation of messages differentially depending upon how much practice a person has had. Wicklund (1975b:267) writes:

> At the earlier, preautomated stages of behavior, the motivational impact of objective self-awareness on performance should be positive. Later, once a sophisticated automization has taken place, the self-focused attention will serve only to interfere.

Wicklund et al. (cited in Wicklund, 1975b:256) had subjects memorize a poem; after memorization the poem was presented under conditions of high and low objective self-awareness. As expected, the objective self-aware state disrupted the presentation of the poem and decreased recall of parts of the poem.

Thus, we might expect that when persons confront a situation in which they anticipate delivering a message, they will become objectively self-aware and will put more effort into the preparation of the message. Furthermore, the objective state may facilitate or hinder the presentation of the message depending upon how well it has been learned.

From the receiver's viewpoint, the objective state should also influence reaction to persuasive messages. In conformity situations, objectively self-aware persons should become more aware of discrepancies between their judgments and the group's judgment. Wicklund and Duval (1971) gave subjects a questionnaire listing nine attitudinal items. After initially reporting their own attitudes, the subjects were given information as to the attitudes of a positive reference group or a negative reference group. Afterwards, they were asked again to indicate their attitudes. Half the subjects heard their own voices prior to receiving information about the reference groups and half did not. As predicted, those who were made objectively self-aware changed their attitudes more in the direction of the positive reference group than those who were not made objectively self-aware. The group receiving the information about a negative reference group tended to change their attitudes less when made objectively self-aware; however, this was not statistically significant. Duval (1976) reports that when subjects perceived themselves to be in the minority on a visual judgment task, they tended to conform to the opinion of others moreso when being videotaped than when no camera was present. Froming (1978) found that conformity to the judgments of a group was influenced by self-awareness, moral judgment, and type of compliance. In situations involving objective self-awareness and minimal requests of compliance, as the level of moral judgment increased conformity to group judgment increased. However, when larger requests of compliance were made and objective self-awareness was increased, moral judgment and conformity were unrelated.

Conformity to group judgments is only one area in which objective self-awareness might influence the persuasion process. Duval et al. (1975) examined the influence of objective self-awareness on self-attribution of responsibility as a result of a persuasive communication. Subjects were exposed to videotapes of their own images either four minutes before, immediately before, immediately after, or four minutes after exposure to a videotape concerning the causes of venereal disease. After the experimental manipulation, subjects filled out a questionnaire concerning the responsibility of the public and themselves for controlling venereal disease. As expected, subjects shown their image immediately before or after the presentation attributed greater responsibility to themselves than subjects in the four-minute before or after conditions. Furthermore, subjects in the immediately before or after conditions indicated a significantly greater willingness to contribute time, money, and energy to the control of venereal disease than did subjects in the four-minute before or after conditions. A replication of the study was done using the topic of poverty in Latin America. A similar tendency for subjects to attribute more responsibility to self for the control of the problem and a resultant commitment of time and money to reduce poverty in Latin America was found for subjects who filled out biographical information immediately before receiving the message than for those who filled out the biographical information four minutes before receiving the message. Similarly, Wegner and Schaefer (1978) observed that people were more likely to comply with requests for help when they were made objectively self-aware by the existence of few other potential helpers or many victims.

Another contribution to persuasion research stems from the prediction that objective self-awareness is a necessary condition for dissonance effects to occur. Since dissonance theory assumes that a person has to be aware of inconsistent cognitions or behaviors before feeling pressure, it is reasonable to assume that objectively self-aware people should be more aware of inconsistency and the resultant dissonance. Wicklund and Duval (1971) examined the influence of objective self-awareness on counterattitudinal advocacy. Half the subjects engaged in counterattitudinal advocacy while in front of an operating videotape recorder which taped their behavior for later viewing by an audience, while the other half only wrote the speeches. As expected, subjects who engaged in counterattitudinal advocacy in front of a camera changed their attitudes to conform to the communication to a greater extent than those who were not taped. In a more complex study, Insko et al. (1973) observed subjects in a counterattitudinal advocacy experiment which manipulated objective self-awareness, choice in expending effort prior to the counterattitudinal advocacy, and amount of effort expended. The greatest attitude change in the direction of the counterattitudinal message was found in two conditions: (1) camera, choice, high effort; and (2) no camera, no choice, low effort. The former cell was considered to be a dissonance cell and verified the prediction. The latter cell was termed a reinforcement condition for which no prediction was made.

Objective self-awareness has also been related to psychological reactance. Carver (1977) examined the relationship between reactions to coercive communications and objective self-awareness. In experiment 1, subjects received a high-threat communication in the presence or absence of a mirror. The results indicated that subjects who received the high-threat communication in the presence of a mirror felt that the communication was significantly more demanding than those who received the communication without the mirror. Experiment 2 concerned the relationship between attitude change and threatening communications in the presence or absence of a mirror. Significant change in the direction of the message occurred for low-threat communications only in the presence of the mirror. Significant persuasion also occurred in the high-threat/no mirror condition. In the high-threat/mirror condition, attitude change was in the direction opposite of that advocated by the message, although the change was not statistically significant. However, Swart et al. (1978) were unable to create a reactance effect in a decision-making situation. Subjects who viewed their image in a mirror tended to comply with the decision of another regardless of the threat to their decision freedom.

Thus, the theory of objective self-awareness suggests that some situations promote an examination of beliefs, attitudes, and behaviors moreso than others. Consequently, those situations which induce objective self-awareness seem to either facilitate or hinder persuasion to a greater extent than those situations which do not induce self-awareness, the critical notion being that people are not always self-aware in every situation.

Langer (1978) presents the most radical position concerning self-awareness. She argues that a great deal of human behavior is mindless in which attention is not paid precisely to those substantive elements that are relevant for the successful resolution of the situation. People who engage in mindless behavior are engaging in scripted behavior. Abelson (1976:33) defines a script as a "highly stylized sequence of typical events in a well-understood situation ... a coherent sequence of events expected by the individual involving him either as a participant or an observer." A person who had engaged in a given behavior many times develops a script for that situation such that encountering that situation in the future does not require a great deal of consciousness to carry out the behavior. Langer writes:

> Philosophers and cognitive psychologists have been concerned with the process of shifting attention from something to something else. However, it may also be the case that in many waking instances, we shift attention from something to nothing else. At those times, we process a minimal amount of information to get us through whatever activity engages us. But, by and large our "minds" are virtually at rest [1978: 40].

From her viewpoint, people find cognitive activity to be exhausting; therefore, they engage in it only when a situation requires action. Cognitive processes occur under five conditions:

1. When encountering a novel situation, for which, by definition they have no script.

2. When enacting scripted behavior becomes effortful, i.e., when significantly more of the same kind of scripted behavior is demanded by the situation than was demanded by the original script.

3. When enacting scripted behavior is interrupted by external factors that do not allow for its completion.

4. When experiencing a negative or positive consequence that is sufficiently discrepant with the consequences of prior enactments of the same behavior.

5. When the situation does not allow for sufficient involvement [Langer, 1978:55-56].

Several studies support Langer's position. Langer et al. (1978) reported three experiments in the area of mindless behavior and compliance to requests. In the first experiment, naive subjects were asked to let another person ahead of them in a line at a photocopying machine. The requests differed on the basis of how much information was provided in support of the request and the amount of photocopying to be done. Analysis of the results indicated that if persons were given a rationale, even if it provided no real information, they were likely to comply with a small request. However, if the request was large, subjects were likely to comply only if a strong rationale was provided.

In experiment 2, an attempt was made to see if people of varying status would respond differently to a request if it was congruent with their experiences with other written communications. It was assumed that congruent written communications included signed requests and unsigned demands and incongruent communications were unsigned requests and signed demands. It was expected that the more educated subjects would comply with congruent communications, whereas less educated subjects would not differ according to congruency. Requests were sent to physicians and subjects randomly selected from a telephone book which asked them to complete and return a questionnaire. Physicians were significantly more likely to return a completed questionnaire when the written communication was congruent (that is, signed requests or unsigned demands). However, the random sample did not differ across conditions of congruency and did not differ in compliance from those physicians receiving an incongruent request.

Experiment 3 examined the likelihood that people would comply with requests that were concistent with their experiences. Secretaries were sent memos requesting them to bring the memo to a room which did not exist; no rationale was presented. Some memos were signed; others were not. Half were requests; the other half were stated as demands. When the secretaries received a memo that was structured in a manner congruent with their previous history (unsigned, request), 90 percent attempted to return it. When the memo was maximally incongruent (signed, demand), 60 percent attempted to return it.

Langer suggests that in many situations people have scripts that suggest what they should do and these scripts do not require cognitive processes. Indeed, the person may respond automatically to the situation without considering the logic of the situation.

The psychology of self-awareness suggests several characteristics of human activity. Higher-order mental processes appear to be beyond the level of awareness. In some cases, changes may occur in cognitive processes without awareness that they occurred or were produced by a given stimulus. While human beings are aware of goals and plan strategies for the attainment of goals, they are not aware of lower-level segments of the strategies. They may use these lower-level behaviors to influence another without being aware they are using them. They may also be influenced by these behaviors without being aware of their influence. Furthermore, some individuals appear to be in greater control of their behavior than others. People who are high in private self-consciousness are more aware of their behavior and thoughts and can more reliably report them. Conversely, people low in private self-consciousness engage in less self-reflection and may be expected to be inaccurate in their self-reports. People high in social anxiety or public self-consciousness are more concerned about their appearance to others and may adapt more readily to the expectations of others. High self-monitors are in greater control of their behavior and tend to conform to the requirements of the situation as a result, high self-monitors may be inconsistent in applying their attitudes to their behavior and vice versa. Low self-monitors are less aware of the requirements of the situation and can be expected to reflect their attitudes in their behavior and vice versa. Finally, people are affected by the situation. Individuals who are forced to focus their attention on their own personal history, attitudes, and behavior tend to be more consistent in attitudes and behaviors. Such individuals are more likely to feel dissonance as a result of being aware of their inconsistencies. People forced to focus attention away from themselves are less concerned with the relationship between their attitudes and behaviors. Since they are less self-aware, they may overlook inconsistencies and be less sensitive to evaluative feedback from others. Some behaviors are so overlearned that they occur with little self-awareness. Only when a situation forces a person to think or expend energy might we expect the person to actively process information in order to achieve a rational behavior.

THE ROLE OF SELF-AWARENESS
IN SOURCE ATTEMPTS TO PERSUADE

Tedeschi et al. (1972) correctly point out that researchers have expended a great deal of effort studying the effects of persuasive messages on receivers but comparatively little effort studying factors that influence the persuader's decision to transmit persuasive messages. Recently, some interest in this area has emerged.

Marwell and Schmitt (1967) examined the intention to use sixteen compliance-gaining techniques. They found five factors which could represent the strategies people would use: rewarding activity, punishing activity, expertise, activation of personal commitments, and activation of impersonal commitments. Miller et al. (1977) found that the original 16 techniques were differentially used in four situations and this situational variation influenced the strategies that might emerge. Roloff and Barnicott (1978, in press) found that the intention to use these strategies were influenced by personality variables and their interactions with the situation. Falbo (1977) developed a taxonomy of 16 power strategies derived from subjects' self-reports. A multidimensional scaling of the responses indicated that they could be evaluated in terms of their openness and rationality.

While this research is useful in describing conscious selections of persuasive techniques, it should be noted that the procedures employed demand that subjects attempt to rationally select strategies. Normally, subjects are given a hypothetical situation which they read and then are asked to select an appropriate strategy. Under such conditions we might expect that a rational model such as that presented by Tedeschi et al. (1972) or Fishbein and Ajzen (1975) might explain a great deal of variance in the selection process. Recently, Roloff (1979) used expectancy value theory to predict intentions to employ Marwell and Schmitt's 16 compliance-gaining techniques. The multiple correlations between attitude toward the behavior and subjective norm and the subject's intentions ranged from .75 to .91. In other words, knowledge of the outcomes that could arise from using a technique and the expectations of significant others about the use of the technique were very good predictors of behavioral intentions. However, the review of the psychology of self-awareness might prompt us to question the generalizability of this finding. In addition to determining the cognitive processes that help us predict the use of persuasive messages, three other questions might be pursued.

First, what processes are subjects aware of in their selection of persuasive messages? The position taken by Nisbett and Wilson (1977a) would suggest that the high multiple correlation between the expectancy value formulation and behavioral intention might be accurate but that subjects are not aware of how they combined the components of the model in order to determine the behavioral intention. Roloff (1979) found differences in the size of beta weights attached to the attitudinal component and the subjective component of the model for the various techniques. It would be interesting to see if subjects generally report such differences in the use of the two components. In addition, the compliance-gaining techniques or power strategies are described at a relatively high degree of abstraction. Specific behaviors are not normally included in the strategy itself. Argyle (1969) would argue that people might be aware of and consciously preplan the use of these higher-level strategies but may be unaware of the lower unit behaviors used to implement them. Nonverbal behaviors in the persuasion situation may not be preplanned and may occur with little recognition.

Second, what effect do individual differences in awareness have on the selection and transmission of the persuasive message? The research concerning self-monitoring would suggest that some people may adapt their persuasive strategies to situations to a greater extent than others. This greater sensitivity to situational cues may facilitate persuasive impacts for high self-monitors. People low in self-monitoring may be more concerned with accurately portraying their attitudes in their communication than being perceived in a desirable light. Furthermore, this greater sensitivity to being viewed as an object or adapting to the demands of the situation may also facilitate the selection of deceptive persuasive strategies to a greater exent than when people are more concerned with accurately presenting their own positions.

Third, what situations prompt the individual to preplan strategies? Certainly, the knowledge that one will be presenting a persuasive message may in itself prompt some preplanning due to objective self-awareness. To that extent, the research employing rational models is accurate and useful since the objective state may prompt such behavior. However, when the person begins to deliver the message, subjective awareness may exist. As a result, the focus shifts from being aware of one's position to simply transmitting the message. Persons may become less adaptive to feedback with limited awareness of their role as persuaders. Consequently, adaptation to the feedback is reduced and the persuasive attempt may be hindered. Moreover, Langer (1978) argues that much of our behavior is scripted. Indeed, the research investigating the use of compliance-gaining techniques may simply be asking subjects what behaviors are part of the script relevant to the situation. Langer also argues that after confronting similar situations repeatedly, the behavior becomes overlearned to the point that it may occur without conscious reflection. Her position suggests several intriguing areas of research. We might become interested in what people expect to occur in persuasive situations. Certainly, stereotypes about "used car dealers" assume that certain strategies will be used by them and that people will respond in a certain manner. Such scripts may provide important insights into the behavioral expectations of persuaders and receivers in various situations. In addition, if such scripts are carried out repeatedly, their use becomes automatic. One can envision door-to-door salespersons who have presented a sales pitch with such regularity that they cannot recall what occurred during a given presentation. If such behaviors are engaged in with little awareness, it may be the case that their quality may also be affected. Does practice of a persuasive message increase its quality up to the point where it becomes so habitual and automatic that its spontaneity is lost? Such a model of overlearned behavior would suggest that the strategy may be so well ingrained that it could be used without consideration of situational variations or feedback.

In any case, a variety of questions might well be raised about source attempts to persuade a receiver if one assumes that both conscious and unconscious processes may be operating.

THE ROLE OF SELF-AWARENESS
IN PERSUASIVE EFFECTS

Considerable research has focused on the reactions of receivers to persuasive messages. Such research has often constructed situations in which subjects were made aware of their beliefs, attitudes, and behaviors in the experiment. While this research has been useful for modeling behavior that is consciously controlled, the psychology of self-awareness would suggest that three additional questions be pursued.

To what extent are people in persuasive situations aware of their mental and behavioral responses to persuasive communications? As indicated earlier, Nisbett and Wilson (1977a) provide evidence that subjects may not be aware of mental processes and changes as a result of persuasive messages. Research in the subliminal area suggests that people may not have to be aware of the stimulus in order to react to it (Dixon, 1971). It may also be useful to examine situational variations producing attitude change of which subjects might not be aware. Indeed, the nonverbal characteristics of the source may prompt responses in the subjects that they cannot reliably report. Nisbett and Wilson (1977b) found that subjects tended to evaluate a person's appearance, mannerisms, and accent as appealing when the person was warm and friendly during an interview. When the person was cold and distant in the interview, subjects tended to evaluate the same appearance, mannerism, and accent as irritating. Interestingly, the subjects were unaware of the influence of the person's behavior on their evaluation of these traits. We might expect such traits to also affect their assessments of the source's credibility and subsequent attitude change.

Second, to what extent do individual differences in self-awareness influence persuasion? The research cited earlier suggests that high self-monitors are less concerned with inconsistencies between attitudes and behaviors. Interestingly, we might also argue that people may differ in their awareness of such inconsistencies. People who are high in private self-consciousness may discover such inconsistencies, whereas people low in private self-consciousness may not. Indeed, one may have had the experience of observing someone who seems totally inconsistent without feeling any dissonance. Such individuals may spend so little time reflecting about themselves that dissonance cannot arise since no inconsistency is ever recognized. However, even more interesting is that individual differences in the type of self-awareness may prompt differential responses to inconsistency. High private self-conscious people may have an increased awareness of inconsistency and may be prompted to reduce such inconsistency because of dissonance arousal. People high in public self-consciousness are more aware of themselves as others may perceive them. They may be concerned about consistency not from a dissonance perspective resulting from intrapsychic pressure, but from an impression management perspective. Tedeschi et al. (1971) argue that the dissonance phenomenon may not result from internal pressures to be consistent but instead result from being perceived as inconsistent by others. Because high private persons are attuned to internal states, we might expect them to behave in a manner consistent with a dissonance formulation. A high public person may behave in a manner consistent with impression management. Kahle (1978) found effects in a counterattitudinal advocacy experiment attributable to both theories. Consistent with dissonance theory, subjects who were high in self-esteem and provided low justification for engaging in counterattitudinal advocacy changed their attitudes in the direction of the message, and subjects who were high in self-esteem and provided high justification for engaging in counterattitudinal advocacy changed their attitudes in the direction of the message. Consistent with impression management theory, subjects who were given the impression that the experimenter agreed with the counterattitudinal essay tended to change in that direction more than when the experimenter gave the impression that he disagreed with the counterattitudinal message. Self-consciousness may provide insight into when either theory might predict persuasive effects.

Third, what situational cues prompt an individual to be self-aware in the persuasion process? A variety of experimental methods seem to increase a person's self-awareness in persuasion experiments. One method that may prompt self-awareness involves recording one's thoughts about a persuasive message. When a person is required to recall thoughts, write them down, and then observe them, we would expect them to be objectively self-aware. Petty and Cacioppo (1977) examined the effects of forewarning people of an impending persuasive message and listing their other thoughts about the message on resistance to attitude change. These authors found that asking forewarned subjects to record their own general thoughts or topic-related thoughts prior to receiving a persuasive message tends to increase counterarguing and subsequent resistance to attitude change.

Greenwald (1968) studied the effect of examining one's own thoughts during the persuasive attempt on attitude change. Greenwald and Cullen (cited in Greenwald, 1968) ran several variations of an experiment in which people were asked to "collect their thoughts" immediately following message reception, but prior to filling out attitude measures. Subjects who generated more agreeing thoughts tended to favor the advocated position, while subjects who generated more disagreeing remarks did not favor that position. Most of the thoughts were reported by the subjects to have been generated by themselves rather than by the message. Love (cited in Greenwald, 1968) asked subjects to record their cognitive responses to a persuasive message after reading it. The best predictor of the effect of the message was recall of these thoughts. Surprisingly, the worst predictor was recall of the persuasive communication.

Roberts and Maccoby (1973) conducted a complex analysis of cognitive reactions to persuasive messages. They found that subjects who listed their thoughts during a communication generated more positive statements about the message, while subjects who listed their thoughts after the message generated more negative statements. In general, subjects who were committed to a position and given the opportunity to counterargue against the message tended to resist influence the most. An inverse relationship was found between counterarguing and persuasion.

Osterhouse and Brock (1970) suggested that the effect of focusing on one's responses to a persuasive message can be disrupted by distraction. Subjects were asked to list their thoughts after receiving a communication under varying degrees of distraction. As we might expect, when a distraction is present, subjects attend less to themselves and produce fewer counterarguments. As the level of distraction increased, counterargument production decreased while communication acceptance increased.

Persuasive messages that focus on self may also affect self-consciousness. Rokeach (1973) argues that people rarely receive objective information about themselves that would allow them to perceive internal contradictions. His position suggests that providing people with information about how they compare with others will lead to value and behavior change. Rokeach and McLellan (1972) provided subjects with information about their own values and the ranking of others on the same values. Furthermore, experimenters encouraged subjects to compare their own scores with the scores of similar others, and then berated the scores of the similar others. In a second condition, subjects were shown the normative responses of the similar others but were not given the opportunity to compare their own responses to the normative responses. Again, the normative responses were berated. The procedures tended to focus the subject's attention on an explicit comparison with others or a more subjective implicit comparison with others. The effect of the two experimental treatments was that subjects changed both their value rankings immediately and four weeks later. Four months after the experimental treatments, subjects continued to engage in a significant behavioral commitment to the new values. Rokeach and Cochrane (1972) induced self-dissatisfaction by comparing subjects' own responses to values with those of similar others. Some subjects received the information under conditions of anonymity and others in a public situation where the experimenter knew their names and responses. The results indicated that self-confrontation changed values immediately and eight to nine weeks after the experiment. The two conditions were not significantly different.

Greenstein (1976) examined the effects of self-confrontation on teachers. Subjects in an experimental group received objective feedback concerning their own values and the values of good and mediocre teachers. Subjects were found to have changed their values more after self-confrontation than did subjects in a control group who received no feedback. These changes in values were related to judges' higher rankings on measures of teaching ability.

Grube et al. (1977) reanalyzed Rokeach's data using path analysis to determine the reason why the self-confrontation techniques were effective. Contrary to Rokeach's theorizing, the major impact of self-confrontation was on subjects whose initial values were congruent with the message but whose behavior was not. In other words, the effectiveness of the techniques seemed to stem from the impact of subjects focusing on their values and comparing them with their previous behavior.

A more complex variable that may affect self-awareness deals with the presence of an audience. Duval and Wicklund (1972) argue that the presence of an audience that scrutinizes one's behavior ought to affect the person's self-evaluation. Cialdini et al. (1974) discovered that people evaluate a receiver of a message according to the receiver's response to a persuasive message. The persuader tends to attribute greater intelligence to a receiver who changes to a position congruent with the persuader's than if the receiver resists. An observer of the persuasive attempt tends to negatively evaluate a receiver who is easily persuaded even if the observer agrees with the position advocated in the message. Research indicates that subjects correctly perceive that they will be differentially evaluated for changing their attitudes by the persuader or an outside observer. Braver et al. (1977) found that subjects perceived that they will be negatively evaluated by an observer if they change their attitudes but will be positively evaluated by the persuader. Consistent with these perceptions, the greatest stated attitude change occurred in the sole presence of the persuader; and intermediate amount was admitted before both the persuader and observer, and the least-admitted attitude change was in the sole presence of the observer. Private attitude change indicated on a questionnaire did not differ significantly across groups but was in the same pattern. Thus, if the target feels observed by the group, differential attitude change will be found.

However, if the group is not focusing on the individual but on a persuader, different effects may occur. Several studies have found that intraaudience effects occur (Hylton, 1971; Monge, 1969; Hocking, 1972; Hocking et al., 1977). Subjects who are part of an audience tend to shape their responses to a message based upon what others are doing. One might argue that this effect is similar to the notion of deindividuation (Zimbardo, 1970; Diener, 1977). Subjects become less self-aware and tend to behave as others around them do. Thus, the presence of a positive audience may induce compliance rather than reduce it.

A variety of factors that are not as obvious as message strategies or an audience may induce self-awareness in the persuasion process. As indicated earlier, several studies have found that self-awareness can be increased through showing subjects their images on a television camera or a mirror. While not all persuaders could employ these techniques, in some cases the use of a mirror or camera may be possible. Certain sale situations often employ a mirror or cameras. When shoppers buy clothes or other apparel, they are often urged by the salesperson to examine how the item looks in a mirror. The mirror examination may have a profound effect on whether or not to buy. If shoppers like what they see, the sale may be finalized. However, the risk of a negative self-evaluation is also heightened by inducing the objective self-awareness state. In addition, security devices which employ camera scanners of shoppers may also increase the objective state. If customers feel they are being observed and someone mistrusts them, sales may decrease.

The focus of this section has been on methods designed to increase self-awareness. According to the analyses provided by Duval and Wicklund (1972) and Langer (1978), this focus is justified. Both positions assume that people either desire or at least tend to spend most of their time in a reduced state of self-awareness. While it is important to examine how people respond to persuasive messages when they are self-aware, it is equally important to examine how they respond when they are not self-aware. Indeed, if we could examine the behavior of people in naturalistic persuasion settings, we might find that they are typically lower in self-awareness than some would expect. One might find that people often comply with a large number of persuasive messages received at work without consciously considering the relevance to beliefs, attitudes, and behaviors. Barnard (1938) suggested that workers have a "zone of indifference" which consists of orders they perceive to be acceptable and require little thought in determining a response. People may simply comply with such requests as part of a typical day.

Even in consumer behavior we may find a dearth of self-awareness. Katona (1960, 1964) suggests that problem-solving behavior such as weighing alternatives and taking into consideration their consequences may be the exception rather than the rule. He suggests that habituated behavior is far more common and that genuine decisions about a purchase only occur under certain conditions.

One might speculate that this lowered state of self-awareness may be a defensive reaction to the large number of persuasive messages received during the day. People are very likely inundated by requests from family, friends, coworkers, and advertisements. For people to respond to each of these requests by comparing them with their beliefs, attitudes, and behaviors would be time consuming. As a result, people may simply respond automatically by complying with some requests and not recognizing others. Indeed, Plummer (1971) has suggested that because of the ever-increasing number of advertisements, recall of the advertisements 24 hours later has been steadily decreasing. People may not even be able to remember a given request for compliance the next day.

Consequently, we need to adjust our theoretical models and research to incorporate the person who is not self-aware. Such models could provide insight into what may be a typical state for most individuals.

CONCLUSION

This chapter has examined the role of self-awareness in the persuasion process. While most approaches to persuasion have characterized both the source and receiver of a message as being maximally aware of their own beliefs, attitudes, and behaviors, this chapter has argued that certain persuasive processes involve minimal reflection upon self. Implications for the contribution of self-awareness to the persuasion process have been presented.

REFERENCES

ABELSON, R. (1976). "Script processing in attitude formation and decision making." Pp. 33-45 in J. Carroll and T. Payne (eds.), Cognition and social behavior. Hillsdale, NJ: Lawrence Erlbaum.

ARGYLE, M. (1969) Social interaction. Chicago: AVC.
——— (1975). Bodily communication. New York: International Universities Press.
ARKIN, R., and DUVAL, S. (1975). "Focus of attention and causal attributions of actors and observers." Journal of Experimental Social Psychology, 11:427-438.
——— DUVAL, S., and HENSLEY, V. (1975). "Attributions of observers as a function of the dynamicity of the actor." (unpublished)
ARKIN, R., GABRENYA, W., Jr., APPELMAN, A., and COCHRAN, S. (1979). "Self-presentation, self-monitoring, and the self-serving bias in causal attribution." Personality and Social Psychology Bulletin, 5:73-76.
BARNARD, C. (1938). The functions of the executive. Cambridge: Harvard University Press.
BEM, D. (1972). "Self-perception theory." Pp. 1-62 in L. Berkowitz (ed.), Advances in experimental social psychology, volume 6. New York: Academic Press.
BERSCHEID, E., GRAZIANO, W., MONSON, T., and DERMER, M. (1976). "Outcome dependency: Attention, attribution and attraction." Journal of Personality and Social Psychology, 34:978-989.
BETTINGHAUS, E. (1973). Persuasive communication. New York: Holt, Rinehart & Winston.
BLANCHE, J. (1975). "Effects of focus of attention, visual and nonvisual perspectives on causal attributions of actors and observers." Ph.D. dissertation, University of Southern California. (unpublished)
BRAVER, S., DINDER, J., CORWIN, T., and CIALDINI, R. (1977). "Some conditions that affect admissions of attitude change." Journal of Experimental Social Psychology, 13:565-576.
BROCKNER, J. (1979). "Self-esteem, self-consciousness, and task performance: Replications, extensions, and possible explanations." Journal of Personality and Social Psychology, 37:447-461.
BROTHEN, T. (1977). "The gain/loss concept and the evaluator: First some good news, then some bad." Journal of Personality and Social Psychology, 35:430-436.
BUSS, D., and SCHEIER, M. (1976). "Self-consciousness, self-awareness, and self-attribution." Journal of Research in Personality, 10:463-468.
BUTLER, S. (1903). The way of all flesh. New York: Window Press.
CARVER, C. (1974). "Facilitation of physical aggression through objective self-awareness." Journal of Experimental Social Psychology, 10:365-370.
——— (1975). "Physical aggression as a function of objective self-awareness and attitudes toward punishment." Journal of Experimental Social Psychology, 11:510-519.
——— (1977). "Self-awareness, perception of threat, and the expression of reactance through attitude change." Journal of Personality, 45:501-512.
——— and GLASS, D. (1976). "The self-consciousness scale: A discriminant validity study." Journal of Personality Assessment, 40:169-172.
CARVER, C., and SCHEIER, M. (1978). "Self-focusing effects of dispositional self-consciousness, mirror presence, and audience presences." Journal of Personality and Social Psychology, 36:324-332.
CIALDINI, R., BRAVER, S., and LEWIS, S. (1974). "Attributional bias and the easily persuaded other." Journal of Personality and Social Psychology, 30:631-637.
CIALDINI, R., LEVY, A., HERMAN, C., and EVENBECK, S. (1973). "Attitudinal politics: The stragegy of moderation." Journal of Personality and Social Psychology, 25:100-108.

DAVIS, D., and BROCK, T. (1975). "Use of first person pronouns as a function of increased objective self-awareness and performance feedback." Journal of Experimental Social Psychology, 11:381-388.

DAVIS, D., and WICKLUND, R. (1972). "An objective self-awareness analysis of communication sets." Pp. 180-184 in S. Duval and R. Wicklund (eds.), A theory of objective self-awareness. New York: Academic Press.

DIENER, E. (1977). "Deindividuation: Causes and consequences." Social Behavior and Personality, 5:143-155.

——— and SRULL, T. (1979). "Self-awareness, psychological perspective, and self-reinforcement in relation to personal and social standards." Journal of Personality and Social Psychology, 37:413-423.

DIENER, E., and WALLBOM, M. (1976). Effects of self-awareness on antinormative behavior." Journal of Research in Personality 10:107-111.

DIXON, N. (1971). Subliminal perception: The nature of a controversy. New York: McGraw-Hill.

DUVAL, S. (1976). "Conformity on a visual task as a function of personal novelty on attitudinal dimensions and being reminded of the object status of self." Journal of Experimental Social Psychology, 12:87-98.

——— and HENSLEY, V. (1976). "Extensions of objective self-awareness theory: The focus of attention-causal attribution hypothesis." Pp. 165-198 in H. Harvey, W. Ickes, and R. Kidd (eds.), New directions in attribution research, volume 1. Hillsdale, NJ: Lawrence Erlbaum.

DUVAL, S., and RITZ, E. (1972). "Perception of control as a function of objective self-awareness." Pp. 35-36 in S. Duval and R. Wicklund (eds.), A theory of objective self-awareness. New York: Academic Press.

DUVAL, S., and WICKLUND, R. (1972). A theory of objective self-awareness. New York: Academic Press.

——— (1973). "Effects of objective self-awareness on attribution of causality." Journal of Experimental Social Psychology, 9:17-31.

DUVAL, S., HENSLEY, V., and NEELY, R. (1975). "Attribution of an event to self and helping behavior as a function of contiguous vs. noncontiguous presentation of self and event." (unpublished)

DUVAL, S., WICKLUND, R., and FINE, R. (1972). "Avoidance of objective self-awareness under conditions of high and low intra-self discrepancy." Pp. 16-21 in S. Duval and R. Wicklund (eds.), A theory of objective self-awareness. New York: Academic Press.

FALBO, T. (1977). "Multidimensional scaling of power strategies." Journal of Personality and Social Psychology, 35:537-547.

FEDEROFF, N., and HARVEY, J. (1976). "Focus of attention, self-esteem and the attribution of causality." Journal of Research in Personality, 10:336-345.

FENIGSTEIN, A. (1979). "Self-consciousness, self-attention, and social interaction." Journal of Personality and Social Psychology, 37:75-86.

——— and CARVER, C. (1978). "Self-focusing effects of heartbeat feedback." Journal of Personality and Social Psychology, 36:1241-1250.

FENIGSTEIN, A., SCHEIER, M., and BUSS, A. (1975). "Public and private self-consciousness: Assessment and theory." Journal of Consulting and Clinical Psychology, 43:522-527.

FISHBEIN, M., and AJZEN, I. (1975). Belief, attitude, intention, and behavior: An introduction to theory and research. Reading, MA: Addison-Wesley.

FROMING, W. (1978). "The relationship of moral judgment, self-awareness, and sex to compliance behavior." Journal of Research in Personality, 12:396-409.

GALSWORTHY, J. (1931). Maid in waiting. New York: Scribner.

GEIZER, R., RARICK, D., and SOLDOW, G. (1977). "Deception and judgment accuracy: A study in person perception." Personality and Social Psychology Bulletin, 3:445-449.

GELLER, V., and SHAVER, P. (1976). "Cognitive consequences of self-awareness." Journal of Experimental Social Psychology, 12:99-108.

GIBBONS, F. (1978). "Sexual standards and reactions to pornography: Enhancing behavioral consistency through self-focused attention." Journal of Personality and Social Psychology, 36:976-987.

——— CARVER, C., SCHEIER, M., and HORMUTH, S. (1979). "Self-focused attention and the placebo effect: Fooling some of the people some of the time." Journal of Experimental Social Psychology, 15:263-274.

GIBBONS, F., and WICKLUND, R. (1976) "Selective exposure to self." Journal of Research in Personality, 10:98-106.

GOETHALS, G., and RECKMAN, R. (1973). "The perception of consistency in attitudes." Journal of Experimental Social Psychology, 9:491-501.

GREENSTEIN, T. (1976). "Behavior change through value self-confrontation: A field experiment." Journal of Personality and Social Psychology, 34:254-262.

GREENWALD, A. (1968). "Cognitive learning, cognitive response to persuasion, and attitude change." Pp. 147-170 in A. Greenwald, T. Brock, and T. Ostrom (eds.). Psychological foundations of attitudes. New York: Academic Press.

GRUBE, J., GREENSTEIN, T., RANKIN, W., and KEARNEY, K. (1977). "Behavior change following self-confrontation: A test of the value-mediation hypothesis." Journal of Personality and Social Psychology, 35:212-216.

HASS, R. (1975). "Persuasion or moderation? Two experiments on anticipatory belief change." Journal of Personality and Social Psychology, 31:1155-1162.

——— and MANN, R. (1976). "Anticipatory belief change: Persuasion or impression management?" Journal of Personality and Social Psychology, 34:105-111.

HOCKING, J. (1972). "The effects of sequentially varied observable audience response." Masters thesis, California State University, San Jose. (unpublished)

——— MARGREITER, D. and HYLTON, C. (1977). "Intra-audience effects: A field test." Human Communication Research, 3:241-249.

HULL, J., and LEVY, A. (1979). "The organizational functions of the self: An alternative to the Duval and Wicklund model of self-awareness." Journal of Personality and Social Psychology, 37:756-788.

HYLTON, C. (1971). "Intra-audience effects: Observable audience response." Journal of Communication, 21:253-265.

ICKES, W., and BARNES, R. (1977). "The role of sex and self-monitoring in unstructured dyadic interactions." Journal of Personality and Social Psychology, 35:315-330.

ICKES, W., LAYDEN, M., and BARNES, R. (1977). "Objective self-awareness and individuation: An empirical link." Journal of Personality, 45:147-161.

ICKES, W., WICKLUND, R., and FERRIS, C. (1973). "Objective self-awareness and self esteem." Journal of Experimental Social Psychology, 9:202-219.

INNES, J., and YOUNG, R. (1975). "The effect of presence of an audience, evaluation apprehension and objective self-awareness on learning." Journal of Experimental Social Psychology, 11:35-42.

INSKO, C., WORCHEL, S., SONGER, E., and ARNOLD, S. (1973). "Effort, objective self-awareness, choice, and dissonance." Journal of Personality and Social Psychology, 28:262-269.

JONES, E., and BAUMEISTER, R. (1976). "The self-monitor looks at the ingratiator." Journal of Personality. 44:654-674.

KAHLE, L. (1978). "Dissonance and impression management as theories of attitude change." Journal of Social Psychology, 105:53-64.

KATONA, G. (1960). The powerful consumer. New York: McGraw-Hill.

——— (1964). "Genuine decision-making." Pp. 289-290 in G. Katona (ed.), The mass consumption society. New York: McGraw-Hill.

LANGER, E. (1978). "Rethinking the role of thought in social interaction." Pp. 35-58 in H. Harvey, W. Ickes, and R. Kidd (eds.), New directions in attribution research, volume 2. Hillsdale, NJ: Lawrence Erlbaum.

——— BLANK, A., and CHANOWITZ, B. (1978). "The mindlessness of ostensibly thoughtful action: The role of 'placebic' information in interpersonal interaction." Journal of Personality and Social Psychology, 36:635-642.

LEFCOURT, H., HOGG, E., and SORDONI, C. (1975). "Locus of control, field dependence and the conditions arousing objective vs. subjective self-awareness." Journal of Research in Personality, 9:21-36.

LIEBLING, B., and SHAVER, P. (1973). "Evaluation, self-awareness and task performance." Journal of Experimental Social Psychology, 9:297-308.

LIEBLING, B., SEILER, M., and SHAVER, P. (1974). "Self-awareness and cigarette-smoking behavior." Journal of Experimental Social Psychology, 10:325-332.

LIEBLING, B., SEILER, M., and SHAVER, P. (1975). "Unsolved problems for self-awareness theory: A reply to Wicklund." Journal of Experimental Social Psychology, 11:82-85.

LIPPA, R. (1976). "Expressive control and the leakage of dispositional introversion-extroversion during role-played teaching." Journal of Personality, 44:541-559.

MARGREITER, D., HOCKING, J. and HYLTON, C. (1974). "An exploratory study of intra-audience effects in small interpersonal settings." Presented at the annual convention of the Central States Speech Association, Milwaukee, April.

MARWELL, G., and SCHMITT, D. (1967). "Dimensions of compliance-gaining behavior: An empirical analysis." Sociometry, 30:350-364.

MAYER, S., HENSLEY, V., and DUVAL, S. (1975). "Causality and commitment." (unpublished)

MILLER, G., BOSTER, F., ROLOFF, M., and SEIBOLD, D. (1977). "Compliance-gaining message strategies: A typology and some findings concerning effects of situational differences." Communication Monographs, 44:37-54.

MONGE, P. (1969). "The effects of variations in observable audience response ratios on attitude change, source credibility, and comprehension." Masters thesis, San Jose State College. (unpublished)

NISBETT, R., and WILSON, T. (1977a). "Telling more than we can know: Verbal reports on mental processes." Psychological Review, 84:231-259.

——— (1977b). "The halo effect: Evidence for unconscious alteration of judgment." Journal of Personal and Social Psychology, 35:250-256.

OSTERHOUSE, R., and BROCK, T. (1970). "Distraction increases yielding to propaganda by inhibiting counterarguing." Journal of Personality and Social Psychology, 15:344-358.

PETTY, R. and CACIOPPO, J. (1977). "Forewarning, cognitive responding and resistance to persuasion." Journal of Personality and Social Psychology, 35:645-655.

PLUMMER, J. (1971). "A theoretical model of advertising communication." Journal of Communication, 21:315-325.

PRYOR, J., GIBBONS, F., WICKLUND, R., FAZIO, R., and HOOD, R. (1977). "Self-focused attention and self-report validity." Journal of Personality, 45:513-527.

RARICK, D., SOLDOW, G., and GEIZER, R. (1976). "Self-monitoring as a mediator of conformity." Central States Speech Journal, 27:267-271.

ROBERTS, D., and MACCOBY, N. (1973). "Information processing and persuasion: Counterarguing behavior." Pp. 269-303 in P. Clarke (ed.), New models for communication research. Beverly Hills, CA: Sage.

ROKEACH, M. (1973). The nature of human values. New York: Free Press.

––– and COCHRANE, R. (1972). "Self-confrontation and confrontation with another as determinants of long-term value change." Journal of Applied Social Psychology, 2:283-292.

ROKEACH, M. and McLELLAN, D. (1972). "Feedback of information about the values and attitudes of self and others as determinants of long-term cognitive and behavioral change." Journal of Applied Social Psychology, 2:236-251.

ROLOFF, M. (1979). "An expectancy value approach to predicting the use of compliance-gaining techniques." (unpublished)

ROLOFF, M., and BARNICOTT, E. (1978). "The situational use of pro- and antisocial compliance-gaining strategies by high and low Machiavellians." Pp. 193-208 in B. Ruben (ed.), Communication yearbook 2. New Brunswick, NJ: Transaction Books.

––– (in press). "The influence of dogmatism on the situational use of pro- and antisocial compliance-gaining strategies." Southern Speech Communication Journal.

RULE, B., NESDALE, A., and DYCK, R. (1975). "Objective self-awareness and differing standards of aggression." Representative Research in Social Psychology, 6:82-88.

SCHEIER, M. (1976). "Self-awareness, self-consciousness, and angry aggression." Journal of Personality, 44:627-644.

––– and CARVER, C. (1977). "Self-focused attention and the experience of emotion: Attraction, repulsion, elation, and depression." Journal of Personality and Social Psychology, 35:625-636.

SCHEIER, M., BUSS, A., and BUSS, D. (1978). "Self-consciousness, self-report of aggressiveness, and aggression." Journal of Research in Personality, 12:133-140.

SCHEIER, M., FENIGSTEIN, A., and BUSS, A. (1974). "Self-awareness and physical aggression." Journal of Experimental Social Psychology, 10:264-273.

SMITH, E. and MILLER, F. (1978). "Limits on perception of cognitive processes: A reply to Nisbett and Wilson." Psychological Review, 85:355-362.

SNYDER, M. (1974). "Self-monitoring of expressive behavior." Journal of Personality and Social Psychology, 30:526-537.

––– and MONSON, T. (1975). "Person, situations, and the control of social behavior." Journal of Personality and Social Psychology, 32:637-644.

SNYDER, M., and SWANN, W., Jr. (1976). "When actions reflect attitudes: The politics of impression management." Journal of Personality and Social Psychology, 34:1034-1042.

SNYDER, M., and TANKE, E. (1976). "Behavior and attitude: Some people are more consistent than others." Journal of Personality, 44:501-517.

SWART, C., ICKES, W., and MORGENTHALER, E. (1978). "The effect of objective self-awareness on compliance in a reactance situation." Social Behavior and Personality, 6:135-139.

TEDESCHI, J., SCHLENKER, B., and BONOMA, T. (1971). "Cognitive dissonance: Private ratiocination or public spectacle?" American Psychologist, 26:685-695.

TEDESCHI, J., SCHLENKER, B. and LINDSKOLD, S. (1972). "The exercise of power and influence: The source of influence." Pp. 287-345 in J. Tedeschi (ed.), The social influence processes. Chicago: AVC.

TURNER, R. (1977). "Self-consciousness and anticipatory belief change." Personality and Social Psychology Bulletin, 3:438-441.

––– (1978a) "Consistency, self-consciousness, and the predictive validity of typical and maximal personality measures." Journal of Research in Personality, 12:117-132.

––– (1978b). "Effects of differential request procedures and self-consciousness on trait attributions." Journal of Research in Personality, 12:431-438.

––– (1978c). "Self-consciousness and speed of processing self-relevant information." Personality and Social Psychology Bulletin, 4:456-460.

––– SCHEIER, M., CARVER, C., and ICKES, W. (1978). "Correlates of self-consciousness." Journal of Personality Assessment, 42:285-289.

TURNER, R., and PETERSON, M. (1977). "Public and private self-consciousness and emotional expressibility." Journal of Consulting and Clinical Psychology, 45:490-491.

VALLACHER, R., and SOLODKY, M. (1979). "Objective self-awareness standards of evaluation and moral behavior." Journal of Experimental Social Psychology, 15:254-262.

WEGNER, D., and SCHAEFER, D. (1978). "The concentration of responsibility: An objective self-awareness analysis of group size effects in helping situations." Journal of Personality and Social Psychology, 36:147-155.

WICKLUND, R. (1975a). "Discrepancy reduction or attempted distraction? A reply to Liebling, Seiler, and Shaver." Journal of Experimental Social Psychology, 11:78-81.

––– (1975b). "Objective self-awareness." Pp. 233-275 in L. Berkowitz (ed.), Advances in experimental social psychology, volume 8. New York: Academic Press.

––– and DUVAL, S. (1971). "Opinion change and performance facilitation as a result of objective self-awareness." Journal of Experimental Social Psychology, 7:319-342.

WICKLUND, R., and ICKES, W. (1972). "The effect of objective self-awareness on predecisional exposure to information." Journal of Experimental Social Psychology, 8:378-387.

YOUNGER, J., and PLINER, P. (1976). "Obese-normal differences in the self-monitoring of expressive behavior." Journal of Research in Personality 10:112-115.

ZIMBARDO, P. (1970). "The human choice: Individuation, reason, and order versus deindividuation, impulse, and chaos." Pp. 237-307 in W. Arnold and D. Levine (eds.), Nebraska Symposium on motivation. Lincoln: University of Nebraska Press.

Chapter 3

... "AND THINKING MAKES IT SO"
Cognitive Responses to Persuasion

Richard M. Perloff and Timothy C. Brock

"There is nothing either good or bad, but thinking makes it so."

Hamlet

Shakespeare may have been one of the cognitive response approach's first proponents if the soliloquies in *Hamlet* are an indication of the bard's attitudes toward persuasion.[1] *Hamlet* contains one of literature's most famous sets of covert counterarguments when Hamlet "collects his thoughts" on the subject of suicide.

The cognitive response approach to persuasion strongly emphasizes the thoughts people have while attending to persuasive communications. This explicit and systematic concern with receivers' cognitive activities is a relatively recent phenomenon, however; it was not so long ago that

AUTHORS' NOTE: The authors are indebted to Anthony Greenwald and Richard Petty for their descriptions and explications of the cognitive response approach. We thank Richard Petty and John Cacioppo for their valuable criticisms of an earlier version of this paper, and Professor Makay of the OSU Department of Communication for generously allowing us to collect data in his introductory communication class. We also appreciate the comments and assistance of Rebecca Quarles, Cheryl Roush, and Kipling Williams.

persuasion research emphasized the impact of variables external to the individual, such as the source, message, and channel (McGuire, 1969). Over the past decade, as communication research has adopted a more cognitive orientation, studies of persuasion have begun to pay more attention to the cognitive and subjective reactions of individuals to persuasive messages.

In 1973, Roberts and Maccoby summarized and extended research on cognitive responses to persuasion. Since their chapter in this annual review series, studies of cognitive responses to persuasion have increased. In this chapter we review a variety of recent investigations that support a cognitive response analysis of persuasion. In addition to providing a state-of-the-art description of recent research on cognitive responses, we suggest new conceptual formulations. These formulations constitute a needed corrective to McGuire's (1968, 1969) approach to attitude change which assigns learning of message content a central role in the persuasion process. Rather than arguing, as McGuire does, that persuasion is in some sense dependent upon comprehension of the persuasive message, the cognitive response approach contends that the impact of situational and individual difference variables on persuasion depends upon the extent to which individuals learn their own idiosyncratic responses to the persuasive communication. Guided by the cognitive response perspective, we offer in this chapter a new formulation linking personality and persuasibility; finally, we suggest practical implications of cognitive response research.

AN EXPLANATION OF
THE COGNITIVE RESPONSE APPROACH

HISTORICAL PERSPECTIVES

In his 1960 dissertation, Brock (1962) had non-Catholic subjects write thoughts on slips of paper. Each slip contained an implication for its owner's "becoming a Catholic." Many of these written implications were, of course, counterarguments to the discrepant behavior of "becoming a Catholic." Brock analyzed these responses to show how cognitive restructuring can be instigated by attitude change pressure. In 1967, Brock showed that student recipients who anticipated a discrepant communication ("increase tuition") listed counterarguments in proportion to the magnitude of discrepancy of the forthcoming persuasive message.

A year later, McGuire (1968), Greenwald (1968), and Weiss (1968) called attention to the important role cognitive responses play in the attitude change process. Over the next decade, cognitive response measures were increasingly employed in accounting for the influences of a variety of independent variables including message discrepancy (Brock, 1967), source credibility (Cook, 1969), distraction (Osterhouse and Brock, 1970; Petty et al., 1976), order of presentation (Insko et al., 1976), and anticipated discussion (Cialdini et al., 1976).

As Roberts and Maccoby (1973) emphasized, cognitive responses were assumed to be intervening variables that explained the effects of a variety of independent variables on communication behavior. Recently, however, cognitive responses have been assigned an even greater role in the persuasion process. Communication researchers appear no longer content to assign cognitive reactions the role of intervening variables, but are increasingly proposing cognitive response-based models of persuasion (Petty, 1977; Calder, 1978; Tybout et al., 1977; Petty et al., in press). Thus, Tybout et al. attempted to integrate Bem's (1967) self-perception theory with the cognitive response approach to persuasion, while Petty and Cacioppo have articulated cognitive response-based explanations of a variety of social psychological phenomena (Petty and Cacioppo, 1977, 1979a, 1979b; Cacioppo and Petty, 1979). At the same time, Brock and his colleagues at Ohio State have formulated a cognitive response analysis of the persistence of belief and attitude changes.

In essence, the cognitive response perspective maintains that individuals are active participants in the persuasion process who attempt to relate message elements to their existing repertoires of information. In so doing, these individuals may consider materials that are not actually contained in the persuasive message. These self-generated cognitions may agree with the position advocated by the source or they may disagree. Insofar as the communication elicits favorable cognitive responses, attitudes should change in the direction advocated by the source. To the extent that the message evokes unfavorable mental reactions, attitude change in the direction advocated by the source should be inhibited.

Cognitive responses, then, are thoughts and ideas that are evoked by persuasive communications and which, in turn, influence individuals' more evaluative, attitudinal responses to these messages. In effect, individuals persuade themselves to adopt the position advocated by the communicator. The advocated position may be consistent with persons' initial attitudes, in which case their thoughts may reinforce and strengthen their initial evaluation. Or the communication may be sufficiently compelling so as to change individuals' beliefs and ideas about the topic. These cognitive reassessments, then, lead to changes in attitude. In addition, an ego-involving message may cause the individual to mentally reevaluate the personal benefits and costs of the communicated position; in turn this reassessment is assumed to affect attitudes.

PERSISTENCE OF ATTITUDE CHANGE

The cognitive response approach maintains that the amount of initial cognitive processing occurring during exposure to the persuasive communication is the critical determinant of the persistence of attitude change. There are two ways individuals may differ in the amount of initial processing of a message: (a) one group may generate more message-relevant thoughts than another group, or (b) both groups may generate an identical number of thoughts at the outset, but one group may rehearse its thoughts while the other does not. In his statement of the cognitive response position, Greenwald (1968) asserted that "cognitive modification of attitudes is dependent upon active rehearsal of thoughts that are relevant to the message when the attitude issue is salient to the person." Greenwald further proposed that this rehearsal and learning of mental responses to communications may provide a foundation for explaining the persisting influences of persuasive messages over time.

Why should the amount of initial cognitive processing be related to the persistence of persuasion? Given the assumption that the cognitive reactions generated during exposure to the message are a determinant of immediate postcommunication attitude (see Petty and Brock, in press, for an extended explanation and justification of this assumption), then insofar as these cognitive responses continue to be salient, attitude at a later time will be similar to the immediate postmessage attitude. The greater the number of cognitive responses or thoughts that individuals generate during exposure to the initial communication, or the more they rehearse these responses, the more initial cognitive reactions they should recall at later points in time and the more the later attitude should resemble the initial attitude. (Cognitive responses have been measured in a variety of ways. See the Appendix.)

A REVIEW OF
COGNITIVE RESPONSE RESEARCH

The diversity of research findings can best be ordered in terms of McGuire's (1969) source, message, context, and destination effects. We substituted Eagly and Himmelfarb's (1978) term "context" for McGuire's "channel."

SOURCE EFFECTS

Source Credibility

The cognitive response approach can predict that under some circumstances a low credibility source will be more influential than a highly credible communicator (Sternthal et al., 1978). When individuals initially support the position being advocated by the communicator, they should be more susceptible to persuasion by a low credibility than a high credibility source; on the other hand, when persons initially disagree with the advocated position, the high credibility communicator should exert a greater impact. Sternthal et al. argue that individuals who favor the advocated position will be more motivated to ensure that their position is being satisfactorily represented when the source is of low credibility than when the source is highly credible. These individuals should, therefore, produce more promessage arguments and, as a result, should be more likely to agree with the position that is advocated by the low credible communicator. By contrast, when individuals disagree with the advocacy at the outset, a highly credible source is more likely to inhibit counterarguing than a low credibility source. Since the reduction of counterarguing stimulates persuasion (Petty et al., in press), the highly credible source should induce more attitude change than the source lacking credibility.

The available evidence is consistent with a cognitive response analysis of source credibility. McGinnes (1973) found that a highly credible communicator was more persuasive than a source with less credibility when the recipient initially opposed the advocated position; however, when the recipient was less opposed to advocacy, there were no credibility effects. Other investigators have reported that a highly credible communicator induced more persuasion when individuals initially opposed the advocated position (Dean et al., 1971; Bochner and Insko, 1966), while a less credible source was more impactful when the issue was relatively close to the recipients' initial opinion (Bochner and Insko, 1966) or was one with which they were likely to agree (Dean et al., 1971). Bock and Saine (1975) observed that a low credibility source was more influential than a highly credible communicator when individuals agreed with advocacy at the outset.

Finally, in a direct test of the cognitive response analysis of source credibility, Sternthal et al. (1978) reported that a moderately credible source induced more agreement and promessage argumentation than a highly credible communicator when subjects initially favored the advocated position and when the source was identified prior to the message. In addition, consistent with cognitive response predictions, a highly credible communicator was more influential when individuals had a negative initial predisposition toward the advocated point of view. The available evidence, then, provides support for the cognitive response model, although it should be noted that there may be other interpretations that are also compatible with the data. (See Tybout et al., 1977, for a self-perception theory explanation.)

MESSAGE EFFECTS

Involvement

Recent research has suggested that involvement increases the likelihood of both rejecting a counterattitudinal communication and of accepting a proattitudinal message (Pallak et al., 1972). To account for these results, Pallak et al. invoked a modified social judgment theory explanation that basically asserts that subjects under high involvement conditions are likely to reject or contrast discrepant message information and accept or assimilate supportive information.

Recently, Petty and Cacioppo (1979b) have articulated an alternative cognitive response-based interpretation of these results. According to Petty and Cacioppo, high issue involvement increases the probability that subjects will carefully ruminate about a persuasive communication. (This notion is based in part on evidence suggesting that increased involvement with a stimulus is related to more extensive processing of the stimulus information [Cialdini et al., 1976; Rogers et al., 1977].)

When the advocated viewpoint is inconsistent with their original attitudes, people are likely to be motivated and capable of producing counter-arguments to the persuasive message. Insofar as high involvement with the issue is related to more thinking about the issue, increased counterargument production and resistance to persuasion should result. By contrast, when the communication presents information that is congruent with individuals' initial attitudes, they are inclined to generate favorable mental responses to the message. To the extent that issue involvement is associated with increased thinking about the communication, enhanced pro-argumentation and susceptibility to influence should occur.

Petty and Cacioppo tested the cognitive response view of involvement in two recent experiments. They varied involvement by informing subjects that a proposed university reform would be instituted at either their own university (high involvement) or an obscure university (low involvement). The results were consistent with the cognitive response explanation of involvement. When both involvement and the direction of advocacy (pro or counter) were varied, increased involvement with the issue reduced persuasion for the counterattitudinal message, but increased persuasion for the proattitudinal communication. These results contradict the original social judgment proposition (Sherif et al., 1965) which predicts that increased involvement invariably decreases persuasion. However, they are consistent with Pallak et al.'s (1972) revised social judgment model.

Petty and Cacioppo conducted a second experiment to pit a cognitive response explanation against the revised social judgment perspective. According to Pallak et al. (1972), the extent to which the message contradicts an individual's initial position is the main determinant of whether involvement will encourage or hinder persuasion. Thus, when the advocated position is inconsistent with the person's initial view, involvement tends to decrease persuasion. By contrast, the cognitive response approach maintains that the position advocated in the message is not as important a determinant of persuasion as the type of thoughts evoked by the message.

While the social judgment approach does not predict that quality of arguments will mediate the effect of involvement on persuasibility, the cognitive response approach predicts that increased issue involvement will result in decreased persuasion only for a message that contains easy-to-counterargue arguments. On the other hand, a message that contains strong or difficult-to-counterargue arguments should lead to increased persuasion. In effect, increased involvement encourages individuals to process message-arguments more diligently. Consequently, while high involvement with an issue may initially increase willingness to reject a counterattitudinal message, in the long run individuals should better recognize the strengths of a high-quality message and the weaknesses of a low-quality communication.

In the second experiment, involvement was varied again, but this time both messages advocated counterattitudinal positions. The results favored the cognitive response interpretation over the revised social judgment model. The compelling, difficult-to-counterargue message evoked predominantly favorable cognitive responses, while the easy-to-counterargue communication elicited primarily counterarguments. High involvement increased persuasion for the difficult-to-counterargue communication, but reduced influence for the weak message. The results suggest that what is important is not direction of advocacy (counter- or proattitudinal), but rather the type and nature of thoughts that are elicited.

Message Repetition

Cacioppo and Petty (1979) argued that while there has been substantial research on the effects of mere exposure (Zajonc, 1968), few studies have investigated the attitudinal and cognitive impact of message repetition. Based on the cognitive response model, they hypothesized that attitude change would parallel the pattern of topic-relevant thoughts generated in response to repeated persuasive communications. The results indicated that message repetition produced increasing, then decreasing agreement with the advocated position; a parallel trend was evidenced by the decreasing, then increasing pattern of counterarguments. However, agreement with the message was not related to recall of message arguments.

Cacioppo and Petty suggested that their results could be interpreted on the basis of a two-step attitude modification model in which the repetition and content of a communication affect the nature and amount of cognitive responses; these mental responses then influence the recipient's attitude toward the topic. According to their analysis, repetition of message arguments provided subjects with increased opportunities to cognitively process the communication and to recognize the cogency of the arguments. Thus, when the communication was repeated a moderate number of times, counterargumentation decreased and agreement increased. However, when the message was repeated many times, boredom and reactance (Brehm, 1966) may have ensued, thereby motivating subjects to criticize the communication. Consequently, counterargumentation increased and agreement declined.

COGNITIVE RESPONSE REHEARSAL VERSUS MESSAGE REHEARSAL

In their classic monograph on persuasion, Hovland et al. (1949) proposed a theoretical account of the persistence of persuasion over time. They contended that a communication would have lasting effects to the extent that message-arguments were remembered. More recently, McGuire (1968) has proposed that under many conditions attention to, and comprehension of, a persuasive message are necessary for persuasion.

Calder et al. (1974) conducted a series of experiments that have bearing on McGuire's postulate. Calder et al. exposed subjects to one or seven arguments favoring the prosecution in a bigamy trial, and either one or seven arguments on behalf of the defense. Belief in the certainty of the innocence or guilt of the defendant constituted the dependent persuasion variable. The results indicated that persuasion was a function of the number of arguments presented, providing evidence for the role of objective information in producing persuasion effects.

In another experiment in this series, Calder et al. (1974) also measured subjects' cognitive responses to the persuasive communications. The results indicated that the number of thoughts favorable to the defense increased when more defense arguments were presented and decreased with more prosecution arguments. Similarly, the number of thoughts favorable to the prosecution increased with more prosecution arguments and decreased when more defense arguments were presented. Beliefs about the defendant's innocence or guilt were significantly associated with the production of favorable or unfavorable thoughts about the defendant. In addition, increasing the number of defense arguments resulted in more favorable beliefs about the defendant, while increasing the number of prosecution arguments yielded the reverse pattern of results. Persistence of these beliefs over time depended on the number of prosecution, but not the number of defense, arguments that were presented.

Calder et al. concluded that the most parsimonious interpretation of the results was that (a) the amount of objective persuasive information is a partial determinant of thoughts about the communication, and (b) these thoughts help determine beliefs about the issue. The authors also suggested that "if comprehension is broadly interpreted so as to imply communication-provoked thoughts," the results support McGuire's (1968) proposition that attention to and comprehension of a communication are determinants of attitudinal acceptance of the advocated position.

On the other hand, if recall of message-arguments is assumed to be a measure of attention and comprehension, then McGuire's hypothesis must be questioned. A variety of studies have found low or nonsignificant relationships between recall of message-arguments and attitudinal acceptance of the advocated position (see Petty, 1977, and Petty et al., in press, for a review of these studies). However, attitudinal acceptance has been significantly associated with the number of subject-generated favorable and unfavorable cognitive responses (Petty et al., in press).

Petty (1977) has provided convincing support for the superiority of the cognitive response model to the message-learning hypothesis. In the first of a series of experiments, subjects were asked to read several arguments about a social dilemma and to list their thoughts on the issue. The experimenter then assessed subjects' ability to recall their own thoughts and the message arguments, as well as their opinions on the two choice dilemma questions, both immediately and a week later. The results showed that students recalled a greater proportion of their own thoughts than the arguments contained in the message. Moreover, ability to recall message arguments was not correlated with the delayed opinion items, even when the arguments were weighted as to judge-rated and subject-rated persuasiveness. On the other hand, there was a significant relationship between the ability to remember one's own thoughts and the delayed measures of opinion.

In another experiment, subjects read five high or low persuasive arguments on the topic of raising the driving age to 21. Subjects listed five thoughts on the subject and were instructed to memorize either their five thoughts or the five arguments. Attitude change was assessed both immediately and a week later by comparing the two experimental groups and a control group that read five neutral statements on the driving issue. The results revealed that regardless of whether they memorized thoughts or arguments, subjects who read the highly persuasive arguments were most favorable to increasing the driving age to 21 when attitudes were measured immediately. Only subjects in the highly persuasive message condition who memorized their thoughts continued to be favorable to increasing the driving age to 21 when attitudes were assessed a week later. The results support the cognitive response prediction that rehearsal of one's own thoughts is a more important determinant of persistence of persuasion than one's rehearsal of message-arguments. A highly persuasive communication apparently elicits favorable cognitive responses which help determine immediate postcommunication attitudes on the driving issue; to the extent that these favorable cognitive responses continue to be salient, attitude at the delayed measurement is similar to the postmessage attitude.[2]

CONTEXT EFFECTS

Distraction

As communication researchers have long known (for example, Festinger and Maccoby, 1964), people are frequently distracted from attending to communications. (Witness also marketers' and broadcast communicators' concern with "clutter.") The communication may itself be accompanied by extraneous and distracting information (as is advertising) or other people may prevent the individual from devoting full attention to the communication, as is the case with much exposure to mass media. There is abundant evidence that when individuals are distracted from attending to a discrepant communication, they generate fewer counterarguments to the position and are consequently more persuaded by the speaker (Roberts and Maccoby, 1973). The cognitive response interpretation holds that distraction interferes with the dominant cognitive response to a persuasive communication. If the dominant response is counterargumentation (that is, if the message presents discrepant information), then distraction will interfere with the generation of counterarguments and will increase the persuasiveness of the communication. If, on the other hand, the dominant response is proargumentation, then the individual will generate fewer supportive arguments and will consequently exhibit less agreement with the message.

An alternative explanation of the distraction research is also plausible. Baron et al. (1973) asserted that individuals who are distracted while they are exposed to a persuasive message must expend more effort to attend to and understand the message than nondistracted individuals; however, the belief that one has voluntarily expended effort to understand a communication should be dissonant with the knowledge that the message advocates a position with which one disagrees. In other words, dissonance is produced when effort is expended on an unpleasant task (listening to a counterattitudinal communication). One way to reduce this dissonance is to change one's attitude in the direction advocated by the message.

Petty et al. (1976) pitted the cognitive response interpretation against the effort justification hypothesis. According to the cognitive response interpretation, distraction should only increase the persuasibility of a counterattitudinal communication that is susceptible to counterarguing; therefore, distraction should not affect acceptance of a difficult-to-counterargue message because, presumably, there are no counterarguments to be blocked (Petty and Brock, in press). The effort justification hypothesis, however, predicts that there will be increasing acceptance of both an easy-to-counterargue and a difficult-to-counterargue message with increasing amounts of distraction (and, therefore, effort). The results of the Petty (1976) experiment supported the cognitive response interpretation. Distraction only increased the persuasibility of a discrepant communication that was susceptible to counterarguing—that is, the easy-to-counterargue message.

FOREWARNING OF COUNTERATTITUDINAL COMMUNICATIONS

McGuire and Papageorgis (1963) asserted that anticipatory counterargumentative responses will be produced when an individual is warned of an upcoming counterattitudinal message. They suggested that when individuals learn they will receive a communication with which they disagree, they will generate arguments that favor their position and refute the opposing point of view. This anticipatory counterargumentation makes the individual less susceptible to persuasion. Indirect evidence supporting the cognitive response interpretation of forewarning has been accumulated by Freedman and Sears (1965) and Hass and Grady (1975). However, cognitive responses were not measured in the early forewarning studies.

More recently, Petty and Cacioppo (1977) conducted a more direct test of the cognitive response interpretation of forewarning. They reasoned that if the cognitive response hypothesis is correct, subjects should exhibit increased counterargumentation and resistance to persuasion when warned that they are about to be confronted with a discrepant communication and when they are simply asked to list their thoughts about the message. The latter condition is of particular interest to the cognitive response position insofar as this viewpoint maintains that it is not forewarning in and of itself that leads to resistance to persuasion, but "the fact that persons are motivated by the warning to more fully consider their own positions, generating arguments supporting their own stands and opposing alternative stands" (Petty and Cacioppo, 1977:650). Thus, resistance should be conferred on unwarned subjects simply by requesting them to list their thoughts about a counterattitudinal message. If anticipatory thinking rather than warning per se confers resistance, these subjects should also be resistant to influence.

The results were consistent with the cognitive response position. They indicated that forewarning of an upcoming counterattitudinal message on an involving topic led to anticipatory counterarguments on the topic and resistance to persuasive influence. Resistance was also demonstrated in a group of people who were instructed to simply list their thoughts about the counterattitudinal message. The results suggest that forewarning about upcoming discrepant communications on involving topics generates resistance to persuasive influence by producing anticipatory counterargumentation. In addition, Petty and Cacioppo (1979a) demonstrated that forewarning of persuasive intent reduced persuasion on involving issues by evoking counterargument production *during* the presentation of the message. Thus, there is evidence that forewarnings of topic and position on involving counterattitudinal issues reduce persuasion by eliciting anticipatory counterarguments (Petty and Cacioppo, 1977), while forewarnings of persuasive intent on involving counterattitudinal issues reduce persuasion by evoking counterarguments during the message (Petty and Cacioppo, 1979a).

DESTINATION EFFECTS

Individual Versus Group Evaluation of Messages

There is abundant evidence that the real or implicit presence of other people inhibits individuals from giving help in emergency situations (Latané and Darley, 1970). Subsequent research has shown that this diffusion of effort effect occurs in nonemergency situations as well. For example, when others are present or available, people are less inclined to pick up coins in an elevator (Latané and Dabbs, 1975), answer an intercom for someone else (Levy et al., 1972), or help themselves to a coupon for a free lunch (Petty et al., 1977).

Recently, Petty et al. (1977) have argued that this diffusion of effort effect is not limited to tasks requiring physical exertion, but may also apply to cognitive activities as well. Petty et al. reasoned that insofar as cognitive effort is perceived as costly and others are capable of lightening the work load, individuals may attempt to reduce their own cognitive effort by sharing task responsibilities. They also proposed that people expend less cognitive effort on a cognitive task when they are part of a group which is responsible for the task than when they are individually responsible. Petty et al.'s results indicated that individual evaluators reported giving more thought to their evaluations of a poem than group evaluators. Unfortunately, only self-reported measures of perceived effort were obtained in this study. These investigators also found that individual evaluators rated the communication more favorably than did group evaluators.

Four different theoretical explanations can be invoked to account for the tendency of individual evaluators to rate communications more positively than group evaluators. First, dissonance theory states that an individual attempts to justify increased effort expenditure by overvaluing the stimuli (Jones and Gerard, 1967; Wicklund et al., 1967). Individual evaluators may have attempted to justify their enhanced expenditure of effort by evaluating the communications in an overly favorable light. Brock's (1968) commodity theory contends that a communication will have more subjective value for individuals the more effort they expend in attending to it. Deindividuation theory might predict that group evaluators would experience a sense of anonymity which would increase their willingness to provide disparaging feedback about the communication. The final explanation is based on a cognitive response approach. According to this viewpoint, increasing mental effort enhances the perceived features of a communication, resulting in the discovery and increased liking of a good communication's strengths and to disliking of a poor message's shortcomings. Thus, in the Petty et al. (1977) study, group evaluators responded favorably to the communications; however, individual evaluators responded even more positively. This explanation is consistent with the cognitive response position that individual evaluators may have engaged in more thought about the positive communication than group evaluators.

A manipulation of the quality of the stimulus to be evaluated makes it possible to determine which of these theoretical processes mediates the effect of group size on favorability of evaluations (Petty et al., 1979). The dissonance, commodity, and deindividuation accounts would all predict that individual evaluators will rate communications more positively than group evaluators, albeit for different reasons. The cognitive response approach, however, would predict that individual evaluators would rate communications more favorably than group evaluators, but only when a high-quality communication is employed. According to the cognitive response view, if individuals put more thought into their evaluations when they are solely in charge of the evaluation, they should be more likely to recognize the strengths of a "good" communication and the weaknesses of a "bad" message.

Petty et al. (1979) exposed subjects individually or in groups to tapes of a client's session with a good or a bad therapist and to strong, weak, or very weak arguments from a newspaper editorial. The results favored the cognitive response interpretation over the competing theoretical accounts. Individual evaluators produced more positive thoughts and evaluated both the therapist tape and editorial more positively than group evaluators when they were evaluating the "good" therapist tape and the strong editorial. On the other hand, individual evaluators generated more unfavorable thoughts and evaluated the stimulus more negatively than group evaluators when they were evaluating a low-quality stimulus. This latter finding held only for the editorial. In sum, group evaluators did not appear to process information as carefully as individuals, and were consequently less inclined to produce thoughts that accurately reflected the nature of the stimulus.

PHYSIOLOGICAL COMPONENTS

A final line of research deserves mention, although it does not fit into our typology of persuasion variables. Recently, there has been increased attention directed to the relationship between physiological variables and cognitive responses to persuasion (Cacioppo, 1979; Cacioppo and Petty, 1979, in press). This recent research is in part an outgrowth of the criticism that instructing individuals to list their thoughts about a message produces responses that do not occur in real life (see Petty et al., in press, and Cacioppo and Petty, 1979, in press, for a discussion of this issue). Until recently there have been few systematic attempts to develop a concurrent measure of cognitive and affective reactions that could be obtained without the subject's knowledge of its purpose and which did not require the subject to emit a voluntary covert response (Cacioppo and Petty, 1979, in press). Cacioppo and Petty developed an electrophysiological instrument to assess affective reactions to a counterattitudinal communication. In a pilot experiment, after subjects were forewarned that they would hear discrepant communications, both their anticipatory counterargumentation and speech muscle activity increased. In the second experiment, in which subjects were exposed to both a pro- and counter-attitudinal message, the affective nature of the covert reactions was reflected by the pattern of facial muscle changes.

More recently, Cacioppo (1979) has investigated the impact of accelerated heart rate on counterargumentation and resistance to persuasion. Cacioppo manipulated heart rate exogenously within the normal span of cardiac activity and without the subject's awareness of the particular trials on which heart rate was accelerated. Subjects were then exposed to highly involving and discrepant communications at the same time that their heart rate was either actually or ostensibly accelerated. The results indicated that more total thoughts and counterarguments were generated when heart rate was accelerated than when it was not accelerated. In addition, resistance to persuasion was significantly associated with the number of counterarguments produced. The physiological approach that Cacioppo has developed provides a method by which researchers can study the impact on communication processes of "actual but unperceived changes in physiological processes" (Cacioppo, 1979).

CONCLUSION

Over the past five years, the cognitive response approach to persuasion has received impressive support from a variety of lines of investigation. A cognitive response analysis can account for source credibility effects, the impact of several types of message variables, contextual influences (such as distraction and forewarning), and destination factors such as group size. In addition, research indicates that there is a relationship between cognitive responses and physiological processes. This accumulated evidence on a variety of research fronts cannot be easily explained by any other theoretical perspective on persuasion. Only the cognitive response approach appears to have the breadth and parsimony to account for these diverse findings. In the next section we shall offer our own theoretical conjectures on some unresolved and fundamental issues in the study of idiosyncratic cognitive responses to persuasion.

CONCEPTUAL EXPLORATIONS

Investigators have consistently reported low or nonsignificant correlations between recall of arguments contained in the message and agreement with the positions advocated in the communication. By contrast, number of self-generated proarguments about a message has been associated with acceptance of the advocated position, and the number of self-produced

counterarguments has been inversely correlated with attitudinal acceptance of the message. Similarly, rehearsal of own favorable thoughts about
a communication has led to more persistence of persuasion than rehearsal
of the message-arguments. We can have confidence in these results because
they have been obtained by different experimenters, using different oper-
ationalizations and different experimental paradigms. In this section we
shall provide theoretical interpretations for the superiority of own-thought
to message-argument rehearsal.

OWNNESS BIAS

Greenwald (1968) reported that his subjects regarded their own cognitive responses as more original than those improvised by another subject.
Greenwald concluded that people appeared to evaluate their own thoughts
about a persuasive communication more positively than others' thoughts.
Slamecka and Graf (1978) also demonstated that subjects are more confident about their performance when they generate words themselves than
when the same words are simply read. Why are self-generated responses so
influential?

We contend that people have a tendency to value products and aspects
associated with the self; consequently, they attach value to their *own*
cognitive responses to persuasive communications. Because these cognitive
responses "belong to" or are associated with the self, they accrue more
value and exert more influence than the arguments contained in the
message.

The "ownness bias" stems from both territorial and nonterritorial
motives. Aspects of one's personal space are valued even though these
aspects may not be otherwise distinguishable. We prefer our own bed, even
though it is the same as other beds in the barracks or dormitory. We prefer
our own place or chair at table. We prefer our towel, although it is
identical to your towel. If *external* objects associated with self can become
so coveted, it is not surprising that internal extensions of the self, such as
thoughts, dreams, fantasies, and the like, can be accorded special value.
Coveting and protecting personal space extends, we assume, to cognitive
components of that space. A territorial perspective is sufficient to account
for an "ownness bias."

A number of nonterritorial motives could cause individuals to assign
greater weight to mental products that they felt they generated themselves. The notion that people value their own products and efforts has
been articulated by psychoanalytic theorists (such as Freud, 1938) who
have long maintained that this egocentric tendency can be traced to basic
inclinations to value extensions of the self—even feces, for example. More

recently, Kohlberg (1966) has contended that children like same-sex objects and characteristics because they have a natural, built-in inclination to like objects and traits that are similar to the self.

A somewhat different explanation can also be put forth to account for this tendency, which we label "the ownness bias." This interpretation finds its roots in the work of Brock (1968) and Fromkin (Fromkin, 1970, 1972, 1973; Fromkin and Brock, 1973).

Brock (1968) generated a series of propositions, which he called commodity theory, suggesting that people have a tendency to value scarce and unavailable resources. Commodity theory suggests that individuals prize scarce and unavailable objects because of scarcity in and of itself, even when no monetary reward or demand is associated with scarcity. One explanation for the prizing of scarce resources is that the possession of scarce commodities enhances one's uniqueness. Fromkin (1970, 1972, 1973) has argued that individuals need to see themselves as different from other people. Thus, individuals value resources associated with the self because they fulfill the desire to perceive the self and its attributes as unique, distinctive, and different.

Uniqueness and commodity theory suggest that own-thought rehearsal is more persuasive than message-argument rehearsal because people place a greater value on products associated with themselves (their own thoughts) than on exogenous products (such as arguments contained in a message). In essence, people may view their *own* thoughts as more unique, original, creditable, and of greater value than arguments contained in *someone else's* persuasive message. Studies by Greenwald (1968) and Slamecka and Graf (1978) lend support to this position. We emphasize that higher valuation of own thoughts is expected to occur, especially in propaganda situations—those in which the individual perceives the intent to persuade.

If individuals attach value to their cognitive responses because these represent their own unique products, then a manipulation that reinforces and enhances this sense of uniqueness should increase the value—and influence—of individuals' cognitive responses. We envision a study to test this proposition: Subjects would be instructed to read a persuasive communication, list their thoughts about the message, and then indicate their attitudes toward the advocated position. If the message is influential, it should elicit favorable thoughts about the topic (Petty, 1977). Following Petty (1977), one group of subjects would be asked to memorize their thoughts, while a second group would be instructed to memorize the arguments in the message.

A third set of subjects would receive the uniqueness manipulation; after writing down their thoughts, individual subjects in this condition, unbeknown to the others, would be informed that their thoughts represented their highly unique, individualistic responses to the message that were unlike the responses of any other subject. Half of these subjects would then memorize their thoughts, while half would memorize the message-arguments. If uniqueness needs are operative, we should find the greatest persuasion among subjects who memorize thoughts that they are convinced are different from others' responses.[3]

This manipulation is purposefully designed to make it salient to individuals that their thoughts are uniquely their own. In real life, of course, individuals vary in the extent to which they regard their cognitive responses as unique. Beliefs about the uniqueness of one's cognitive products are fairly stable attributes, though they may vary somewhat from situation to situation. Consequently, people do not need chronic public feedback about their cognitive responses in order to believe (or not believe) that their thoughts are uniquely or distinctively their own. This is important because research on cognitive responses typically asks subjects to *privately* list their thoughts about a communication.

If people regard their thoughts as weak, rehearsing these thoughts probably will not be more persuasive than rehearsing the arguments in the message. (See the Personality and Persuasibility section of this chapter for a further discussion of this point.) In addition, there are undoubtedly individual differences in the need to be unique; consequently, not everyone will attach more value to their own cognitive responses because these enhance a sense of uniqueness. Furthermore, people sometimes change their minds about an issue to escape the uncomfortable feeling when they adopt an unpopular or unusual position. In these situations, individuals may attach the greatest value to cognitive responses that reflect the viewpoint of others.

Other determinants of the "ownness bias" already have been suggested—the psychoanalytic proposition regarding instinctual libidinal investment in extensions of the self and Kohlberg's idea that individuals have an innate tendency to value like-self objects. Still other factors could be involved; for example, subjects may attribute persuasive intent to the communicator and therefore be suspicious about the communicator's arguments. By contrast, subjects do not ascribe any hidden motives to themselves when they list their own thoughts as more credible than those that appear in the message. Compared with the message-arguments, the subject's thoughts may possess freshness and originality that are not tainted by any attribution of persuasive intent.

By this point the reader may be wondering how anyone is ever persuaded about anything. After all, if people's own thoughts about a message are always more persuasive than communicator's arguments, then they would never change their attitudes about anything. But, of course, people are persuaded to adopt different positions. It turns out that this is really not a problem for the cognitive response approach. Our position is that once communicators have started to change people's minds about an issue, then they can be most assured that this change will persist if audience members rehearse their own thoughts about the message rather than the speaker's arguments. If people begin to think more favorably about the issue, then attitude change—and persistence of this change—is aided and abetted by the production and rehearsal of self-generated favorable thoughts.

In this section we have suggested that one reason why own-thought rehearsal is more persuasive than learning of message-arguments is that people tend to value and respect their own thoughts more than the arguments in the communication. In the next section, we shall offer a more cognitive explanation for the apparent superiority of own-thought to message-argument rehearsal. These explanations will attempt to account for the finding that self-generated cognitive responses are better *remembered* than those produced by someone else (Greenwald, 1968) or those that are presented to be read by an experimenter (Slamecka and Graf, 1978). After offering some explanations for these findings, we shall return to the question of why self-generated responses are more *persuasive* than message-arguments.

SELF-SCHEMATIC PROCESSING

Individuals remember more of their self-generated arguments to a communication than those improvised by another subject (Greenwald, 1968). They also remember more of the thoughts they generated about the message than the arguments contained in the communication itself (Petty, 1977). Additional support for the finding that people learn their own cognitive responses better than equivalent statements produced by someone else has been recently provided by experimental psychologists (Slamecka and Graf, 1978).

In a series of intriguing experiments, Slamecka and Graf demonstrated that individuals remembered words better when they generated the words themselves than when words were simply presented to be read. This finding held for measures of cued and uncued recognition and free and cued recall. It persisted across variations in rules for encoding, self-paced or timed presentation, presence or absence of test information, and between- subjects or within- subjects designs. These results extend the generalizability of the cognitive response findings to the arena of human learning and memory, suggesting the fundamental nature of these results.

Why are self-generated cognitive responses better learned than the statements contained in a message or provided by an experimenter? One explanation may be located in recent research on the self (Markus, 1977; Rogers et al., 1977). Markus has asserted that people possess a better-developed cognitive schema for self-related information than for other types of information. Thus, information about the self or associated with the self (such as one's thoughts) can be more extensively processed than information from other sources (such as from the message).

In essence, one's own pro- or counterarguments are more meaningfully and extensively processed than the arguments that are contained in the message. An example from everyday experience may clarify this point. We have all read over our colleagues' manuscripts and have been dismayed to discover the presence of obvious typographical errors. And yet it is our colleagues who have the last laugh, for when we read over our own papers, we invariably skip over typographical errors as well. Why are we our own worst proof-readers? Because we read our own material for content and meaning, not for surface attributes. Analogously, when we rehearse our own thoughts about a persuasive communication, we engage in more extensive processing than when we rehearse the arguments in the message.

Other interpretations may also be advanced to explain why subjects remember self-generated material (thoughts) better than information produced externally (for example, the message-arguments). Slamecka and Graf (1978:603) explained their findings on this subject by suggesting:

> Initial recall confers beneficial consequences upon a subsequent memory test on the same material. As applied to the present paradigm, it would suggest that the act of generation is really an instance of recall, with the source being semantic memory. . . . In contrast, a reading task involves no recall-based episodes, since all responses are given.

In addition, Slamecka and Graf suggest that generation involves extensive "tagging of nodes in the associative network, thus increasing access routes" (p. 603).

Whatever the reasons, there is evidence suggesting that self-generated thoughts appear to be more extensively processed and better remembered than message-arguments. We now turn to the issue of how these findings relate to the evidence that own thoughts are more influential than message-arguments.

Brock (1962) showed clearly that own thoughts processed for *meaning* were more influential than own thoughts processed for *grammar and syntax*. Since own arguments about a communication are more likely to be processed for meaning than are the arguments in the message itself, own arguments or thought rehearsal should be more persuasive than rehearsal of the message-arguments. Stated somewhat differently, attention is a necessary condition for persuasion (Osterhouse and Brock, 1970); because we probably direct more and "deeper-level" attention to our own thoughts than to the arguments in the message, we more thoroughly learn the persuasive arguments contained in our own thoughts than the arguments that are contained in the message.

Needless to say, this is an empirically testable proposition. We propose a study to test our hypotheses. Subjects would read a persuasive communication and then list their thoughts about the issue. (If the communication is persuasive, it should elicit favorable thoughts from subjects: Petty, 1977; Petty and Cacioppo, 1979b.) They would next read a second persuasive message on a very similar issue and list the arguments in the message.[4] Attitudes toward both issues would then be measured. If self-schematic processing is operative, subjects should remember more of their thoughts than the arguments in the communication. Since learning of persuasive material can facilitate persuasion (McGuire, 1969; Osterhouse and Brock, 1970), subjects should be more persuaded by the first message—about which they listed their thoughts—than the second communication.

SUMMARY

In this section we have suggested two explanations for the finding that own-thought rehearsal is more influential than the rehearsal of message-arguments. We have proposed that people possess an "ownness bias" which leads them to value and respect their own products and efforts. It was suggested that this bias may derive from natural tendencies to value extensions of the self, need to be unique, or other, possibly attributional, processes. We subsequently focused on the related finding that individuals remember self-generated cognitive responses better than those provided by someone else. A self-schematic processing explanation as well as several other interpretations were invoked. We then suggested how more extensive processing of cognitive responses might help explain their relative influence and persuasive powers. Throughout this section we have proposed methods of testing our hypotheses and propositions.

THEORETICAL FORMULATION OF PERSONALITY AND PERSUASIBILITY

In the preceding sections we have mentioned in passing several issues that have interesting implications for personality and persuasibility. Although there has been abundant research on individual differences in susceptibility to persuasion, the yield has not matched the expenditure of research energies. After over 20 years of research, we still are not certain of the impact of individual difference variables on persuasion; nor do we know which personality variables exert the greatest influence on persuasibility, and why.

We suggest that attention be directed to the role that uniqueness motivation plays in the persuasibility process. For example, individuals who have a strong need to be unique may be more sensitive to their own cognitive responses than individuals low in uniqueness needs. Subjects high in uniqueness needs should be especially motivated to regard their thoughts about a message as "unique, and distinctively their own." They should attach greater value and respect to these thoughts and may even be more confident about their cogency and intellectual value than subjects low in uniqueness needs. As a result, cognitive responses should predict attitudes better for these subjects than for subjects low in uniqueness needs. Individual differences in the extent to which people are biased toward their own products may have interesting implications for research on personality and persuasibility. For example, to the extent that a good self-image involves the favorable evaluation of one's own cognitive products, high self-esteem subjects should regard their own cognitive responses to a persuasive message as more original and of higher overall quality and importance than low self-esteem subjects. We predict that high self-esteem individuals will be more persuaded by a message when they rehearse their own proarguments than when they rehearse the favorable arguments contained in the communication. The opposite prediction is made for low self-esteem persons, who are likely to attach less value to their own arguments than to those generated by someone else.

A caveat needs to be added here. We believe that only a particular dimension of self-esteem may affect own cognitive responses and subsequent susceptibility to persuasion (Hedges, 1974; Perloff, 1978). It is possible, for example, that only individuals who have a high regard for their own intellect and cognitions will be most persuaded by a communication when they rehearse their own thoughts, and that only persons who have a low regard for their cognitive skills will be most influenced when they rehearse the arguments in the message. In essence, then, noncognitive dimensions of the self-concept (such as self-esteem about social skills) should not affect the value people attach to their own cognitive responses to communications.

Note that our approach differs somewhat from McGuire's (1968) information-processing formulation of individual differences in persuasibility. McGuire contended that learning and comprehension of the content of a persuasive communication mediate the impact of a personality variable on susceptibility to persuasion. McGuire asserted that a personality variable's impact on persuasion will vary as a function of the complexity of the persuasive message and the individual's comprehension of the message. According to McGuire, comprehension and message learning are likely to mediate the impact of individual difference variables on persuasion when the message allows for variance in people's comprehension of the message—that is, when the communication is complex and subtle.

McGuire's approach must be questioned, however, in view of the repeated evidence that message learning is only weakly correlated with attitudinal acceptance of the communication. The documented importance of cognitive responses in persuasion suggests an alternative proposition. Rather than solely emphasizing the mediating role of message comprehension and learning, we conjecture that the impact of individual difference variables on persuasion is also mediated by the value people attach to their own cognitive responses to persuasive communications.

Individuals who are at high and low levels of a personality variable should place differential value on their arguments with a counterattitudinal communication. Thus, to the extent that a good self-image involves the favorable evaluation of one's accomplishments, products, and thoughts, high self-esteem persons should perceive that their counterarguments are of relatively high quality; believing that they effectively refuted the advocated position, they should be relatively immune to persuasion. On the other hand, low self-esteem subjects, who have a lower image of their overall competence, should perceive their counterarguments to be of relatively low quality; given their belief that they have not effectively criticized the speaker's position, they should be prime candidates for attitude change and persuasion.

Personality variables like self-esteem, then, are believed to impact upon susceptibility to persuasion because they affect the value that individuals attach to their own cognitive responses to persuasive communications. Other individual difference variables—particularly developmental variables such as age and cognitive-developmental stage—may also exert predictable effects on resistance to persuasion to the extent that they influence the value attached to own thoughts about the persuasive communication. On the other hand, there may be other dispositional variables that do not influence resistance to persuasion because they do not affect the perceived value or quality of own mental responses to the communication (for example, sex).

PRACTICAL APPLICATIONS

How can communicators benefit from the finding that own thought rehearsal induces more persuasion than message-argument rehearsal? At present, communication theorists and practitioners (Cutlip and Center, 1971) tend to operate on the basis of the common-sense assumption that a highly effective way to persuade someone is to teach them—and teach them well—the contents of the persuasive message. For example, public relations experts and advertisers employ the well-touted principle of message repetition when they repeat the same phrase or theme time and again during a broadcast. Our research suggests that it may be more effective in the long run if communicators (a) developed communications that are sufficiently persuasive to evoke favorable thoughts from people, and (b) induced individuals to rehearse and remember these favorable thoughts. This approach, if adopted, has intriguing implications for physical and mental health.

PHYSICAL HEALTH

Behavioral scientists have become increasingly interested in determining how their theories and research can be employed to improve the state of people's physical and psychological health. For example, in the past five years, both the International Communication Association and the American Psychological Association have added health to their list of divisions. The cognitive response approach outlined in this chapter, we believe, has some interesting implications for health communication.

Over the past several years, "self-help" clinics and "patient-teaching" workshops have rapidly increased in number (Schwartz, 1977; Tracy and Gussow, 1976). There are clinics to help cancer patients cope with the physical and psychological traumas of cancer, groups to aid smokers in their efforts to quit smoking, as well as more traditional groups such as Weight Watchers and Alcoholics Anonymous. At the same time, nursing and hospital personnel are increasingly concerned with teaching patients preventive medical strategies and orientations, such as exercise and regularly taking prescribed medications. These clinics are all involved, in one way or another, in the business of persuasion; they are seeking to change people's health-related attitudes, beliefs, and behaviors.

Our implicit emphasis on "self-persuasion" has some interesting implications for patient self-care. Specifically, the cognitive response approach suggests that patients might be persuaded to take pills, jog frequently, and the like if they could be induced to process and rehearse favorable thoughts about these behaviors. Rather than lecturing about the virtues of self-care, a self-help clinic might employ the following strategy: Individuals would listen to a persuasive communication which graphically explains the benefits of various self-help strategies (for example, taking medications). Patients could then be asked to take a few minutes to collect their thoughts and list all the reasons why it is important to engage in that behavior. Individuals would then be instructed to regularly think about and rehearse these reasons. Well-established principles of memory might be employed to induce self-persuasion (for example, use of phrases or catchwords that make one's own thought easier to remember). In effect, people would persuade themselves about the advantages of a particular self-care strategy.

MENTAL HEALTH

Cognitive strategies, such as those we have suggested, may also be useful to clinicians. For example, cognitive response techniques might be used to aid students who are convinced their poor performance in math courses is due to their lack of intelligence and ability. The students might be asked to simply write down and rehearse all the reasons why their attribution is likely to be false (for example, failure is also due to poor instruction, difficulty of tests; in the case of women, their lack of effort in math because they erroneously believe that because they are females they lack basic quantitative skills). While a therapist might help students to believe that these are viable explanations of their problems, the students would list and write down these explanations and thoughts *in their own words*. Cognitive response research suggests that the students' production and rehearsal of their own responses to the problem would be a first step toward persuading them that their failure in math can be overcome.

These strategies are similar in many ways to the cognitively based attributional strategies suggested by Valins and Nisbett (1971). The difference is that our approach emphasizes the production and rehearsal of the client's *own* thoughts and attributions, not the passive acceptance of the therapist's explanations. Needless to say, this strategy is not likely to be successful unless the patient or client is motivated to engage in favorable thought-processing and self-persuasion. Yet many of the people who attend self-help clinics are already motivated to change their health-related beliefs, attitudes, and behaviors. Given this motivation, the cognitive response strategy may be a particularly fruitful way to induce attitude change.

NOTES

1. Shakespeare's comment is also consistent with Tesser's (Tesser and Cowan, 1977) studies, which show that time to think about a topic is associated with polarization of attitudes on the issue. There is a subtle difference between Tesser's

position and the cognitive response approach in that the latter emphasizes the production of positive and negative thoughts about an issue. The cognitive response approach asserts that it is not length of time to think about a persuasive communication that determines attitude change; rather, persuasion is determined by the number of pro- or counterarguments that are generated, the cogency or implausibility of the message-arguments, and the perceived personal benefits and costs of the advocated position. However, if one takes Shakespeare's remark about thinking in its most general sense and also considers the production of counterarguments in Hamlet's famous "To be or not to be" soliloquy, then Shakespeare is indeed an early advocate of the cognitive response approach.

2. It should be noted that recent covariance analyses lend further support to both the association of cognitive responses and persuasion and the lack of relationship between persuasion and recall of message-arguments. Cacioppo and Petty (1979) conducted several analyses of covariance using cognitive responses and recall as covariates. When both counterarguments and favorable thoughts served as the covariate, the original significant main effect of the independent variable on agreement was reduced to nonsignificance. On the other hand, the F for agreement remained significant when message recall served as the covariate.

3. Uniqueness will have to be varied in such a way that related, but confounding, processes like self-esteem are not simultaneously manipulated.

4. Order of presentation would be randomized such that half of the subjects listed thoughts first and half listed the message-arguments first.

Appendix

METHODS OF MEASURING COGNITIVE RESPONSES

Hovland et al. (1949) were the first to assess cognitive responses to persuasive communications. They provided subjects with a set of push buttons during the presentation of a movie and instructed them to press one button during parts of the movie they liked and the other during segments they did not like. A similar technique, called "signal-stopping," has been developed recently by Carter et al. (1973). At the same time, Cacioppo (1979) has employed physiological measures of cognitive responses, while Lingle and Ostrom (in press) have made use of reaction time measures.

However, the most common method to measure cognitive responses has been the thought-listing technique developed by Brock (1967) and Greenwald (1968) (see below for illustration of thought-listing procedure). This procedure requires subjects to read or listen to a persuasive message and then report the thoughts that crossed their minds as they attended to the communication. A series of spaces is provided for subjects to list their thoughts or reactions to the message. A major benefit of this procedure is that it provides a rich set of information about people's ongoing thoughts, ideas, and mental responses to a persuasive communication.

It should be noted that since the procedure was developed, other investigators have modified or altered the thought-listing technique. For example, some researchers instruct subjects to list their thoughts while listening to the message, while others employ the original procedure in which subjects list their thoughts after exposure to the message. Another procedure has been employed by Greenwald (1968), who has instructed subjects to classify their thoughts on the basis of whether they fit several categories. For example, Greenwald's subjects classified their thoughts as to whether they were (a) externally originated (having their source in the communication); (b) recipient-modified (reactions to and qualifications of the communication materials); or (c) recipient-generated (responses that cannot be directly traced to the communication). (See Roberts and Maccoby, 1973, for a description of the various methods used to assess cognitive responses. Also see Petty et al., in press, for a discussion of the reliability and validity of cognitive response measures.)

SAMPLE THOUGHT-LISTING PROCEDURE

We now want to probe deeper into your feelings about a campus issue. Specifically, we are interested in your thoughts on the topic of comprehensive exams for seniors. The next few pages contain the form we have prepared for you to use to record your thoughts and ideas. Simply write down the first idea on the topic that comes to mind in the first box, the second idea that occurs to you in the second box, etc. Please put only one idea or thought in a box. You might have ideas all on one side of the issue or the other, or a mixture of the two. Any of these is fine. Please state your thoughts and ideas as concisely as possible; a phrase is sufficient. IGNORE SPELLING, GRAMMAR, and PUNCTUATION.

You will have *three minutes* to write your ideas. We have deliberately made the booklets longer than we think most people will need to ensure that everyone will have plenty of room to write his or her ideas, so don't worry if you aren't able to fill every box. Just put down as many ideas as occur to you on the topic during the time allowed. *DO NOT BEGIN WRITING UNTIL INSTRUCTED.* Remember, in this section you will have three minutes to write your ideas on required comprehensive exams for seniors.

PLEASE WRITE ONLY ONE IDEA PER BOX

REFERENCES

BARON, R.S., BARON, P.H., and MILLER, N. (1973). "The relationship between distraction and persuasion." Psychological Bulletin, 80:310-323.

BEM, D.J. (1967). "Self-perception: An alternative explanation of cognitive dissonance phenomena." Psychological Review, 74:183-200.

BOCHNER, S., and INSKO, C. (1966). "Communication discrepancy, source credibility and opinion change." Journal of Personality and Social Psychology, 4:614-621.

BOCK, D., and SAINE, T. (1975). "The impact of source credibility, attitude valence and task sensitization on trait errors in speech evaluation." Speech Monographs, 37:342-358.

BREHM, J. (1966). A theory of psychological reactance. Morristown, NJ: General Learning Press.

BROCK, T.C. (1962). "Cognitive restructuring and attitude change." Journal of Abnormal and Social Psychology, 64:264-271.

——— (1967). "Communication discrepancy and intent to persuade as determinants of counterargument production." Journal of Experimental Social Psychology, 3:296-309.

——— (1968). "Implications of commodity theory for value change." In A.G. Greenwald, T.C. Brock, and T.M. Ostrom (eds.), Psychological foundations of attitudes. New York: Academic Press.

CACIOPPO, J.T. (1979). "The effects of exogenous changes in heart rate on the facilitation of thought and resistance to persuasion." Journal of Personality and Social Psychology, 37:489-498.

——— and PETTY, R.E. (1979). "Effects of message repetition and position on cognitive responses, recall, and persuasion." Journal of Personality and Social Psychology, 37:97-109.

——— (in press). "Attitudes and cognitive responses: An electrophysiological approach." Journal of Personality and Social Psychology.

CACIOPPO, J.T., GLASS, C.R., and MERLUZZI, T.V. (1979). Self-statements and self-evaluations: A cognitive-response analysis of heterosocial anxiety." Cognitive Therapy and Research, 3: 249-262.

CACIOPPO, J.T., HARKINS, S.G., and PETTY, R.E. (in press). "The nature of attitudes and cognitive responses and their relationships to behavior." In R.E. Petty, T.M. Ostrom and T.C. Brock (eds.), Cognitive responses in persuasion: A text in attitude change. Hillsdale, NJ: Lawrence Erlbaum.

CALDER, B.J. (1978). "Cognitive response, imagery and scripts: What is the cognitive basis of attitude?" In H.K. Hunt (ed.), Advances in consumer research, volume 5. Ann Arbor, MI: Association for Consumer Research.

———, INSKO, C.A., and YANDELL, B. (1974). "The relation of cognitive and memorial processes to persuasion in a simulated jury trial." Journal of Applied Social Psychology, 4:62-93.

CARTER, R.F., RUGGELS, W., JACKSON, K., and HEFFNER, M. (1973). "Application of signaled stopping technique to communication research." In P. Clarke (ed.), New models for communication research. Beverly Hills, CA: Sage.

CIALDINI, R., LEVY, A., HERMAN, P., KOZLOWSKI, L., and PETTY, R. (1976). "Elastic shifts of opinion: Determinants of direction and durability." Journal of Personality and Social Psychology, 34:663-672.

COOK, T.D. (1969). "Competence, counterarguing, and attitude change." Journal of Personality, 37:342-358.

CUTLIP, S.M., and CENTER, A.H. (1971). Effective public relations. Englewood Cliffs, NJ: Prentice-Hall.

DEAN, R., AUSTIN, J., and WATTS, W. (1971). "Forewarning effects in persuasion: Field and classroom experiments." Journal of Personality and Social Psychology, 18:210-221.

EAGLY, A., and HIMMELFARB, S. (1978). "Attitudes and opinions." In L. Porter and M. Rosenzweig (eds.), Annual review of psychology, 29. Palo Alto, CA: Annual Reviews, Inc.

FESTINGER, L. (1957). A theory of cognitive dissonance. Evanston, IL: Row, Peterson.

——— and MACCOBY, N. (1964). "On resistance to persuasive communications." Journal of Abnormal and Social Psychology, 68:359-366.

FREEDMAN, J., and SEARS, D. (1965). "Warning, distraction, and resistance to influence." Journal of Personality and Social Psychology, 1:262-266.

FREUD, S. (1938). The basic writings of Sigmund Freud. New York: Modern Library.

FROMKIN, H.L. (1970). "The effects of experimentally aroused feelings of undistinctiveness upon valuation of scarce and novel experiences." Journal of Personality and Social Psychology, 16:521-529.

——— (1972). "Feelings of interpersonal undistinctiveness: An unpleasant affective state." Journal of Experimental Research in Personality, 6:178-185.

——— (1973). The psychology of uniqueness: Avoidance of similarity and seeking of differentness. Paper No. 438 Institute for Research in the Behavioral, Economic, and Management Sciences, Purdue University.

——— and BROCK, T.C. (1973). "Erotic materials: A commodity theory analysis of availability and desirability." Journal of Applied Social Psychology, 3:219-231.

GREENWALD, A.G. (1968). "Cognitive learning, cognitive response to persuasion, and attitude change." In A.G. Greenwald, T.C. Brock, and T.M. Ostrom (eds.), Psychological foundations of attitudes. New York: Academic Press.

HASS, R.G., and GRADY, K. (1975). "Temporal delay, type of forewarning and resistance to persuasion." Journal of Experimental Social Psychology, 11:459-469.

HEDGES, N. (1974). "Attitude change as a function of confidence in counterargumentation." Personality and Social Psychology Bulletin, 1:141-143.

HOVLAND, C., LUMSDAINE, A.A., and SHEFFIELD, F.D. (1949). Experiments on mass communication. Princeton: Princeton University Press.

INSKO, C.A., LIND, E., and LATOUR, S. (1976). "Persuasion, recall, and thoughts." Representative Research in Social Psychology, 7:66-78.

JONES, E.E., and GERARD, H.B. (1967). Foundations of social psychology. New York: John Wiley.

KOHLBERG, L. (1966). "A cognitive-developmental analysis of children's sex-role concepts and attitudes." In E. E. Maccoby (ed.), The development of sex differences. Stanford: Stanford University Press.

LATANÉ, B., and DABBS, J.M. (1975). "Sex, group size, and helping in three cities." Sociometry, 38:180-194.

LATANÉ, B., and DARLEY, J.M. (1970). The unresponsive bystander: Why doesn't he help? New York: Appleton-Century-Crofts.

LATANE, B., WILLIAMS, K.D., and HARKINS, S.G. (1979). "Many hands make light the work: The causes and consequences of social loafing." Journal of Personality and Social Psychology, 37:822-832.

LEVY, P., LUNDGREN, D., ANSEL, M., FELL, D., FINK, B., and McGRATH, J.E. (1972). "Bystander effect in a demand-without-threat situation." Journal of Personality and Social Psychology, 24:166-171.

LINGLE, J. and OSTROM, T.M. (in press). "Principles of memory and cognition in attitude formation." In R.E. Petty, T.M. Ostrom, and T.C. Brock (eds.), Cognitive responses in persuasion: A text in attitude change. Hillsdale, NJ: Lawrence Erlbaum.

MARKUS, H. (1977). "Self-schemata and processing information about the self." Journal of Personality and Social Psychology, 35:63-78.

McGINNES, E. (1973). "Initial attitude, source credibility, and involvement as factors in persuasion." Journal of Experimental Social Psychology, 9:285-296.

McGURIE, W.J. (1968). "Personality and attitude change: An information-processing theory." In A.G. Greenwald, T.C. Brock, and T.M. Ostrom (eds.), Psychological foundations of attitudes. New York: Academic Press.

––– (1969). "The nature of attitudes and attitude change." In G. Lindzey and E. Aronson (eds.), Handbook of social psychology, volume 3. Reading, MA: Addison-Wesley.

––– and PAPAGEORGIS, D. (1963). "Effectiveness of forewarning in developing resistance to persuasion." Public Opinion Quarterly, 26:24-34.

OSTERHOUSE, R.A., and BROCK, T.C. (1970). "Distraction increases yielding to propaganda by inhibiting counterarguing." Journal of Personality and Social Psychology, 15:344-358.

PALLAK, M.S., MUELLER, M., DOLLAR, K., and PALLAK, J. (1972). "Effect of commitment on responsiveness to an extreme consonant communication." Journal of Personality and Social Psychology, 23:429-436.

PERLOFF, R.M. (1978). "An attributional and cognitive response approach to personality and persuasibility." Doctoral dissertation, University of Wisconsin-Madison. (unpublished)

PETTY, R.E. (1977). "A cognitive response analysis of the temporal persistence of attitude changes induced by persuasive communications." Doctoral dissertation, The Ohio State University. (unpublished)

––– and BROCK, T.C. (in press). "Thought disruption and persuasion: Assessing the validity of attitude change experiments." In R.E. Petty, T.M. Ostrom, and T.C. Brock (eds.), Cognitive Responses in Persuasion: A Text in Attitude Change. Hillsdale, N.J.: Lawrence Erlbaum.

PETTY, R.E., and CACIOPPO, J.T. (1977). "Forewarning, cognitive responding, and resistance to persuasion." Journal of Personality and Social Psychology, 35:645-655.

––– (1979a). "Effects of forewarning of persuasive intent and involvement on cognitive responses and persuasion." Personality and Social Psychology Bulletin, 5: 173-176.

––– (1979b). "Issue involvement can increase or decrease persuasion by enhancing message-relevant cognitive responses." Journal of Personality and Social Psychology, 37:1915-1926.

PETTY, R.E., HARKINS, S.G., and WILLIAMS, K.D. (1979). "The effects of diffusion of cognitive effort on attitudes: An information processing view." Journal of Personality and Social Psychology.

PETTY, R.E., OSTROM, T.M., and BROCK, T.C. (eds., in press). Cognitive responses in persuasion: A text in attitude change. Hillsdale, NJ: Lawrence Erlbaum.

PETTY, R.E., WELLS, G.L., and BROCK, T.C. (1976). "Distraction can enhance or reduce yielding to propaganda: Thought disruption versus effort justification." Journal of Personality and Social Psychology, 34:874-884.

PETTY, R.E., HARKINS, S.G., WILLIAMS, K.D. and LATANÉ, B. (1977). "The effects of group size on cognitive effort and evaluation." Personality and Social Psychology Bulletin, 3:579-582.

PETTY, R.E., WILLIAMS, K.D., HARKINS, S.G., and LATANÉ, B. (1977). "Social inhibition of helping yourself: Bystander response to a cheeseburger." Personality and Social Psychology Bulletin, 3:575-578.

ROBERTS, D.F. and MACCOBY, N. (1973). "Information processing and persuasion: Counterarguing behavior." In P. Clarke (ed.), New models for communication research. Beverly Hills, CA: Sage.

ROGERS, T.B., KUIPER, N.A., and KIRKER, W.S. (1977). "Self-reference and the encoding of personal information." Journal of Personality and Social Psychology, 35:677-688.

SCHWARTZ, J.L. (1977). Motivating for health—The self-care/self-help concept. Sacramento: Office of Planning and Program Analysis.

SHERIF, M., and HOVLAND, C. (1961). Social judgment. New Haven: Yale University Press.

SHERIF, C.W., SHERIF, M., and NEBERGALL, R.E. (1965). Attitude and attitude change. Philadelphia: W.B. Saunders.

SLAMECKA, N.J. and GRAF, P. (1978). The generation effect: Delineation of a phenomenon. Journal of Experimental Psychology: Human Learning and Memory, 4:592-604.

STERNTHAL, B., DHOLAKIA, R., and LEAVITT, C. (1978). "The persuasive effect of source credibility: Tests of cognitive response." Journal of Consumer Research, 4:252-260.

TESSER, A., and COWAN, C. (1977). "Some attitudinal and cognitive consequences of thought." Journal of Research in Personality, 11:216-226.

TESSER, A., and LEONE, C. (1977). "Cognitive schemas and thought as determinants of attitude change." Journal of Experimental Social Psychology, 13:340-356.

TRACY, G.S., and GUSSOW, Z. (1976). "Self-help health groups: A grass roots response to a need for services." Journal of Applied Behavioral Science, 12:381-396.

TYBOUT, A.M., STERNTHAL, B., and CALDER, B.J. (1977). "A two-stage theory of information processing in persuasion: An integrative view of cognitive response and self-perception theory." In H.K. Hunt (ed.), Advances in consumer research, volume 5. Ann Arbor, MI: Association for Consumer Research.

VALINS, S., and NISBETT, R.E. (1971). "Attribution processes in the development and treatment of emotional disorder." In E.E. Jones, D. Kanouse, H.H. Kelly, R.E. Nisbett, S. Valins, and B. Weiner (eds.), Attribution: perceiving the causes of behavior. Morristown, NJ: General Learning Press.

WEISS, W. (1968). "Modes of resolution and reasoning in attitude change experiments." In R. Abelson, E. Aronson, W. McGuire, T. Newcomb, M. Rosenberg, and P. Tannenbaum (eds.), Theories of cognitive consistency: A sourcebook. Chicago: Rand McNally.

WICKLUND, R.A., COOPER, J., and LINDER, D. (1967). "Effects of expected effort on attitude change prior to exposure." Journal of Experimental Social Psychology, 2:416-428.

ZAJONC, R.B. (1968). "The attitudinal effects of mere exposure." Journal of Personality and Social Psychology Monograph, 9(2, Pt.2)

Chapter 4

THE JUDGMENT OF COMMUNICANT ACCEPTABILITY

Gary Cronkhite and Jo R. Liska

THE FACTOR ANALYSIS of semantic differential "credibility" scales by Berlo, Lemert, and Mertz was a major event in the early history of communication research. (The date of publication was 1969; actually, the paper had been around in mimeographed form for almost a decade before it was published.) The credibility construct was peculiar to communication, not borrowed from social psychology or sociology as were so many early variables. Berlo, Lemert, and Mertz treated the construct using a new and sophisticated statistical tool, factor analysis, which was only then becoming feasible as a result of sudden advances in computer technology. It was a proud day in the history of communication research.

Unfortunately, researchers dealing with source credibility seem to have been transfixed by the Berlo, Lemert, and Mertz technique. In the succeeding 15 years little was done with the credibility construct other than to factor analyze similar sets of semantic differential scales used by a variety of subject populations to rate a variety of potential sources.[1]

The present writers have elsewhere bemoaned the sins of that era (Cronkhite and Liska, 1976; Liska, 1978). We do not propose to repeat the entire litany, but a brief summary should be instructive. In our review of the factor analytic studies of source credibility we found that rating scales were generally selected haphazardly, sometimes from the researchers' own imaginations, but more frequently from previous studies.

They were seldom generated by the subjects themselves. The danger with this approach is that the array of factors may have been limited artificially; listeners may, in fact, use factors of judgment which go undetected because they are given no scales representing those factors. We found that semantic differential scales were used almost exclusively, probably because they are so easy to construct, whereas Likert-type scales and behavioral differential scales (Triandis, 1964), for example, which might elicit more subtle and/or more specific responses, were virtually ignored. We found that the same factor names were frequently applied to factors which loaded on quite dissimilar sets of scales, giving the illusion of continuity and similarity where none existed. We found that, in the search for generalizable factors of source credibility, factor structure differences among rater populations, among sources rated, and among communication topics/situations were largely ignored. We also found a number of problems with the factoring procedures and their interpretation.

A RECONCEPTUALIZATION OF "SOURCE CREDIBILITY"

In addition to the preceding difficulties, the major problem we observed was that the factor analytic approach seems to have exerted a stultifying effect upon conceptualization of the function of credibility in the process of communication in general and persuasion in particular. Apparently, it is so easy to find semantic differential scales which seem relevant to sources, so easy to name or describe potential/hypothetical sources, so easy to capture college students to use the scales to rate the sources, so easy to submit those ratings to factor analysis, so much fun to name the factors when one's research assistant returns with the computer printout, and so rewarding to have a guaranteed publication with no fear of nonsignificant results that researchers, once exposed to the pleasures of the factor analytic approach, rapidly became addicted to it. More difficult research approaches requiring the mental effort of conceptualization and theorizing, the risk of advancing hypotheses, and the labor of constructing actual messages or observing actual communication languished for years while credibility researchers concentrated on factor analysis.

CREDIBILITY AND PROCESS

The factor analytic research paradigm has severely alienated the construct of credibility from the process in which it participates. Asking someone to contemplate and rate a potential source (for example, "Ted Kennedy") or a hypothetical source who is described, without describing the topic or the situation and without presenting or at least describing an actual communication, radically violates the concept of communication as process. In such a paradigm the potential source is assumed to be static, the rater (who is not even a listener) is assumed to be static, and the situation and the communication are nonexistent.

Part of the difficulty in fitting the construct of credibility into the process of persuasion is that a tautology seems to be operating. Of course listeners are more likely to believe those who are credible; whom else would they believe? But the construct treated in this way begins to take on an identity independent of the research findings and begins to obscure other important and interesting variables. For example, McCroskey (1966) long ago banished the "dynamism" dimension from consideration because it does not seem to fit the construct of credibility, and has done the same with several of Norman's (1963) factors which seem to be dimensions of person perception in general but do not fit an a priori conception of credibility.

Despite its exile, who would deny that dynamism plays a part in the process of persuasion, even though it may not be a semantic subset of "credibility"? And what of reluctant witnesses? Are they "credible"? Certainly not in the sense of being necessarily competent or trustworthy, but certainly in the sense of being believable so long as they are testifying against their own biases and best interests. And what of well-liked and/or famous sports figures who endorse products about which they know very little but from which they profit a great deal? Is it possible the millions spent on this sort of advertising is being wasted simply because the celebrities are not competent and trustworthy?

We could continue at length in this vein, but let us come to the point: *People choose to participate in the process of persuasion with others who are most likely to satisfy needs and achieve goals which are most salient and important at the moment of choice.* The construct of "credibility" simply fails to cover all that is important about the participants in the process of persuasion.

SOURCE AND PROCESS

We further limit ourselves if we insist on considering only character-istics of "sources." For one thing, we limit the analysis to persuasion which occurs in the mass media or public speaking, since those are the only formats in which sources are more or less identifiable and capable of being somewhat reliably distinguished from receivers. In fact, a great deal of persuasion occurs in face-to-face interaction in dyads, triads, and small groups and organizations, with all participants playing both source and receiver roles. In such cases, interpersonal bargaining for mutual need satisfaction becomes an inherent part of the process of persuasion. We can deal with interpersonal bargaining and other interpersonal phenomena relevant to persuasion only if we deal with *participant* characteristics rather than merely *source* characteristics.

But suppose we give a bit more thought to the phenomena of mass media and public speaking. Do listeners always attend to public speakers and television commercials because they consider the sources to be believable? Sometimes that is the reason, of course, but persuasion in such formats also proceeds as a matter of mutual need satisfaction. Sometimes the listener needs are satisfied by sources who are competent and trustworthy, but frequently they are not; likeability, novelty, and entertainment are often valued more highly.

Source needs are equally important in public speaking and mass media, and satisfaction of those needs depends on listener characteristics. People choose to speak in public in order to satisfy certain needs: money, votes, and acclamation, among others. Those needs usually will be satisfied by attempting to persuade listeners having certain specific characteristics, seldom by persuading some random aggregation. Mass media persuaders must also remain aware of the specific characteristics of their audiences if they are to satisfy their needs. It is no accident that commercials for Mattel toys and Kellogg cereals are scheduled for Saturday mornings rather than for prime time or weekdays—they are aimed at children who need something to do while their parents recover from Friday night. The persuaders schedule the persuasion at the appointed time and the persuaders gather at the appointed time because it is mutually satisfying.

Thus, the characteristics of sources are of no greater import to a dispassionate scholarly observer trying to analyze the total process of persuasion than are the characteristics of receivers, and that is true regardless of the context or format in which the persuasion is occurring.

Of course, listener *characteristics* have always interested persuaders, and thus analysts, who have usually looked at persuasion from the persuader's point of view. In much the same way, hunters are interested in the characteristics of rabbits so they can find and convert the animals to their own use, and one who proposes to instruct novice hunters is going to have similar interests. But that view of listener characteristics is extremly myopic for a scholar studying persuasion as a process.

We propose to consider also the extent to which the achievement of listeners' needs/goals is facilitated or blocked by various source characteristics. In fact, we propose to express most source and listener characteristics as needs/goals, as indicative of needs/goals, or as causative of needs/goals, and then describe how various combinations of participants' needs/goals may or may not be mutually facilitative.

INFORMATION AND ATTRIBUTION

We have concluded that there is more to assessing the relevant characteristics of participants involved in persuasive transactions than can be subsumed under the restricted construct of credibility. We have also concluded it is not merely the characteristics and needs/goals of sources which must be assessed. Still, if we abandon the term "source credibility," the construct it represents, and the linear effects-oriented model upon which it is based, what are we to use in its stead?

Eagly and Himmelfarb (1978) wrote in the *Annual Review of Psychology* last year that research on attitudes and opinions seems to be attracting interest again after a period of dormancy, and attributed this

> to a more promising outlook for the attitude-behavior relationship and a widely shared interest in information-processing views about attitude formation and change. Information processing is a major theme, especially in the persuasion literature, and may account for the renewed interest investigators are showing in many classic research problems [1978:517].

Then, regarding the construct of credibility in particular, they wrote:

> Studies by speech communication researchers have repeatedly demonstrated that credibility judgments are based on multidimensional criteria (e.g., 23 [Berlo et al., 1969]), but recent work (55 [Cronkhite and Liska, 1976]) suggests that the components of credibility may not be transsituationally valid because they depend on the identity of the communicator and the role a communication is expected to perform [1978:522].

If information-processing approaches are moving opinion theory in general out of the doldrums, perhaps a similar approach can do the same for credibility. That was the direction in which we were pointing in the 1976 paper (Cronkhite and Liska, 1976), and that is the sort of conceptualization we would like to develop here, but one which also takes advantage of attribution theory.

The conceptualization we have in mind is one in which an individual attributes certain unobservable characteristics to others on the basis of observed characteristics. The individual then evaluates the others by comparing these attributed characteristics to criteria for desirable communicators which have been derived from the needs/goals which are salient in the specific communication situation. Figure 1 is our attempt to represent this conceptualization graphically and simply.

Because of the linear nature of the print medium, we are going to have to discuss this process as if it occurs in three phases, although we are

Figure 1 Diagram of the Process by which an Individual Judges the Acceptability of Another Individual

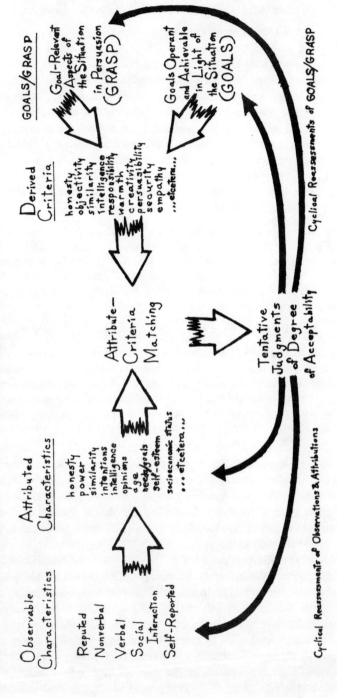

relatively certain it does not. We will deal first with the process of attributing characteristics to other communicators, then with the process of deriving the criteria for desirable communicators from needs/goals salient in a communication situation, and finally with the process of comparing the attributed characteristics to the derived criteria. In fact, we presently assume the three processes proceed simultaneously. This assumption is especially important because it retains the probability that early selection and matching of criteria to initial attributed communicator characteristics will affect subsequent perceptions of both communicators and situations.

CHARACTERISTICS OF COMMUNICANTS

Classic studies by Asch (1951, 1956) and Sherif (1935, 1936) demonstrated early and persuasively that humans have a tendency to "construct" social "reality," and much of social psychology and communication research since then has consisted of reaffirmation of that conclusion. However, we believe there exists such a rich array of objectively observable human characteristics that much of what has been attributed to autistic construction can be attributed instead to our observation of this array of characteristics. In fact, the existence of such a quantity of observable information makes all the more remarkable those instances of autistic perceptual construction which do occur. We propose first to survey this array of social information and then consider the ways in which people attribute more abstract characteristics to their potential communicants on the basis of that information.

THE SOCIAL ARRAY

The array of available social information can be subdivided into at least five types, according to the epistemological conditions governing its perception. These five types we will discuss briefly under the following headings: (1) reputed characteristics, (2) nonverbal characteristics, (3) verbal characteristics, (4) characteristics of social interaction, and (5) self-reported characteristics.

Reputed Characteristics

The reports of others regarding potential communicants constitute a major source of information. Such reports may concern observable, verifiable characteristics such as height and specific instances of nonfluency, or reporters may make their own attributions of abstract characteristics such as attractiveness or honesty. In either case, it is the *report* which constitutes a part of the observable social array, and not the characteristics which reporters claim are descriptive of the potential communicator.

We mention this first in part because many, if not most, of the studies dealing with impression formation, interpersonal attraction, person perception, and consensus[2] have manipulated *reputed* characteristics of fictitious people or *bogus* characteristics purported to describe people the subjects had met earlier or would meet later in the course of the experiment. Researchers conducting such studies have sometimes exposed their subjects to actual human others, but they have seldom manipulated the characteristics of those others, since that sort of manipulation is made difficult by problems of control on the one hand and ethics on the other.

The problems involved in creating and/or presenting a stimulus person in studies of person perception have been dealt with elsewhere (Tagiuri, 1971), and we do not intend to belabor them. The point is that a special set of epistemological constraints apply when a communicant is described rather than (or even in addition to) being directly observed. The most obvious of these constraints is that persons who describe the potential communicants become themselves also communicants, so that their own characteristics become an important part of the process. If experimenters or one of their cohorts are the reporters, then experimenter credibility becomes an important factor and a possible target for communication research.

Nonverbal Characteristics

These can be viewed as consisting of two types, symptomatic and symbolic.[3] Symptomatic nonverbal characteristics are those which bear a natural relationship to some biological state of the communicant. Changes in respiration and pupil size, for example, are generally symptomatic of biological states; they are not ordinarily under the (conscious) control of the communicant. They are not part of a rule-governed symbol system created for the purpose of communicating. Obviously, however, they may provide one communicant with valuable information about another. In fact, they may provide particularly valuable information because they are *not* ordinarily under the conscious control of the communicant, and thus not as likely to be manipulated for the purpose of deception. Symptomatic nonverbal characteristics are the only communicant characteristics observed directly, without the mediation of other communicants or common symbol systems. Thus, they constitute an epistemologically unique category of characteristics.

Symbolic nonverbal characteristics are significant because they are part of a rule-governed symbol system shared by the communicants. An upraised middle finger, an upraised or downturned thumb, a pointing finger drawn across the throat, a nod of the head, are symbolic nonverbal acts (momentary characteristics) which can be used as bases for attribution. Wearing particular types of clothing or maintaining certain distances among communicants can be more properly termed "characteristics" because of their longer duration, and both are symbolic in that they depend for their significance upon common symbol systems.

Not all nonverbal acts/characteristics are so easily categorized, especially because of the human propensity to appropriate or exaggerate symptoms into their symbol systems. For example, forming a fist may in some cases be a preparation for a violent encounter, in which case it is a symptom. In other cases, it may be a symbolic threat. In many cases it is partly one and partly the other. Thus, it is probably useful to say that many, if not most, nonverbal acts/characteristics are both symptomatic and symbolic in varying degrees. The distinction is important, not for the merely academic purpose of categorization, but because the attribution of intent may depend upon the extent to which a given act/characteristic is perceived as symbolic rather than symptomatic.

We do not propose to provide a summary of the research on nonverbal communication, since thorough treatments are available elsewhere.[4] Rather, our purposes are two: first, to provide some substantiation of our contention that the social array is rich with information, and, second, to provide a basis for a subsequent discussion of the process by which more abstract characteristics are attributed. Other treatments of nonverbal communication generally use categories or communicant acts/characteristics such as these: (1) general appearance, including aspects which are relatively permanent and those which are to some extent under the control of the communicant; (2) kinesics, including changes in facial expressions and bodily movements; (3) paralanguage or vocalics; (4) proxemics, including perceptions and preservation of personal space, marking and defense of territory, and the arrangement of communicants, objects, and environmental features within limited spaces; (5) chronemics, including especially the timing of communicative acts in relation to other events; (6) iconics, or the use and display of physical objects as images and symbols; and (7) tactilics, or the use and effects of intercommunicant touching.

One need not read far in any of the multitude of volumes which have dealt with nonverbal communication to see that the acts and characteristics in each of these categories provide a tremendous quantity and variety of information. But with respect to our second purpose, there appear to be at least three dimensions of nonverbal acts/characteristics which determine the extent to which they are useful as bases of attribution.

The first of these is their capacity for information transmission. Ekman and Friesen (1967, 1969), in a well-known analysis, have pointed out that a communicant's face is a rich source of information (in the information-theory sense) because the overwhelming complexity of the facial muscula-ture creates such an array of available states. The feet and legs, however, are capable of being altered into relatively few states, making them a limited source of information.

A second dimension is the extent to which a nonverbal act/charac-teristic can be, or ordinarily is, monitored by other communicants. Ekman and Friesan (1967, 1969), again, have noted that the feet and legs are more likely to be used as a channel for the leakage of emotions which are socially unacceptable because they are not closely and frequently observed by others. Thus, a communicant who wants to conceal nervousness may maintain a "poker face" but is likely to express the nervousness in high leg and foot activity. Ekman and Friesen's *specific* observations regarding these body areas have not always held up, probably because their cate-gories (face versus legs) are too gross, but the general concept of moni-toredness as a dimension seems a useful one.

The third dimension is the extent to which the communicant has (or is perceived to have) control over a given nonverbal act or characteristic. Some characteristics such as pupil dilation, piloerection, and micromomen-tary facial expression obviously cannot be willfully controlled by a com-municant without training in biofeedback techniques, while gross motor movements are easily controlled. Facial expression, respiration, and muscle tension are nearer the center of the continuum in that they are control-lable with some effort. One can also describe this dimension as repre-senting the extent to which nonverbal acts/characteristics are manageable by the communicant rather than given or unmanageable. These terms seem more applicable to physical characteristics, grooming, and attire. The terms "symptomatic" and "symbolic," as defined earlier, are highly redun-dant with these, although they carry some additional implications. To the extent that an act or characteristic is symptomatic, it is less likely to be controlled, and to the extent that it is symbolic it is more likely to be not only manageable but managed.

Verbal Characteristics

Verbal characteristics of communicants share their epistemological basis with symbolic nonverbal characteristics, in that their perception must be mediated by a perceiver's knowledge of a rule-governed symbol system.

Gibson, the psychologist who has most forcefully advocated the position that there is direct sensory pickup of environmental characteristics in human perception, has made an exception in the case of language, granting that its perception is indirect (Mace, 1974). (Actually, we believe all symbol systems to be rule-governed, but that is a discussion for another paper.) By a *rule* we mean an algorithm or segment of an algorithm (an instruction) for operating on elements of a symbol system such that if the algorithm/instruction is not followed, one is not, in fact, operating within that symbol system. That is, a set of rules *defines* a symbol system.

A rule-defined symbol system, because it is used by people in social situations, also tends to accumulate *norms* which, while they do not define the system, nevertheless create strong expectations regarding the ways in which it will be used. Analogically, the game of bridge has a set of rules by which it is defined. If one breaks the rules (for example, if one deals unequal numbers of cards to players, or plays out of turn), one is simply not playing the game of bridge. However, there are also norms which apply at least when the game is played on social occasions: One is expected to refrain from drastically overbidding one's hand merely to prevent opponents from taking a profitable bid, for example, even though that might be an effective strategy and might, in fact, be used in a duplicate bridge tournament. To violate the *norm* does not invalidate the game, however; it merely brings social sanctions.

This rule-norm distinction is important for our purposes because the consequences for a communicant's image are likely to be different when a language rule rather than a language norm is violated. (We will consider this in more detail in the next section. Basically, when people violate rules, they will be assumed to have a defective understanding of the language. Violation of a norm, however, is more likely to give the impression the communicant is not willing to play the language game fairly or by accepted social standards.) Another set of distinctions which is important for our purposes consists of those among phonemic, syntactic, semantic, and pragmatic language levels. Briefly, the phonemic level has to do with the sounds which are used in a language and the allowable juxtapositions of sounds; the syntactic level has to do with the combination of sounds into strings or sentences; the semantic level has to do with the relation between the symbol system and entities outside that system; and the pragmatic level has to do with language use and effects.

Both rules and norms exist at each of the first three levels. If one violates the phonemic rules of a language by using sounds or sound combinations which are not part of the language, one is simply not speaking the language. However, there is an allowable range of phonemic variation which makes room for dialectical norms. Phonemic norms may be characteristic of geographical areas, social classes, and subcultures. Those are certainly part of what is perceived about the communicant.[5]

Rules at the syntactic level specify what constitute complete sound strings in a language. Within the range of acceptable sound strings (sentences, utterances) there will usually be a vast number of alternative constructions, however. Different syntactic alternatives are normative or expected for different social groups, different verbal tasks, and different social occasions.

Semantic rules specify how the words and utterances of a language relate to nonlanguage entities (or, in the case of metalanguage, how a language relates reflexively to itself). Violating semantic rules may produce semantic anomalies such as "The five-year-old bachelor . . .," or may produce varying degrees of inaccuracy. Again, however, there exists such a variety of alternative ways of expressing any given idea that there is plenty of room for the development and violation of semantic norms within the boundaries of semantic rules.

There are no rules at the pragmatic level as we have defined it, but there are ethical norms and strategies based on psychological principles. Communicants are perceived with respect to how ethically and effectively they use the language strategies available to them to achieve their desired effects. The pragmatic level also has somewhat of an executive function with respect to the other language levels, since decisions regarding the extent to which one will conform to phonemic, syntactic, and semantic norms are pragmatic decisions.

Characteristics of Social Interaction

The epistemological bases for the observation of social interaction are similar to those for verbal characteristics in that such interaction seems to be rule-governed and thus symbolically significant. However, the interactions observed may be either verbal or nonverbal. We refer specifically to such aspects of social interaction as the total amount of communication in which communicants are observed to participate, the ratio of communication produced to that received, the number of others with whom they communicate, the types of others to whom messages are sent and the types of others from whom messages are received, and the types of messages sent to and received from various types of others.

Self-Reported Characteristics

The epistemological basis for observation of these characteristics is interestingly and uniquely reflexive, since the observer is in the position of having to decide, for example, whether communicants are lying when they say they are not lying. Thus, the process builds upon itself, although it is apparently affected by the sort of introduction the communicant receives (Biddle, 1966).

Of course, any sort of characteristic can be self-reported or revealed, but there are some which are especially amenable to self-report and especially relevant to persuasion. Obvious among those are communicants' reports of their past experiences and future plans, their reported perceptions, significant experiences, and behavior under various conditions. Opinion statements on significant issues, statements regarding the communicants' opinions of the listener, and statements of the communicants' opinions of others are likely to be monitored especially closely. Finally, self-reports of a particularly disclosive nature, of incidents or opinions which are especially intimate and revealing, are assigned particular importance.

When one really begins to consider how much information is available on which to make judgments of others, it is easy to see we are not dealing with a process in which impressions must be fabricated from fleeting snatches of experience. There is no question that we sometimes *do* construct our views of others somewhat independently of what we actually observe, but it is also clear that that does not happen by default.

INFERRED ATTRIBUTES

What we are about to discuss concerns the ways in which communicants infer from observable characteristics and attribute to one another such abstract characteristics as power, similarity, intentions, emotions, ethics, and personality. The problem is a familiar one in communication, but usually it has not been discussed under the heading of persuasion; it seems to have been driven out by the concept of credibility. Rather, it is usually discussed as a problem of more concern in interpersonal communication (Miller, 1976). It is even more familiar in social psychology, where it is studied under the rubrics of impression formation, acquaintance processes, interpersonal attraction, and, probably most generally, person perception.

A considerable body of theoretical and empirical literature has grown up around this issue. However, it is an open question whether by giving it a place in persuasion we have just stumbled upon a treasure chest or unlocked a Pandora's box. Certainly the credibility construct was less complicated, there being fewer (if any) theories designed to explain it and fewer research paradigms designed to explore it.

Some Available Theories

Each of the available theories would lead us to view the process of perception somewhat differently—to emphasize different parts of the process. Bruner's (Bruner and Tagiuri, 1954; Bruner et al., 1956, 1958) approach would lead us to observe acts of categorization, for example, with special attention to cues to category formation and category assignment, and to the effects of stereotyping. Adopting Kelly's (1955) personal construct theory, we would study the perceiver as a sort of lay scientist who advances perceptual hypotheses, tests them, and tries to construct theories regarding the universe, people in general, and, in this present regard, what specific people are like and how they are likely to act.

A number of theories emphasize the constructive nature of the process, so that we would tend to focus on interaction, altercasting, role-playing, role-testing, and negotiation. Of special importance among these are Goffman's (1956) descriptions of self-presentation and Mead's (1934) symbolic interactionism (see Stone and Farberman, 1970). Gestalt theories of perception (see, for example, Arnheim, 1949) hold that people are perceived as meaningful wholes or patterns or "psychic structures" rather than as combinations of items of sensory data.

Broadbent's (1958) book, on the other hand, describes a system of perception internal to the individual and traces the routes of information through that system. This and other information-processing models tend to characterize the perceiver as less actively involved, being more akin to a collection of circuits and filters or of mathematical functions. Ajzen (1977) has attempted to distinguish between mechanistic and constructive information-processing models, but his distinction seems to be rather fine.

Some Relatively Atheoretical Data

Cook (1971) has discussed the possibility of discovering "identification rules that tell us how to recognize people who have particular attributes," as distinguished from "association rules that tell us which attributes or traits are associated" (p. 60). Perhaps that is what is needed in this area—a program of research designed to discover and characterize the relationships which seem to hold between the observable characteristics of communicants and the attributes observers infer from them. We might borrow the approach taken by the contributors to the Rappoport and Summers (1973) volume, *Human Judgment and Social Interaction.* Those scholars organized their research around Brunswik's (1956) Lens Model of perception based on the theory he termed "probabilistic functionalism." They have tried to describe how humans in some rather circumscribed experimental circumstances use cues they are given to make certain judgments. The cues are not characteristics of humans, although they could be. The judgments have to do with matters less conceptual than the inferred attributes we are discussing, but that is a problem for only a part of the Lens Model, and no problem at all for us.

Probably the clearest example of a research program designed to produce such identification rules is that of Addington (1967), who conducted a study of selected vocal characteristics. Speakers produced a variety of vocal characteristics such as "breathiness," "nasality," and variations in rate and pitch. Judges rated the voices on 40 semantic differential scales representing attributes of personality. Judges rated stimulus persons who simulated nasality as having a considerable collection of undesirable personality attributes, and rated those simulating a great deal of pitch variety as having predominantly desirable personality attributes.

Clearly, these identification rules do not operate independently; rather, they are confounded by the rules of association which operate among the inferred attributes. Thorndike (1920) reported, for example, that he observed a correlation of +.64 between ratings of "character" and ratings of "intelligence," and of +.63 between ratings of (apparently pleasantness of) "voice" and ratings of intelligence. The old factor analyses of "credibility" scales depended on just such redundancies among inferred attributes, and they may yet prove useful to us if reinterpreted in that light.

The interactions of identification rules with association rules produce what Warr and Knapper (1968) term "combination rules," which are rules for inferring sets of attributes given a variety of observed characteristics. The whole collection of identification, association, and combination rules upon which a given perceiver operates seems to be more or less equivalent to what others have termed the perceiver's "implicit personality theory," although the rules do not involve merely personality attributes.

There is much discussion of these notions in works dealing with person perception, interpersonal attraction, and impression formation. There is also much research reported which deals with the *accuracy* (veridicality) of attribute inference and its presumed opposite, selective perception, as well as a wealth of research investigating the characteristics of the perceiver which contribute to or detract from such veridicality, under headings such as "individual differences" or "perceptual ability."[6]

But the research coverage of the identification rules themselves has been rather spotty. Rules dealing with nonverbal characteristics have been covered most thoroughly, especially in the areas of voice, facial expressions, bodily activity, and attire.[7] Regarding verbal characteristics, research is beginning to accumulate which relates various dialects and characteristics of style to perceiver judgments of communicants,[8] but such research is only getting underway.

There is very little research on identification rules for characteristics of social interaction and for self-reported characteristics. There is a great deal of research dealing with reputed characteristics, but that has generally been an accident of research design, and most of it is hopelessly confounded. What has happened, as we noted in our earlier discussion, is that most early researchers in social perception—and, for that matter, many present researchers—have adopted the technique of giving their subjects lists of characteristics and attributes of fictitious others, or short, paragraph-long descriptions of fictitious others, or bogus feedback from others, in order to study a variety of effects on subjects' perceptions of those others. This meets our definition of "reputed," although we certainly did not intend experimenters or their assistants to be the reporters. It would be more informative if the reports had come from peers or had been reported in the mass media. Further, these studies did not distinguish between reputed *objective characteristics* and reputed *inferred attributes,* so the results are a confounded and confusing mixture of identification and association rules.

An Attributive Model

In fact, as Schneider et al. (1979) point out, inferred characteristics are frequently related, as if they were physically observable, in attempts to describe people. Yet these authors insist that the distinction is important and provide what we consider to be the best recent model to describe how perceivers bridge the gap between the two. They argue that a number of processes are involved, which they list in the following order—insisting, however, that they are not linear and sequential: (1) attention, (2) snap judgment, (3) attribution, (4) trait implications, (5) impression formation, and (6) behavior prediction in classes of situations.

The first of these processes has occupied volumes in the literature, so we will not dwell on it. The second process is probably what Addington was studying when he manipulated vocal characteristics, and it is probably about all that research aimed at discovering identification rules could hope to deal with. The third process, however, introduces some new considerations.

The authors note that attribution theory seems to have been introduced by Heider in a 1974 paper and a 1958 book, but owes a great deal to Brunswik's (1956) concept of "probabilistic functionalism." They list the following as important assumptions Heider made: (1) People perceive behavior as being caused. (2) The causal locus lies either in the person or in the environment. (3) "An action outcome is perceived to be an additive function of the effective environmental force and the effective person force." (4) "The person force is in turn a multiplicative function of the other's power or ability and the effort he exerts."

Jones and Davis (1965) have tried to simplify the Heider description and make it more explicit. What seems to be most important for our purposes is that Jones and Davis introduce the concepts of "social desirability" and "noncommon effects." They hold that insofar as an individual's action is socially desirable (or "normal"), it really tells very little about that individual. It is when an action deviates from what is ordinarily expected that we learn something about the actor. Jones and Davis also argue that observers attempt to determine the cause (or intent) of an action by asking what makes that action unique among the alternatives the actor might have chosen; thus the concept of "noncommon effects" as a basis for attribution.

Jones and McGillis (1976) have made it clear that attributions are based on *information gain* with respect to an actor. They believe that we depend upon *category-based* and *target-based* expectancies regarding an actor and a given action tells more about the actor to the extent that it deviates from those expectancies.

The name of Harold Kelley (1967, 1972a, 1972b, 1973; Kelley and Thibaut, 1978) is that which has become most closely associated with attribution theory in recent years. There seem to be three Kelley models. Schneider et al. (1979) label the first two of these the *Covariation Model* and the *Causal Schemata Model.* The third Kelley presents with Thibaut in their new book, published in 1978, to which Schneider et al. apparently did not have access at the time their manuscript was submitted.

The Covariation Model takes into account how *consistent* an actor's behavior has been with respect to a given entity over time and contexts; how *distinctive* the behavior is with respect to this entity as compared with other entities, and to what extent this actor's behavior deviates from the *consensus* of others' behavior toward this entity. Thus, the model depends upon the observer having some history of experience with and/or knowledge about the actor.

Kelley's Causal Schemata Model, however, like that of Jones and Davis (1965), is designed to deal with those situations in which an observer perceives only a single instance of an actor's behavior. Kelley assumes that observers carry about with them sets of causal schemata which, he says "reflect the individual's basic notions of reality and his assumptions about the existence of a stable external world" (1972a:153). When observers refer to their causal schemata first to determine what *could have been* the causes of the behavior and then to decide what, under the known present circumstances, *was/were most likely the cause(s)*.

The Kelley and Thibaut (1978) model deals with the situation in which actor and observer have the opportunity to interact. They assume that observers will actively test their perceptions of others during such interaction. A second assumption, that people choose to associate with others depending upon some congruence between their own needs and the others' resources, is, of course, also the basic assumption of this chapter.

The differences among the models become important when applied to the choice or evaluation of communicants in a situation involving persuasion. The Jones and Davis model and Kelley's Causal Schemata Model are applicable when two (or more) communicants encounter one another for the first time and must assess one another on the basis of initial communications. Kelley's Covariation Model is more applicable to a situation in which one has had experience with a potential communicant and is trying to decide whether to initiate or accept further communication. The Kelley and Thibaut model does not have so much to say about past experience; its predictions have more to do with the continuing and future mutual behaviors and evaluations of communicants.

The three remaining processes mentioned by Schneider et al.—trait implications, impression formation, and behavior prediction—clearly relate to those communication situations in which the communicants have some experience with one another and in which they anticipate continued association.

A List and an Example

At this point it may be most helpful for us to provide a list of what we mean by inferred attributes, accompanied by speculative examples of some possible identification rules. While we hope these are educated speculations, they are speculations nevertheless meant primarily for the purpose of illustration.

Our list of inferred attributes includes the following, some of which certainly overlap others: honesty, power, physical attractiveness, similarity to the perceiver (especially opinion and goal similarity), reward potential, intentions, needs/goals, intelligence, creativity, sex, sexual preference, sexuality, age, warmth, politeness, compliance/persuasibility, responsibility, potential for reciprocity, dogmatism, self-esteem, tendency to manipulate others, opinions on important issues, liking for the perceiver, empathic ability, need for affiliation, need for intimacy, extroversion/introversion, bias, security, aggressiveness, state of stress/activation/anxiety, educational level, and socioeconomic status. Obviously, the list does not exhaust the possibilities of even general attributes, not to mention those which are situation-specific.

The first of these, honesty, has appeared in two of our studies (Liska, 1978; Cronkhite, 1977) to be of special importance, so we will use it in our first hypothetical example. From what observable characteristics might honesty be inferred? For referential clarity, we will name our hypothetical communicant Roger Clarion.

First, it may be inferred from reputed characteristics. Reporters may express their own opinions regarding Roger's honesty. Then the grounds of our inference will depend on our assessment of the believability of those reporters. Frequently, however, they will testify to their observations of Roger's past behavior, including incidents which we will have to judge for ourselves, and frequently including incidents from which we will have to make attributions.

Second, Roger's honesty or lack of it may be inferred from his non-verbal acts and characteristics. Some of these inferences are obvious and stereotypical: certain types of attire, gaze direction, and certain vocal characteristics are stereotypically associated with honesty/dishonesty. Our suspicion is, however, that it is more often the inconsistencies among nonverbal acts and inconsistencies between nonverbal acts and verbal assertions that produce the inference of dishonesty. A "polite smile," for example, is an inconsistency, in that, as a smile, it is supposed to be indicative of friendship and interest, but its rigidity and lack of spon-taneity indicate that it is being maintained at a conscious level with some effort—that it is being used as a symbol without symptomatic support. Additionally, Roger may express interest verbally, but we may (at a tacit level, of course) process his lack of pupil dilation, lack of muscle tension, sighs, certain micromomentary facial expression, and the shuffling of his feet and make two inferences: first, that he is *not* interested and, probably more important, that he is not *honest* since his verbal expression of interest appears to be a lie.

Third, we may infer the extent of Roger's honesty from observation of his verbal characteristics. At the pragmatic level, his reports of "facts" may be inconsistent with what we have experienced or heard from other sources we consider reliable, in which case we must attribute his inaccur-acies and inconsistencies to lack of knowledge, poor memory, or deliberate attempts at deception. We may also observe him using pragmatic devices which we do not consider honest, devices such as concealing his intent to persuade when we have inferred that intent from other information. He may exhibit semantic dishonesty by using excessively emotive language or by using language in violation of semantic norms for apparently deceptive rather than stylistic purposes. He may attempt to adopt vocabulary, syntax, and dialect with which he is not familiar and comfortable, and we may detect the signs of discomfort and infer that he is faking for the purpose of ingratiation or condescension, from which we may further infer, among a host of other attributes, some degree of dishonesty.

Fourth, we may base our inference on observation of Roger's social interactions with others as well as with ourselves. If he interacts with us only in the presence of certain others or with certain others only when he believes we are not around, we may draw from that some inferences about his honesty. If he interacts frequently, favorably, and apparently voluntarily with influential others whom he professes to dislike, that may give us pause regarding his honesty.

Fifth, we may infer a great deal from his self-reports, although we will probably infer very little from his direct statements regarding his honesty— unless, of course, he "doth protest too much." Rather, we will make our inferences on the basis of inconsistencies among his self-reports and inconsistencies between his self-reports and information we have gained from the first four sources.

Finally, we must form some holistic impression and consider the way it does or does not "add up," the extent of consistency of the total presentation. Very little of this will be done at an explicit level, of course, unless Roger makes major and obvious errors or unless we are acquainted with him for some time. Rather, we will usually be left with a feeling that Roger is honest or dishonest to some degree, a feeling which may be supported by good reasons at a tacit level, but reasons we could make explicit only with considerable effort.

CHOICE OF CRITERIA

It is our position that the perception of communicants or potential communicants—that is, the inference of certain attributes on the basis of the array of observable characteristics—is only one facet of the evaluation process. The second facet involves the choice of criteria by which evaluation can proceed. (We deliberately avoid terming this the second "phase," because we want to avoid implying any particular chronological order.)

Life was much simpler under the credibility regime; we could make the simplistic assumption that there were two important criteria, competence and trustworthiness, and could then spend our time arguing over the importance of dynamism. Liska (1978) demonstrated that most of the criteria for believability change from one topic/situation to another, but that suspicion had been gaining on us for some time.

We believe that the criteria by which we judge the acceptability of potential participants in the process of persuasion, be they predominantly persuaders or persuadees, depend upon the constraints of the situation and the goals we wish to achieve within those constraints. Unfortunately, the term "situation" is perhaps the most conveniently vague in all of social science, and the term "goals" is not far behind. We will not attempt to destroy that vagueness in general, but we may be able to clear it up to some extent for our specific purpose.

SITUATIONAL CONSTRAINTS ON CRITERIA

There appear to be five types of definitions of situations offered by others who are interested in the relationship between situational properties and behavior. The first type defines situation as everything. Unfortunately, this type of definition, which suffers from terminal vagueness, does little toward accomplishing the goal of identifying situational characteristics or redundancies which distinguish among types or categories of situations. We began to more fully comprehend the problem when we set about listing the social, spatial, and temporal characteristics which constrain or facilitate communication. Our list included such characteristics as number of participants, amount of space, arrangement of space, accessibility of others, extent to which participants share language/culture/experiences/needs and goals, extent to which purpose is defined, task difficulty, liking for situation, liking of other participants, and power distribution—just to name a few. Clearly, this approach was not proving very useful.

Anthropologists, sociologists, and sociolinguists are the primary originators of the concept of culturally defined or culturally significant situations—the second type of definition of situation. Instances of culturally significant situations include funerals, weddings, classrooms, religious rituals, cocktail parties, and the Navaho stomp dance. Culturally significant situations are "collective representations," usually staged, ritualized events—governed by "a set of rules which regulate how the elements of an event should be assembled, arranged, manipulated and controlled" (Stone and Farberman, 1979:150). An example might be useful: We use a get-acquainted exercise called "cocktail party" in our basic course for the purpose of encouraging students to get acquainted with one another. The usual cocktail party physical setting (living room, den, or patio) and props (drinks, chips, and dips) are not necessary to create the situation. In fact, students require little instruction beyond the name of the game to know what kind of behaviors are appropriate or expected. Neither is it difficult for a bystander to guess what the situation is.

The third type of definition of situation is concerned with the physical environment or staging of the situation, including such matters as light, sound, temperature, props (furniture, dress), and arrangement of space, and how those variables influence interaction. Researchers focusing on group behavior have been especially interested in staging.

For proponents of the fourth type of definition of situation social interaction is the defining characteristic. According to this definition, two people arguing or quizzing one another for an exam or sharing the latest gossip constitute a situation in and of itself; cultural rules or physical environment need not be considered a part of this definition.

We have observed that people frequently describe and discuss situations in terms of activity they are engaged in, even though it may not be a primarily social activity. That is, activities such as watching television, answering correspondence, talking on the telephone, and driving to work all constitute specific situations. The fifth type of definition of situation then places activity in the center and the activity defines the situation.

Now we believe that no single type of definitions described above is adequate for explaining the relationship between situation and behavior. The first type of definition is far too broad to be useful, while the others are too narrow. We suggest that a more useful definition of situation would include environmental aspects, social interaction, and activity.

While we believe this definition is an improvement over any one of the five types of definitions by itself, we are not yet satisfied. An example might illustrate our point. Consider the following scenario: Person A is currently employed by a particular university but is not happy with his position and is looking for another. Person B is a professional friend and has displayed interest in Person A's search for another position. In fact, Person B has offered his assistance to Person A on a number of occasions. Person B calls Person A and asks: "How's your situation?" It seems reasonable to guess that Person B is not asking about everything in Person A's life. Indeed even close personal friends or family may not wish to obtain such an answer to "How's your situation?" It also seems likely that Person B was not asking about Person A's culturally significant situations nor about his physical environment. Person B could, however, want to know about Person A's present social interaction—that is, is Person A free to talk or should they agree to talk at some future time, or about what professional activities Person A is currently engaged in. We believe, however, that there is a better interpretation. Specifically, Person B most likely wants to know about aspects of the situation which are relevant to A's goal of obtaining a new position.

This example points to a subset of situations: those aspects that are relevant to (constrain or facilitate) one's goals at a particular moment.

We are especially interested in the goal-relevant aspects of situations, and since this book is especially concerned with persuasion, we intend to focus on the Goal-Relevant Aspects of Situations in Persuasion (GRASP). Situations probably are to be defined more broadly, but there are certain aspects of a situation which are important in persuasion and we will henceforth refer to these aspects as GRASP. While the acronym might be considered merely "cute," we intend it to be a shorthand mnemonic device. It is fairly common to refer to a person's "grasp of the situation," by which is ordinarily meant the extent to which that person understands how certain aspects of that situation may facilitate or frustrate the realization of salient goals.

We are not suggesting that the situation is entirely defined by the goals of those involved, but no matter what overall definition of situation is used, it is those aspects of the situation most relevant to those goals which are most important. Generally, what we intend in saying that a situational aspect is "relevant" to a goal is that the aspect must be taken into account because it constrains or facilitates goal-achievement. Since we are putting so much emphasis on goals in this conceptualization, suppose we consider them more specifically.

MOTIVATIONAL CONSTRAINTS ON CRITERIA

To present an exhaustive review of the literature relevant to goals and the ways people go about accomplishing those goals is beyond the scope of this chapter. Nonetheless, we would like to briefly consider some physical, social, and psychological needs that may develop from the situation (intrinsic) or may occur for reasons extrinsic to the situation.

Physical Needs

Satisfaction of physical needs such as those for food, water, warmth, avoidance of pain, security, and so forth are essential to the general well being and survival of an individual. If those needs are not adequately provided for, other needs such as those Maslow (1962) identifies as social needs, ego needs, and self-fulfillment needs may not be attained. On the one hand, people use communication to try to achieve their goals by persuading others to assist them. On the other hand, people attempt to persuade others to do what they want them to do by convincing them that complying will help achieve their physical goals. In civilized societies it is frequently necessary to achieve economic goals in order to achieve these physical goals as well as many of the social goals, which we will discuss next.

Social Goals

People seek to achieve social rewards in that they wish to be loved, liked, belong, command respect, and they seek to avoid social punishment such as withholding affiliation or outright rejection. Persuaders have these social goals and they seek to achieve them by influencing others to affiliate with them, to approve of their opinions, and to join them in their actions. Persuaders also know that their listeners have these goals and they seek to take advantage of them by assuring their listeners with varying degrees of subtlety that their social goals will be realized if only they accept the persuaders' proposals.

Psychological Goals

People need to express their self-concepts, maintain the central values that define their self-concepts, and defend their egos against guilt and threats. While appeals to physical needs can be quite blatant and appeals to social needs only somewhat less so, persuaders' appeals to psychological needs are generally more subtle if they are to be effective.

Some advertising is directed toward building or reinforcing one's identity or self-concept. The Virginia Slims cigarette commercial may serve as an example. It would probably be most ineffective for a commercial to say: "If you smoke Virginia Slims you'll appear to be a liberated woman." Instead, we see advertisements in which Cheryl Tiegs or some other attractive and apparently liberated woman is smoking Virginia Slims or we see that Virginia Slims sponsors a women's tennis tournament. The implication is obvious: Liberated women smoke Virginia Slims; if you consider yourself to be a liberated woman, you will smoke Virginia Slims.

One commercial that seems to be directed at the second of these psychological needs, what one of us had identified elsewhere as ego-maintenance, is the commercial for Merrill Lynch, the stock brokerage firm, which uses the slogan "We're bullish on America." Obviously, Merrill Lynch believes that the people who are likely to seek out their services are also likely to believe that America has a bright future. It would be foolish for this brokerage firm to say explicitly that people ought to use their brokerage services because they believe in some of their listeners' central values, but that is certainly what they are attempting to say more subtly.

The third type of psychological need we want to discuss is ego-defense. By ego-defense we mean protecting oneself against internal conflicts and external threats to one's ego. Generally, the mechanisms one uses to combat threat and fear are, by definition, in psychoanalytic theory, not known to the user. But we feel that this is too restrictive a definition and it presumes too rigid a barrier between the conscious and the unconscious. We feel that it is more useful to assume a continuum of awareness and to conceive of ego-defense mechanisms falling along this continuum from total unawareness through some sort of twilight awareness and even to the conscious use of such devices for the purpose of deceiving others. For example, it is not unusual for someone who is insecure about relations with the opposite sex to date only others who are married, thus providing a built-in rationalization in case of rejection. This device may be used totally unconsciously, semiconsciously, or it may be used totally consciously to provide an explanation to others in case the relationship goes sour. In any case, appeals to such goals are going to have to be very subtle—either because the listener will not admit to himself/herself that he/she harbors such goals or because he/she doesn't want to admit it to others.

Not only do persuaders appeal very subtly to these goals, but they also use persuasion to attempt to accomplish them for themselves, again at various levels of awareness.

All these goals can be accomplished by means of persuasion, and may be used in order to accomplish persuasion. But in any given situation there are only certain goals which are salient and capable of being achieved. In a situation-specific conceptualization such as this, those goals are obviously the ones with which we are concerned. Begging the reader's indulgence, we would once again like to take advantage of an acronym to make it easier to refer to this subset of goals: they are Goals Operant and Achievable in Light of the Situation, henceforth simply GOALS.

GENERATION OF CRITERIA

The criteria for assessing, evaluating, and choosing our coparticipants in the process of persuasion spring out of the intersection of these two subsets of situational aspects and goals. Persuasive situations can be divided into a variety of types on the basis of the GOALS each participant wishes to achieve. We are under no delusion that pure types such as these exist in reality, but it does seem useful to have such a typology so as to make it possible to characterize those situations one encounters. The purpose of characterizing persuasive situations in this way is to see how criteria differ depending upon the GOALS of the participants.

We are going to assume it is given by definition that at least one participant in a situation must have persuasion as a goal; otherwise it will not be a persuasive situation. Obviously, opinion change is frequently produced by messages whose sources had no persuasive intent, but we simply do not wish to label such opinion change "persuasion."

Thus, we can say that at least one of the participants in any persuasive situation will have the set of general criteria common to any persuader evaluating potential persuaders. First, persuaders will want persuadees who are *accessible* or who are willing to make themselves accessible in return for something the persuader has to offer. Second, persuaders will want persuadees who are *susceptible* to persuasion *in general*. Third, persuaders will look for those who are *susceptible* to their influence *in particular*. Fourth, they will want persuaders to have GOALS which can be satisfied by the proposal or which can be made to appear to be capable of being satisfied by the proposal. Fifth, persuaders will want persuadees to be capable of executing the proposal, which may involve their having access to and control over certain resources, and may involve their being agents by whom others can be influenced.

As we have said, these are general criteria persuaders are likely to use in all persuasive situations; they are criteria for choosing those persuadees who are most likely to be persuaded. Other criteria are more specific to the GOALS and GRASP of particular situations or types of situations.

The first general type of persuasive situation is that in which the persuadees' GOALS are to be *informed* by the persuader's message(s). This is frequently the case in public speaking, for example. Persuadees will vary in the extent to which they are aware of the source's persuasive intent. To the extent that they are aware, they are essentially agreeing to submit themselves to the risk of being persuaded in return for the information they hope to gain. This is the situation for which the concept of "credibility" was invented, and that to which it best applies. Because the persuadees want reliable information, one of their criteria for a satisfactory informant is going to be *competence*. To the extent that they suspect that this prospective "informant" may also want to persuade them, and thus to the extent they fear the informant may be so motivated to persuade that deception and misinformation may be put to use, another of their criteria is going to be *trustworthiness*.

More detailed lists of criteria for this quite common type of persuasive situation include:

(1) [The persuader/informant] is or was in a position to observe the facts;
(2) He is or was capable of observing, in the sense of:
    (a) being physically capable,
    (b) being intellectually capable,
    (c) being psychologically or emotionally capable,

     (d) being sensitive to the facts in question, and
     (e) having had experience in making such observations;
  (3) He is motivated to perceive and report accurately, in that he:
     (a) has nothing to gain by deceiving, and
     (b) has goals similar to or compatible with [those of the persuadee];
  (4) He has reported accurately in the past on this and other topics; and
  (5) He is responsible in the sense of being in a position to be held accountable for the testimony [Cronkhite, 1977].

What is most important to note here is that these criteria spring out of the intersection of the persuadees' GOALS of information-gathering with the GRASP that the information is being provided by a persuader. If the persuadees' GOALS did not include information-gathering, the criteria would be different; if the GRASP did not include the information being provided by a persuader (for example, being provided, alternatively, by a more neutral informant), the criteria would be different.

Consider, for example, a second very common type of persuasive situation: that in which two or more parties confront one another, each with the GOALS of persuading the other(s). To the extent they are aware of one another's persuasive intent, they are essentially striking a bargain in which each party exposes himself or herself to the risk of being persuaded in return for the possibility of persuading the other(s). Here the criteria listed as those persuadees use to evaluate persuaders/informants in the case above do not apply, since none of the parties seeks to gather information. Rather, the general criteria persuaders use to evaluate potential persuadees are the ones which apply here, since each party expects to be the persuader. In addition to these general criteria, since each party is exposed to the risk of being persuaded by the other(s), to the extent each party fears being persuaded, each will choose other communicants who are inept at persuasion.

One might conclude that the type of persuasive situation we have just described is a debate, but that is not what we intend. In a debate, two (or possibly more) participants confront one another, not with the GOALS of persuading one another, but with the GOALS of defeating one another in the view of some third party or parties who are observing and thus persuading the third party. Communicant choice in a debate situation, our third type, is more complex. Each of the debaters must choose opponents and an audience. The audience probably will be chosen on the basis of the general criteria for choosing persuadees. Ordinarily (that is, in the pure case as we have defined it), a debater does not care whether he or she persuades those he or she considers opponents. One's primary criterion for choosing an opponent will be the level of persuasive ability in comparison to one's own: One generally seeks a *"worthy"* opponent but an opponent somewhat less capable than oneself. If the opponent is too weak, the audience is less likely to attend or to believe that the opposing side has been fairly represented. But the audience also has criteria for choosing debaters. Those criteria depend on the reasons they have for attending. The reason for attending may be information-gathering, but there may be many others, including all those we will enumerate as operant in succeeding situation-types, and of course each listener will have his or her own combination of GOALS. For each participant, debater or listener, the criteria are determined by the GOALS and the GRASP which are applicable in a debate.

A fourth type of persuasive situation, which we will label "dialectic" (with apologies to those who have defined that term otherwise), is that in which the GOALS and criteria described in situation-types one and two are mixed for each participant. That is, each participant wishes to persuade the other(s), but would also like to gather reliable information. Consequently, all the general criteria for choosing persuadees are relevant here, but so are the criteria for choosing reliable persuader/informants. In any given case, for any given participant, the total set of criteria will be some balance or mixture of these two subsets. This situation-type is close enough to the common characterization of dialectic as a search after truth by means of verbal confrontation that we believe that term to be at least minimally appropriate even though not entirely accurate by all definitions.

In our remaining descriptions of persuasive situation-types we must distinguish between GOALS and thus criteria which are intrinsic and those which are extrinsic to a persuasive message. In some situations persuaders may be said (metaphorically, at least) to "bribe" persuadees to attend to their messages by offering GOALS-satisfaction which is to be achieved not by means of the persuasive message itself, but rather by actions of the persuaders which are contingent upon the persuadees attending to that message. These persuasive situations we will identify as involving extrinsic GOALS-satisfaction for the persuadees, and as involving extrinsic criteria. When GOALS-satisfaction is to be achieved by the persuasive message itself, we will identify the GOALS-satisfaction and the criteria as intrinsic.

The descriptions themselves will probably clear up this distinction. In our first type of situation, we described persuadees as attending to persuasive messages because they wanted information *from those messages.* In that case the GOALS-satisfaction and the criteria were intrinsic. But many of us attend to persuasive messages—commercials—on television as we gather information from the evening news. Not to malign (—well, yes, let's be honest—to malign) the quality of the average television commercial, the GOALS-satisfaction here usually has little to do with the persuasive messages themselves. We watch the commercials primarily because they are difficult to avoid while one is gathering information from the newscast. Of course, we obtain information from the commercials, but we do not generally attend to them for that purpose, and we do not choose to watch them on the basis of their conformity to information-gathering criteria. We, at least, do not know anyone who watches the CBS Evening News because it has a better class of commercials than does the NBC Nightly News. Once we have been lured into watching them, however (assuming we have our wits about us), we may apply the information-gathering criteria to whatever "sources" we can identify. We advance this as our fifth persuasive situation-type because in this case the GOALS have to do with information-gathering, but the information-gathering criteria are not applied to the source of the persuasive message, so that the message and its source are chosen on the basis of extrinsic criteria.

A sixth type of persuasive situation is that in which the persuadees' GOALS have to do with entertainment which is provided by the persuasive message itself, as in the plays of Shaw or some of the political satire of the television show "Saturday Night Live" or—more pervasively and subtly— by almost every dramatic or comedy show on television. The "willing suspension of disbelief" on the part of persuadees in such situations involves, in part, the substitution of entertainment criteria for the informa- tion-gathering criteria they would be likely to impose if they were fully aware of the extent of the persuasion being visited upon them.

A seventh type of persuasive situation is that in which the reward for the persuadee is entertainment achieved extraneously to the persuasive message. Again the most familiar examples probably come from the mass media, where we find persuasive messages in the form of commercials interspersed with shows designed to be entertaining and in the form of advertisements interspersed throughout our favorite magazines. Still, the mass media did not invent this situation-type. The familiar "message from the sponsor" occurs in many contexts in which the monetary price of admission is inadequate to cover the cost of the entertainment, so that part of the "price of admission" becomes the persuadees' willingness to risk being persuaded by the sponsor. Television entertainment (and infor- mation) is unusual only in that *all* its costs are borne by a bargain struck between sponsors and viewers in which viewers give sponsors nothing more than the opportunity to persuade them. And for our purposes the situa- tion becomes distinctive in that the criteria by which persuadees choose their persuaders become largely extrinsic to the persuasive messages and thus largely extrinsic to the persuaders.

Rather than belabor this further, let us merely suggest some of the remaining types of persuasive situations. Two more have to do with social reward and punishment, the eighth intrinsic and the ninth extrinsic.

Flattery, for example, may be provided by the other communicant as *intrinsic* social reward. But those who attend a church service or a political rally hoping to be seen there choose their communicants on the basis of *extrinsic* social reward. If ego-defense needs are satisfied by the chosen communicant(s), the satisfaction is intrinsic, and it constitutes our tenth situation-type; if the ego-defense is achieved extrinsically to the chosen communicant(s), this constitutes an eleventh situation-type. What we have numbered our twelfth and thirteenth situation-types have to do with intrinsic and extrinsic physical reward/threat, and the fourteenth and fifteenth with intrinsic and extrinsic economic reward/threat.

We could make the list longer or shorter depending on how finely or coarsely we divided the possible needs of persuadees, but basically what we have here is a set of situations in which needs such as those for information, entertainment, social reward and threat avoidance, ego defense, physical and economic reward, and threat avoidance are satisfied either intrinsically by or extrinsically to the other communicant(s). That accounts for a dozen of our proposed situation-types. In addition there are three special situation-types: mutual persuasion (which, if we had the nerve, we could label "dialogue"), "debate," and "dialectic."

JUDGING CHARACTERISTICS ON CRITERIA

Given this background, our thesis can be stated fairly simply: *We choose as communicants in a given persuasive situation those people whose characteristics most nearly satisfy the criteria we have established for that situation.*

This thesis is basically that which Kelley and Thibaut (1978) apply to interpersonal "interaction" in general, although they develop it much differently. That work, *Interpersonal Relations: A Theory of Interdependence,* describes the process in terms of "interdependence matrices":

> The interdependence matrix for a dyad describes the way in which the two persons control each other's outcomes in the course of their interaction. It is constituted by specifying the behaviors important to the relationship that each of them may enact and by assessing the consequences for both persons of all possible combinations of their respective behaviors. . . . On the one hand, it reflects the various ways in which psychological and situational factors impinge on the pair. The pattern of interdependence summarizes the consequences for the pair of the abilities, needs, and evaluative criteria each person brings to the dyad as well as the manner in which these two sets of personal dispositions engage with each other. . . . On the other hand, the interdependence matrix describes the joint and individual prob-

lems the two persons face in their relationship and certain of the means available to them for solving these problems. Thus the matrix portrays the kinds and degrees of power they have over each other by means of outcome control and the bases they have for influence through threats, appeals to social norms, and other communications [Kelley and Thibaut, 1978:3].

This technique for analysis and measurement appears to be compatible with the model described here, in that it provides a means for describing how the characteristics and criteria of two communicants "engage with each other," and how the engagement facilitates or inhibits mutual influence.

However, the technique depends upon an observer's knowledge of the interaction of two people over some period of time, so that it is best suited to the description and analysis of interpersonal persuasion.

THE LENS MODEL AS A RESEARCH PARADIGM

More traditional persuasive situations require some framework which will allow for the evaluation of a potential communicant on the criteria we have described. An adaptation of Brunswik's (1956) Lens Model seems to provide that framework.

Rappoport and Summers (1973) have adapted the Lens Model to four different cases of perceptual judgement: (1) the 1-System Case, in which a subject is presented with cues generated by an unknown environmental system and makes judgments in response to those cues; (2) the 2-System Case, which is identical to the 1-System Case except that the environmental system is known; (3) a 3-Systems Case, which is identical to the 2-System Case except that two subjects make judgments; and (4) an n-Systems case, which is identical to (2) and (3) except that a number of subjects greater than two make the judgments.

The case with which we are dealing here is the first, since there is no known objective "environmental system" against which subjects' perceptual judgments of communicants can be validated. That 1-System Case is diagrammed in Figure 2. The term "criterion" as used in this diagram refers to a known and objectifiable distal event rather than "bases for judgment," which is the way we have used it in this chapter.

Using this model, it is easy to visualize how research can be conducted to determine the ways in which subjects are using cues to produce the judgments: to determine the differential weights they are giving the cues and the shape of the functions they are maintaining between the cues and the judgments. Slovic and Lichtenstein (1973) and Wiggins (1973) describe how regression analysis, ANOVA, factor analysis, and multidimensional scaling can be used in such research.

However, we have described two acts of judgment which we believe occur in the process of communicant choice/assessment in persuasive situations: The observer attributes general characteristics to another communicant on the basis of observable characteristics (cues), and then uses the newly attributed characteristics as cues on which to base a judgment of the other communicant's acceptability under the circumstances (given the GOALS and GRASP). Thus, we need a double lens model or, if you will, a Bifocal Lens Model, as diagrammed in Figure 3.

Notice that, applying regression techniques to this model, one might first attempt to determine the correlations between subjects' judgments of each observable characteristic and of each attributed characteristic. (See Naylor and Wherry, 1965; Hoffman, 1960; Goldberg, 1970). Such correlations would represent the "identification rules" which Cook (1971) describes. But the observable characteristics are themselves intercorrelated, which correlations represent Cook's "association rules," so it would be necessary to use multiple regression techniques to eliminate these redundancies and determine formulas by which the perceptions of observable characteristics are most reliably related to judgments of the attributed characteristics: the "combination rules" of Ware and Knapper (1968).

A second set of intercorrelations will represent the extent to which the attributed characteristics are related to one another and to the judgments of communicant suitability. Multiple regression formulas can then be used

Figure 2   Diagram of the Brunswik (1956) Lens Model 1-System Case*

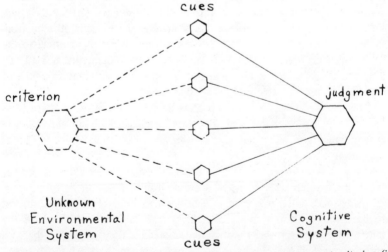

*In this process, the relations between the cues and the environment criterion (if any) is unknown and the relations between the cues and the judgment are being investigated.
NOTE: The term "criterion" as used in this diagram refers to an objectively identifiable feature of the environment. The term is used differently in the text to mean "bases for judgment."

Figure 3   An Adaptation of the Brunswik (1956) Lens Model

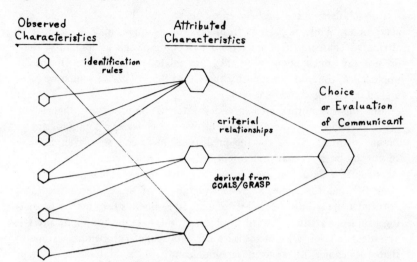

to identify that combination of attributed characteristics which subjects seem to be using to judge communicant suitability in that situation. We can also compare these formulas from one situation to another and from one type of situation to another and from one type of subject to another.

The functions relating the characteristics and judgments may not be linear, of course, but we can test for that. Regression analysis is not the only statistical technique we can use, either; we mentioned ANOVA, factor analysis, and multidimensional scaling as other useful techniques. Multidimensional scaling would be necessary to detect individual differences among subjects.

The *criteria* we described in the second major section of this chapter, however, may seem to have fallen into a crack between our description of our own model and our modification of the Lens Model. Not so; they are alive and well in the functions relating the attributed characteristics to communicant acceptability. "Honesty," for example, may be a characteristic attributed to communicants, but if it is given a strong weight in determining communicant acceptability (either by an individual subject or as a regression weight based on a number of subjects), then it also constitutes a *criterion*. Of course, some theorists in some cases may want to describe such weighted characteristics as *reflective of* criteria rather than *constituting* criteria.

SOME RELEVANT THEORIES

For scholars who especially enjoy theorizing, this model should be a playground. While regression formulas, for example, may describe *how* attributed characteristics are related to communicant acceptability, they do not say much about *why* they are related as they are. Of special importance, they do not identify the GOALS and GRASP which we have argued determine those relationships.

But this is another area in which information-processing theories of attitude change are potentially useful. We can consider a communicant to be an "attitude object" or the predisposition to choose a given communicant to be a "behavioral intention" (see Fishbein and Ajzen, 1975). At a surface level we can treat the attributions of characteristics as "beliefs" and the subjects' evaluative ratings of those characteristics as "attitudes toward the attributes" and apply Fishbein's formula for predicting a subject's attitude toward an object, in this case the communicant. Or, at a deeper level, we can measure subjects' belief (probability estimate) that the choice of a given communicant will facilitate each of their GOALS and measure also subjects' attitudes toward each of those GOALS (in a specific GRASP-defined situation). Then we can use Fishbein's later formula for predicting the strength of subjects' behavioral intention to choose that communicant. As soon as we define the problem in these terms, all the Subjective Expected Utility models (theories) and others based on the Bayes Theorem,[9] many of the other information-processing models described by Eagly and Himmelfarb (1977), and many of the behavioral decision theories described by Slovic et al. (1977) become relevant, useful, and testable.

CONCLUSION

In our earlier critique of factor-analytic approaches to the study of credibility we found many problems with that research, but, although we provided a brief description of a possible direction for future research, we did not really provide a very clear alternative. In this chapter we have tried to provide a better (at least a more detailed) conceptualization which we hope will be more useful to future researchers. We believe this present approach has the advantages of treating "credibility" as a process itself, of restoring it to a function in the more general process of persuasion, of providing a conceptualization applicable to all the participants in persuasion, of emphasizing its relation to established bodies of research in person perception and attitude theory, and, above all, of moving it in the direction of theory and moving it away from its previous dependence on the vagaries of fishing in the doldrums for correlations.

Of course, our success in this endeavor depends entirely on the extent to which future researchers find it useful to discuss credibility in terms of observed characteristics, attributed characteristics, criteria generated by the convergence of Goals Operant and Achievable in Light of the Situation and Goal-Relevant Aspects of the Situation in Persuasion, attribute-criterion matching, and communicant acceptability.

NOTES

1. McCroskey (1966), Bowers and Phillips (1967), Markham (1968), Whitehead (1968), McCroskey et al. (1971, 1972a, 1972b, 1973a, 1973b, 1974), Baudhuin and Davis (1972), Applbaum and Anatol (1973), Falcione (1974), Tuppen (1974).

2. See, for example, reviews by Walster and Abrahams (1972), Schneider et al. (1979), Kelley and Thibaut (1978), Tagiuri (1971), Berscheid and Walster (1978), Bruner and Tagiuri (1954), Tedeschi (1972), Huston (1974), Cook (1971), Warr and Knapper (1968), Livesley and Bromley (1973), Duck (1977), and Moscovici (1976). A paper by Tedeschi et al. (1972) argues a position very similar to that which we are taking here.

3. What we mean by a "symptom" has been termed a "signal" by many other writers. In nontechnical language, however, the distinctions among "sign," "signal," and "symbol" are at best vague and generally nonexistent. A "symptom," however, seems much more easily distinguished from a "symbol" in common parlance.

4. See especially Knapp (1978), Ekman and Friesen (1975), Davitz (1964), Mehrabian (1972), Weitz (1974), Birdwhistell (1970), Ashcraft and Scheflen (1976), and von Cranach and Vine (1973).

5. Two excellent books have recently been published covering perceptual correlates of language variables at all four language levels. See Sandell (1977) and Giles and Powesland (1975).

6. See note 2, especially Cook (1971).

7. See note 4.

8. See note 5.

9. Two recent reviews, Eagly and Himmelfarb (1978) and Slovic et al. (1977), have covered these theories. Wyer (1974) and Fishbein and Ajzen (1975) are also highly recommended.

REFERENCES

ADDINGTON, D. W. (1967). "The relationship of selected vocal characteristics to personality perception." Speech Monographs, 35:492-503.

AJZEN, I. (1977). "Information processing approaches to interpersonal attraction." In S. Duck (ed.), Theory and practice in interpersonal attraction. New York: Academic Press.

APPLBAUM, R.L., and ANATOL, K.W.E. (1973). "Dimensions of source credibility: a test for reproducibility." Speech Monographs, 40:231-237.

ARNHEIM, R. (1949). "The Gestalt theory of expression." Psychological Review, 56:156-171.

ASCH, S.E. (1951). "Effects of group pressure upon the modification and distortion of judgments." In H. Guetzkow (ed.), Groups, leadership, and men. Pittsburgh: Carnegie Press.

ASCH, S.E. (1956). "Studies of independence and conformity: A minority of one against a unanimous majority." Psychological Monographs, 70:Issue 416.

ASHCRAFT, N., and SCHEFLEN, A.E. (1976). People space: the making and breaking of human boundaries. Garden City, NY: Anchor.

BAUDHUIN, E.S., and DAVIS, M.K. (1972). "Scales for the measurement of ethos: Another attempt." Speech Monographs, 39:296-301.

BERLO, D.K., LEMERT, J.B., and MERTZ, R.J. (1969). "Dimensions for evaluating the acceptability of message sources." Public Opinion Quarterly, 33:563-576.

BERSCHEID, E., and WALSTER, E.H. (1978). Interpersonal attraction. Reading, MA: Addison-Wesley.

BIDDLE, P.R. (1966). "An experimental study of ethos and appeal for overt behavior in persuasion." Ph.D. dissertation, University of Illinois.

BIRDWHISTELL, R.L. (1970). Kinesics and context. Philadelphia: University of Pennsylvania Press.

BOWERS, J.W., and PHILLIPS, W.A. (1967). "A note on the generality of source credibility scales." Speech Monographs, 34:185-186.

BROADBENT, D.E. (1958). Perception and communication. New York: Pergamon.

BRUNER, J.S., GOODNOW, J.J., and AUSTIN, G.A. (1956). A study of thinking. New York: John Wiley.

BRUNER, J.S., SHAPIRO, D., and TAGIURI, R. (1958). "The meaning of traits in isolation and in combination." In R. Tagiuri and L. Petrullo (eds.), Person perception and interpersonal behavior. Stanford: Stanford University Press.

BRUNER, J.S., and TAGIURI, R. (1954). "The perception of people." In G. Lindzey (ed.), Handbook of social psychology. Reading, MA: Addison-Wesley.

BRUNSWIK, E. (1956). Perception and the representative design of psychological experiments. Berkeley: University of California Press.

CRONKHITE, G.L. (1977). "Scales measuring general evaluation with minimal distortion." Public Opinion Quarterly, 41:65-73.

CRONKHITE, G., and LISKA, J.R. (1976). "A critique of factor analytic approaches to the study of credibility." Communication Monographs, 43:91-107.

COOK, M. (1971). Interpersonal perception. New York: Viking.

DAVITZ, J.R. (ed., 1964). The communication of emotional meaning. New York: McGraw-Hill.

DUCK, S. (ed., 1977). Theory and practice in interpersonal attraction. New York: Academic Press.

EAGLY, A.H., and HIMMELFARB, S. (1978). "Attitudes and opinions." Annual Review of Psychology, 29:517-554.

EKMAN, P., and FRIESEN, W. (1967). "Head and body cues in the judgment of emotion: a reformulation. Perceptual and Motor Skills, 24:711-724.

――― (1969). "Nonverbal leakage and clues to deception." Psychiatry, 32:88-106.

――― (1975). Unmasking the face. Englewood Cliffs, NJ: Prentice-Hall.

FALCIONE, R.L. (1974). "The factor structure of source credibility scales for immediate superiors in an organizational context." Central States Speech Journal, 25:63-66.

FISHBEIN, M., and AJZEN, I. (1975). Belief, attitude, intention, and behavior. Reading, MA: Addison-Wesley.

GILES, H., and POWESLAND, P.F. (1975). Speech style and social evaluation. New York: Academic Press.

GOFFMAN, E. (1956). The presentation of self in everyday life. Edinburgh: Social Sciences Research Centre.

GOLDBERG, L.R. (1970). "Man versus model of man: A rationale, plus some evidence, for improving on clinical inference." Psychological Bulletin, 73:422-434.

HEIDER, F. (1944). "Social perception and phenomenal causality." Psychological Review, 51:358-374.

––– (1958). The psychology of interpersonal relations. New York: John Wiley.

HOFFMAN, P.J. (1960). "The paramorphic representation of clinical judgment." Psychological Bulletin, 57:116-131.

HUSTON, T.L. (1974). Foundations of interpersonal attraction. New York: Academic Press.

JONES, E.E., and DAVIS, K.E. (1965). "From acts to dispositions: The attribution process in person perception." In L. Berkowitz (ed.), Advances in experimental social psychology. New York: Academic Press.

JONES, E.E., and McGILLIS, D. (1976). "Correspondent inferences and the attribution cube: A comparative reappraisal." In J.H. Harvey, W.J. Ickes, and R.F. Kidd (eds.), New directions in attribution research. Hillsdale, NJ: Lawrence Erlbaum.

KELLY, G.A. (1955). The psychology of personal constructs. New York: Norton.

KELLEY, H.H. (1967). "Attribution theory in social psychology." In Nebraska symposium on motivation. Lincoln: University of Nebraska Press.

––– (1972a). "Causal schemata and the attribution process." In E.E. Jones et al. (eds.), Attribution: Perceiving the causes of behavior. Morristown, NJ: General Learning Press.

––– (1972b). "Attribution in social interaction." In E.E. Jones et al. (eds.), Attribution: Perceiving the causes of behavior. Morristown, NJ: General Learning Press.

––– (1973). "The process of causal attribution." American Psychologist, 28:107-128.

––– and THIBAUT, J.W. (1978). Interpersonal relations: A theory of interdependence. New York: John Wiley.

KNAPP, M.L. (1978). Nonverbal communication in human interaction. New York: Holt, Rinehart & Winston.

LISKA, J.R. (1978). "Situational and topical variations in credibility criteria." Communication Monographs, March 1978:85-92.

LIVESLEY, W.J., and BROMLEY, D.B. (1973). Person perception in childhood and adolescence. New York: John Wiley.

MACE, W.M. (1974). "Ecologically stimulating cognitive psychology: Gibsonian perspectives." In W.B. Weimer and D.S. Palermo (eds.), Cognition and the symbolic processes. Hillsdale, NJ: Lawrence Erlbaum.

McCROSKEY, J.C. (1966). "Scales for the measurement of ethos." Speech Monographs, 33:65-72.

––– HOLDRIDGE, W., and TOOMB, J.K. (1974). "An instrument for measuring the source credibility of basic speech communication instructors." Speech Teacher, 23:26-33.

McCROSKEY, J.C., JENSEN, T., and TODD, C. (1972a). "The generalizability of source credibility scales for public figures." Presented at the Speech Communication Association Convention, Chicago, Illinois.

McCROSKEY, J.C., JENSEN, T., and VALENCIA, C. (1973a). "Measurement of the credibility of mass media sources." Presented at the Western Speech Communication Association Convention, Albuquerque, New Mexico.

—— (1973b). "Measurement of the credibility of peers and spouses." Presented at the International Communication Association Convention, Montreal, Quebec.

McCROSKEY, J.C., SCOTT, M.D., and YOUNG, T.J. (1971). "The dimensions of source credibility for spouses and peers." Presented at the Western Speech Communication Association Convention, Fresno, California.

McCROSKEY, J.C., JENSEN, T., TODD, C., and TOOMB, J.K. (1972b). "Measurement of the credibility of organization sources." Presented at the Western Speech Communication Association Convention, Honolulu, Hawaii.

MARKHAM, D. (1968). "The dimensions of source credibility of television newscasters." Journal of Communication, 18:57-64.

MASLOW, A. (1962). Toward a psychology of being. Princeton, NJ: Van Nostrand-Rinehold.

MEAD, G.H. (1934). Mind, self, and society. Chicago: University of Chicago Press.

MEHRABIAN, A. (1972). Nonverbal communication. Chicago: AVC.

MILLER, G.R. (ed., 1976). Explorations in interpersonal communication. Beverly Hills, CA: Sage.

MOSCOVICI, S. (1976). Social influence and social change (C. Sherrard and G. Heinz, trans.). New York: Academic Press.

NAYLOR, J.C., and WHERRY, R.J., Sr. (1965). "The use of simulated stimuli and the 'JAN' technique to capture and cluster the policies of raters." Educational and Psychological Measurement, 25:969-986.

NORMAN, W.T. (1963). "Toward an adequate taxonomy of personality attributes: Replicated factor structure in peer nomination personality ratings." Journal of Abnormal and Social Psychology, 66:574-583.

RAPPOPORT, L., and SUMMERS, D.A. (1973). Human judgment and social interaction. New York: Holt, Rinehart & Winston.

SANDELL, R. (1977). Linguistic style and persuasion. New York: Academic Press.

SCHNEIDER, D.J., HASTORF, A.H., and ELLSWORTH, P.C. (1979). Person perception. Reading, MA: Addison-Wesley.

SHERIF, M. (1935). "A study of some social factors in perception." Archives of Psychology, 27:187.

—— (1936). The psychology of social norms. New York: Harper & Row.

SLOVIC, P., and LICHTENSTEIN, S. (1973). "Comparison of Bayesian and regression approaches to the study of information processing in judgment." In L. Rappoport and D.A. Summers (eds.), Human judgment and social interaction. New York: Holt, Rinehart & Winston.

SLOVIC, P., FISCHHOFF, B., and LICHTENSTEIN, S. (1977). "Behavioral decision theory." Annual Review of Psychology, 28:1-39.

STONE, G.P., and FARBERMAN, H.A. (1970). Social psychology through symbolic interaction. Waltham, MA: Xerox.

TAGIURI, R. (1971). "Person perception." In G. Lindzey and E. Aronson (eds.), Handbook of social psychology. Reading, MA: Addison-Wesley.

TEDESCHI, J.T. (ed., 1972). Social influence processes. Chicago: AVC.

—— BONOMA, T., and SCHLENKER, B. (1972). "Influence, decision, and compliance." In J. Tedeschi (ed.), Social influence processes. Chicago: AVC.

THORNDIKE, E.L. (1920). "A constant error in psychological ratings." Journal of Applied Psychology, 4:25-29.

TRIANDIS, H.C. (1964). "Exploratory factor analysis of the behavioral component of social attitudes." Journal of Abnormal and Social Psychology, 68:420-430.

TUPPEN, C.J.S. (1974). "Dimensions of communicator credibility: An oblique solution." Speech Monographs, 41:253-260.

VON CRANACH, M., and VINE, I. (eds., 1973). Social communication and movement. New York: Academic Press.

WALSTER, E., and ABRAHAMS, D. (1972). "Interpersonal attraction and social influence." In J. Tedeschi (ed.), Social influence processes. Chicago: AVC.

WARR, P.B., and KNAPPER, C. (1968). The perception of people and events. New York: John Wiley.

WEITZ, S. (ed., 1974). Nonverbal communication. New York: Oxford University Press.

WHITEHEAD, J.L. (1968). "Factors of source credibility." Quarterly Journal of Speech, 54:59-63.

WIGGINS, N. (1973). "Individual differences in human judgments: A multivariate approach." In L. Rappoport and D.A. Summers (eds.), Human judgment and social interaction. New York: Holt, Rinehart & Winston.

WYER, R.S., Jr. (1974). Cognitive organization and change: An information-processing approach. Hillsdale, NJ: Lawrence Erlbaum.

Chapter 5

PERSUASIVE MESSAGE STRATEGIES

Michael Burgoon and Erwin P. Bettinghaus

INTRODUCTION

One cannot begin a chapter on persuasive message strategies, let alone be enthusiastic about doing research in such an area, without feeling a bit amused, bemused, and even a little cynical. First, if communication scientists expend effort to determine the most effective ways to present persuasive messages to intended audiences, they will be labeled at best as "suddenly traditional" and at worst "hopelessly out of date" by many people in the discipline. Miller and Burgoon (1978), perhaps being a little of both, have discussed the apparent decline in interest in persuasion research in general and much traditional message research in particular by communication scholars. We believe that they have also made an excellent case for the contention that interest in this problem area is essential to our eventual understanding of human communication.

The apparent decline in research interest in persuasive message strategies probably can be attributed to three separate but unequal influences. First, faddish trends have attempted to replace traditional research concerns with alleged methodological innovations. Some people in the communication sciences appear to be more concerned with a particular methodology than with whether their data have any isomorphism with prevailing theory, past research, or common sense. For instance, specific mathematical models presently in vogue rule out any concern with the structure or quality of persuasive messages as inconsequential in obtaining attitude change.

Second, another school of thought has suggested the "holy grail" of understanding human communication can be unearthed only by measuring "interaction," "talk," or "conversation," depending on their metaphysical leanings, and/or present place of employment. They feel that creating and assessing persuasive messages is "easy" but trivial, while measuring their particular brand of communication is difficult but important. Obviously, certain variables in persuasive messages are relatively easy to control and study. The assumptions that some message structures should prove more effective than others, that some types of evidence should be more easily learned than others, or that some kinds of appeals will be more persuasive than others are relatively amenable to empirical verification. Other variables provide more knotty problems. The most difficult variable to control has been the topic of the message. Controlling for topic differences in messages seems to be an obvious requirement, but our review in this area suggests a number of perils that are far from obvious. Suppose we create two messages on the same topic using different organizational patterns, and one turns out to be a minute longer than the other. Can attitudinal differences be readily attributed to differences in arrangement, or is the additional material primarily responsible? If we study the effects of internal refutation, we have to create messages that differ in length or add new material to one of the versions. Is that addition a change in "topic?" Questions and problems such as these have made research into message strategies in all communication contexts very difficult. Furthermore, these same questions and problems severely limit the generalizability of much of the research in this area. Such complex problems probably have also led to a decline in the number of people willing to attempt needed research in persuasive message strategies. Therefore, we reject the claim that such interests are easy to handle but trivial, while conceding that others face important obstacles in measuring important communication events.

A third problem has been the somewhat myopic orientation of people engaged in persuasion research. Those problems are discussed in various sections of this chapter, but we would suggest that the tendency to view persuasion as an activity reserved for one-to-many speaking situations and as a linear, unidirectional communicative activity concerned only with measures of attitude change has put much research out of step with the current thinking in the discipline of communication. An expanded view of what constitutes persuasion research has been suggested by Miller and

Burgoon (1978). This chapter argues for such an expanded definition of what might constitute persuasive message research.

We have reviewed two broad research areas that we feel should be included in any work on persuasive messages: logical/rational message strategies and affective message strategies. Much of the research reviewed in those sections was completed more than a decade ago. For a variety of reasons, more recent research is not available. While we do not claim that these sections are an exhaustive review of all message research, we do think that the reviewed research provides a springboard for identifying areas for future research. Moreover, this chapter identifies two areas of research activity that traditionally have not been labeled message strategies: positioning of persuasive messages and messages as distractors and/or conditioners. We believe that these areas fit nicely into an expanded view of what constitutes persuasive message strategies.

CREATING EFFECTIVE PERSUASIVE MESSAGES

The questions of what to include in and how to arrange persuasive messages have generated considerable research. The first general question concerns just how rational one must be to be persuasive.

MESSAGE STRATEGIES– BEING RATIONAL

One of the oldest controversies in communication is whether a persuasive speaker is better advised to construct messages based on people's emotional needs or their rational bent. The basic argument can be traced to the ancient Greek philosophers, but it has surfaced at frequent intervals in the centuries since Plato and Aristotle formulated their rhetorical positions. The argument stems from a fundamental difference in the way proponents of the two positions view the nature of humanity. Those who adopt a strict rationalist position argue that when faced with emotional arguments versus rational arguments, receivers tend to respond best to well-constructed, logical arguments. A rationalist position argues that "at heart" people are rational beings who respond favorably to emotional messages only when rational alternatives are not available. In contrast, those who argue for a nonrationalist position say that a person is essentially an emotional being, swayed by cleverly constructed messages that appeal to patriotism, love, self-interest, and other feelings that may not be rational in nature. Such a position would say that the use of evidence, logical structure, or tight organization is not persuasive unless the evidence, or structure, is used to make an appeal to the emotions.

We have painted an extreme picture in order to obtain a clear conception of the essential difference between the two camps. Actually, few scholars would argue that people behave either all "rationally" or all "emotionally." The question still remains, however, as to whether the best advice one can give a prospective communicator is to structure a message so as to emphasize rational appeals—that is, the use of logic or evidence—or to emphasize the appeals made to various emotions. We begin by examining three kinds of studies which (1) use the syllogism as a vehicle for testing response, (2) examine the effectiveness of varying kinds of evidence, and (3) vary message structure along several dimensions.

Judging Syllogisms

A number of studies have attempted to determine whether receivers are more affected by logical or emotional factors by utilizing the classical, three-line syllogism as a research vehicle. These prior studies (McGuire, 1960, Miller, 1969) assumed that there might be variables which affect a receiver's ability to judge whether a syllogism was logically valid. Presumably, if receivers made errors in judging syllogistic validity, they would be in the direction of a receiver's prior beliefs if emotion were to rule. If logic were to prevail, the errors would be random and independent of prior belief. Many studies (Feather, 1964; Janis and Frick, 1943; Lefford, 1946; Morgan and Morton, 1953; Thouless, 1959) have shown that prior attitudes do affect the ability to make validity judgments. McGuire (1960) argues that in making logical judgments people try to maintain attitudinal consistency. Thus, an individual who is attitudinally in favor of the conclusion of an invalid syllogism has a higher probability of judging it to be valid, while an individual who disagrees with the conclusion of a valid syllogism is more likely to judge it invalid.

Two more recent studies have used syllogisms to explore the possibility that personality factors might influence logical judgments and that the complexity of an argument may also affect a receiver's judgmental ability. Bettinghaus et al. (1970) found that dogmatism affects the ability to make logical judgments, although the results are closely allied with the perceived credibility of the source of the syllogism and the type of syllogism used. Highly dogmatic persons make more errors than low-dogmatic people in the case of valid syllogisms attributed to negative sources.

The findings of this study, however, suggested that one of the major sources of variance might be due to the inherent complexity of the logical form. In fact, almost all of the errors made by subjects were made on one particular syllogistic form. This finding triggered a subsequent study (Steinfatt et al., 1974) which attempted to explore the inherent logical ambiguity in a syllogism as it might be related to judgments of validity. Syllogisms differ in complexity, and some forms have more potential conclusions than others. Such syllogistic forms may be said to be more ambiguous. The results of the study clearly indicated a direct relationship between the degree of difficulty of judging the validity of a syllogism and the ambiguity of the premise combination associated with the syllogism. The inherent difficulty of the syllogism was far more important than any other variable. Receivers made few errors on "easy" syllogisms and more errors on "hard" syllogisms.

The research history using the classical syllogism does not lead to firm conclusions regarding the rationality of man. The research says that prior attitudes affect judgments, that perceived credibility affects judgments, and that even personality may affect judgment. None of these results give one much faith in people's inherent ability to "behave rationally." The Steinfatt et al. (1974) results, however, show a different picture. If receivers really do make errors in judging logical forms primarily because of the inherent difficulty of the form and not because of any content in that form, it is easier to suggest that the rules of logic are aligned with the rules of thought, and homo sapiens would appear to be far more rational beings.

Most people, of course, have never seen a syllogism in a message; syllogisms are encountered in textbooks and research articles, but seldom in persuasive messages. Their absence from everyday persuasive discourse suggests the kind of research efforts that seem needed in the future. There are other systems of logic than the class logic represented by the classical syllogism. Propositional calculi of the type developed by Whitehead and Russell (1927) would seem to be far more closely related to actual arguments than the syllogism. There has been no research in which various arguments are constructed and manipulated on the basis of their propositional characteristics. Such research might go a long way toward answering arguments about humanity's rationality.

A second line of potential research stems from the work of Toulmin (1958). Toulmin argues that the syllogism does not represent the way in which people actually think, nor the way in which they may be affected by arguments. He provides a system of analyzing arguments which can be applied to both the analysis and the construction of any argument. The system has been widely used in communication texts (Ehninger and Brockriede, 1963; Bettinghaus, 1972), but it has never been subjected to careful empirical study. Toulmin's is a "people's logic," and a careful examination of Toulmin's forms versus standard logical structures would be extremely useful.

A final line of research that seems promising stems from the approach taken by Marwell and Schmitt (1967). Rather than manipulating various message forms and then testing those forms on receivers, they place individuals in dyadic communication situations and ask them to construct a persuasive message appropriate to that situation. Marwell and Schmitt have identified five major categories of persuasive strategies, none of which can be considered a logical category. However, the nature of the dyadic situations used may have made the development of logical messages unlikely. It would be extremely useful to utilize situations in which one might expect logical messages to be used and, through experimentation to see whether people do develop the expected messages. Alternatively, one might utilize similar situations, but provide instructional sets that would emphasize the creation or noncreation of logical messages. The results of such studies might help to answer the question of whether people are essentially logical or emotional.

Using Evidence

A second major approach to the question of whether rational messages are more effective than emotional messages raises the issue of the importance of *evidence* in a message. We consider as rational those messages using evidence that supports the probable truth of a given proposition; we also consider as emotional those messages simply pointing out the desirable consequences that might follow from a proposition. The question of whether to use evidence or emotional appeals has obvious practical consequences for many communication situations. Should defense lawyers review the evidence in a summation, or should they attempt to play upon the emotions of the jury? Should the opposition try to get a zoning ordinance defeated by telling the city council about the potential loss of wildlife, or by pointing to the venality of the company wanting the change?

There is a surprising paucity of research in this area. In two separate reviews of the literature, McGuire (1969) and McCroskey (1969) are able to identify fewer than two dozen studies. Few of these studies actually test the use of nonuse of evidence in communication situations, but examine evidential use as a by-product of other research interests. Cathcart (1953) and Bettinghaus (1953) report some positive results, although the Bettinghaus study does not directly test the use of evidence. Many studies report nonsignificant findings (Chen, 1935; Knower, 1935; Dresser, 1962).

Those few studies that directly test between emotional appeals and appeals using evidence generally report negative findings (Eldersveld, 1956; Hartmann, 1936; Menefee and Granneberg, 1940).

In our judgment, however, none of the prior research provides very clear data about the effectiveness of the use or nonuse of various types of evidence. Almost all of the studies used audiences composed entirely of college students. That may not be a shortcoming when one is looking at general aspects of human behavior, but if one suspects that a variable may be differentially affected by age, education, or other similar factors, it is a fatal flaw. In addition, almost all of the studies looked at evidence as a secondary issue to the examination of other variables. As a result, research designs were complicated, and many of the early studies did not adequately separate out the effects of other variables. Since interactions between the use of evidence and other variables are quite common (for example, credibility: McCroskey, 1969), it seems desirable to design studies simply looking at evidence as a main effect variable. This approach has not been pursued.

We think that the study of evidence has been neglected and suggest that a fruitful research program could be mounted in this area. Several topics of importance can be identified.

(1) The use of evidence is clearly dependent on the topic of the message. One would not expect detailed evidence if the message were designed to get a receiver to purchase a particular brand of soft drink. Use of testimony or simply an appeal to the senses is probably more persuasively effective in this situation. Yet, we have no studies that attempt to outline exactly what kinds of topics would be suitable for particular kinds of evidence. The Marwell and Schmitt (1967) approach seems to be potentially useful in this area.

(2) Audiences may differ with respect to many variables: for example, age, sex, education, and other similar dimensions. One might well expect that evidence persuasive to one audience would not be persuasive to others. Such differences may help account for some of the mixed empirical results abounding in the literature. Identifying some of the interactions between the use of evidence and various audience characteristics would be a distinct help to the field.

(3) Current classification systems for evidence have been derived from the legal system (Newman and Newman, 1969; Bettinghaus, 1972). There is absolutely no evidence that these legally derived classification systems are related to how people behave toward the use of evidence. For example, we can distinguish between direct evidence and negative evidence. That distinction may be vital in the legal setting, but may make no difference at all if we are concerned with persuading an audience to stop smoking. The

development of a classification system for evidence based on behavioral criteria, rather than a legal system, might help spur research interest.

Serious empirical studies on evidence in communicative situations seems to have halted abruptly following the publication of review articles on the topic some ten years ago. We do not wish to suggest that those efforts "put the kiss of death" on the area, but one can look in vain for research since that time. Our own analysis, however, suggests that this is still a potentially fruitful area of study, and we hope future scholarly efforts will be directed to it.

Message Structure

One of the few areas that yields some fairly clear findings concerns the effects of message structure on behavior. Although a few studies suggest that a structured message may be no more effective than an unstructured one, most researchers have concluded that structured messages are more effective than unstructured ones. However, prior research is somewhat inconclusive about the precise effects of message organization. Thompson (1960) concluded that organization was important for learning, but not for attitude change. Darnell (1963), however, concluded after a careful study using written messages that message disorganization must be severe before learning is affected, but that only slight deviations from normal organizational patterns were enough to influence attitude change. The Darnell results were similar to those of Sencer (1965), who found that adding serious grammatical errors to a message affected attitude toward the message, but had little effect on learning.

These and other results (see a review by Petrie, 1963) may seem inclusive, but taken as a whole they strongly suggest that a structured message is preferable to an unstructured one. Put differently, no studies reveal a preference for disorganized messages over organized ones.

To say that a reader or listener prefers an organized message over some random combinations of words is, of course, to take only the very first step in a research area. The first step, however, has been the last step when we look at the literature in message organization. No studies have investigated *what* kinds of structure are useful in particular situations. Should the communicator use a problem-solution order for a topic, or a deductive approach? The literature is silent on this question. Almost every communication text has a section on message organization; typically, these sections provide the student with a number of standard types of organizational patterns. No one has attempted to make comparative studies of any of these patterns. Darnell (1963) concluded that perhaps the variable involved was familiarity—that is, any organizational pattern would be acceptable as long as it was one that had some degree of familiarity to an audience. He viewed the problem as one of violation of expectations. An unfamiliar pattern would be a negative violation of expectations to the audience member, with the likely reaction one of attitudinal rejection.

We accept the plausibility of the familiarity explanation. Nevertheless, considerable work has been left undone. Some of the obvious questions to us include the following.

(1) Are there hierarchies of acceptable patterns? Certainly, audiences encounter problem-solution orders more frequently than they do space patterns. Can we assume that acceptability is directly related to frequency of use? An answer would help give advice to communicators that is not now found in our prescriptive textbooks.

(2) Do different receivers react differently? This is a simple question, but audiences can be divided along various lines (for example, race, sex, education, or occupation). Might we find that males prefer inductive patterns, while females prefer deductive patterns? Or would the reverse be true? Are people with college educations more likely to be influenced by messages cast into problem-solution patterns, and people with eighth-grade educations more apt to be influenced by a pattern such as a motivated sequence?

(3) Are there any naturally preferred patterns of organization? A teacher could easily assign students a number of topics over a term and leave the organization of topic reports or speeches to the students. The number of different kinds of organizational patterns chosen for different kinds of topics would make a very interesting study. To our knowledge, no one has attempted such a study. In fact, there is no research that attempts to compare what the "experts" tell us with what people actually do when faced with a task of organizing a quantity of material.

(4) How does the nature of the situation affect message structure? Textbooks typically list a number of possible structures for organizing a speech. One would expect, however, that a message to be delivered to a group of five people sitting around a table might be organized differently than one to be delivered to an audience of 600 people in a large auditorium. Similarly, one might expect that a speech delivered over television would have a different structure than one delivered in a face-to-face situation. We can find no sound studies that make such comparisons, nor even any mention of expected differences.

Structured messages are to be preferred to unstructured messages. Familiar structures seem to be more effective than unfamiliar ones. But after making these general conclusions, the research on message structure tells us little. It is still an area ready for development.

AFFECTIVE MESSAGE STRATEGIES–BEING EMOTIONAL

Throughout our discussion of logical and rational approaches to message use, we have implicitly suggested that the alternative to logical message appeals lies in appeals to various emotions. Thus, we can talk about fear appeals, intense appeals versus mild appeals, appeals to self-interest, and the like. In this section, we examine several affective message strategies that have generated a significant body of research.

Fear Appeals

Is it more effective to "just give the facts" to a receiver in a persuasive situation, or should the source attempt to "scare" the receiver into compliance? Behind this question lies a sizable body of research into fear appeals. The classic study by Janis and Feshback (1953) compared high fear messages and low fear messages in a situation designed to induce high school students to brush their teeth. Their results indicated that low levels of fear were more successful in changing attitudes than the high-fear appeal messages. A few studies have tended to confirm the Janis and Feshback findings (DeWolfe and Governale, 1964; Goldstein, 1959; Janis and Terwilliger, 1962). Many studies find the reverse—that is, that high fear is more effective than low levels of fear—or they report mixed results, positive in some situations and negative in others. (Snider, 1962; Miller and Hewgill, 1964, 1966; Chu, 1966)

McGuire (1969) argues that the research suggests the existence of a nonmonotonic, inverted "u-shaped" relationship. He posits an interaction between the receiver's level of anxiety (arousal) and opinion change. Such an interaction was found in several studies (Niles, 1964; Leventhal and Watts, 1966; Powell, 1965; Millman, 1965). We agree with McGuire that there is no simple, monotonic relationship between persuasibility and level of fear appeal. Still, we doubt that McGuire's further explanation of a nonmonotonic theory—that is, that the effect of the fear appeal is directly related to the simplicity of the message—is adequate.

We believe there is a series of alternative explanations that need to be explored carefully before coming to conclusions about the persuasive impact of fear appeals. For example, Goldstein (1959) suggested that levels of fear appeal might be related to personality type. A second type of explanation may relate to the importance of the topic. Colburn (1967) found that high levels of fear appeal increase in effectiveness as the topic becomes increasingly important to the receiver. A third kind of explanation was suggested by Miller and Hewgill (1964, 1966), who related fear appeals to credibility; they found that high levels of fear were effective when identified with a relatively credible source.

Obviously, the findings in this area are confusing, and research is needed to further parse out the effects of important variables. A simplistic explanation is unlikely to result. We would like to suggest one further area that deserves examination. The nature of the communication situation seems extremely important to the use of fear appeals. A role-playing study by Mann (1967) underscores the importance of the situation as a variable. He created three types of situations: a high-fear situation, a shame situation, and a cognitive situation. His results suggested that the fear situation played a more important role in attitude change than did the cognitive situation. Miller and Burgoon (1973) utilized the Mann study to point to the possible use of fear appeals in counterattitudinal advocacy situations where people are actively encoding messages that are contrary to their private beliefs. We suggest that other important situational variables include (1) the presence or absence of other receivers in a situation; (2) whether the situation involved interposed communication; (3) the size of the audience receiving the message; and (4) the importance of other audience members to the receiver.

The issue of the persuasive impact of fear appeals benefited from a strong beginning series of research efforts. The initial results suggested that parsing out the important relationships would be difficult. Unfortunately, we have seen relatively little research in this area in the decade just past. We suggest that it still remains a fruitful area of research. In these times, the use of fear in suasory communication is unlikely to diminish even if research efforts fade away.

The Use of Intense Language

People make choices about the kinds of language they will use to develop persuasive appeals. A great deal of evidence suggests that these language choices exert an impact on whether the persuasive attempt succeeds or fails. The level of language intensity one chooses to use in any persuasive message is clearly one important language variable. Language intensity has been defined as the perceptual distance between a persuasive claim and some neutral position. The level of language intensity of a persuasive message can be systematically varied in several ways.

One way to manipulate language intensity is to insert qualifiers in a persuasive appeal. A qualifier like "certainly" is apt to be perceived as more intense than a word like "probably." Qualifiers which indicate extremity such as "extremely dislike" indicate more intensely held positions than do phrases like "don't care for." A second way to increase intensity of language is to use metaphors, especially those with sexual or violent connotations (Bowers, 1964). Although much of the teaching in communication would lead students to believe that highly intense language leads to more acceptance of a communicator's position, the research evidence does not suggest such a simplistic view.

Bowers (1963) found an unexpected "boomerang effect" such that messages using relatively low intense language were more persuasive than messages arguing very intensely. Burgoon and King (1974), among others, have presented evidence that people react somewhat negatively to persuasive messages which are perceived as too intense. Jones and Burgoon (1975) found that people under stress were especially likely to be receptive to messages employing low levels of language intensity while tending to reject highly intense persuasive messages. People under stress were significantly more sensitive to language differences than people in more normal message reception conditions.

Burgoon and Stewart (1975) discovered another factor that mediates the effects of language intensity in the persuasion process. They suggest that people develop expectations about what is "appropriate" communication behavior on the part of any given communicator. At least in this culture, males can apparently use much more intense language and still be persuasive, while females are more effective when they use language relatively low in intensity. If this culture expects males to be aggressive and to demonstrate their aggressiveness by using forceful language, then males using highly intense language would not violate any expectations about appropriate communication behavior. Conversely, to the extent that such language behavior by females is not normative in this society, females who choose to use highly intense language negatively violate expectations and reduce their persuasive impact. Burgoon (1975) demonstrates that highly credible sources, perhaps because they are expected to be forceful and dynamic, can be effective with language higher in intensity than can low-credible sources. In other words, males and highly credible sources tend to have a wider range of language choices that will not reduce their persuasiveness. People lower in credibility and females are restricted by the norms of the society and have less latitude in language usage if they desire to be maximally persuasive.

Burgoon (1970), Burgoon and Miller (1971), and Burgoon and King (1974) present interesting evidence suggesting that the above conclusions about highly intense language only apply to situations in which some communicator is delivering a message to potential persuadees who are relatively passive receivers. This is, of course, a typical context in which persuasion attempts occur. However, in the counterattitudinal advocacy or forced compliance paradigm, where people are enticed to actively encode messages that deviate from their private beliefs, different results are obtained. In those active encoding situations, the more intense the language used by speakers, the more the speakers will change their private beliefs to conform to the position advocated. In other words, the more intensely persons say something counter to their attitude, the more they will come to believe the position advocated in the persuasive message (we come to believe our own lies, especially if we tell them with enough forcefulness).

Opinionated language is similar to intense language and has comparable effects on persuasion. Opinionated language usually expresses two separate messages: the persuasive claim and the communicator's attitude toward those who agree or disagree with the claim. An opinionated rejection statement derogates those who disagree with the persuasive appeal, while an opinionated acceptance statement praises those who agree with the claim or show acceptance of the communicator. A statement that merely expresses the communicator's attitude toward the topic (for example, "racial discrimination is bad") is not what is generally called an opinionated statement as no opinion is expressed toward those who agree or disagree with the claim.

Research indicates that opinionated statements are perceived as more intense than nonopinionated statements. Miller and Lobe (1967) and Miller and Baseheart (1969) found that highly credible sources could use opinionated rejection statements more effectively than could sources low in credibility. Mehrley and McCroskey (1970) reported that opinionated rejection language is more effective than nonopinionated language when the receiver is neutral on the topic being discussed. However, when people are highly involved and hold intense attitudes toward the topic, non-opinionated language is significantly more persuasive.

Unlike some of the perviously discussed areas of interest, research on the effects of specific language variables seems alive and somewhat well. Perhaps this research interest has continued because of the dramatic mediating effects of these language variables in a number of persuasion contexts. Continued research efforts are likely to provide added insight into the degree to which people's use of language affects persuasiveness.

STRATEGIC USES OF PERSUASIVE APPEALS

As the previous discussion indicates, the lion's share of research on persuasive messages has been more relevant to those more interested in how to structure a message than in how to use a message to induce compliance. Selecting message appeals, based both on logic and emotion, and making strategic decisions about what to include in what order has been the focus of most persuasive message research. The limitations of such a narrow research focus are manifest. First, most of the previously discussed research findings are primarily translatable to those situations in which persuasion is attempted in a one-to-many communication context. Miller and Burgoon (1978) have argued that exclusive attention to this one-to-many communication context is one of the reasons for the apparent decline in persuasion research. They argue for extending the notion of persuasion to include the recognition that social influence is an essential ingredient of *all* communication transactions.

In addition to much of the message appeal and message structure research having limited utility in nonpublic speaking contexts, little is offered to one interested in actually using messages to induce compliance in a variety of social situations. While one cannot deny the utility of research devoted to message structure and content, it seems reasonable to ask, "Is that all there is to message research?" Two recent lines of inquiry, one dealing with size of initial request and the other with message distraction effects, indicates that there is more—much more—and that research on message strategies will provide a complement to existing research. The first life of research deals with the question of how much a message should ask for or what are the effects of the size of an initial request in a social influence attempt. The so-called "foot-in-the-door technique" centers on gaining compliance without pressure. This procedure requires the preparation of messages that obtain a person's compliance with a small request in order to substantially increase the probability of that person's compliance with a subsequent larger request. The "door-in-the-face technique" is a radically different procedure for gaining compliance. Unlike the foot-in-the-door strategy, this approach first uses a message that requests a large demand which presumably will be refused; a second persuasive message makes a smaller request with which the target person is more likely to comply. These two techniques rely on different explanations for the efficacy of different persuasive messages facilitating compliance.

Both techniques merit detailed discussion for several reasons: (1) the research is novel and raises many questions for those interested in persuasive messages, and (2) both approaches are useful in a broad range of communication contexts other than the one-to-many situation.

THE FOOT-IN-THE-DOOR-TECHNIQUE:
COMPLIANCE WITHOUT PRESSURE

A common approach to persuasion is to apply considerable pressure on individuals or groups to induce them to comply with the wishes of a communicator, regardless of whether such compliance is in their best interest. Certainly, the ongoing credibility research (Kelman and Hovland, 1953; Berlo et al., 1969; McCroskey et al., 1972) attempts to delineate those source characteristics most likely to enhance the pressure on individuals to comply with the wishes of a communicator. Asch (1951) presents compelling evidence of the effects of group pressure on conformity. Even the modeling research of Bandura et al. (1963) dealing with the power of the modeled person provides evidence on the effects of conformity pressures. Clearly, the previously discussed material on logical and emotional appeals is chiefly concerned with optimal strategies for pressuring people to change. All of this research suggests a direct, linear relationship between external pressure to comply and obtained compliance by the communicator.

However, there are times when the goal of a communicator is to produce compliance with a minimum of perceived external pressure. In many interpersonal transactions, power, credibility, and status differentials are sufficiently small among the people involved as to be ineffectual sources of pressure to comply. Moreover, as Freedman and Fraser (1966) suggest, there may be moral and ethical reasons for applying minimal external pressure to gain compliance. Finally, there may be times when it is possible, but not wise, to apply great external pressure to induce compliance.

The major assumption underlying the foot-in-the-door technique is that a powerful predictor of future compliance is past compliance; that is, a person who has been induced to comply with a small request is more likely to comply with subsequent, larger demands. This knowledge is certainly intuitive to those in the advertising world. Many campaigns attempt gradually to induce people to become regular buyers by initially asking them to respond to requests even if the response is simply evaluating a product.

Freedman and Fraser (1966) report two experiments demonstrating that people who comply with initial small requests are more likely to comply with subsequent larger demands. The first study showed that people who initally comply with a first request are more likely to comply with a second, larger request from the same communicator. The second study provides more intriguing and dramatic evidence of the effects of the foot-in-the-door strategy. The effect was quite strong, even when a different person made the larger request and the two requests were substantially different. Specifically, people were asked to place a small sign in their window or sign a petition on the issues of keeping their state beautiful or safe driving. Two weeks later a different person returned and asked the homeowners to place a large, ugly sign promoting auto safety on their front lawns for two weeks. Subjects who complied with the initial request were much more likely to comply with the larger request. Snyder and Cunningham (1975) and Pliner et al. (1974) provide evidence of the replicability of Freedman and Fraser's (1966) findings.

Freedman and Fraser explain their results in the following manner:

> What may occur is a change in the person's feelings about getting involved or about taking action. Once he has agreed to a request, his attitude may change. He may become in his own eyes a person who does this sort of thing, who agrees to requests made by strangers, and who takes actions on things he believes in, who cooperates with good causes [1966:201].

This explanation is seen as congruent with Bem's (1970) theory of self-perception, which posits that people infer their attitudes from self-observation of behavior. Kelley's (1973) attribution theory is also compatible with the above explanation. According to attribution theory, people often make self-attributions about their attitudes/dispositions on the basis of their overt behavior and the context in which they performed the behavior.

Pliner et al. (1974), in addition to replicating the earlier foot-in-the-door findings, found that compliance with both small and moderate initial requests yielded more compliance with subsequent larger requests. Seligman et al. (1976) refined the earlier research by testing four plausible explanations of the foot-in-the-door paradigm. First, Freedman and Fraser (1966) imply that compliance to any initial request produces later, more substantial compliance. An explanation more consistent with Bem's (1970) self-perception notions would suggest that prior compliance produces later compliance only if appropriate self-perceptions occur. This position would argue that the larger the initial request complied with, the greater the likelihood of subsequent larger compliance. A third explanation suggests that every person has a fixed amount of commitment on any given issue; thus, the larger the size of the first request complied with, the less likely the compliance with the later request. A fourth explanation suggests a curvilinear relationship between size of the first request and compliance with a second request. The results suggested that the self-perception explanation was most useful. The first request must be of a minimally sufficient magnitude to commit the individual to further compliance.

Taken as a whole, this research clearly demonstrates the interdependent nature of persuasive messages in sequential message reception conditions. We now turn to a discussion of door-in-the-face techniques and will then discuss needed message research to incorporate these paradigms in ongoing persuasion research.

THE DOOR-IN-THE-FACE TECHNIQUE:
RECIPROCAL CONCESSIONS PROCEDURES

The door-in-the-face technique has been called the exact opposite of the foot-in-the-door procedure. The door-in-the-face approach begins with a persuasive message advocating/requesting an action which is sure to be rejected, followed by a subsequent message requesting a more moderate outcome. Obviously, the second, moderate behavior is what is desired from the inception of the influence attempt. The door-in-the-face procedure is based on evidence from two different research areas.

The first line of research centers on reciprocation. Gouldner (1960) says reciprocity involves giving benefits to those who give you benefits. Cialdini et al. (1975:206) posit what they call a reciprocal concessions corollary to the norm of reciprocity. This corollary implies that you should make concessions to those who make concessions to you. Reciprocity is obviously a major factor in many interpersonal communication transactions. Often interpersonal transactions begin with positions which are unacceptable to one or both parties. Mutual concession is a mechanism to prevent termination of the communication according to Cialdini et al. (1975). The principle of reciprocal concessions allows interactants to initiate compromise attempts with the expectation that reciprocal concessions will occur.

The second area of research deals with negotiation. Chertkoff and Conley (1967) found that in a bargaining situation, the more frequently an opponent makes concessions, the more frequently the other interactant also gives ground. Komorita and Brenner (1968:18) concluded

> in a bargaining situation, if one party wishes to reach an agreement at a "fair" price, clearly a strategy of making an initial offer at that level and remaining firm thereafter is not an effective means of reaching an agreement.

Cialdini et al. (1975) present the results of three experiments which support their reciprocal concessions model. The first experiment demonstrated that people who had initially rejected an extreme request were more vulnerable to a more moderate second request than those only exposed to the smaller moderate request. In the second experiment, a large request followed by a smaller one was made by the *same* person in one condition. A second condition involved a large request and a subsequent smaller request made by a *different* person. The reciprocal concessions model would predict that only when the extreme and smaller favors were asked by the same person would compliance be enhanced. The findings supported the reciprocal concessions model.

The third experiment added an equivalent second-request condition to rule out the explanation that sheer persistance in making requests leads to increased compliance. In the rejected extreme-moderate request sequence, the persuader is seen as making concessions and reciprocal concessions are offered. When a person makes an initial large request, is refused, and then makes an equally large second request, there should be no perceived concession. The results suggested that only when the second request was *smaller* (not necessarily small) was compliance enhanced.

Even-Chen et al. (1978: 140) further suggest the following necessary conditions for occurrence of the door-in-the-face effect:

(a) the original request must be rejected by the person;
(b) the original request should be large enough so that its rejection will be perceived by the target person as irrelevant for making self-attribution;
(c) the original request should not evoke in the target person resentment, anger or hostility;
(d) the second request must be unambiguously smaller than the first one.

PERSUASIVE MESSAGE STRATEGIES TO FACILITATE FOOT-IN-THE-DOOR AND DOOR-IN-THE-FACE PROCEDURES

It is obvious that both of these persuasive strategies have potential utility for the person interested in designing persuasive messages to enhance compliance. The foot-in-the-door procedure suggests the following message strategies:

(a) The first message in a sequential message reception must make an unambiguously smaller request than subsequent requests and the initial request must induce compliance.
(b) The first message must make a request of sufficient magnitude to trigger self-perceptions that commit the person to future compliance. In other words, the initial request should not be trivial, for it

must prompt the person to infer attitudes from behaviors, thus heightening the likelihood of subsequent compliance.

(c) A communicator can take advantage of previous compliance gains even if someone else were responsible for the initial compliance. Persons who find themselves in the position of following someone who succeeded in gaining compliance to a smaller request can often gain even more compliance with that person's wishes.

The door-in-the-face technique operates on different principles and requires different persuasive message strategies:

(a) The second message in a sequential message reception must make an unambiguously smaller request than the initial request and the initial request must be rejected.
(b) The first request must be so large that persons do not perceive rejection of that request as a reflection of their attitudes. In other words, self-perception must not operate and the request must not be so large as to make rejection reasonable.
(c) The initial request must not be so large and absurd as to evoke hostility or no subsequent compliance will occur.
(d) A communicator must be seen as making concessions or compliance will not result. Therefore, one communicator will not necessarily benefit from the rejection of another person's larger demands.
(e) The second requests do not have to be small or trivial, but must be perceived as smaller than the first request.

DISTRACTION AS A PERSUASIVE MESSAGE STRATEGY

The second line of research deals with the effects of distraction in the compliance-gaining process. Some might find it questionable to include elements that distract a listener during the reception of a message in a chapter on persuasive message strategies. Nevertheless, it can be argued that attempts to distract receivers are a strategic activity that can enhance or inhibit compliance. Moreover, potential and actual distractions are very much a part of most social influence attempts. Some distractions are unintentional, from the point of view of people engaged in persuasive communication, and will not be dealt with in this section. However, many distractions are deliberate attempts to manipulate outcomes and become persuasive message strategies in themselves.

Festinger and Maccoby (1964) and Osterhouse and Brock (1970) are among those who have emphasized that when exposed to persuasive messages, people actively subvocalize counterarguments against the position advocated by the message. This subvocalization process is presumed to create resistance to the persuasive arguments directed at the listener. Counterarguing can take several forms. First, persons can covertly generate arguments supporting their initial position. Another strategy is to rehearse arguments refuting the position advocated by the persuasive message. Finally, the listener can also derogate the competence and/or character of the communicator.

This interest in counterarguing as a mediator of attitude change has led to research focusing on the effects of inhibiting counterarguing, primarily through the presentation of some form of distraction concurrent with a persuasive message. Since counterarguing is presumed to create critical resistance, when distractors interfere with these cognitive exercises, counterarguing should be decreased, as should critical resistance leading to greater acceptance of the position advocated by the persuasive message. It should be noted that an alternative theoretical position suggests that distraction from the content of a persuasive message decreases rather than increases the effectiveness of that message. McGuire (1966) points out that a learning theory approach implies that distractors presented during a persuasive message should interfere with the learning of a new argument and thus attitude change should be reduced.

The direct relationship between distraction and attitude change has been supported by Festinger and Maccoby (1964), Rosenblatt (1973), and Osterhouse and Brock (1970). Haaland and VenKatesen (1968) found that both visual distractors and behavioral distractors decreased the impact of a persuasive message. Vohs and Garrett (1968) found that both recall and attitude change were inhibited by distraction. Breitrose (1966) and Gardner (1966) independently found that distraction reduced learning (recall) but had no effects on shifts in attitudinal position.

These confusing, often seemingly contradictory results prompted researchers to focus attention on the kinds of distractions being used to mediate attitude change. A myriad of distractors have been used, including flashing lights; multichannel, multimessage competition; attachment to EKG hardware; irrelevant tasks; and many others. Zimbardo et al. (1970) found that an irrelevant, distracting task performed concurrently with receipt of a persuasive message *increased* attitude change when the receivers were set to attend primarily to the persuasive message. However, when receivers were set to primarily attend to the task, attitude change was *inhibited*.

Regan and Cheng (1973) found that the nature of the persuasive message mediated the effects of distraction. In conditions where the messages were relatively unconvincing but simple, distraction increased attitude change. When the persuasive message was difficult to understand but convincing if understood, distraction reduced the persuasiveness of the complex message. Obviously, the nature of the distractor and the persuasive message are important predictors of attitude change.

Burgoon et al. (1978) attempted to expand knowledge of the effects of distraction to include situations other than one-shot influence attempts. Moreover, they attempted to deal with distractors that might realistically occur in a number of communication contexts. First, they looked at the effects of distraction during an initial persuasive message to predict vulnerability to a subsequent persuasive message arguing the same position as the initial message. Thus, they examined sequential message reception conditions. Distractors were manipulated by inducing people to attend to either positive or negative characteristics of the source of the initial message or the arguments contained in that message. Given that people are predisposed to criticize or praise a communicator and/or a message with which they initially disagree, these kinds of distractions are quite comparable with naturally occurring social influence attempts.

Burgoon et al. (1978) argue that when people are asked to critically evaluate attributes of a communicator and to look for negative source and/or delivery characteristics, they are vulnerable to later persuasive attempts. These authors claim that attention to negative communicator characteristics minimizes the threat involved by having beliefs attacked in the initial persuasive message. Furthermore, attention to negative communicator characteristics should prove to be distracting. Both the minimization of threat and the distraction effects should inhibit counterarguing and leave people vulnerable to forthcoming persuasive messages. Conversely, attention to positive communicator characteristics should enhance the effectiveness of an initial persuasive message and create expectations in receivers' minds that future speakers may effectively argue for positions opposing their private beliefs. This should prompt counterarguing and cause people to *revert* to more negative attitudes after receiving a second persuasive message.

Likewise, when people initially are encouraged to attend to the content of persuasive messages, there is less distraction, inhibition of counterarguing, and susceptibility to later persuasive attempts. However, people who are initially induced to be negative toward message content will be less threatened, counterargue less, and be somewhat more susceptible to later persuasive messages than people initially set to positively evaluate message content. Burgoon et al. (1978) present evidence that confirms these predictions while demonstrating that strategies of distraction dramatically influence the effectiveness of sequentially received persuasive messages.

Miller and Burgoon (1979) extended and refined the Burgoon et al. (1978) model by incorporating knowledge about confirmation and disconfirmation of expectancies about persuasive messages in their predictions. Miller and Burgoon argue that people develop expectations about the nature of persuasive messages they will receive. When those expectations are violated in a positive manner (for example, expecting strong arguments and receiving moderate appeals), the effect of an initial persuasive message is enhanced. However, the realization that persuasive arguments counter to one's beliefs can be advanced in a reasonable manner should threaten the individual and increase the motivation to counterargue. Thus, upon exposure to a second persuasive message on the same side of the issue, attitudes should revert to their original negative positions.

When message expectancies are negatively violated (for example, receiving unexpectedly strong appeals), distraction from message content occurs. Persuasive information can be resisted by derogating the communicator or the writing/speaking style and counterarguing that each statement is unnecessary. Therefore, a person in this condition should be vulnerable to future persuasive messages given the initial inhibition of counterarguing. Miller and Burgoon (1979) found support for all of these predictions.

It is clear that communicators can intentionally use distraction as a persuasive strategy. Messages designed to distract a receiver from a concurrent message often have unintended salutory effects on the message which the distractor intended to inhibit (such as heckling a speaker). At other times, distractions are offered concurrently with another message with the express purpose of enhancing the persuasiveness of that persuasive appeal. The nature of the distraction and the kind of persuasive message being presented mediate the effects of distraction strategies.

Distractions do not have to take the form of whirring noises, flashing lights, or attachment to alien hardware. Potential distractors are present in many communication situations. Competing messages and/or channels can be used as distractors. Evidence also suggests that the kinds of critical sets people have can distract them in persuasive message reception situations. Much of the discipline's attention to evaluation/criticism of communicator characteristics may have the unintended effect of producing more generally gullible receivers (Miller and Burgoon, 1973). Finally, people develop expectations about the nature of forthcoming persuasive messages, and positive or negative violations of those expectations can provide distracting effects, thus affecting the impact of persuasive attempts.

Finally, the research indicates that distraction can operate to enhance or inhibit a concurrent persuasive message. However, recent research also strongly suggests that distraction not only affects the impact of a simultaneous persuasive message but also can affect the success of subsequent influence attempts. It is hoped that this section has been suggestive of many strategies to produce change or induce resistance to persuasion.

Future research will undoubtedly shed additional light on methods for effectively using this persuasive message strategy.

Miller and Burgoon (1978) have argued for an expanded view of the persuasion process that would redirect research effort. The inclusion of the foot-in-the-door, door-in-the-face, and distraction research is in keeping with their stated criteria for needed persuasion research. First, all of these techniques investigate influence attempts in a variety of communication situations other than the one-to-many context that has typified much of the prior persuasion research. Second, all of these techniques approach the issue of message strategies from a different point of view than most traditional persuasion research; they deal with studies that center on message choices made by the communicator. A communicator must make choices about the size of initial request and the effects of such requests on subsequent influence attempts. Also, distractions and potential critical response sets can be manipulated by the choices a communicator makes. These lines of research also exemplify three additional crucial criteria. First, this research demonstrates how one persuasive message can potentially influence subsequent persuasive attempts. Since messages rarely, if ever, exist in a vacuum in our information-saturated society, it is important to consider the effects of persuasive messages on later persuasive messages. All of these studies look at persuasion as a result of miltiple persuasive messages received over time. Finally, these lines of research deal with important questions for people who have to make everyday decisions about persuasive message strategies. People operate in situations where distractors are present whether because of the intentional behavior of the persuader or not. People attempt to persuade others who have been bombarded with earlier, similar requests. Individuals often enter negotiation and bargaining transactions, and reciprocal concession appears to be an aspect of many communication situations.

RECENT RESEARCH DEALING WITH
COMPREHENSIVE PERSUASIVE STRATEGIES

Several recent studies have sought to develop comprehensive typologies of persuasive message strategies, as well as to discover how people vary in their use of these strategies across persuasive situations. As discussed earlier, Marwell and Schmitt (1967) suggest that a great deal of research has centered on the use of specific message strategies (for example, evidence, fear appeals, and the like) not on a comprehensive set of strategies. They identified 16 general persuasive message strategies. Marwell and Schmitt asked subjects to indicate how they would use each of the strategies in four different dyadic situations: a job situation, in the family, a sales situation, and a situation involving a roommate. Five primary factors emerged from the 16 items and were labeled: (1) rewarding activity, (2) punishing activity, (3) activation of impersonal commitments, (4) activation of personal commitments, and (5) expertise. Their study suggests that comprehensive message strategies can be developed in any given situation. Communicators may threaten others if they do not comply (punishment) or cause those persons to have a more negative self-concept if compliance is not gained. While both of these specific appeals may be based upon fear of noncompliance, their motivational base is different. Moreover, a communicator may make promises of rewards for compliance or remind people that others will think better of them if they comply (activation of impersonal commitments). Several different strategies can be used in any given influence attempt, and each strategy requires differing kinds of persuasive messages. This study is a reminder of the multidimensionality of many constructs such as fear appeals and reinforcement.

Miller et al. (1977) used the Marwell and Schmitt typology to determine the likelihood of using various strategies in interpersonal and non-interpersonal situations (Miller and Steinberg, 1975). Subjects tended to prefer socially acceptable, reward-oriented strategies in all persuasive situations. However, people were more likely to suggest that they would use a greater variety of persuasive strategies in noninterpersonal situations. Miller et al. (1977) suggest that people tend to say they will use more strategies in noninterpersonal contexts than in interpersonal contexts because they are less sure about what strategy will work in the former context. Roloff (1976:181) has suggested a set of prosocial and antisocial communication strategies. Prosocial strategies "reflect people's attempts to obtain relational rewards by techniques that facilitate understanding of their attitudes and needs." Antisocial strategies "represent people's attempts to obtain relational rewards by imposing their position on another through force or deception." Research is needed to specify the potential persuasive messages that could be used as part of a more comprehensive prosocial or antisocial communication strategy. Moreover, research on the persuasive efficacy of all of these differing comprehensive strategies is at present lacking. We know something about how people choose strategies but less about the effectiveness of these strategies.

REFERENCES

ASCH, S.E. (1951). "Effects of group pressure upon the modification and distortion of judgments." In H. Guetzkow (ed.), Groups, leadership and men: Research in human relations. Pittsburgh: Carnegie Press.

BANDURA, A., ROSS, D., and ROSS, S.A. (1963). "A comparative test of the status envy, social power, and secondary reinforcement theories of identificatory learning." Journal of Abnormal and Social Psychology, 67:527-534.

BEM, D.J. (1970). Beliefs, attitudes, and human affairs. Belmont, CA: Brooks/Cole.

Berlo, D.K., LEMERT, J.B., and MERTZ, R.L. (1969). "Dimensions for evaluating the acceptability of message source." Public Opinion Quarterly, 33:563-576.

BETTINGHAUS, E. (1953). "An experimental study of the effectiveness of the use of testimony in an argumentative speech." Master's thesis, Bradley University. (unpublished)

––– (1972). The nature of proof. New York: Bobbs-Merrill.

–––, MILLER, G., and STEINFATT, T. (1970). "Source evaluation, syllogistic content, and judgments of logical validity by high- and low-dogmatic persons." Journal of personality and Social Psychology, 16:238-244.

BOWERS, J.W. (1963). "Language intensity, social introversion and attitude change." Speech Monographs, 30:345-352.

––– (1964). "Some correlates of language intensity." Quarterly Journal of Speech, 50:415-420.

BREITROSE, H.S. (1966). "The effect of distraction attenuating counterarguments." Doctoral dissertation, Stanford University. (unpublished)

BURGOON, M. (1970). "Prior attitude and language intensity as predictors of message style and attitude change following counterattitudinal communication behavior." Doctoral dissertation, Michigan State University. (unpublished)

––– (1975). "Empirical investigations of language intensity: III. The effects of source credibility and language intensity on attitude change and person perception." Human Communication Research, 1:251-254.

––– and KING, L.B. (1974). "The mediation of resistance to persuasion strategies by language variables and active-passive participation." Human Communication Research, 1:30-41.

BURGOON, M., and MILLER, G.R. (1971). "Prior attitude and language intensity as predictors of message style and attitude change following counterattitudinal advocacy." Journal of Personality and Social Psychology, 20:246-253.

BURGOON, M., and STEWART, D. (1975). "Empirical investigations of language. I. The effects of sex of source, receiver, and language intensity on attitude change." Human Communication Research, 1:244-248.

BURGOON, M., COHEN, M., MILLER, M.D., and MONTGOMERY, C.L. (1978). "An empirical test of a model of resistance to persuasion." Human Communication Research, 5:27-39.

CATHCART, R.S. (1953). "An experimental study of the relative effectiveness of four methods of presenting evidence." Speech Monographs, 22:227-233.

CHERTKOFF, J.M., and CONLEY, M. (1967). "Opening offer and frequency of concession as bargaining strategies." Journal of Personality and Social Psychology, 7:185-193.

CHEN, W.K.C. (1935). The influence of oral propaganda material upon students' attitudes. New York: Archives of Psychology.

CHU, G.C. (1966). "Fear arousal, efficacy and imminency." Journal of Personality and Social Psychology, 5:517-524.

CIALDINI, R.B., VINCENT, E.J., LEWIS, K.S., CATALAN, J., WHEELER, D., and DARBY, L. B. (1975). "Reciprocal concessions procedure for inducing compliance: The door in the face technique." Journal of Personality and Social Psychology, 31:206-215.

COLBURN, C. (1967). "An experimental study of the relationship between fear appeal and topic importance in persuasion." Doctoral dissertation, University of Indiana. (unpublished)

DARNELL, D. (1963). "The relation between sentence order and the comprehension of written English." Speech Monographs, 30:97-100.

DeWOLFE, A.S., and GOVERNALE, C.M. (1964). "Fear and attitude change." Journal of Abnormal and Social Psychology, 69:119-123.

DRESSER, W.R. (1962). "Audience reaction to various types of evidence." Presented at Central States Speech Association Convention, Chicago.

EHNINGER, D., and BROCKRIEDE, W. (1963). Decision by debate. New York: Dodd, Mead.

ELDERSVELD, S.J. (1956). "Experimental propaganda techniques and voting behavior." American Political Science Review, 50:154-165.

EVEN-CHEN, M., YINON, Y., and BIZMAN, A. (1978). "The door in the face technique: Effects of the size of the initial request." European Journal of Social Psychology, 8:135-140.

FEATHER, N.T. (1964). "Acceptance and rejection of arguments in relation to attitude strength, critical ability, and intolerance of inconsistency." Journal of Abnormal and Social Psychology, 69:127-136.

FESTINGER, L., and MACCOBY, N. (1964). "On resistance to persuasive communications." Journal of Abnormal and Social Psychology, 68:359-366.

FREEDMAN, J.L., and FRASER, S.C. (1966). "Compliance without pressure: The foot in the door technique." Journal of Personality and Social Psychology, 4:195-202.

GARDNER, D.M. (1966). "The effect of divided attention on attitude change induced by a marketing communication." In R.M. Haus (ed.), Science, technology, and marketing. Chicago: American Marketing Association.

GOLDSTEIN, M.J. (1959). "The relationship between coping and avoiding behavior and response to fear arousing propaganda." Journal of Abnormal and Social Psychology, 58:247-252.

GOULDNER, A.W. (1960). "The norm of reciprocity: A preliminary statement." American Sociological Review, 25:161-178.

HAALAND, G.A., and VENKATESAN, M. (1968). "Resistance to persuasive communications: An examination of the distraction hypothesis." Journal of Personality and Social Psychology, 9:167-170.

HARTMANN, G.W. (1936). "A field experiment on the comparative effectiveness of 'emotional' and 'rational' political leaflets in determining election results." Journal of Abnormal and Social Psychology, 31:99-114.

JANIS, I.L., and FESHBACH, S. (1953). "Effects of fear-arousing communications." Journal of Abnormal and Social Psychology, 48:78-92.

JANIS, I., and FRICK, F. (1943). "The relationship between attitudes toward conclusions and errors in judging logical validity of syllogisms." Journal of Experimental Psychology, 33:73-77.

JANIS, I.L., and TERWILLIGER, R. (1962). "An experimental study of psychological resistance to fear-arousing communication." Journal of Abnormal and Social Psychology, 65:403-410.

JONES, S.B., and BURGOON, M. (1975). "Empirical investigations of language intensity: II. The effects of irrelevant fear and language intensity on attitude change." Human Communication Research, 1:248-251.

KELLEY, H.H. (1973). "The process of causal attribution." American Psychologist, 28:107-128.

KELMAN, H.C., and HOVLAND, C.I. (1953). " 'Reinstatement' of the communicator in delayed measurement of opinion change." Journal of Abnormal and Social Psychology, 48:327-335.

KNOWER, F.H. (1935). "Experimental studies of changes in attitudes: I. A study of the effect of oral argument." Journal of Social Psychology, 6:315-347.

KOMORITA, S.S., and BRENNER, A.R. (1968). "Bargaining and concession making under bilateral monopoly." Journal of Personality and Social Psychology, 9:15-20.

LEFFORD, A. (1946). "The influence of emotional subject matter on logical reasoning." Journal of General Psychology, 34:127-151.

LEVENTHAL, H., and WATTS, J.C. (1966). "Sources of resistance to fear-arousing communications on smoking and lung cancer." Journal of Personality, 34:155-175.

McCROSKEY, J.C. (1969). "A summary of experimental research on the effects of evidence in persuasive communication." Quarterly Journal of Speech, 55: 169-176.

———, JENSEN, T., and TODD, C. (1972). "The generalizability of source credibility scales for public figures." Presented at the Speech Communication Association Convention, Chicago.

McGUIRE, W.J. (1960). "A syllogistic analysis of cognitive relationships." In C.I. Hovland and M.J. Rosenberg (eds.), Attitude organization and change. New Haven: Yale University Press.

——— (1966). "Attitudes and opinions." Annual Review of Psychology, 17:475-514.

——— (1969). "The nature of attitudes and attitude change." In G. Lindzey and E. Aronson (eds.), The handbook of social psychology. Reading, MA: Addison-Wesley.

MANN, L. (1967). "The effects of emotional role playing on desire to modify smoking habits." Journal of Experimental Social Psychology, 3:334-348.

MARWELL, G., and SCHMITT, D.R. (1967). "Dimensions of compliance-gaining behavior: An empirical analysis." Sociometry, 30:350-364.

MEHRLEY, R.S., and McCROSKEY, J.C. (1970). "Opinionated statements and attitude intensity as predictors of attitude change and source credibility." Speech Monographs, 37:47-52.

MENEFEE, S.C., and GRANNEBERG, A.G. (1940). "Propaganda and opinions on foreign policy." Journal of Social Psychology, 11:393-404.

MILLER, G.R. (1969). "Some factors influencing judgments of the logical validity of arguments: A research review." Quarterly Journal of Speech, 55:276-286.

——— and BASEHEART, J. (1969). "Source trustworthiness, opinionated statements and response to persuasive communication." Speech Monographs, 36:1-7.

MILLER, G. R., and BURGOON, M. (1973). New techniques of persuasion. New York: Harper & Row.

——— (1978). "Persuasion research: Review and commentary." In B.D. Ruben (ed.), Communication yearbook II. New Brunswick, NJ: International Communication Association.

MILLER, G.R., and HEWGILL, M.A. (1964). "The effects of variations in nonfluency on audience ratings of source credibility." Quarterly Journal of Speech, 50:36-44.

––– (1966). "Some recent research on fear-arousing message appeals." Speech Monographs, 33:377-391.

MILLER, G.R., and LOBE, T. (1967). "Opinionated language, open- and closed-mindedness and responses to persuasive communications." Journal of Communication, 17:333-341.

MILLER, G.R., and STEINBERG, M. (1975). Between people: A new analysis of interpersonal communication. Chicago: Science Research Associates.

MILLER, G.R., BOSTER, F., ROLOFF, M., and SEIBOLD, D. (1977). "Compliance-gaining message strategies: A typology and some findings concerning effects of situational differences." Communication Monographs, 44:37-50.

MILLER, M.D., and BURGOON, M. (1979). "The relationship between violations of expectations and the induction of resistance to persuasion." Human Communication Research, 5:301-313.

MILLMAN, S. (1965). "The relationship between anxiety, learning and opinion change." Doctoral dissertation, Columbia University. (unpublished)

MORGAN, W., and MORTON, A. (1953). Logical reasoning: With and without training." Journal of Applied Psychology, 37:399-401.

NEWMAN, R.P., and NEWMAN, D.R. (1969). Evidence. Boston: Houghton-Mifflin.

NILES, P. (1964). "The relationship of susceptibility and anxiety to acceptance of fear-arousing communications." Doctoral dissertation, Yale University. (unpublished)

OSTERHOUSE, R.A., and BROCK, T.C. (1970). "Distraction increases yielding to propaganda by inhibiting counterarguing." Journal of Personality and Social Psychology, 15:344-358.

PETRIE, C. (1963). "Informative speaking: A summary and bibliography of related research." Speech Monographs, 30:79-91.

PLINER, P., HART, H., KOHL, J., and SAARI, D. (1974). "Compliance without pressure: Some further data on the foot in the door technique." Journal of Experimental Social Psychology, 10:17-22.

POWELL, F.A. (1965). "The effects of anxiety-arousing messages when related to personal, familial and interpersonal referents." Speech Monographs, 32:102-106.

Regan, D.T., and CHENG, J.B. (1973). "Distraction and attitude change: A resolution." Journal of Experimental Social Psychology, 9:138-147.

ROLOFF, M.E. (1976). "Communication strategies, relationships, and relational change." In G.R. Miller (ed.), Perspectives on interpersonal communication. Beverly Hills, CA: Sage.

ROSENBLATT, P.C. (1973). "Persuasion as a function of varying amounts of distraction." Psychonomic Science, 5:85-86.

SELIGMAN, C., BUSH, M., and KIRSCH, K. (1976). "Relationship between compliance in the foot in the door paradigm and size of first request." Journal of Personality and Social Psychology, 33:517-520.

SENCER, R. (1965). "An investigation of the effects of incorrect grammar on attitude and comprehension in written English messages." Doctoral dissertation, Michigan State University. (unpublished)

SNIDER, M. (1962). "The relation between fear-arousal and attitude change." Dissertation Abstracts, 23:1802.

SNYDER, M., and CUNNINGHAM, M.R. (1975). "To comply or not comply: Testing the self-perception explanation of the 'foot-in-the-door' phenomenon." Journal of Personality and Social Psychology, 31:64-67.

STEINFATT, T.M., MILLER, G.R., and BETTINGHAUS, E.P. (1974). "The concept of logical ambiguity and judgments of syllogistic validity." Speech Monographs, 41:317-328.

THOMPSON, E. (1960). "An experimental investigation of the relative effectiveness of organizational structure in orgal communication." Southern Speech Journal, 26:59-69.

THOULESS, R. (1959). "Effects of prejudice on reasoning." British Journal of Psychology, 50:290-293.

TOULMIN, S. (1958). The uses of argument. New York: Cambridge University Press.

VOHS, J.L., and GARRETT, R.L. (1968). "Resistance to persuasion: An intergrative framework." Public Opinion Quarterly, 32:445–462.

WHITEHEAD, A.N., and RUSSEL, B. (1927). Principia Mathematic, volume III. Cambridge, England: University Press.

ZIMBARDO, P., SNYDER, M., THOMAS, J., GOLD, A., and GURTWITZ, S. (1970). "Modifying the impact of persuasive communications with external distraction." Journal of Personality and Social Psychology, 16:669-680.

Chapter 6

ALTERED PHYSIOLOGICAL STATES
The Central Nervous System
and Persuasive Communications

Robert N. Bostrom

THE PHENOMENON OF persuasive communication has fascinated serious thinkers in almost every society. In few of these, however, has the interest exceeded that shown in contemporary American culture. In any growing society change is necessary, and if the society also values personal freedom, then noncoercive influence becomes very important. Where freedom of choice is less valued, other methods of bringing about change are less offensive. But contemporary American culture exhibits a strong and continuing interest in persuasion, and most of us would agree with Nilsen (1958) that preserving individual liberties is best done by a system in which persuasion plays a major part.

The study of social psychology since World War II certainly reflects this interest, since one of its major topics has been the study of communication and attitude change. Since 1950 hundreds of research reports have appeared exploring the various facets of source credibility, message construction, and receiver variables. Recently, however, the nature of this research has changed. Miller and Burgoon (1978) have observed that contemporary interest in persuasion has shifted away from the unidirectional, one-to-many, manipulative process that occupied much academic attention in the 1950s and 1960s, and has given way to emphasis on the persuasive "transaction." More researchers are now interested in the way communicators influence each other; the way change is likely to occur in the evaluations of persons rather than "attitude objects"; and changes in behavior, cognition, and affects rather than "attitudes." Much of this altered interest is due to the failure of early research to produce clear and unambiguous theories of persuasion, but some of the change has been due to inherent distaste for the attempts of government and large organizations to manipulate others.

In spite of the differences created by this new shift in emphasis, one element remains fairly constant. Persuasion is still thought of as a process in which *change* occurs. The change may involve reevaluations of sources rather than objects, may center on specific behaviors rather than verbal responses, and indeed may only involve potential behavior. But change is clearly the one element that distinguishes persuasion from other forms of communicative activity. In addition, we usually assume that this change is the result of communicative activity and not some other influence. When other factors influence this change persuasion researchers usually dismiss them as being of less interest than the communicative act.

But when we examine persuasive interactions carefully, we see that seldom can the communicative activity itself be considered solely responsible for the nature of the changes that take place. For example, one individual may seek to persuade another to donate to the Red Cross, and be helped in this task by the fact that the Internal Revenue Service allows such donations to be exempted from income tax. The persuader may not even include in the message the information that such charitable contributions are deductible. Yet, without the influence of the IRS the attempt might not have been successful. In addition, the message may have been presented when the receiver was in a particularly good mood. Any number of factors could be considered as important causes of the successful conclusion of this persuasive attempt, and the original communicative effort may not even have been the most important one. In fact, persuasive communication may be only the "trigger" that sets off behavioral and attitudinal effects that were already probable, even without further stimuli.

A great deal of research has been concerned with some of these "extraneous'. factors in persuasion. Many of them include frustration (Carmichael and Cronkhite, 1965), personality (Bostrom and Tucker, 1968), sex (Scheidel, 1963), and age (Janis and Rife, 1959). In each of these studies the interaction of persuasive message and noncommunicative factors has a strong effect on subsequent attitude change.

Let us consider an entirely different kind of example. Janis et al. (1965) asked individuals to read a message designed to change attitudes concerning the future of three-dimensional movies. The readers were divided into two groups: one was served soft drinks and some peanuts to consume while reading the message; the other group received no refreshment. The group that ate and read exhibited more attitude change than did the other group. Janis et al. attributed this differential effect to a more "positive attitude", toward the experimenter when the food was present, which these authors assume would create a differential effect. Insko (1967) attributes the differences in the two groups to a "reinforcing" effect, but does not specify what was supposedly reinforced. Learning theories usually state that reinforcement operates upon a *response* being performed. Once reinforced, the response is likely to appear more often. In this experiment, the subjects were reading and conceivably could have been responding either positively or negatively. No opportunities for responses (at least overt ones) were present in the experiment. Why, then, would eating a small snack create the additional attitude change?

Perhaps the answer can be found in some theoretical explanation other than reinforcement. In discussing contemporary attitude theories, Fishbein and Azjen (1975) list (in addition to learning or reinforcement theories) expectancy-value theories, consistency theories, and attribution theories. The expectancy-value theories are informational in nature and predict that attitudes change when information changes concerning the potential utility of the attitude to the receiver. It is difficult to see how a bottle of soda and a package of peanuts would add to these portions of the respondents' information systems. Consistency theories might explain the effect, *if* we can assume that Janis et al. are correct and the subjects attributed more positive affect to the experimenters as the result of the food, *and* that the experimenters were perceived as the source of the persuasive messages. Neither of these assumptions can be made in this case, at least not with any confidence. The attribution theories hold that external cues cause us to "attribute" attitudes to ourselves and to others. Bem's example (1965) of the use of "external" cues as measures of internal states cites the case of an individual who, when asked "Do you like brown bread?" responds, "I guess I do, I'm always eating it." Someone in the Janis et al. study could have been asked "Do you find this message convincing?" and then answered "I guess it is, I feel pleasant and relaxed here."

All in all, the theories of attribution, reinforcement, consistency, and expectancy-value do not provide a really satisfactory explanation of the phenomenon of "eating while reading." There are, of course, many other theories of attitude change, and we could continue to look for explanations of the Janis et al. experiment from other theories, none of which seem any more satisfactory than the four discussed above. How, then, do we explain this experiment?

To begin with, at least two elements were involved, one cognitive and the other physiological. Any theory that is employed to explain Janis et al.'s results should involve an altered physiological state. The incorporation of physiological state, communicative attempt, and resulting attitude change could result in a more general theory of communication and persuasion.

Altered physiological states can produce altered states of awareness, arousal, and methods of information processing. These states would seem to be very important in the context of persuasive communication. For the most part, however, theories of communication and persuasion have ignored the possible presence of fatigue, psychosis, pain, and the many possible states arising from the use of drugs. These inherently interesting psychological states have clear correlations in altered behavior. Why, then, have most researchers ignored these variables while studying persuasion? At least part of the answer to this question lies in the way in which we think persuasion ought to work in our society.

A primarily manipulative model of persuasive communication creates some ethical problems in many persons, but these problems are minor compared with those created by the coupling of persuasion and physiological control. A manipulative model involving only words is quite different from a manipulative model involving physiological states. When we hear that a standard technique utilized by Chinese interrogators in the Korean war was to deprive the subject of food and reward him with a potato when the desired response was obtained (Schein, 1956), we are horrified. This technique seems to us to be morally equivalent to "persuading" someone with a blackjack. Rewards for "correct" behavior seem acceptable for modern child-rearing, for our economic system, and even in the annual merit review procedures of a university. But to alter the reception of a message through the use of hunger or drugs is quite distasteful to most of us. Nonetheless, the exploration of altered physiological states as they relate to attitude change is an interesting problem and should not be ignored simply because of our aversion to its use. Certainly, some segments of our society have used physiological manipulation to enhance acceptance or rejection of ideas. A popular "consciousness raising" course (est) involves some physical deprivation as part of its systematic "teaching" of self-awareness (Gorden, 1979). Participants in this program apparently find it effective.

At the roots of the problem is our strong reaction to the study of phenonema which we find unpleasant. Most of us wish to believe that our behavior is not determined by extraneous forces beyond our control. Unfortunately, many forces shape our beliefs and attitudes that are out of our control and of which we may not even be aware. B. F. Skinner, who has been interested in this kind of control for many years, has repeatedly stated that studying behavioral manipulation is certainly not the same as advocating it. Control, to Skinner, is a fact of life and should be studied. As long ago as 1955 he wrote:

> We cannot make wise decisions if we continue to pretend that human behavior is not controlled, or if we refuse to engage in control when valuable results might be forthcoming. Such measures weaken only ourselves, leaving the strength of science to others. . . . The first step in a defense against tyranny is the fullest possible exposure of the controlling techniques [1955: 15].

Reactions to Skinner's interest in control are varied but usually negative. One typical response appeared in a popular magazine when the writer admitted he knew little about psychology, but did "know something about freedom and dignity!" (Pearce, 1972).

Altered physiological states occur in persons for reasons entirely separate from persuasive attempts, and could interact with persuasive communication in interesting ways. Tranquilizers, for example, are widely used by a variety of persons and it is usually impossible to detect their use. Tranquilizers might well influence the audience of persuasive attempts. Menstrual cycles have a good deal of influence in the general outlook of women, yet this condition is seldom, if ever, discussed in public-speaking texts under the heading of audience analysis! All in all, it seems short-sighted to ignore the relationships between physiological conditions and attitude change out of fear that such study will hasten the onset of the brave new world. On the contrary, we ought to seek better understanding so that we cope with the phenomenon of persuasion in a number of widely varied circumstances.

It is often a surprise to students of communication to discover that there is a well-developed literature on the manipulation of human behavior. For example, Gottschalk (1961) explored the possible use of some of the common drugs used in psychotherapy as facilitators of police interrogations. Kubzanksy (1961) similarly speculated how stimulus deprivation affects behavior, especially in "suggestibility."

Nonetheless, most research done on the process of attitude change has been done using individuals (subjects) whose thought processes are considered "normal" and in situations in which central nervous system (CNS) activity will not be altered. When we examine the "ordinary" world, however, we see that we cannot safely assume that these conditions will prevail. Alcohol, for example, is extremely widely used—over 100 million Americans use alcohol in some form or another (Straus, 1976). Tobacco is another drug that significantly alters the CNS; over 50 million Americans use tobacco in the form of cigarettes, and these users are exposed fairly constantly to its effects.

Tranquilizers are another substance that enjoy fairly wide use, and the exact proportion of our population using them is not known. Estimates run as high as 10 million daily users of a tranquilizing substance. Then when we add the users of controlled substances, epinephrines, marijuana, and other drugs, we are forced to conclude that the possibility of encountering an individual whose CNS activity has been altered by chemical means is quite high.

Other conditions significantly alter the CNS level. Fatigue, psychosis, pain, and many other physiological variants are important. A substantial portion of our population is overweight and is involved in various dieting methods. Hunger significantly affects the CNS and might affect attitude change. In short, the assumption that potential audiences for persuasive communications will be "normal" with respect to CNS activity is probably a naive one. On the other hand, the probability than an ordinary audience will be affected in some way by altered CNS condition seems rather high.

In this chapter, we will examine some of the factors that create alteration of the CNS, together with the possible influences that these alterations might have on the process of persuasion. First, we will explore some of the effects of CNS arousal, subject awareness of this arousal, and the relationship of these factors to attitude change. Then the effects of CNS depression will be explored. Following this discussion, we will examine some of the specific causes of alterations in CNS states, such as epinephrine, caffeine, ethanol, tobacco, and other drugs; then we will examine some of the effects of the environment, such as the presence of others, hunger, and fatigue. Prior to all this will be a brief discussion of the attitude-behavior problem, primarily because a good bit of attention has been given to it in the past, and clear distinctions are necessary when discussing possible CNS involvement. When the word "attitude" is used in this chapter, it will be taken to indicate cognitive and affective elements primarily, and possible behavior change subsequent to attitude change will be considered less important.

ATTITUDES AND BEHAVIORS

Much of the recent disenchantment with the study of attitude change has stemmed from the difficulties inherent in linking attitudes with be-

Bostrom / Altered Physiological States   177

havior. La Piere's study (1934) of response inconsistency is probably the example cited most often. La Piere traveled around the country with a Chinese couple and then wrote to the establishments (hotels and restaurants) to ask if they served Chinese guests. He found that many places of business wrote that they did not serve Chinese guests, when in fact they had served them when they appeared in person. (Since La Piere's conclusions were based on the inconsistencies between letters written describing future discrimination and the face-to-face interactions with the same Chinese couple, we might just as easily assume that the attitudes were constant but that the interaction modes were different).

Dillehay (1973) has pointed out some of the difficulties inherent in taking La Piere's study too seriously; nonetheless, there still exist some problems in connecting "attitudes" and behavior, if only because other theorists in this area have made it so. Attitudes are often defined in terms of predispositions to respond (Doob, 1947), cognitive elements such as beliefs and behavioral intentions (Fishbein and Ajzen, 1975), affective elements and conative behavior. It makes little sense to say that an attitude is a predictor of behavior and then define an attitude as that which preceded behavior, so that conative definition probably ought not to be included. Affective and cognitive dimensions are simply two different ways of defining "predisposition to respond." The principal ways in which attitudes should be defined rest in the cognitive and affective elements. Not surprisingly, a "behavioral intention" is a better predictor of subsequent behavior than either one of these elements. After a careful review of the literature concerning attitude-behavior correspondence (or lack of it), Ajzen and Fishbein (1978) conclude that "action, context, target, and time'. are four crucial factors influencing correspondence between attitudes and behaviors. "A person's attitude," they conclude, has a consistently strong relation with his or her behavior when it is directed at the same target and when it involves the same action" (1978: 912). But the problem is clouded by yet another factor that has been overlooked to some extent—behavioral potential.

After hearing a persuasive message urging me to vote for a particular candidate for water commissioner, I may feel more kindly toward the candidate (affective component), see in him many good qualities (belief component), decide that I am going to vote for him (behavioral intention), and the sum of these might be described as my "predisposition" to get out and vote. Unfortunately, before I actually vote there are a number of other factors that influence me. I may not be registered, so that voting would be impossible. I may have a job that keeps me a significant distance from the polling booth; the election may take place during the week that I have already scheduled for my vacation, and so on. Even if all those obstacles were not present, I may not know where the polls are located. The sum of all these factors that are necessary to elicit the behavior may be called the behavioral *potential,* and it should be clear that it is quite different from behavioral *intention.*

Given a high behavioral potential, the other components of attitude probably ought to lead to the behavior in question. Some responses to persuasive communication would have inherently high behavioral potentials, while some would be low. For example, if I were to attempt to persuade someone to take a vacation trip to Iran, the political unrest there and the high cost of airfare are going to create a low behavioral potential no matter how effective my persuasive communication might be. Going to Florida, on the other hand, is quite different. In other words, it is probably unreasonable to include actual behavior as a meaningful indicator of attitude in almost all instances; I may honestly prefer to go to Tehran but still end up in Miami. The expectation of attitude-behavior consistencies has been a serious obstacle to the study of attitude change. If attitude change brings about behavioral change, the persuader would, of course, be gratified. But the expectation that these two events would be linked most of the time is probably unreasonable.

EFFECTS ON AROUSAL

One of the most popular explanations of the effects of persuasive communication stems from consistency theories, in which the inconsistent elements in the message are held to create a psychological state similar to drive, or motivation (Festinger, 1957). "Dissonant" elements do not always unequivocally create physiological effects (Cronkhite, 1965), but, by and large, there is ample evidence to indicate that dissonance and arousal may be said to be similar states (Pallak and Pittman, 1972). This would lead us to believe that arousal should have a simple effect on the process of persuasion—enchanced arousal ought to lead to an enhanced attitude change, and the lack of arousal should have the opposite effect. Unfortunately, the relationship is not that simple. A crucial element in the process is the degree to which the individual being aroused is aware of the arousal, and the source to which the arousal is attributed.

An interesting demonstration of the role of awareness and arousal was done by Schacter and Singer (1962). In an experiment where subjects were told that the principal purpose was a test of vision, the experimenters injected the subjects with a solution of epinephrine bitartrate, a sympathomimetic drug whose effects bear a marked similarity to activation of the central nervous system. These subjects were told that they were to receive an injection of a vitamin supplement designed to affect their vision. Some subjects were correctly informed of the effects of epinephrine, some subjects were not told of any effects, and a third group was misinformed— that is, they were told to expect symptoms of an entirely different nature. Then all subjects were placed in an emotion-producing condition, in which a confederate of the experimenters attempted to produce either euphoria or anger. Following the inducement, each subject was asked to report his or her emotional state. Both emotions were induced, but, interestingly enough, the group that was misinformed of the possible effects of the epinephrine reported that they felt much more euphoric than the informed group. In other words, subjects were more susceptible to the confederate's moods when they had no explanation of their own bodily states than when they did. In the anger inducement, subjects were measured as to amount of angry behaviors present following the inducement. Again, more behaviors were present when the subjects were ignorant of the possible effect of the epinephrine on their own bodily states. The attribution of the source of arousal, then, seemed to be a crucial factor in the evaluation of the situation.

In a similar experiment, Schacter and Wheeler (1962) injected subjects with both epinephrine and chlorpromazine. Following an appropriate period for the drugs to take effect, they showed an amusing film to subjects and measured the number of behavioral indications of positive affect—smiles, laughter, and so forth. The epinephrine had produced more responses than the placebo, but fell short of significance. Both groups were far more stimulated than those with the chlorpromazine. The degree of amusement was interpreted to be directly related to the degree of CNS activation. Schacter (1964) sums up the results of both of these studies:

> Given a state of sympathetic activation, for which no immediately appropriate explanation is available, human subjects can be manipulated into states of euphoria, anger, and amusement at a movie. Varying the intensity of sympathetic activation serves to vary the intensity of variety of emotional states in both rat and human subjects [1964:69].

Often, however, we are aware of CNS arousal when we experience it, and are accustomed to interpret it. But what happens when we think that we are experiencing CNS arousal even if we are not? Kerber and Coles (1978) conducted an experiment to answer this question. Subjects were led to believe that they were aroused when actually they were not. In this study, individuals were monitored on two physiological measures—heart rate and skin conductivity—while they judged the attractiveness of nude females. The heart rates were "fed back" so that the subjects could monitor their own responses. In one group, a false feedback gave the impression of increased CNS activity, and this false feedback produced higher rates of perceived attractiveness than did the ordinary feedback. Actual physiological measures (both heart rate and skin conductivity) had little relation to judgments. This, of course, is direct support for Bem's self-perception theory (1965).

In a similar study, Mintz and Mills (1971) gave subjects pills containing caffeine and either told them about the true effect of the drug or described an irrelevant side-effect. All then read a fear-arousing communication. Subjects who were not told of the effects of the drug were significantly more persuaded than those who were informed of the drug's effects.

These studies provide support for consistency interpretations of attitude change, but whether the individuals in these studies are aware of the affective inconsistencies is not entirely clear. It may be that CNS arousal is associated with attitude change, and that a simple association is enough to explain the effect. Results of this kind seem to be fairly consistent across many kinds of CNS arousal. For example, Pittman (1975) created CNS arousal by placing subjects in a situation that appeared threatening. The threat interacted with the other elements of the dissonance-producing situation in much the same manner as did the drug-induced arousals in the Schacter studies and the Mintz and Mills experiment. In other words, CNS arousal seems to be quite general in its effects, whether it is induced by epinephrine, caffeine, fear, or false feedback. If individuals are aware of the source of the arousal, then no particular effects care be attributed to the CNS. If, however, individuals attribute the CNS arousal to the stimuli which they have experienced, then CNS arousal will significantly affect the result in attitude change.

This process of attribution provides the first really adequate explanation of the Janis et al. study mentioned earlier. The individuals experienced heightened CNS arousal as a result of the snack and could possibly have attributed it to the message. We might consider this a special case of attribution theory, or might even label it a special kind of "misattribution" that has cognitive consequences, especially on attitudes.

The nature of this misattribution is not always clear. Worschel and Arnold (1974) showed that arousal from other sources is easily misattributed to dissonance. This misattribution seems to be reversible. Zanna and Cooper (1974) placed subjects in situations which would create dissonance-related attitude change. Then they gave subjects a pill (a placebo) and told them that "it would make them tense." When the pill was given, no attitude change resulted. The pill did not reduce the tension, but only explained it for the participants. In a more complete study of these misattributions, Cooper et al. (1978) placed subjects in a forced compliance situation and varied the decision freedom in order to vary the amounts of dissonance produced. Then they gave subjects either a tranquilizer, a placebo, or an amphetamine. The results are shown in Table 1. The placebo results are similar to other dissonance experiments in that the high decision freedom resulted in more change. The effect was enchanced in the amphetamine condition and was nonexistent in the tranquilizer condition.

The effects of CNS arousal and its attribution seem consistent. Small changes in CNS states lead to rather pronounced attitudinal consequences, and the strongest of these is when the CNS change is attributed falsely to the attitudinal stimuli. Most of the studies previously cited, however, are of situations in which communication has not played a prominent part in bringing about the attitude change. Can we see the same effects in a more usual communication experiment? Harris and Jellison (1971) provide evidence that these processes apply to communicative situations. They studied the interaction of a fear-arousing communication and false feedback of CNS condition. One group of their subjects was given false feedback indicating arousal during the portion of the message in which the fear appeals was contained; then were given false feedback indicating that the arousal was diminished during the section of the message in which the recommendations were contained. This group experienced a substantial degree of attitude change compared with the other groups in the study.

CNS arousal, then, cannot by itself be said to be a significant factor in attitude change. Only when the arousal is either created by the message or when it is attributed to the message does arousal have an effect. In those instances, its effects are quite strong—in most cases it nearly doubled the effect of the messages alone. Persuasive messages addressed to persons

Table 1   Attitude Change Resulting from the Interaction of Various Drug Conditions and Decision Freedom

	Tranquilizers	Placebo	Amphetamine
HIGH DECISION FREEDOM	8.6_a	14.7_b	$0\ 20.2_e$
LOW DECISION	8.0_a	8.3_a	13.9_b

(Means whose subscripts are different are significantly different from one another. After Cooper, Zanna, and Taves (1978)).

already experiencing some sort of CNS arousal are likely to be effective—especially if the individuals are not aware of the source of the arousal.

EFFECTS OF DEPRESSION

Depressing the CNS logically should have the reverse effect of arousal on attitude change. Some evidence for this reversal is furnished by two of the studies cited above. Schacter and Wheeler (1962) administered chlorpromazine as a "blocking" agent and Cooper et al. (1978) used tranquilizing substances. In both of these studies the drug produced less attitude change than in the normal subjects. We might interpret these effects as simply the absence of arousal—if arousal creates attitude change, then any tranquilizing substance merely prevents that effect.

Probably the clearest indication of the effects of CNS depression on attitude change is found in a study conducted by Bostrom and White (1979). Their subjects were informed that they were involved in a study concerned with gathering data on the relationship between information retention and alcohol consumption, and that they might be asked to drink an alcoholic beverage. All subjects completed an inventory which measured their attitudes toward three "cultural truisms" adapted from those employed by McGuire (1961). All were then given a large glass of a soft drink (Fresca) but some received a high alcohol dose (.770 ml per kg body weight), others a moderate dose (.517 ml per kg), and others received none. Then all subjects viewed a film (a 20-minute animated feature concerning conformity) while they consumed their drinks.

Each subject then read three messages attacking the validity of the cultural truisms. Each of these was a short, 500-word essay containing factually oriented material which attacked the truism in question. Following the essays were factual questions concerning their general sobriety and motivation level. Last, the individuals were asked to identify counterarguments, if any, that had occurred to them while reading the essays. Two additional "control" groups were used, one which had no drinks or movies but which read the messages, and one which only took the posttest.

The results for these groups are shown in Figure 1. Clearly, the presence of alcohol in the drinks had a deleterious effect on attitude change, but it is interesting to note that even the high alcohol condition produced more attitude change (though not significantly so) than the control group with the messages alone. The soft drinks apparently served as the same kind of social facilitator that the drinks and peanuts did for Janis et al. (1965), and the alcohol served to diminish the effect. No differences were observed in the number of counter-arguments formed, but the subjects' perception of their motivational levels were higher for the two alcohol groups than for the no-alcohol condition. In other words, subjects with high alcohol dosages felt "motivated" but simply did not exhibit the attitude change that ought to accompany high motivation. Here we have an interesting contrast to the role of awareness in the CNS arousal states. CNS depression—at least when it is due to alcohol—produces an entirely opposite effect.

The state of the central nervous system would seem to be an extremely important factor in the determination of subsequent attitude effects arising from persuasive communications. However, the practical value of some of the conclusions might be less interesting to many of us—after all, it would be unusual to inject a receiver with epinephrine prior to hearing a persuasive speech and then tell that same receiver that the injection would be harmless, so that misattribution could occur. But the use of drugs that affect the CNS is certainly not rare, as observed earlier in this chapter; it may be rarer to find individuals whose CNSs have *not* been affected in some way by some drug. In addition, our environment has clear effects on CNS states, and these certainly have a potential influence on the process of attitude change. If we are to include the less formal interpersonal inter-actions as an integral part of our study of persuasion, then the use of

Figure 1   Amounts of Attitude Change in Various Conditions

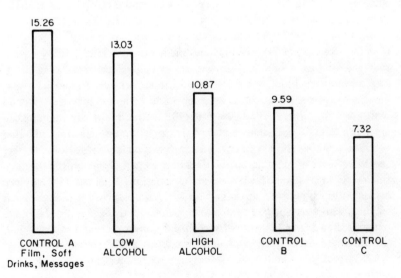

tobacco, alcohol, tranquilizers, and even marijuana becomes more important for the study of persuasion. In the next section, some specific substances commonly used by large segments of our population will be briefly discussed, together with the possible effects that they might cause in the persuasive interaction. Following this substance inventory, specific environmental effects such as the presence of others, hunger, and sensory deprivation will also be examined.

SPECIFIC DRUGS AND THEIR EFFECT ON THE CNS

TOBACCO

Although public use of tobacco is under attack by various groups, it is probably safe to say that it remains one of the most commonly used drugs in social situations and, by extension, in communicative interactions. The active agent in tobacco use is nicotine, and it is through the effects of nicotine that tobacco has its strongest effect on the CNS. Nicotine is readily absorbed through the mucous membranes, not only in the lungs, but in the oral and gastrointestinal tract as well as the skin, (Goodman and Gilman, 1958). This means that cigar and pipe smokers, as well as cigarette smokers, are probably ingesting some amount of nicotine through tobacco usage. The principal method of deciding whether or not an individual is addicted seems to lie in the frequency of use and the effects of deprivation, not the method of ingestion.

What are the physiological effects of tobacco use? The U.S. Surgeon General's Report (1964) was quite specific about CNS effects. They report that smoking even one cigarette evinces strong effects: increasing heart rate, respiration, blood sugar level, and cardiac output. These symptoms are exactly the same as those experienced in "emotional states" (Woodworth and Schlosberg, 1958). Nesbitt (1972) found that chronic smokers are more "emotional" than nonsmokers, so it would seem that the link between smoking and CNS activity is fairly well established. However, the specific effects of nicotine on the CNS depend to a degree on whether the smoker is in a state of withdrawal or satiation. Schacter (1978) cites evidence to show that smokers who were not allowed to smoke and smokers who were allowed to smoke only low-nicotine cigarettes showed a much greater degree of irritability than did nonsmokers and smokers that were allowed as many high-nicotine cigarettes as they wished. Schacter (1978) finds that addiction is the only psychological construct that entirely explains the effect of smoking:

Again and again, then, one finds the same pattern. Smoking does not improve the mood or calm the smoker or improve his performance when compared with the nonsmoker. However, not smoking or insufficient nicotine makes him considerably worse on all dimensions. Given this persistent fact, how, then, to account for the fact that the smoker smokes more when he is stressed? One can, obviously, account for the generally debilitating effects of no or low nicotine by assuming the deprived smoker is in withdrawal, but this assumption alone cannot account for the effects of stress on smoking rate unless one assumes that stress in some way depletes the available supply of nicotine [Schacter, 1978:439].

Schacter goes on to demonstrate that when stress is present, the urine is acid, and when the urine is acid, more nicotine is excreted, leading to nicotine deficiency and more smoking.

In addition, tobacco affects the fashion in which information is acquired. Kleinman et al. (1973) found that 24-hour deprived smokers learned better on high meaningful tasks but did more poorly on low meaningful tasks. They explained their finding by assuming that withdrawal of nicotine created CNS arousal which facilitated performance on the easy task but retarded it on the difficult one. Anderson and Hockey (1977) found that serial learning was not affected by the presence of nicotine but incidental memory was affected. In general, then, there seem to be at least two ways in which nicotine affects the CNS—as an immediate stimulus to CNS activity when the nicotine content of the body falls below acceptable levels, and as a depressant to the CNS in anxiety-related situations. The effects of the CNS arousal-depression should therefore have considerable influence on the evaluation of persuasive messages *if* individuals are aware of them and can attribute the CNS arousal to the effects of nicotine. If users are not aware of the effects, then they should "attribute" the effects to the persuasive message and therefore experience more attitude change.

Do smokers have a clear knowledge of the effects of smoking on different physiological measures? To determine, at least partially, the extent of such knowledge, a questionnaire was given to 97 undergraduate students at the University of Kentucky. Of these students, 65 classified themselves as nonsmokers or as smokers using less than five cigarettes per day. Thirty-two reported that they used more than five cigarettes per day. They were asked if the use of cigarettes raised or lowered heart rate, respiration rate, blood sugar, general emotionality, and irritability. The results are tabulated in Table 2. Smokers differ slightly from nonsmokers in the proportion of their responses, but the discrepancies are not significant. Most smokers correctly respond that smoking raises heart rate, but only half correctly responded that smoking raises respiration rate. Only 31.2 percent of the smokers correctly identified a rise in emotionality with smoking; 37.5 percent felt that emotionality decreased; 31.2 percent did not know. A separate sample of faculty members and adults produced proportions very similar to those in Table 2.

While the sample reported certainly would not meet the requirements of a national poll, it seems reasonable to assume that a substantial number of persons who use tobacco are at least unaware of a portion of the effects it produces and would fit well into the paradigm of aroused-ignorant receivers, with the subsequent enhancement of attitude change. Interestingly, a large proportion of smokers seem to know that smoking increases heart rate but also feel that it reduces "emotionality," which they may be identifying as stress. This is consistent with Schachter's analysis of the interaction of nicotine and stress (1978).

CAFFEINE

Caffeine appears in an amazing number of foods commonly consumed and many consumers are ignorant of the specific caffeine content in most foods. An ubiquitous source of caffeine is coffee. Some individuals drink up to 20 cups daily—a heavy dose of caffeine in the bloodstream. Another source of caffeine is cola-type soft drinks; in some of these, the caffeine content often is the equivalent of several cups of coffee. Television ads promoting decaffeinated coffee should lead us to believe that heavy coffee drinkers might attribute their emotional state to the caffeine intake, but most soft drink consumers seem unaware of the caffeine content of the beverages.

Mintz and Mills (1971) provide the best direct evidence of the effects of caffeine, showing that individuals ingesting caffeine but misattributing the effects to a persuasive message exhibited much more attitude change than did individuals ingesting caffeine, but attributing their arousal to the drug. Although caffeine is a CNS stimulant, Franks and his associates (1975) found that it could not counteract the depression introduced by ethanol. Thus, in terms of its cognitive effects, caffeine must be described as a very mild stimulant, but one whose presence will enhance attitude change, especially if the recipient of the message has no knowledge of its effects.

CANNABIS

Cannabis, or marijuana, usually produces the following physiological effects:

Table 2 Proportions Responding to Questionnaire of Physiological Effects of Cigarettes

	Percent Responding "raises"		Percent Responding "lowers"		Percent Responding "don't know"	
	Non-Smokers (n=65)	Smokers (n=32)	Non-Smokers (n=65)	Smokers (n=32)	Non-Smokers (n=65)	Smokers (n=32)
Heart Rate	64.6	84.3	10.7	6.2	24.6	9.3
Respiration Rate	60.0	50.0	21.5	25.0	18.4	25.0
Blood Sugar	18.4	12.5	30.7	50.0	50.7	37.5
General Emotionality	27.6	31.2	29.2	37.5	43.0	31.2
Irritability	35.3	31.2	29.2	50.0	35.3	18.7

[An] increase in the pulse rate, a slight rise in blood pressure, and conjuctival vascular congestion; the cardiovascular system is otherwise unaffected. The blood sugar and basal metabolic rate are elevated, but usually not beyond the upper limits of normal. (Goodman and Gilman, 1958, p. 172).

Marijuana apparently acts as a mild CNS stimulant; thus, its effects would be similar to caffeine. However, other effects usually accompany the marijuana "high." Salzman et al. (1976) report that marijuana decreased hostility, both in verbal aggression and in reported "inner feelings." Hill et al. (1974) found that marijuana increased sensitivity to painful and nonpainful stimuli, and reduced the general tolerance for pain.

There is some evidence of particular effects that marijuana has on cognitive functioning as well. Crockett et al. (1976) report that marijuana disrupts cognitive processes and "emotional tone." Miller et al. (1977) found that marijuana dosages significantly decreased immediate and final free recall but only slightly influenced recognition memory. In a study to determine possible long-term effects of heavy cannabis use, Weckowitz et al. (1977) studied 24 heavy users. They found evidence for more field dependence, and users had better control of attention processes than did 24 matched nonusers. The users also did slightly better on tasks designed to measure originality, cognitive flexibility, and general cognitive functioning. It is entirely possible that the 24 users differed from the nonusers in these characteristics prior to the heavy cannabis use; no real causal attribution can be drawn from these data.

The effects of marijuana on the reception of a persuasive message are problematical at best. The most salient characteristic of the use of the drug is the factor of subject awareness—in fact, Schachter (1964) suggests that whatever pleasurable sensations arise from its use are at least partially determined by the user's expectations and the socialization inherent in the situation. So it seems apparent that one principal effect on persuasion would be to diminish perceptions of arousal and to attribute these sensations to the use of the drug. Another would certainly be inattention and lack of acquisition memory (Abel, 1971). All in all, it would seem that marijuana would seriously diminish persuasibility.

ALCOHOL

Most researchers agree that alcohol acts as a depressant on the CNS. Beyond this generalization, however, the effects of alcohol on cognitive tasks is less well known. A review of 41 studies involving alcohol dosages concluded that cognitive and perceptual activities are affected more than are psychomotor tasks (Levine et al., 1975). Nor are the CNS effects without ambiguity—Crow and Ball (1975), for example, found that alcohol dosage increased heart rates, although the effect depended on order of dosage. But in general, alcohol dosage affects cognitive tasks rather markedly. Carpenter (1962) demonstrated that alcohol increases response latency on a variety of tasks, and Moskowitz and Burns (1973) produced this same effect on an information-processing task. Alcohol has a deleterious effect on immediate and short-term memory (Tarter et al., 1971), but does not seem to affect the forgetting rate as much as the learning rate (Wickelgren, 1975). Experience, or familiarity, seems to mitigate some of these effects (Jones, 1972).

McGonnel and Beach (1968) found that alcohol reduced subjects' anxiety about a 50-watt shock, and Smart (1965) found that alcohol reduced anxiety in conflict situations.

Alcohol definitely seems to decrease general affect. The study by Bostrom and White (1979) clearly indicated that the act of ingesting any kind of drink enhanced persuasive effects, but that the presence of alcohol in such drinks decreased persuasive effects so that an alcoholic drink was approximately equal to no drink at all. Alcohol per se, then, inhibits persuasion, but drinking in general enhances it.

TRANQUILIZERS

Many kinds of tranquilizing substances are commonly available today to most segments of the population, even though most of them require a physician's prescription. Kleikecht and Smith-Scott (1977) report, for example, that over 37 percent of college students in their sample used tranquilizing substances in one form or another. It may well be that college students are subject to particular forms of anxiety which makes their use of tranquilizers less representative than a true national sample, but even so, it seems reasonable to assume that the national proportion is high. Tranquilizers generally depress the CNS, but have a milder depressant effect than does alcohol. They produce state-dependent learning, which may influence the retention of the persuasive message. But their primary influence is to lessen the amount of CNS arousal and subsequently lessen the impact of a persuasive message.

In addition, there is some evidence that tranquilizers may inhibit memory processes as well. Tranquilizers as well as alcohol produce state-dependent learning (Carpenter and Ross, 1965; Goodwin, 1969). Material acquired in one state is poorly remembered if the same state is not present during the recall period. The total effect of tranquilizers on persuasibility should be that of a strong inhibitor.

AMPHETAMINES

Another very common drug, amphetamines are normally used to allay fatigue and relieve pain. Dieters use them to combat the debilitating effects of hunger. In large doses, however, they have the capacity to bring on the symptoms of paranoid schizophrenia. According to Marshall (1979), professional football players who received large doses of amphetamine could be induced into a state of rage, and were less reluctant to perform when tired or injured. Schachter's demonstration of the interaction of epinephrine and behavioral inductions probably best illustrates the effects of amphetamines. When individuals taking the drug fully understand its effects, then the result on persuasive communication is likely to be minimal. However, when they either expect no particular arousing effect or expect one that is less than is likely to occur, the probability is high that they will attribute the arousal state to the act of persuasion and as a consequence experience a heightened effect.

EFFECTS OF THE ENVIRONMENT ON CNS

There are many environmental effects that strongly influence the reception of persuasive communications, and these effects are especially interesting since most of them are not perceived by the individual experiencing them. As most of them heighten CNS activity, we can say usually that most of these environmental effects would increase the effectiveness of a persuasive message.

THE PRESENCE OF OTHERS

Zajonc (1965) was one of the first to note that the presence of others could create CNS arousal. He cited instances of increased level of hydrocortisone in the bloodstream of individuals who were performing in groups rather than alone, and also observed that this enhancement inhibited the acquisition of new responses but facilitated the performance of previously learned activities. A similar effect was recently reported by Markus (1978), who studied the performance of individuals who operated either alone or in a situation where they were watched by others. When watched, people's performance on a well-learned task was facilitated, but more complex tasks were hindered.

The presence of others may inhibit CNS arousal when the arousal comes from another source. For example, pain typically creates CNS arousal, but Kleck and others (1976) showed that the presence of others not only inhibits overt expressions of pain but also inhibits the CNS arousal that usually accompanies pain.

The nature of the effect of the presence of others is not universally agreed upon. Many researchers attribute it to a kind of anxiety, but Fish et al. (1978) make a strong case for calling it an embarrassment effect. In an interesting attempt to resolve some of this ambiguity, Rajecki et al. (1977) tested individuals in the presence of others who were blindfolded and therefore could not observe the individual performing. They found that the presence of a nonblindfolded peer reduced the error rate on a cognitive task, but that the presence of a blindfolded peer caused individuals to complete the trials faster and make fewer errors than in isolation. These authors conclude that observation is an important effect but that mere presence is also efficacious in bringing about increased performance. Since little of these effects, if any, are known to most individuals, we would expect a strong facilitation of persuasive effect in the presence of others. While this may seem contradictory (persuasive interactions per se seem to imply the presence of at least one other person), the effects of others' presence can be detected in the situation where the persuasive message is read rather than delivered in person.

HUNGER

During the latter part of World War II, 36 young men volunteered for a study involving semistarvation at the University of Minnesota. After six months of a sharply attenuated diet, the volunteers were carefully studied, and marked changes were noted.

> They had become distractable, unable to study effectively. . . . They had become inefficient in other tasks as well. They were irritable, unable to control their actions for social acceptability, although somewhat recovered in this respect from a nadir during semistarvation. A number of them had become addicted to activities that had not figured in their earlier lives—to drinking tea and coffee, smoking tobacco, and chewing gum. Most of them had also become addicted to eating as much as possible and had ceased to display earlier discriminative tastes in doing so. Their table manners were neglected [Easterbrook, 1978:51-52].

Where we would expect hunger to be simply an actuator or a creator of drive (Hull, 1943), it appears that prolonged hunger produces an entirely different set of reactions. While no specific evidence is available, we would expect a mild amount of hunger to facilitate persuasion and a prolonged amount to inhibit it.

THE DDD "SYNDROME"

DDD is the acronym given by Farber et al. (1957) to the factors present in prison camps—debility, dependence, and dread. The three factors inter-act to produce a situation in which the individual experiences a generalized state of hyporesponsiveness, a loss of time concept, and self-disorganiza-tion. The similarity to the hunger symptoms presented above is responsible for its inclusion here. And while we might expect individuals in a "nor-mal" environment to be free of these characteristics, it is entirely possible that many persons at particular times are experiencing the DDD syndrome. Medical students, for example, may neglect their nutrition because of the extreme anxiety caused by a scheduled examination, and fear their profes-sors in much the same way that prisoners fear their guards. Older persons often report the same kinds of reactions to the threats of decreasing resources, a hostile environment, and inactivity. Persons experiencing the DDD syndrome are extremely persuasible when the source of the message is one of the sources of the DDD. According to news reports, American hostages held by Iranian students in 1979 showed signs of the DDD syndrome, and were consequently more persuadable.

OTHER FACTORS

There are a number of other factors that could possibly affect the CNS and the reception of persuasive communication. Boredom (Heron, 1972), biorhythms (Lane, 1971), fatigue, and even meditation strongly affect the CNS. However, the lack of strong evidence for consistent effects in each of these sources of CNS alterations should lead one to be cautious about possible effects. However, each of these is an important factor and should be considered.

CONCLUSION

We have seen that altered CNS states are common in ordinary audi-ences, and even that "normal" CNS states might be the exception to the rule. The use of cigarettes, alcohol, and tranquilizers are very common. In addition, environmental factors such as hunger, fatigue, and the presence of others have significant effects on the CNS. All of these effects are easily classifiable into two categories: stimulants and depressants. Depressants inhibit persuasive effects because they apparently inhibit cognitive pro-cessing and the subsequent discomfort caused by attitude-discrepant mes-sages. Stimulants enhance persuasive effects if and only if the individual does not attribute the arousal to the drug or the environment; then the arousal is apparently attributed to the persuasive message and persuasion is enhanced. Most persons do not seem to understand the physiological effects of common drugs on their central nervous systems, and so we might expect the overall effect of CNS arousal to be facilitative.

The implications of this information are profound. A successful persuasive strategy might include the presence of a small amount of hunger, some sort of CNS stimulant administered in the form of a social ritual, and attribution of the subsequent arousal to the persuasive communication. It is a common practice at my university, for example, to invite candidates for new positions to faculty cocktail parties, to lunches, dinners, coffees, and many other social functions. This practice usually is designated as "hospitality," but its implications could easily be seen as somewhat more sinister. Fortunately, few, if any, of the interviewers involved in these practices have any Machiavellian purpose in mind. Many political figures have favorite theories about the proper time of day for political broadcasts. Dinnertime would seem to be an effective choice, since persons usually eat their meals in groups and can experience arousal while eating and smoking. Franklin Roosevelt made effective use of dinnertime speeches on Thanksgiving and Christmas. Who knows how much of Walter Cronkite's popularity might be due to the time of his broadcasts?

Probably the most important potential use of this kind of information lies in our understanding of the persuasive process. In an area where "inoculation" was once thought of as a topic of major importance, we ought to see clear implications of knowledge concerning CNS arousal as an inoculating device. When correct attributions about arousal are made, then subsequent persuasive effects will be minimized, and, when present, would be due solely to the messages-sources interaction. Such understanding ought to be an important part of any educational effort where the persuasive process is involved.

REFERENCES

ABEL, E.L. (1971). "Marijuana and memory: Acquisition or retrieval?" *Science*, 173:1038-1040.

AJZEN, I., and FISHBEIN, M. (1978). Attitude-behavior relations: A theoretical analysis and review of empirical research." *Psychological Bulletin*, 84:888-912.

ANDERSSON, K., and HOCKEY, G.R. (1977). "Effects of cigarette smoking on incidental memory." *Psychopharmacology*, 52:223-226.

BEM, D.J. (1965). "An experimental analysis of self-persuasion." *Journal of Experimental Social Psychology*, 1:199-218.

BOSTROM, R.N., and TUCKER, R.K. (1968). "Evidence, personality, and attitude change." *Speech Monographs*, 34:22-27.

BOSTROM, R.N., and WHITE, N.A. (1979). "The effects of alcohol ingestion on the processing of attitude-discrepant messages." *Journal of Communication*, forthcoming.

CARMICHAEL, C., and CRONKHITE, G. (1965). "Frustration and language intensity." Speech Monographs, 32:107-111.

CARPENTER, J.A. (1962). "Effects of alcohol on some psychological processes." Quarterly Journal of Studies on Alcohol, 23:274-314.

––– and ROSS, B.M. (1965). "Effects of alcohol on short-term memory." Quarterly Journal of Studies on Alcohol, 26:561-579.

COOPER, J., ZANNA, M.P., and TAVES, P.A. (1978). "Arousal as a necessary condition for attitude change following induced compliance." Journal of Personality and Social Psychology, 36:1101-1106.

CROCKETT, D., KLANOFF, H., and CLARK, C. (1976). "The effects of marijuana on verbalization and thought procedures." Journal of Personality Assessment, 40:582-587.

CRONKHITE, G.L. (1965). "Autonomic correlates of dissonance and attitude change." Speech Monographs, 33:392-399.

CROW, L.T., and BALL, C. (1975). "Alcohol state-dependency and autonomic reactivity." Psychophysiology, 12:702-706.

DILLEHAY, R.C. (1973). "On the irrelevance of the classical negative evidence concerning the effect of attitudes on behavior." American Psychologist, 28:887-891.

DOOB, L. (1947). "The behavior of attitudes." Psychological Review, 54:135-156.

EASTERBROOK, J.A. (1978). The determinants of free will. New York: Academic Press.

FARBER, I.E., HARLOW, H.F., and WEST, L.J. (1957). "Brainwashing, conditioning, and DDD." Sociometry, 20:271-283.

FESTINGER, L. (1957). A theory of cognitive dissonance. Stanford: Stanford University Press.

FISH, B., KARABENICK, S., and HEATH, M. (1978). "The effects of observation on emotional arousal." Journal of Experimental Social Psychology, 14:256-265.

FISHBEIN, M., and AJZEN, I. (1975). Belief, attitude, intention, and behavior. Reading, MA: Addison-Wesley.

FRANKS, H.M. et al. (1975). "The effect of caffeine on human performance alone and in combination with ethanol." Psychopharmacologica, 45:177-181.

GOODMAN, L.S., and GILMAN, A. (1958). The pharmacological basis of therapeutics. New York: MacMillian.

GOODWIN, D.W. (1969). "Alcohol and recall: State-dependent effects in man." Science, 163:1358-1360.

GORDEN, W.I. (1979). "Experiental training: A comparison of t-groups, tavistock, and est." Communication Education, 28:39-48.

GOTTSCHALK, L.A. (1961). "The use of drugs in interrogation." In A.D. Biderman and H. Zimmer (eds.), The manipulation of behavior. New York: John Wiley.

HARRIS, V. and JELLISON, J. (1971). "Fear arousing communications, false physiological feedback and the acceptance of recommendations." Journal of Experimental Social Psychology, 7:269-279.

HERON, W. (1972). "The pathology of boredom." In T.J. Teyler (ed.) Altered states of awareness. San Francisco: W. H. Freeman.

HILL, S.Y., SCHWIN, R. GOODWIN, D.W., and POWELL, B. (1974). "Marijuana and pain." Journal of Pharmacology and Experimental Therapeutetics, 188:415-418.

HULL, C.L. (1943). Principles of behavior. New York: Appleton-Century-Crofts.

INSKO, C.A. (1967). Theories of attitude change. New York: Appleton-Century-Crofts.

JANIS, I.L., and RIFE, D. (1959). "Persuasibility and emotional disorder." In C.I. Hovland and I.L. Janis (eds.), Personality and persuasibility. New Haven: Yale University Press.

JANIS, I.L., KAYE, D., and KIRSCHNER, P. (1965). "Facilitating effects of 'eating while reading' on responsiveness to persuasive communication." Journal of Personality and Social Psychology, 1:181-186.

JONES' B.M. (1972). "Cognitive performance during acute alcohol intoxication: The effects of prior task experience on performance." Psychonomic Science, 26:327-329.

KERBER, K.W., and COLES, M.G.H. (1978). "The role of perceived physiological activity in affective judgements." Journal of Experimental Social Psychology, 14:419-433.

KLECK, R.E. et al. (1976). "Effects of being observed on expressive subjective, and physiological responses to painful stimuli." Journal of Personality and Social Psychology, 14:1211-1218.

KLEINKNECHT, R.A., and SMITH-SCOTT, J. (1977). "Prevalence, sources, and uses of tranquilizers among college students." Journal of Drug Education, 7:249-257.

KLEINMAN, K.W., VAUGHN, R.L., and CHRIST, S. (1973). "Effects of cigarette smoking and smoking deprivation on paired-associate learning of high and low meaningful nonsense syllables." Psychological Reports, 23:963-966.

KUBZANSKY, P.E. (1961). "The effects of reduced environmental stimulation on human behavior: A review." In A.D. Biderman and H. Zimmer (eds.), The manipulation of behavior. New York: John Wiley.

LANE, L.L. (1971). "Communicative behavior and biological rhythms." Speech Teacher, 20:16-20.

LAPIERE, R.T. (1934). "Attitudes vs. actions." Social Forces 13:230-237.

LEVINE, J.M., KRAMER, G.C., and LEVINE, E.N. (1975). "Effects of alcohol on human performance: An integration of research findings based on an abilities classification." Journal of Applied Psychology, 60:285-293.

McGONNEL, P.V., and BEACH, H.D. (1968). "The effects of ethanol on the acquisition of a conditioned gsr." Quarterly Journal of Studies on Alcohol, 29:845-855.

McQUIRE, W.J. (1961). "Resistance to persuasion conferred by active and passive prior refutation of the same and alternative counterarguments." Journal of Abnormal and Social Psychology, 63:326-332.

MARKUS, H. (1978). "The effect of mere presence on social facilitation." Journal of Experimental Social Psychology, 14:389-397.

MARSHALL, E. (1979). "Drugging of football players curbed by central monitoring system." Science, 203:626-628.

MILLER, G.R., and BURGOON, M. (1978). "Persuasion research: Review and commentary." In B.D. Reuben (ed.), Communication Yearbook, volume II. New Brunswick, NJ: Transaction/International Communication Association.

MILLER, L.L., McFARLAND, D., CORNETT, T.L., and BRIGHTWELL, D. (1977). "Marijuana and memory impairment: Effect on free recall and recognition memory." Pharmacology, Biochemistry, and Behavior, 7:99-103.

MINTZ, P.M., and MILLS, J. (1971). "Effects of arousal and information about its source upon attitude change." Journal of Experimental Social Psychology, 7:5 61-570.

MOSKOWITZ, H., and BURNS, M. (1973). "Alcohol effects on information processing time with an over-learning task." Perceptual and Motor Skills, 37:835-839.

NESBITT, P.D. (1972). "Chronic smoking and emotionality." Journal of Applied

Social Psychology, 2:187-196.

NILSEN, T.R. (1958). "Free speech, persuasion, and the democratic process." Quarterly Journal of Speech, 64:235-243.

PALLAK, M.A., and PITTMAN, T.S. (1972). "General motivational effects of dissonance arousal." Journal of Personality and Social Psychology, 21:349-358.

PEARCE, D. (1972). "God is a variable interval." Playboy, 19:81-86, 171-176.

PITTMAN, T.S. (1975). "Attribution of arousal as a mediator in dissonance reduction." Journal of Experimental Social Psychology, 11:53-63.

RAJECKI, D.W., ICKES, W., CORCORAN, C., and LENERZ, K. (1977). "Social facilitation of human performance: Mere presence effects." Journal of Social Psychology, 102:297-310.

SALZMAN, C., vanderKOLK, B.A., and SHADER, R. (1976). "Marijuana and hostility in a small group setting." American Journal of Psychiatry, 133:1029-1033.

SCHACTER, S. (1964). "The interaction of cognitive and physiological determinants of emotional state." In L. Berkowitz (ed.), Advances in experimental social psychology, volume 1. New York: Academic Press.

――― (1978). "Second thoughts on biological and psychological explanations of behavior." In L. Berkowitz (ed.), Cognitive theories in Social Psychology. New York: Academic Press.

――― and SINGER, J. (1962). "Cognitive, social, and physiological determinants of emotional state." Psychological Review, 69:379-399.

SCHACTER, S., and WHEELER, L. (1962). "Epinephrine, chlorpromazine and amusement." Journal of Abnormal and Social Psychology, 65:379-399.

SCHEIDEL, T. (1963). "Sex and persuasibility." Speech Monographs, 30:353-358.

SCHEIN, E.H. (1956). "The Chinese indoctrination program for prisoners of war: A study of attempted brainwashing." Psychiatry, 19:149-172.

SKINNER, B.F. (1955). "Freedom and the control of men." American Scholar, 25:47-65.

SMART, R.G. (1965). "Effects of alcohol in conflict and avoidance behavior." Quarterly Journal of Studies on Alcohol, 26:187-205.

STRAUS, R. (1976). "Alcoholism and problem drinking." In R.K. Merton and R. Nisbet (eds.), Contemporary social problems. New York: Harcourt Brace Jovanovich.

TARTER, R.E., JONES, B.M., SIMPSON, C.D., and VEGA, A. (1971). "Effects of task complexity and practice on performance during acute alcohol intoxication." Perceptual and Motor Skills, 33:307-318.

U.S. Department of Health, Education, and Welfare, Public Health Service (1964). Smoking and health (Public Health Service Publication No. 1103). Washington, DC: U.S. Government Printing Office.

WECKOWITZ, T.E., COLLIER, G., and SPRENG, L. (1977). "Field dependence, cognitive functions, personality traits and social values in heavy cannabis users and nonuser controls." Psychological Reports, 41:291-302.

WICKELGREN, W. (1975). "Alcoholic intoxication and memory storage dynamics." Memory and Cognition, 3:385-389.

WOODWORTH, R.H., and SCHLOSBERG, H. (1958). Experimental psychology. New York: Holt, Rinehart & Winston.

WORSCHEL S., and ARNOLD, S.E. (1974). "The effects of combined arousal states on attitude change." Journal of Experimental Social Psychology, 10:549-560.

ZANNA, M.P., and COOPER, J. (1974). "Dissonance and the pill: An attribution approach to the arousal properties of dissonance." Journal of Personality and Social Psychology, 29:703-274.

ZAJONC, R.B. (1965). "Social facilitation." Science, 149:269-274.

Chapter 7

POWER AND THE FAMILY

Charles R. Berger

Perhaps the surest key to understanding the problems of the nuclear family is the concept of power—in particular the power of parents over children.

Arlene S. Skolnick and Jerome H. Skolnick

On the whole, however, power is a disappointing concept. It gives us surprisingly little purchase in reasonable models of complex systems of social choice.

James G. March

When researchers think about social contexts within which theory and research concerned with communication and persuasion might be applied, it seems as if the areas of marketing and advertising are among the first which come to mind. The obvious relevance of these applied persuasion areas tends to overshadow other social arenas in which persuasion and social influence processes assume considerable importance. One social context in which persuasion and social influence processes play an important role is that of the family. The recent revitalization of the feminist movement has highlighted the problems with power relationships between males and females in general and husbands and wives in particular. Who *does* influence whom and who *should* influence whom concerning which issues and under what conditions in male-female relationships has become a major concern of social scientists, social critics, and public policy makers. In addition, increasing attention to the rights of children has raised the question of how power is and should be distributed among family members. The general purpose of this chapter is to review theory and research concerned with power in family relationships. It is hoped that this review will demonstrate the potential that the family has as a laboratory for the study of social influence processes.

Over the past two decades the construct of power has enjoyed a prominent role in the theory and research of family sociologists. In addition, the power construct, along with such related concepts as dominance, control, influence, and authority, has been central to those psychiatrists, clinical psychologists, and other helping professionals who hold that the psychological problems of one family member are generally symptomatic of more general family problems in such areas as communication and control. This chapter first considers some problems associated with both conceptualization and measurement of the family power concept. As the reader can gather from the above quotations, opinion is divided concerning the theoretical usefulness of power as an explanatory concept. The second part of the chapter summarizes the research on family power done by both family sociologists and family therapists. It should be noted that there is relatively little interchange between these two groups of researchers; even though they are interested in explaining similar phenomena. Finally, some recommendations for future research will be made from the point of view of communication theory. Here again, it is interesting to note that communication researchers have devoted minimal attention to the family power literature. As we shall see, a number of conceptual and methodological issues are common to these two research areas.

CONCEPTUALIZATION AND MEASURE OF FAMILY POWER

The most influential conceptual and operational definitions of power for family power research done by family sociologists in the 1960s and early 1970s were employed by Blood and Wolfe (1960) in their survey of 909 Detroit-area housewives. They defined power as "the potential ability of one partner to influence the other's behavior" (1960:11), as in the case of a person influencing a family decision. Blood and Wolfe also distinguished between power and authority, asserting that authority is "legitimate power, i.e., power held by one partner because both partners feel it is proper for him [her] to do so" (1960:11). Although the two concepts are similar, the difference between them lies in the fact that persons may have authority to influence certain decisions but fail to use it, or they may exert considerable influence without the authority to do so. This distinction between power and authority resembles one presented by Wolfe (1959). Furthermore, in his discussion of family power and authority, Wolfe emphasized that power is not an attribute of an individual, but rather a property of a relationship between two or more persons.

Wolfe (1959) discusses three additional concepts which are related to power and authority in the family. *Resources* are properties of persons or groups which can be transferred socially to others for satisfaction of their needs or attainment of their goals. Wolfe pointed out that for an individual to have power over another, the other must have goals or needs which can only be fulfilled with the help of this particular individual's resources, and the other must perceive this individual as having the critical resources. *Relative authority* concerns the number of behavioral areas over which the husband and the wife can potentially exercise their authority. As the range of authority of one spouse exceeds that of the other, the spouse with the greater range has higher relative authority. Finally, *shared authority* concerns the proportion of the family's behavioral region over which both husband and wife have joint authority. The degree of relative authority determines whether the husband or wife is dominant or whether they are equal. Wolfe distinguishes between two kinds of equality. When the degree of shared authority is high, the family is said to exhibit a *syncratic* type of authority pattern. When the degree of shared authority is low—that is, when the husband and wife have equal relative authority but have low levels of overlap in the areas where authority is shared—the family exhibits an *autonomic* authority type. Thus, according to Wolfe, there are four possible authority types: Wife Dominant, Husband Dominant, Autonomic, and Syncratic. The foregoing concepts of resources, relative power, and shared power play a critical role in what has come to be known as the *resource theory* of marital power. In short, the principal proposition of this theory asserts: "The balance of power will be on the side of that partner who contributes the greater resources to the marriage." (Blood and Wolfe, 1960:12).

Blood and Wolfe (1960) measured family power—or, more accurately, *conjugal power*—by having wives indicate the extent to which they or their husbands made decisions in the following eight areas: (1) what job the husband should take, (2) what car to get, (3) whether or not to buy insurance, (4) where to go on vacation, (5) what house or apartment to take, (6) whether the wife should go to work or quit, (7) what doctor to have when someone is sick, and (8) how much money the family can afford to spend per week on food. The researchers tried to select decisions of importance to the family and to balance them with respect to which spouse might typically make the decision. For each item, respondents were given the following choices: "husband always," "husband more than wife," "husband and wife exactly the same," "wife more than husband," or "wife always." These responses were summed to arrive at a total score reflecting the overall balance of power in the family. In addition, scores reflecting shared authority were computed so that syncratic and auto- nomic authority types could be identified. The findings of this, and several related studies, will be summarized in the next section of this chapter.

Numerous studies conducted both within and outside the United States have used Blood and Wolfe's (1960) conceptual and methodological approach to investigate conjugal power (Blood, 1967; Burchinal and Bauder, 1965; Buric and Zecevic, 1967; Burr et al., 1977; Centers et al., 1971; Cromwell and Cromwell, 1978; Kandel and Lesser, 1972; Lamouse, 1969; Lupri, 1969; Michel, 1967; Price-Bonham, 1976; Safilios-Roths- child, 1967; Turk and Bell, 1972). The relatively large mass of studies following the Blood and Wolfe tradition has produced a number of critiques of both their conceptualization and measurement of family power. First we will examine some of the conceptual problems; next we will consider several measurement issues.

CONCEPTUAL ISSUES IN FAMILY POWER

Heer (1963) raised a number of conceptual problems related to Blood and Wolfe's (1960) study. He pointed out that a conception of *family power* which involves only the marital dyad obviously excludes the poten- tial power of children. While it might be tempting to assume that children exert little power relative to their parents, Strodtbeck (1958) found that sons had power levels almost as high as their mothers when attempting to resolve revealed differences (Strodtbeck, 1951) within father-mother-son triads. Moreover, later studies of interaction in both normal and disturbed families found that children can exert considerable conversational control through interruptions and other conversational power strategies (Mishler and Waxler, 1968; Turk and Bell, 1972). Thus, if one focuses upon conjugal power but excludes the role children may play in decision- making, one may be making a critical error.

A second problem raised by Heer (1963) is that power is a multidimen- sional concept and that family decision-making is but one facet of power. In addition, he asserted that whether or not decisions were contested and how these conflicts were resolved might be significant dimensions of power. In her literature review, Safilios-Rothschild (1970) also suggested that power is a multidimensional construct and that such dimensions as outcome of decision-making, patterns of tension and conflict management, and the type of division of labor in the family would all have to be studied to understand power in the family. Olson and Rabunsky (1972) distinguished among five types of family power: outcome power, predicted power, process power, retrospective power, and authority. However, as Sprey (1972) points out, Olson and Rebunsky failed to coordinate these five facets of power to the general concept of family power. Sprey further suggests that looking at family relationships from the perspectives of *conflict and exchange* is likely to be more productive than generating various measures of power.

Smith (1970) has noted that while there have been conceptual differences among power theorists concerning the nature of power, they all tend to agree that social power is an individual's potential for exerting force toward change in another person, and that power is not a personal attribute, but depends upon the conditions which govern the interdependence of individuals in social relationships. Building on Smith's first proposition, Rollins and Bahr (1976) distinguished between power and control. For them, *power* is the ability or potential of one person to influence or control the behavior of another. *Control attempt* is the actual behavioral manifestation of attempted influence. *Control* involves the degree of compliance with the actual influence attempt. They agree with Phillips (1967) that power and control only become relevant issues in a marriage when the goals of the couple are in conflict. Finally, Burr et al. (1977) have distinguished among power, control, and authority. For these theorists, *power* is the ability of potential to exert control or influence on another person's behavior. *Control* represents the actual behavioral attempt to induce change. A person might have a high level of power but attempt to exert little influence and thus have a low level of control. Finally, these researchers view *authority* as power which is legitimated by social norms which indicate who should have power.

While it is generally recognized that power is multidimensional and that in any one study of family or conjugal power several measures of different facets of power might be appropriate, discussions of these various dimensions of power and the ways in which they might relate are difficult to come by. One exception is the Rollins and Bahr (1976) study, which depicts authority as a causal antecedent to power and power as a causal antecedent to both control and control attempts. However, this model is obviously oversimplified, since it is reasonable to assume that through repeated exertion of control one's authority is established—that is, the targets of influence come to believe that the role incumbent has the right to exercise influence over them. Moreover, making conceptual distinctions among power, authority, and control tells us little about the bases of power in the family. It is obvious that in family life a considerable number of alternative bases of power are employed to gain control. Rather than asking the currently popular question of whether the husband or the wife has greater power, it seems more important to ask in what relevant domains family members exert what kind of power and upon what bases that power rests. The heavy reliance on decision-making in studies of family power represents a very narrow conceptualization of the construct. The husband may exert considerable influence in deciding which car to purchase; however, when the car breaks down, the teenage son may exert considerable power by virtue of being able to repair it. Note that in this example no overt "decision" is necessarily involved. The son may repair the car without any discussion; he may exert considerable control over his father's behavior by having his father help him in the role of a less competent subordinate. Even younger children can exercise considerable control over their parents by learning skills that their parents have not acquired. (For example, when the new math was in vogue, many children became mentors for their parents.) Thus, depending upon the domain of behavior focused upon, the pecking order of the family may be over-turned.

Most studies of family power carried out by sociologists of the family have used wives as respondents; a few employed both husbands and wives. The obvious neglect of the role of the child in the family power structure was noted previously. This situation emphasizes one very important difference between the study of conjugal power and the study of family power. When one studies families consisting of only husbands and wives, it is unnecessary to consider the possibility of coalitions. Obviously, coalitions with relatives and in-laws are possible within the larger context, but within the nuclear unit no coalitions are possible. The introduction of one child immediately raises the possibilities of various family coalitions. Caplow (1968), who has discussed coalitions in nuclear families with from three to five members, proffers the general principle that persons are more likely to form and maintain coalitions with similar persons. This principle would suggest that mother-daughter and father-son coalitions would be more frequent than unlike-sex coalitions; however, Caplow also points out that within the family there are *generational* similarities and differences which also determine how alike family members are. Thus, coalitions between parents and children of like gender are rendered less stable by their age differences. Of course, coalitions among children of like gender and generation are possible, but, even here, the two children may vary on other attributes. Upon moving beyond the three-person family, it is possible to have coalitions involving more than two persons, thus making the task of studying coalition formation more difficult. However, the central point is that the family power literature has largely ignored the processes of coalition formation and change. Even granting the possibility that the study of decision outcomes à la Blood and Wolfe (1960) provides a useful picture of family power, the responses given by wives and/or husbands on such decision items may be conditioned by coalitions which exist in the family. Thus, when the husband indicates that he has a great deal of influence in car-purchasing, the actual power may reside in the father-son (or sons) coalition and not in the father alone. Self-report decision-making instruments given to husbands and wives cannot detect these kinds of family power arrangements.

A final conceptual issue, raised by both Heer (1963) and Safilios-Roths-child (1970), concerns the view of resources taken by Blood and Wolfe (1960). These critics argue that married persons may make comparisons between their current spouse and potential alternative marital partners. They suggest that such comparisons may be more important in determining marital power than relative resources themselves. This concept is similar to Thibaut and Kelley's (1959) comparison level for alternatives notion and suggests a broadening of resource theory in the direction of social exchange theories (Adams, 1965; Altman and Taylor, 1973; Blau, 1964; Homans, 1974; Thibaut and Kelley, 1959). Indeed, Edwards (1969) has taken a step in that direction by showing how family authority relationships can be analyzed with social exchange principles. In addition to the necessity for some notion of comparison level for alternatives, both Safilios-Rothschild (1970) and McDonald (1977a) have argued that some concept akin to Waller's (1938) "principle of least interest" is needed in the study of conjugal power relationships. Waller's principle of least interest asserts that the person who demonstrates the greater level of emotional involvement in the relationship is likely to be less powerful than the person who is least interested in the relationship. The rationale for this principle is simply that the more intensely involved person is likely to be open to the manipulative attempts of the less involved person because of his or her admiration for the less involved person.

MEASUREMENT ISSUES IN FAMILY POWER

Heer (1963) and Safilios-Rothschild (1969, 1970) have pointed to measurement problems in both Blood and Wolfe (1960) and many subsequent studies. These problems arise from the fact that only wives were interviewed, a procedure defended by Blood and Wolfe (1960) on the grounds that wives could give accurate estimates of influence for both spouses. Unfortunately, evidence indicates that estimates of husbands, wives, and children concerning the relative power of family members do not necessarily agree (Burchinal and Bauder, 1965; Buric and Zecevic, 1967; Douglas and Wind, 1978; Heer, 1962; Larson, 1974; Olson and Rabunsky, 1972; Turk and Bell, 1972). Some of these differences appear to be due to item ambiguity (Douglas and Wind, 1978).

A second criticism (Heer, 1963; Safilios-Rothschild, 1970) concerns the kinds of decisions used and their weighting. Briefly, it is argued that the decision areas sampled by Blood and Wolfe (1960) should be both more extensive and weighted according to their importance to the person. Centers et al. (1971) added decision areas in order to correct what they deemed to be an antifemale bias in the Blood and Wolfe item set. Their findings did show an increase in the wives' power with the new items, but the general findings of Blood and Wolfe were replicated. Price-Bonham (1976) weighted scores according to their perceived importance and found little difference between weighted and unweighted scores when both sets were correlated with the other variables of the study.

A third measurement issue concerns the comparability of various ways of indexing family or conjugal power. A number of studies have assessed the relationship between self-report and behavioral measures of power. Usually these measures have been taken within the context of some decision-making task. Kenkel (1963) found little agreement between self-reports of expected influence and actual influence during a decision-making task. Olson (1969) also found no relationship between predicted power, as assessed through self-report, and actual power, as determined by influence exerted by each spouse on the final decision of the couple; however, couples with high levels of empathy showed significantly higher levels of congruence between predicted and actual power. In a multiphase study of conjugal power, Olson and Rabunsky (1972) had couples indicate on self-report measures the extent to which they would have power in a series of decision-making tasks (*predicted power*). A second prediscussion, self-report measure assessed the perceived right of each spouse to exercise power (*authority*). Using Strodtbeck's (1951, 1954) revealed differences technique, in which couples discuss issues on which they have been shown to disagree from independent measures of their opinions, the degree of influence exerted on each issue discussed was measured by whose preference prevailed. This behavioral measure was labeled *process power*. A second behavioral measure was constructed by comparing the direction of initial disagreement on each issue discussed and the direction of the final decision. This measure was called *outcome power*. Finally, a postdiscussion questionnaire assessed *retrospective power* by having participants indicate who exercised influence on each of the issues discussed. These researchers found no relationship between predicted power, process power, retrospective power or authority, and the criterion measure of outcome power. Significant relationships were found between authority and the process and retrospective power variables, but process and retrospective power were not related to each other. These findings suggest that self-reports of retrospective power such as the Blood and Wolfe (1960) measure are related to authority but not to actual decision-making behavior. It appears that persons are able to report accurately *what* decisions are made but not *who* makes them.

In an extensive study of 211 families, Turk and Bell (1972) had husbands, wives, and children complete a number of self-report measures of power and participate in two decision-making tasks in order to measure power. Turk and Bell used the Blood and Wolfe (1960) self-report measure and two additional self-report measures of power. One developed by Heer (1958) asked who usually won when there was a disagreement between the spouses. Finally, respondents were asked the question, "Who is the real boss in your family?" In addition to these measures, families were asked to decide how they would spend a gift of three hundred dollars. Power was measured by the percentage of items to be purchased that each family member initially suggested. A second interactional task used in the study was the previously discussed revealed differences technique. Points were allocated to family members according to whether or not their position prevailed at the end of the discussion. Four additional power indices were computed from the two discussion tasks: (1) relative number of units of action initiated, (2) relative number of instrumental acts initiated, (3) index of directive control (Bales, 1950), and (4) relative number of interruptions initiated by each family member.

Turk and Bell (1972) compared their findings on the Blood and Wolfe (1960) measure and the Heer (1958) measure with the power distributions found in these two studies. There were similar distributions of power among the Turk and Bell sample and the other two; however, comparisons of the responses of mothers, fathers, and children within the Turk and Bell sample revealed numerous discrepancies among their perceptions of conjugal power on these measures. The "Who is the real boss of the family?" self-report measure produced a relatively high level of agreement between husbands and wives and wives and children, but the degree of agreement between husbands and children was relatively low. Both the Blood and Wolfe and Heer measures correlated moderately with the "boss" item (r = .54 and r = .40, respectively), but the two measures did not correlate well with each other. The "boss" item was the only self-report item to show a relationship to any of the measures of power derived from the interactions. The "boss" item correlated moderately well (.65) with relative number of units initiated and considerably less well with relative number of instrumental acts initiated (.37). However, there were virtually no significant relationships among the interaction measures, with the exception of a very strong correlation (.94) between number of units initiated and relative number of instrumental acts initiated. This correlation is probably spuriously high because of the likelihood that the person who enacts more units is more likely to initiate more instrumental acts. Most important, none of the four interaction process measures correlated well with either of the two decision outcome measures. Thus, there was no relationship between conversational control and the final decisions reached by the groups. These latter findings conflict with those of Strodtbeck (1951), who found that the spouse who spoke most tended to "win" in the revealed differences procedure.

Based upon the above findings, Turk and Bell (1972) concluded that both the conceptualization and measurement of power need to be rethought, and Turk (1974) suggested some lines along which power might be reconceptualized. It is frequently assumed that persons have goals or ends clearly in mind when they enter group interaction situations. While this may be a viable assumption in *specific* relationships, such as the relationship between a salesperson and a customer, in the *diffuse* relationships which characterize the family it is unreasonable to assume that persons are aware of their goals before or during interactions with each other. As Turk (1974) points out, psychoanalytic theory suggests that interaction goals are frequently unknown by both interactants and observers. As an alternative to studying family power from the perspective of individuals who have the ability to attain goals, Turk (1974) proposed that family power be studied as emergent action from the group as a whole; *patterns* of interaction among family members should be studied, not the ability of individual family members to attain their individual goals in the group. Turk (1974:49) further suggests that

> while previous work has ascribed both single-mindedness and clarity of purpose to group members, this approach treats these as problematic. That is, neither the clarity of purpose nor an individual's dedication to an end can necessarily be assumed (let alone knowable) in any given instance.

These assumptions led Turk (1974) to propose that intensive studies of small numbers of families be made rather than relatively less intensive investigations of large numbers of families.

In yet another study designed to examine the relationships between outcome and process measures of power, Hadley and Jacob (1973) studied the interactions of 20 middle-class families. Only parents and their high-school-age sons were studied for each family. The process measures of power were total talking time and successful interruptions, while the outcome measures were success in an unrevealed differences task and the number of points won in a coalition game. Results revealed a significant positive relationship between the two process measures, but no relationship between the two outcome measures. Moreover, no significant relationships were found between process and outcome measures. These findings reinforce those of Turk and Bell (1972) and raise further questions about the dimensions of power tapped by outcome and process measures of power.

Cromwell and Wieting (1975) investigated the dimensional structure of the Blood and Wolfe (1960) decision outcome type measures in a number of different samples representing three different cultures. Factor analyses of these scales revealed that they are not unidimensional and thus not additive, as Blood and Wolfe (1960) and other researchers have assumed in their studies. Furthermore, the factor structures obtained from the different samples were not comparable. This finding led Cromwell and Wieting to conclude that it would be extremely difficult to develop a self-report measure of outcome power which would not be sensitive to differences in context. While this study suggests that the lack of relationship between self-report- and interaction-based measures of power may be due to the lack of internal consistency of self-report measures of power, more recent research using a unique self-report technique to measure power found significant relationships between self-reported perceptions of power and power as measured in interaction situations (Klopper et al., 1978). These investigators measured what they called "prominence" in the family by having family members independently arrange cloth figures representing each member of the family on a felt board just prior to their interaction with each other. Prominence was measured by indexing figure placement order and figure placement height. It was assumed that figures placed on the left side and figures placed higher were thought of as more "prominent" by the respondent. Since the families were in therapy, they were asked to discuss ways in which the family should change. Before the discussion, each family member indicated five ways he or she would like to see the family change. The family members then were asked to decide five goals which would represent the entire family.

The decision outcome measure of this study was the number of individual goals included in the final decision. The two process measures of talk time and amount of communication received were used as additional measures of prominence. Figure placement order and figure placement height both correlated significantly with all three measures of prominence constructed from analyses of the interactions. Figure placement order (left

to right) correlated positively with talk time (r = .62), received communication (r = .46), while prominence as measured by figure placement height
also correlated positively with the same three variables (talk time, r = .68;
received communication, r = .52; and goals included, r = .61). The correlations among the three interaction measures ranged from .55 to .66, and
the correlation between the figure order and figure placement measures
was .64.

These findings suggest that it is possible to find significant correlations
between self-report measures of power and interaction indices of power.
Moreover, they indicate that process measures of power such as talk time
and communication received do correlate with outcome power measures as
indexed by the extent to which the group product manifests the influence
of individual group members' inputs. The critical questions are, why were
such relatively strong relationships found between the various measures of
power in the study discussed above, and why were relatively weak or null
relationships found in earlier studies? There are several possible explanations for these differences, including the fact that the populations sampled
in the studies were quite dissimilar. However, there are two additional
differences which may be especially critical. In the Turk and Bell (1972)
study, for example, persons were given quite different interaction tasks. In
one of the tasks, a family was asked how it would spend a gift of $300,
while in the other the family was asked to resolve revealed differences. In
the Klopper et al. (1978) study, the families all worked on issues which
were neither hypothetical nor of low relevance. These families presumably
wanted to change and the task they were given was directly relevant to this
goal. A second important difference between the two studies concerns the
way in which power was measured by self-reports. Turk and Bell (1972)
asked decision-making questions: a "who wins when there is a disagreement" question, and a "who is the real boss in the family" question.
Klopper et al. (1978) used more projective self-report measures of power.
The relative success of the projective measures may be due to a reduction
in the tendency to give socially desirable responses, which might be more
frequent on more obtrusive verbal self-report measures. In addition,
encoding the phenomenal experience of power through verbal language
may be difficult. Perhaps the use of figures and their relative placements to
index power provides a symbol system more iconic to the experience of
power relationships in real life. Thus, these kinds of measures correlate
better with noncontent aspects of communication behavior than do self-
report measures relying heavily upon verbal language.

This brief review of the conception and measurement of family power
underscores numerous problems which plague the concept. Like many
areas of research in the social sciences, researchers are so preoccupied with

finding *relationships* between and among variables that they spend too little time on issues of conceptualization and measurement. Furthermore, as evidenced by this review, some of the most frequently used measures of family power are of questionable reliability and therefore unknown validity. Perhaps the most optimistic statement that can be made about the measurement of family power is that all of the measures we have reviewed here seem to be tapping some facet of the general construct. Even when self-report- and interaction-based indices do not correlate with each other, we are in no position to assert that one is "right" and the other is "wrong," for both could be valid measures of different facets of power. Moreover, the temptation to argue that power measures based upon interaction behavior are somehow more meaningful than self-reports with which they do not correlate ignores the fact that persons' perceptions of their power may be more important in some situations than the actual ability of those people to exercise power. Thus, as the findings of family power research are reviewed in the next section, the reader should avoid the tendency to discount one line of research in favor of another because of measurement differences. Lines of research based upon different measurement approaches simply may not be comparable.

POWER, POWER, WHO'S GOT THE POWER?

This section will examine the family power literature from two different perspectives: First, the research stimulated by Blood and Wolfe's resource theory will be reviewed; second, the literature concerning power and family pathology will be discussed. It was noted earlier that these two groups of researchers operate relatively independently, although there are some signs that family sociologists are beginning to take a closer look at the family therapy literature for both conceptual and measurement ideas (see Cromwell and Olson, 1975).

RESOURCE THEORY AND RESEARCH

The genesis of this line of research is the previously discussed Blood and Wolfe (1960) study of 909 Detroit-area housewives. These investigators argue that spousal power arises from one of two sources, cultural ideology or, more pragmatically, the relative amount of resources each partner contributes to the marriage. They reason that if conjugal power is primarily determined by cultural ideology, certain subgroups of the population should display a patriarchal pattern of power more frequently than other segments of the population. Specifically, they hypothesized that farm families, Catholic families, immigrant families, older couples, and less educated couples would display a higher level of "traditional" husband dominance on their eight-item decision-making index. Blood and Wolfe's data revealed no differences between these groups and their counterparts in the direction of husband dominance; in fact, the power of the husband relative to the wife actually increased with increasing levels of education. Based upon these findings, Blood and Wolfe abandoned their search for evidence of cultural ideology as a source of conjugal power and focused their attention upon the resource explanation of conjugal power differences.

Resources which can be brought to a marriage include material goods and money as well as social skills and interpersonal competencies. To determine the effects of resource contributions on power balance, Blood and Wolfe (1960) examined the relationships between the income, educational level, and occupational prestige of the husband and the extent of his power. In all three cases there was a positive relationship; however, the *absolute* number of resources a person brings to the marriage does not determine his or her power, but rather the *relative* contribution of resources to the relationship. Comparing the relative education and level of organizational participation of the spouses with their levels of power yielded the same pattern of results as previous comparisons: The higher the husband's relative education and level of organizational participation, the greater his power. Also, consistent with the relative resources explanation of power differences, working wives displayed greater power than their nonworking counterparts, and the longer a wife worked the more power she tended to have. Finally, the power of husbands was found to peak when the family contained preschool children. After this point in the family life cycle, the power of husbands decreased. Presumably, wives' increased dependency when small children are part of the family was responsible for the increase in the husband's power. Blood and Wolfe (1960) conclude that the patriarchal family, in which the husband sustains his power on the basis of a cultural ideology which asserts that the male has the legitimate right to make the decisions, is essentially a myth in the United States. While Blood and Wolfe (1960) did find that husbands had higher overall levels of power than did wives, they point out that the great majority of couples in their study displayed equalitarian patterns (51 percent). The remaining 49 percent split about evenly between husband-dominated and wife-dominated relationships.

A number of subsequent studies sought to replicate Blood and Wolfe's (1960) findings both within the United States and abroad. The positive relationship between the husband's level of education and his level of power has been replicated in Belgium (Laplae, 1968), Denmark (Kandel and Lesser, 1972), France (Michel, 1967), Germany (Lupri, 1969), Japan (Blood, 1967), and the United States (Centers et al., 1971). In another German study, Lamouse (1969) found a positive relationship between education and power for males but a negative relationship for females. Also, three studies have reported inverse relationships between husbands' educational levels and power. One of these studies was conducted among Cuban immigrants living in the United States (Richmond, 1976), one in Greece (Safilios-Rothschild, 1967), and the other in Yugoslavia (Buric and Zecevic, 1967). The positive relationship between husbands' incomes and their levels of power reported in the Blood and Wolfe (1960) study was also found by Blood (1967), Lupri (1969), Michel (1967), and Richmond (1976); however, Kandel and Lesser (1972) found no relationship, and Lamouse (1969) reported that husbands at middle income levels had greater power than husbands at either extreme. Again, Buric and Zecevic (1967) and Safilios-Rothschild (1967) found inverse relationships between income level and power. The positive relationship found by Blood and Wolfe (1960) between occupational status and power has been replicated by Centers et al. (1971), Lupri (1969), Michel (1967), and Richmond (1976). Kandel and Lesser (1972) reported that husbands with middle-status occupations had the most power, while Blood (1967), Buric and Zecevic (1967), and Safilios-Rothschild (1967) all found inverse relationships between occupational status and power. Only one of these studies attempted to replicate the relationship between organizational participation and power and that attempt was successful (Lupri, 1969). In addition, Lupri found that social status as estimated by interviewers was positively related to husbands' power. All of the studies cited above, with the exception of Centers et al. (1971), found that the level of the husband's power was reduced when his wife worked. This relationship was strongest in the Richmond (1976) study when the husband's resources were moderate.

In general, most of the studies reviewed here provide support for resource theory, but there are some notable exceptions. Kandel and Lesser's (1972) Denmark study did reveal a positive relationship between educational level and power, but failed to find any relationship between income and power. Moreover, Kandel and Lesser also found a curvilinear relationship between occupational status and power, such that moderate levels of status were associated with the highest levels of power. Possibly, some of these differences appear because Denmark has a more equalitarian conjugal power structure than some other Western European countries and the United States. But why this particular difference might produce the kinds of relationships obtained by Kandel and Lesser (1972) is not immediately apparent. Even more contrary to resource theory predictions are the findings of the studies done in Greece (Safilios-Rothschild, 1967) and Yugoslavia (Buric and Zecevic, 1967): in both studies consistent inverse relationships were found between resource variables and power.

In an attempt to explain the inverse relationships between resources and power obtained in the Greece and Yugoslavia studies, Rodman (1967, 1972) developed the theory of resources in cultural context. He contends that in societies which lean toward equalitarian ideology in marital relationships there is considerable freedom to negotiate the amount of influence each spouse should have in decision-making. Of course, this does not mean that spouses will necessarily overtly negotiate the distribution of power or authority. These arrangements may arise through processes of which the spouses are unaware. In societies where equalitarian ideology is relatively weak and patriarchal ideology is strong, there is relatively less flexibility to negotiate the distribution of power. The power the husband holds is obtained through the legitimized authority structure of the society. In equalitarian societies, flexibility in the distribution of decision-making power allows resources to influence the power of the individual in the relationship. By contrast, societies with patriarchal family power structures do not provide the latitude for resources to operate to enhance power. This explanation accounts for the positive relationships between resource variables and power in more developed countries which tend to have more equalitarian power structures, but it also suggests a lack of relationship between power and resources in less developed countries. However, since affluent persons in developing countries are more likely to be exposed to better educational opportunities, they should develop more equalitarian attitudes about marital power than their less educated counterparts. Thus, in patriarchal societies we would expect to see a diminution of the husband's level of power as his social status increases.

Burr (1973) generated a number of propositions from Rodman's theory, and Burr et al. (1977) tested some of them. Their study found no support for the proposition that resources are more strongly related to power when norms about authority are equalitarian. In fact, weak trends in the opposite direction were found. Nevertheless, at least one problem with this study deserves mention. The group used in the study was a r. nrandom sample of college students, 93 percent of whom were Mormon. Although the authors argue that this was an ideal sample in which to test Rodman's propositions, since Mormon culture is generally considered to be somewhat patriarchal, the fact remains that the amount of variability on the authority structure dimension was probably not as great as that which would be obtained by comparing samples from Western Europe and the United States with samples from countries with strong patriarchal ideologies.

Buehler et al. (1974) measured Catholic high school students' perceptions of conjugal power in five different countries: Mexico, Puerto Rico, Spain, West Germany, and the United States. Correlations between the degree of industrialization of the countries and the fathers' conjugal power scores for male and female respondents, respectively, were $r_s = .30$ and $r_s = .40$. Students in less industrialized countries tended to attribute greater power to the father than did students in more industrialized countries. Correlations between husbands' education and occupational status and perceived power were positive and significant for the United States students in St. Paul, Minnesota, schools but not for students in New York schools and students in the other countries. An inverse correlation was found between husband's occupational status and power among female students in Spain; however, no other correlations between husband's education and occupational status and the power variable were significant. Significant inverse correlations were found between wife's employment and husband's power among Puerto Rican and Mexican males. No other correlations involving wife's employment were significant, although most coefficients were negative across countries. Finally, a significant inverse correlation was found between the wife's education and the husband's power among males in New York. While these findings provide limited support for Rodman's resources in cultural context theory, the authors of this study note that most of their correlations were probably depressed because of lack of variability in the independent variables of the study.

Both of the studies designed to test the impact of cultural differences on the relationship between resources and power involved the use of children's perceptions of conjugal power. While these two studies failed to produce consistent relationships between resources and power, a study by Bahr et al. (1974) reported significant relationships between resource variables and conjugal power as measured from the perspective of adolescent children. This study revealed a positive relationship between the educational level of the father and his perceived power, a positive relationship between occupational status and the power of the father, and a reduction in father's power when the wife worked. These results not only provide additional support for resource theory, but they also indicate that children's perceptions of their parents' levels of power correlate with resource variables in ways similar to those obtained when parental responses are used to index power. The findings are not consistent with those of Turk and Bell (1972), who found considerable numbers of discrepancies between parents and children on self-report measures of conjugal power. Nevertheless, the findings of the Bahr et al. (1974) study suggest that the failure of Burr et al. (1977) to support Rodman's theory and the relatively weak correlations between resources and power found in the Buehler et al. (1974) study of high school students in five nations are not due to the fact that relationships between resource variables and power change when children give estimates of their parents' power levels. Other explanations for the failure of these studies to provide strong support for Rodman's theory must be sought.

The research reviewed above generally provides support for resource theory, but more work obviously needs to be done on Rodman's proposed modification of resource theory. In addition, most of the studies reviewed here fail to provide us with estimates of the *magnitudes* of relationships between resource variables and power. It is important to know what proportion of variance in power is explained by resources so that additional resource variables can be isolated and included in future research and other determinants of power which are not related to resources can be explored. If resource variables themselves account for a very large proportion of variance in power, then it might not be fruitful to explore alternative possibilities, unless resource variables themselves are confounded with still other, more basic explanatory variables. Finally, the ways in which resources have been measured seem to be extremely limited. The focus has been largely upon economic resources with some attention to social prestige; however, it is obvious that persons can bring a multitude of other resources to a marital relationship. Interpersonal skills and personality orientations such as dominance, physical attractiveness, and a sense of humor are examples of resources which might enable an individual to gain some degree of control in a relationship. While some of these variables have been investigated within the context of general social psychological theory, they have only rarely appeared in family research. In short, it is very likely that if conjugal power is to be understood, additional resource variables will have to be considered.

OTHER DETERMINANTS OF CONJUGAL POWER

This section will briefly consider some additional variables which have been linked to conjugal power either theoretically or empirically. These variables are typically not considered resources, but appear to have some impact on marital power. For example, in her critique of resource theory, Safilios-Rothschild (1970) pointed out that while a husband might be highly successful in his occupation, thus giving him a high level of resources to exercise considerable power, his wife might still be able to wield considerable power by fixing or failing to fix his favorite foods, granting or withholding sexual intercourse, being a great hostess to the husband's guests or being a miserable shrew, and so on. Furthermore,

Safilios-Rothschild (1970) suggests that perhaps the most critical determinant of power in the marital dyad is the extent to which one spouse loves and needs the other. The spouse who has the strongest feelings for the other is essentially in the less powerful position. This idea is closely akin to the principle of least interest mentioned earlier which asserts that the person with the least interest in the relationship is in the best position to exploit the other person. Finally, Safilios-Rothschild (1970), in agreement with Heer (1963) argues that some consideration must be given to the alternative relationship possibilities of each spouse. Spouses who consider divorce a real possibility and who have other potential marital partners readily available (perhaps even waiting in the wings) are obviously in a position of power vis-à-vis their current partner. Of course, the power that may be derived from this situation is dependent upon the level of commitment of the other partner. The mere existence of alternatives does not ensure increased power for the spouse who has them; in addition, the other spouse must have some degree of commitment to the relationship so that the alternatives of the other spouse represent a real threat.

In addition to control of valued resources, Centers et al. (1971) suggest the following five sets of variables which affect relative conjugal power: (1) role patterning, (2) personality, (3) cultural factors, (4) relative competence, and (5) relative involvement. With reference to role patterning, they point out that both Blood and Wolfe (1960) and they themselves found consistent sex differences in who made certain kinds of decisions. For example, decisions related to the family car and the husband's clothes are male decisions, while decisions concerning house decoration and the wife's clothing are female-oriented decisions. Centers et al. (1971) included a measure of authoritarianism in their study to examine relationships between that factor and conjugal power. They found that individuals in husband-dominant and wife-dominant families had significantly higher levels of authoritarianism than did persons in equalitarian families. Thus, their data support the notion that personality variables play a role in conjugal power. We have already seen that cultural factors condition the relationship between resources and power and that conjugal power balance does vary with culture. In addition, Richmond (1976) found that among Cubans who had immigrated to the United States, those more highly exposed to Americans had lower levels of commitment to a male-dominance ideology. While it is difficult to infer causal direction in this case, these data suggest that exposure to equalitarian cultural norms may influence the power balance of the family. Centers et al. (1971) included a measure in their study designed to tap self-competence; however, no relationship was found between that and conjugal power balance. While this evidence suggests that the role of relative competence in the marital power balance might be slight, it seems that relative competence might be so specific to particular areas that a general measure, such as the one employed by Centers et al., might not adequately index the construct. Finally, we have already mentioned the role that relative involvement in the relationship might play in the relational power balance.

To the above list of conjugal power determinants could be added such variables as coalition formation, communication style, and perhaps physical factors such as height and weight. The important point of this discussion is that the focus upon resource theory as an explanation of marital power balance has directed attention away from variables which might be at least as important as resource distribution in determining conjugal power. In addition, even if we grant the ability of resource variables to account for variations in conjugal power, we must concern ourselves with the question of how these resources are actually exchanged in the relationship; for example, how does a husband with high income actually translate that resource into some kind of pragmatic strategy for exercising power? Does he say, "Since I make a lot of money, we will do what I say," or does his wife accept his increased influence based solely upon her knowledge of his income level? How does the working wife translate her working status into a set of power strategies? Does she say, "We should do it my way because I contribute money to the family," or does her increased power derive from the mere fact that her husband is aware of her contribution to the family income? Thus, the communicative processes involved in resource exchange must be examined before we can learn how power is distributed between spouses and within larger families.

FAMILY PROCESS THEORY AND RESEARCH

Three general characteristics of family process research are important to keep in mind as this body of literature is reviewed. First, in contrast to the family sociology literature, there is a much greater commitment to observation and measurement of ongoing interaction among family members. Second, in most of the studies to be reviewed here, husbands, wives, and some or all of their children are the foci of inquiry, not just the conjugal dyad. Finally, all of these studies contrast interaction in disturbed families with interaction in normal families, with the object of determining how patterns of communication differ between normal and disturbed families. Since many of the researchers in this area feel that patterns of *control* in families are important in explaining family pathology, this body of literature is of obvious interest to those persons interested in family power relationships. While family power will be the focus of this review, it should be noted that family researchers are also interested in such family phenomena as communication accuracy, conflict, and expression of affect. These latter three areas will not be touched upon in this discussion.

Family process researchers have indexed family power through a variety of interaction measures. Frequency of talk, talk time, length of each talk period, and the amount of talk received have been used to measure power. Persons who talk most frequently and for the longest periods of time are assumed to be the most dominant group members. In addition, persons receiving the most communication are also assumed to be most powerful. Other indices of power used in this research are frequency of interruptions, question-asking, and outcome measures such as amount of influence on the group decision. In the typical study, family members are given various discussion tasks, usually involving a group decision of some kind, and their interactions are recorded. The various measures of power are then developed from analyses of recordings.

Power and the Schizophrenic Family

Haley (1959) noted that families containing schizophrenic members frequently show a pattern of behavior which suggests that no member of the family will allow another member to govern his or her behavior. Closely tied to this notion is the observation that while family members might wish to exercise influence over each other, they cannot express their influence attempts in a *direct manner*. Since messages always include a command or directive component (Bateson et al., 1956; Haley, 1962; Watzlawick et al., 1967), this would lead to a consistent incongruity between command and content aspects of messages. An early study by Haley (1962) examined these notions by predicting that families with schizophrenic children would have more difficulty forming coalitions in order to win points in a game than would normal families. Haley (1962) found support for this proposition and also reported that normal families spent longer periods of time in coalitions with each other. Finally, in normal families, the parents and the child won the game about an equal number of times, while in the schizophrenic families the father won most and the disturbed child rarely won.

In another study of coalition formation in schizophrenic and normal families, Mishler and Waxler (1968) found that in normal families interactions between parents and their sons produced a father-mother-son dominance hierarchy, but when parents interacted with their daughters, mothers and daughters tended to form coalitions with each other. In families containing a schizophrenic male child, mothers and sons tended to form coalitions against fathers, a pattern which violates both the traditional notion that the husband is the instrumental leader in the family

(Parsons, 1955) and Caplow's (1968) prediction that family coalitions tend to form between family members of the same sex. Finally, in families which contained a schizophrenic daughter, the coalition pattern isolated the daughter from the parents. Since children are expected to gain their self-identities through identification with their like-sex parent, the coalition patterns in schizophrenic families act to subvert these identification processes. It is of further interest to note that Blood and Wolfe (1960) found that wives were happiest in equalitarian marriages, not much less happy in husband-dominant marriages, but least happy in wife-dominant marriages. Centers et al. (1971) replicated this finding for both husbands and wives. Thus, it appears that when the wife makes most of the family decisions, both her husband and the wife herself are least happy. This finding may be related in some way to the finding that normal families have a more dominant father, while in schizophrenic families with sons the mother takes a more dominant role.

In the Mishler and Waxler (1968) study, a distinction was made between power gained through *attention control* and power attained through *control of the other person*. Participation rate, who speaks to whom, and statement length were employed as measures of attention control. Interruptions and questions were used, respectively, as measures of direct and indirect person control. The coalition findings discussed above were based upon the attention control measures. In terms of person control, normal families used more interruptions than schizophrenic families and schizophrenic families used more questions. This finding was interpreted as consistent with Haley's (1959, 1962) notion that schizophrenic families tend not to make direct influence attempts on each other, even though they may wish to influence each other in some way.

Other studies have examined the role that one or both parents play in the schizophrenic family. Caputo (1963) examined the hypothesis that the combination of a powerful, dominant mother and a passive, ineffectual father would produce schizophrenic children. In this study, only parents of schizophrenics were placed in an interaction situation. Caputo (1963) found that mothers produced no more communicative acts than did fathers. Also, he found no evidence that mothers denigrated fathers any more than the fathers denigrated the mothers. In fact, Caputo (1963) concluded that there were more bilateral expressions of hostility in schizophrenic families. In a related study, Cheek (1964) examined Fromm-Reichmann's (1948) notion of the "schizophrenogenic mother." Fromm-Reichmann (1948) argued that it was the cold, aloof, and rejecting mother who was responsible for the development of schizophrenia in her children. Contrasting interaction in normal and schizophrenic families revealed that the mothers of schizophrenic children were more withdrawn in the interaction sessions, emitted lower rates of positive social-emotional behavior, and did not appear to be overly domineering. Moreover, higher rates of agreement were found in normal families and evidence suggested the existence of a mother-father coalition in normal families, but a tendency for mother-schizophrenic child coalitions to form in the schizophrenic families. Cheek (1964) generally concluded that there is some support for the characterization of the schizophrenogenic mother as cold and rejecting.

Power and the Distrubed Nonschizophrenic Family

Numerous studies have compared interaction in normal families with interaction in families which contain a disturbed but not schizophrenic individual. For example, Murrell and Stachowiak (1967) asked clinic and nonclinic families to perform four group tasks. Analyses of family interaction during task performance revealed that (1) nonclinic families distributed their statements less evenly across family members, (2) nonclinic families were more productive on certain tasks, and (3) clinic families were less likely to define leadership roles. In general, there was less cooperation in clinic families. In terms of units of interaction sent and received, mothers in nonclinic families had higher rates, and older children in clinic families had higher rates. Rates for fathers did not differ between family types. Within disturbed families, rates of interaction received did not differ between parents or between parents and the older children; however, in nonclinic families both parents received more acts than their children.

In another study contrasting clinic and nonclinic families, Leighton et al. (1971) found that in terms of number of times talked, total time talked, and average duration of time talked, fathers in normal families had higher rates than fathers in disturbed families, mothers in disturbed families had higher rates than mothers in nonclinic families, and the children in clinical families had higher rates than nonclinic children. There were more interruptions in the interactions of clinic families and there were fewer instances of simultaneous speech in normal families. In general, the mother appeared to be more dominant in clinic families but her influence was not accepted. In normal families the father was more dominant.

Jacob (1975) has provided an excellent evaluative review of these and other studies which examined interaction in both schizophrenic families and disturbed nonschizophrenic families. He notes that there are a number of inconsistent findings, most likely due to the failure to control the sex of the participating child and the diagnostic status of the family. However, two general conclusions regarding the relationship between dominance in the family and family disturbance are supported by the research findings.

First, the family power structure appears to be more differentiated in normal than in disturbed families. Second, the role of the *father* in the power structure appears to discriminate between normal and disturbed families most often. Fathers are more influential in normal families than are fathers in disturbed families, especially in relationship to their children.

WHITHER THE CONCEPT OF FAMILY POWER?

For power to become a more useful construct from which to launch inquiry into communication in the family in particular and interpersonal communication in general, there are several problems which have to be addressed. First, more work needs to be done to explicate the concept of power at the theoretical level. As we have seen in this overview, much power research has focused upon the generation of empirical indicators of power, many of which appear to be unrelated to each other. Since these uncorrelated power indices do correlate significantly with other variables, the various measures of power apparently are tapping different dimensions of power. Still, although these empirical data have been available for a number of years, there have been few attempts to trace the conceptual consequences of this measurement morass. Most often, reliability and validity studies have ended by cautioning that one cannot assume a particular empirical indicator is a measure of power and that more research is needed on measurement issues. The position advocated here is that more *thinking* is needed about the nature of power at the conceptual level, not more research.

Second, once a seemingly useful conceptualization of power is achieved, the next task will be to develop a set of propositions which deal with both the antecedents and the consequences of power. The emphasis of family sociologists has been upon the antecedents of conjugal power— for example, resources or ideology—while family process researchers have tried to study dominance patterns as an antecedent to family disturbance. Of course, in the case of family researchers, the kinds of research designs they are able to employ severely limit their ability to make any kind of statement regarding the causal role of family interaction in the production of symptoms of disturbance in individual family members. Nevertheless, these difficulties at the empirical level should not impede the development of theoretical propositions. Furthermore, efforts should be made to relate family power to variables other than resources and family disturbance. McDonald (1977b) has taken a step in this direction by proposing that children identify with and imitate the more powerful parent rather than identifying with the same-sex parent. He presents data which partially support his position. This study represents a move toward expanding the domain of consequences of differential family power.

It is almost a sure bet that an adequate theory of power in groups or a theory of family power will be relatively complex. Thus far, most of the research in the family area has confined itself to relatively simple designs involving a few variables, such as comparisons between normal and disturbed families. Obviously, an approach to family power which ignores its complexity is bound to explain little variance. For example, in many of the family process studies no effort has been made to differentiate among families whose disturbed members differ with respect to diagnostic category. There are a number of different types of schizophrenia and an even larger range of additional psychological disturbances. Is it reasonable to assume that deviant dominance patterns in the family are equally responsible for all of these different psychological disturbances? Similarly, the research on resource theory generally fails to go beyond socioeconomic determinants of conjugal power. This kind of myopia may be justified when a research area is in its beginning stages; however, it is imperative that a new set of lenses be developed which enable us to see both finer gradations of existing variables and new variables which are theoretically and empirically relevant. Once these variables are isolated, they will most likely have to be brought into relatively complex relationships with existing variables. In short, adequate power theory will no doubt contain numerous variables with nonrecursive relationships.

Finally, it is obvious from this review that communication variables of various kinds have played a large role in family power research. Several empirical indicators of power are based upon interaction measures. While this state of affairs might tend to make one bullish about the prospects of doing significant communication research in the area of family power, the difficult task remains of showing exactly how communication variables influence and are influenced by such variables as power and authority. This process is bound up in the problems of the conceptualization of power and the construction of power theories outlined above. We have yet to see whether the plethora of power-related terms in everyday discourse justifies the attention they have received as scientific constructs.

REFERENCES

ADAMS, J.S. (1965). "Inequity in social exchange." In L. Berkowitz (ed.), Advances in experimental social psychology, 2. New York: Academic Press.

ALTMAN, I., and TAYLOR, D.A. (1973) Social penetration: The development of interpersonal relationships. New York: Holt, Rinehart and Winston.

BAHR, S.J., BOWERMAN, C., and GECAS, V. (1974). "Adolescent perceptions of conjugal power." Social Forces, 52:357-367.

BALES, R.F. (1950). Interaction process analysis. Reading, MA: Addison-Wesley.

BATESON, G., JACKSON, D.D., HALEY, J., and WEAKLAND, J. (1956). "Toward a theory of schizophrenia." Behavioral Science, 1:251-264.

BLAU, P. (1964). Exchange and power in social life. New York: John Wiley.

BLOOD, R.O. (1967). Love match and arranged marriage: A Tokyo-Detroit comparison. New York: Free Press.

――― and WOLFE, D.M. (1960). Husbands and wives: The dynamics of married living. New York: Free Press.

BUEHLER, M.H., WEIGERT, A.J., and THOMAS, D.L. (1974). "Correlates of conjugal power: A five culture analysis of adolescent perceptions." Journal of Comparative Family Studies, 5:5-16.

BURCHINAL, L.G., and BAUDER, W.W. (1965). "Decision-making and role patterns among Iowa farm and non-farm families." Journal of Marriage and the Family, 27:525-530.

BURIC, O., and ZECEVIC, A. (1967). "Family authority, marital satisfaction, and the social network in Yugoslavia." Journal of Marriage and the Family, 27:325-336.

BURR, W.R. (1973). Theory construction and the sociology of the family. New York: John Wiley.

――― AHERN, L., and KNOWLES, E.M. (1977). "An empirical test of Rodman's theory of resources in cultural context." Journal of Marriage and the Family, 39:505-514.

CAPLOW, T. (1968). Two against one: Coalitions in triads. Englewood Cliffs, NJ: Prentice-Hall.

CAPUTO, D.V. (1963). "The parents of the schizophrenic." Family Process, 2:339-356.

CENTERS, R., RAVEN, B.H., and RODRIGUES, A. (1971). "Conjugal power structure: A re-examination." American Sociological Review, 36:264-278.

CHEEK, F.E. (1964). "The 'schizophrenogenic mother' in word and deed." Family Process, 3:155-177.

CROMWELL, R.E., and OLSON, D.H. (1975). "Multidisciplinary perspectives of power." In R.E. Cromwell and D.H. Olson (eds.), Power in families. Beverly Hills, CA: Sage.

―――― and WIETING, S.G. (1975). "Multidimensionality of conjugal decision making indices: Comparative analyses of five samples." Journal of Comparative Family Studies, 6:139-152.

CROMWELL, V.L., and CROMWELL, R.E. (1978). "Perceived dominance in decision-making and conflict resolution among Anglo, Black and Chicano couples." Journal of Marriage and the Family, 40:749-759.

DOUGLAS, S.P., and WIND, Y. (1978). "Examining family role and authority patterns: Two methodological issues." Journal of Marriage and the Family, 40:35-47.

EDWARDS, J.N. (1969). "Family behavior as social exchange." Journal of Marriage and the Family, 31:518-526.

FROMM-REICHMANN, F. (1948). "Notes on the development of treatment of schizophrenics by psychoanalytic psychotherapy." Psychiatry, 11:263-273.

HADLEY, T., and JACOB, T. (1973). "Relationship among measures of family power." Journal of Personality and Social Psychology, 27:6-12.

HALEY, J. (1959). "The family of the schizophrenic: A model system." Journal of Nervous and Mental Disease, 129:357-374.
——— (1962). "Family experiments: A new type of experimentation." Family Process, 1:265-293.
HEER, D.M. (1958). "Dominance and the working wife." Social Forces, 36:341-347.
——— (1962). "Husband and wife perceptions of family power structure." Marriage and Family Living, 24:65-67.
——— (1963). "The measurement and bases of family power: An overview." Marriage and Family Living, 25:133-139.
HOMANS, G.C. (1974). Social behavior: Its elementary forms. New York: Harcourt Brace Jovanovich.
JACOB, T. (1975). "Family interaction in disturbed and normal families: A methodological and substantive review." Psychological Bulletin, 82:33-65.
KANDEL, D.B., and LESSER, G.S. (1972). "Marital decision-making in American and Danish urban families: A research note." Journal of Marriage and the Family, 34:134-138.
KENKEL, W.F. (1963). "Observational studies of husband-wife interaction in family decision-making." In M.B. Sussman (ed.), Sourcebook in marriage and the family. Boston: Houghton Mifflin.
KLOPPER, E.J., TITTLER, B.I., FRIEDMAN, S., and HUGHES, S.J. (1978). "A multi-method investigation of two family constructs." Family Process, 17:83-93.
LAMOUSE, A. (1969). "Family roles of women: A German example." Journal of Marriage and the Family, 31:145-152.
LAPLAE, C. (1968). "Structure des taches domestiques et du pouvoir de decision de la dyade conjugale." In P. de Bie et al. (eds.), La dyade conjugale. Bruxelles, Belgique: Editions Vie Ouvriere.
LARSON, L.E. (1974). "System and subsystem perception of family roles." Journal of Marriage and the Family, 36:123-138.
LEIGHTON, L., STOLLAK, G., and FERGUSON, L. (1971). "Patterns of communication in normal and clinic families." Journal of Consulting and Clinical Psychology, 36:252-256.
LUPRI, E. (1969). "Contemporary authority patterns in the West German family: A study in cross-national validation." Journal of Marriage and the Family, 31:134-144.
McDONALD, G.W. (1977a). "Family power: Reflection and direction." Pacific Sociological Review, 20:607-621.
——— (1977b). "Parental identification by the adolescent: A social power approach." Journal of Marriage and the Family, 39:705-719.
MICHEL, A. (1967). Comparative data concerning the interaction in French and American families." Journal of Marriage and the Family, 29:337-344.
MISHLER, E.G., and WAXLER, N.E. (1968). Interaction in families: An experimental study of family processes in schizophrenia. New York: John Wiley.
MURRELL, S., and STACHOWIAK, J. (1967). "Consistency, rigidity and power in the interaction patterns of clinic and nonclinic families." Journal of Abnormal Psychology, 72:265-272.
OLSON, D.H. (1969). "Measurement of family power by self-report and behavioral methods." Journal of Marriage and the Family, 31:545-550.
——— and RABUNSKY, C. (1972). "Validity of four measures of family power." Journal of Marriage and the Family, 34:224-234.

PARSONS, T. (1955). "Family structure and the socialization of the child." In T. Parsons and R.F. Bales, Family, socialization and interaction processes. New York: Free Press.

PHILLIPS, C.E. (1967). "Measuring power of spouse." Sociology and Social Research, 52:35-49.

PRICE-BONHAM, S. (1976). "A comparison of weighted and unweighted decision-making scores." Journal of Marriage and the Family, 38:629-640.

RICHMOND, M.L. (1976). "Beyond resource theory: Another look at factors enabling women to affect family interaction." Journal of Marriage and the Family, 38:257-266.

RODMAN, H. (1967). "Marital power in France, Greece, Yugoslavia and the United States: A cross-national discussion." Journal of Marriage and the Family, 29:320-324.

――― (1972). "Marital power and the theory of resources in cultural context." Journal of Comparative Family Studies, 3:50-69.

ROLLINS, B.C., and BAHR, S.J. (1976). "A theory of power relationships in marriage." Journal of Marriage and the Family, 38:619-627.

SAFILIOS-ROTHSCHILD, C. (1967). "A comparison of power structure and marital satisfaction in urban Greek and French families." Journal of Marriage and the Family, 29:345-352.

――― (1969). "Family sociology or wives' family sociology? A cross-cultural examination of decision-making." Journal of Marriage and the Family, 31:290-301.

――― (1970). "The study of family power structure: A review 1960-1969." Journal of Marriage and the Family, 32:539-552.

SMITH, T.E. (1970). "Foundations of parental influence upon adolescents: An application of social power theory." American Sociological Review, 35:860-872.

SPREY, J. (1972). "Family power structure: A critical comment." Journal of Marriage and the Family, 34:235-238.

STRODTBECK, F.L. (1951). "Husband-wife interaction over revealed differences." American Sociological Review, 16:468-473.

――― (1954). "The family as a three person group." American Sociological Review, 19:23-29.

――― (1958). "Family interaction, values, and achievement." In D.C. McClelland et al. (eds.), Talent and society. Princeton: Van Nostrand.

THIBAUT, J.W., and KELLEY, H.H. (1959). The social psychology of groups. New York: John Wiley.

TURK, J.L. (1974). "Power as the achievement of ends: A problematic approach in family and small group research." Family Process, 13:39-52.

――― and BELL, N.W. (1972). "Measuring power in families." Journal of Marriage and the Family, 34:215-222.

WALLER, W. (1938). The family: A dynamic interpretation. New York: Cordon.

WATZLAWICK, P., BEAVIN, J.H., and JACKSON, D.D. (1967). Pragmatics of human communication. New York: Norton.

WOLFE, D.M. (1959). "Power and authority in the family." In D. Cartwright (ed.), Studies in social power. Ann Arbor: Research Center for Group Dynamics.

Chapter 8

COMMUNICATION IN BARGAINING AND NEGOTIATION

James T. Tedeschi and Paul Rosenfeld

BARGAINING REFERS to the process by which two or more persons attempt to reach agreement about the terms of exchange between them. An agreement stipulates how each party will behave in the future. Bargaining involves positive, giving, or rewarding behavior as well as negative, deprivation, or punishing behavior. Children's agreement to eat all their vegetables may be exchanged for the promise of their parents not to spank them; this example shows that bargaining may be an important dimension in most human relationships. However, most people think of bargaining as occurring only in such formal settings as union-management negotiations or in the high-level discussions of nations.

Because of the need for laboratory control over variables, the scientific study of bargaining has tended to produce a static and improverished view of the process. Perhaps the most neglected aspect of bargaining has been the role of various kinds of communications. Bargainers probe and explore each other's values, make commitments of various kinds, engage in impression management tactics, and attempt to influence each other in direct and indirect ways. In the present chapter we will focus on the role of communications in bargaining and will give only a brief description of the structure of the bargaining situation and several illustrative scientific theories of the bargaining process. Readers who want a more comprehensive review of the bargaining and negotiation literature are referred to

Schelling (1960), Walton and McKersie (1965), Rubin and Brown (1975), Tedeschi et al. (1973), and Druckman (1977).

Scientists have tended to focus on situations which are formally and collectively defined as bargaining. However, we view many of the processes characteristic of formal bargaining situations as applicable to a wide range of human interactions. These latter situations may be referred to as informal bargaining, and are characterized primarily by the fact that the parties involved do not overtly acknowledge (and often do not covertly believe) that they are involved in bargaining. A number of social scientists employ a bargaining metaphor in the analysis of everyday encounters. Scott and Lyman (1968) view actors in social situations as in a constant process of negotiating identities, while Nieburg (1969) interprets most political behavior in terms of bargaining.

The basis of all bargaining is that two or more persons are interdependent for their rewards. There is very little of value that we can obtain for ourselves without the help of others—we want food, power, respect, safety, love, entertainment, and much more. It is seldom the case that others are willing to provide these rewards without some form of quid pro quo. In many cases the terms of exchange have been worked out in advance (standardized) and one either agrees to the terms or does not. Thus, either one is willing to pay $1.50 for a gallon of gas or else one does not drive to the grocery store. In other instances, such as an open-air market in the Middle East, haggling or other means of influence may be brought to bear to affect the terms of exchange and potential agreement.

We have seen, then, that bargaining may be formal and labeled as such or it may be informal and not recognized generally as a bargaining situation. The range of human interactions interpretable by a bargaining metaphor is immense; it may be applicable whenever the outcomes of two or more persons are interdependent. Bargaining can be over material commodities, such as money, production of goods, or reduction of a stockpile of nuclear weapons, or it can be over such intangibles as the identities ascribed by the parties to each other.

A distinction is often made between bargaining and negotiation. According to Rubin and Brown (1975), bargaining refers primarily to interactions among individuals, while negotiation is best applied to similar interactions among more complex social entities, such as representatives of unions, management, or government agencies. The legendary haggling among customers and shopkeepers on New York City's Lower East Side or the give and take between a salesman and a potential customer in a used car lot are examples of bargaining, while attempts by heads of state to reach agreement on arms control is an example of negotiation. An important difference between bargaining and negotiation is that in the latter the party must not only come to terms with another party but he or she must also do so in a manner satisfactory to those he or she represents. Thus, bargainers represent only themselves, but negotiators represent constituencies.

The course of bargaining depends to some extent on the structure of the situation. The dynamic aspects of bargaining involve various kinds of communications. Explicit or tacit communications may serve one of four major purposes: (1) discovery of the preferences and values of the other party; (2) disguise the communicator's own preferences and values; (3) influence the opponent's behavior; and (4) alter such basic relationships as the attractiveness or trust between the bargainers. After examining the structure of bargaining situations, we will describe these communication functions in more detail.

THE STRUCTURE OF BARGAINING SITUATIONS

Some degree of conflict between the parties is a feature of most formal bargaining situations. In order to obtain the value desired, the bargainer must also be willing to give something of value. Hence, for every gain there is a cost. The question to bargainers is how much they are willing to relinquish for the amount conceded by their adversaries. In other words, one party's gain is typically the other party's loss. Walton and McKersie (1965) refer to this kind of situation as *distributive bargaining*.

Researchers have found it useful to identify the parameters of distributive bargaining by use of a technical vocabulary. We may refer to a structure for the bargaining situation because it is within the context of the goals and expectations of the two contending parties that the dynamics of the bargaining process will occur. Let's examine a hypothetical bargaining situation between a tourist and an Arab merchant in a busy outdoor market in the Middle East.

Among the most sought-after commodities by foreign tourists in the open-air markets of the Middle East are the handmade backgammon sets found in many shops. Suppose that an Arab merchant has acquired an exquisite backgammon set at a cost to him of $50.00. In addition, he has overhead expenses and wants to make a profit. Of course, he would like to get as much as possible for the set, but the least he will take is $75.00. This minimum sale price is typically not revealed to a customer, but is referred to in technical terms as the merchant's *resistance point*. Now suppose an American tourist takes a fancy to the backgammon set and is privately willing to pay as much as $150.00 for it. This maximum price that the buyer is willing to pay is *his* resistance point. These two resistance points set the boundaries within which the bargain will be reached and is referred to as the *bargaining range*. Of course, if the seller will take nothing less than $160.00 for the backgammon set or the buyer is not willing to spend more than $70.00 for it, no agreement will be reached, since both positions are outside the bargaining range. The failure to reach agreement leaves each party at a *status quo point*—that is, they leave the interaction with exactly the same resources as when they began bargaining. However, since each spent time and effort in the haggling process and each is disappointed with the failure to achieve his goal, there is a sense in which the failure to reach an agreement leaves both of them worse off than before they had interacted.

The bargaining range in the above example is between the resistance points of the buyer and seller—in this case, between $75.00 and %150.00. Of course, the buyer would like to pay less than the maximum he is grudgingly willing to pay, and the seller would like to receive more than the minimum he would painfully accept. This is, both bargainers may realistically seek an agreement more in their own favor and closer to the other party's resistance point. Typically, the two parties do not know what the other's resistance point is; hence, each makes offers or counter-offers, probes the other's values system, and attempts to influence the other.

Each party may have a realistic *level of aspiration* with regard to a preferred agreement. For example, the merchant may have a level of aspiration of receiving $125 for the backgammon set and the tourist may believe that if he bargains well he can buy the set for $100. Since these two values are within the bargaining range and both parties can, through some ultimate compromise, nearly achieve their levels of aspiration, it could be predicted that a mutually satisfactory bargain would be achieved. The status quo point, resistance point, and level of aspiration make up a bargainer's *utility schedule*. As indicated in our example, bargainers typically try to find out what the other party's utility schedule is without divulging their own.

This analysis of the structure of a bargaining situation has assumed the simplest possibility: two parties bargaining over a single commodity. Consider the complexity of negotiations between union and management which involves production rates, wages, grievance procedures, vacations, retirement, medical plans, and so on. Furthermore, the failure to reach agreement may mean a strike or a lockout, a status quo point that is costly to both sides. In such situations it seems clear to both parties that they would be better off reaching some kind of agreement than if no solution is found. Nevertheless, each will have a resistance point and damaging failure to reach agreement sometimes occurs.

THEORIES OF BARGAINING

The focus of most theories of bargaining is the structure of the situation. For example, game theory (von Neumann and Morgenstern, 1944) is a mathematical formulation of the bargaining process which examines the structure of payoffs that can occur to the two parties (that is, the bargaining range and utility schedules) and the relationship of various strategies to the payoff structure. A strategy may consist of a series of concessions and counteroffers, threats, and promises which may have the effect of altering the outcomes. For example, if a party threatens the other (with a strike, for example), then the value of the status quo outcome is worsened, provided, of course, that the threatener means what he or she says. Game theory makes predictions about the nature of the agreement that should be reached by the parties given the structure of the situation. Note that we used the word "should," not "will," in the previous sentence; this is because game theory makes prescriptions about what a totally rational decision maker should do and does not make predictions about what real people do. Nevertheless, game theory has been quite useful in providing a conceptual framework within which much research has been done on behavior of people in highly simplified bargaining situations. Much of what we have to say about bargaining later in this chapter has been obtained from research stimulated by game theory.

Many laboratory studies of bargaining limit the communications between the parties to making bids, counteroffers, and refusals. It is not surprising, therefore, that some theories focus upon the rate of concessions made by the parties in making predictions about the agreement that will be reached. Initial bids by both parties are interpreted as exploratory and unrealistic and each is likely to scale back his or her demands in a stepwise fashion. A tough bargaining stance of few concessions, if adopted by both parties, is likely to lead to a failure to reach agreement, but if one party continues to make concessions, the tough bargainer will stand to gain a great deal. On the other hand, if both bargainers tend to reciprocate the kind of concessions made by the other, the likelihood of agreement would be great and a clear prediction about its nature could be made (Siegel and Fouraker, 1960; Bartos, 1974).

Bargainers operate in a world that contains exemplars, norms, and power. When steel workers negotiate with management, they know what kind of agreement aluminum workers have obtained, and vice versa. This kind of social comparison provides a standard about what constitutes a fair agreement; management could argue that by comparison steel workers produce less or that the costs of raw materials are higher. Standards of fairness are also set by certain rules of distributive justice. One such rule is *equality*; that is, if there are good profits to the corporation, then they should be equally divided between management and labor. Management may argue for the *principle of equity*; that is, each party to negotiations should receive a share of the profits that is proportional to their contribution toward earning them. A government arbitrator might argue for a *social welfare principle* that a certain agreement is in the best interests of the community as a whole for reasons of "keeping a lid on" inflation, providing maximum incentive for saving and investment, or to bolster the overall economy.

Komorita and Chertkoff (1973) have offered a theory that takes into account both the power of the bargainers and the norms that will tend to dictate the bargaining outcome. While the theory is presented in mathematical form, it essentially suggests that bargainers' power can be measured in terms of the amount of resources they control and that the most powerful bargainers will expect an agreement that reflects their relative power (that is, equity). Weaker bargainers will adhere to an equality norm. In order for agreement to be reached, the powerful party must accept something less than equity and the weak party must accept less than equality. A compromise in norms is postulated by the theory and hence a split-the-difference solution is predicted. That is, the agreement will be approximately midway between equity and equality outcomes. This prediction of the theory has frequently been supported in simplified laboratory versions of bargaining situations.

While we certainly agree that the structure of the bargaining situation, the relative power of the parties, the concessions they make, as well as the norms that regulate the distribution of outcomes are factors affecting the bargaining process, our present thesis contends that the dynamic communicative interplay between the parties is of paramount importance. Although an adequate scientific theory of communications in bargaining has yet to be proferred, nevertheless, we can take a functional approach. Specifically, we will examine the role that various types of communications play in bargaining and negotiations. In accordance with Walton and McKersie (1965) and Smith (1968), we see the function of communications in bargaining and negotiation to include discovering the opponent's utility schedule, manipulating the adversary's bargaining position, and fostering different fundamental relationships with other parties outside the bargaining situation.

DISCOVERING THE OPPONENT'S UTILITY SCHEDULE

Commonsense would suggest that knowing the resistance point and level of aspiration of your bargaining opponent would provide you with an advantage in reaching an agreement. Presumably, if the opponent does not know your utility schedule and you know his, you can hold out for an agreement that is close to his resistance point and your own level of aspiration. Schelling (1960) has noted that where parties are mutually ignorant of each other's utility schedule an initial discovery phase will take place. Many tactics can be employed in this discovery phase of bargaining. Initial offers may be made more to probe the reactions of the adversary than as a serious attempt to reach an agreement. A calculated set of concessions may also serve this purpose. Written and/or oral communications may also probe the values and resolution of the opponent.

Contrary to common sense, Schelling (1960) has claimed that knowledge of opponents' utility schedules might cause bargainers to temper their own demands and hence actually place them at a disadvantage. Knowledgeable parties might be constrained by their own allegiance to norms of fairness and hence adjust their level of aspiration to a point that represents the standards they employ (for example, equity or equality). The uninformed party, having no way of judging whether the informed party's offers are fair, may interpret the latter's concessions as tacit communications of weakness and as a consequence toughen his own stand. In support of this reasoning Cummings and Harnett (1969) found that informed bargainers offered more concessions than uninformed ones. Harnett and Cummings (1968) found that uninformed bargainers usually began with higher initial bids, took longer to reach agreement, and gained a greater advantage in their agreements than did informed bargainers. These results suggest that actors should not rely on information about their opponent's utility schedule as a means of increasing their own profits, and should they acquire such information the implication is that it might be judicious to voluntarily reveal their own utility schedules. As Schelling (1960) argues, weakness is strength in bargaining. Possessing more information than the other should place the opponent in a weak bargaining position, but his very weakness is his strength, since the informed party is hampered by the knowledge he possesses and norms of fairness that often·prevent him from exploiting his advantage. It is more usual, however, that both bargainers are ignorant regarding the other's utility schedule and devote a great deal of energy and time to concealing their own preferences from the adversary.

DISGUISING ONE'S OWN UTILITY SCHEDULE

Each party is cognizant that his or her bids and concessions may tacitly communicate his or her utility schedule to the adversary and this affects bargaining behavior. Research has established that most subjects in bargaining situations make high initial demands (Tedeschi et al., 1973). A tough strategy involving a high initial demand and then making few small concessions may be adopted, but, as we have already indicated, this gives rise to the *bargainer's dilemma*. Behavior directed toward appearing tough interferes with a flexible strategy which is responsive to the adversary's concessions with the result that the chances of reaching an agreement are decreased. On the other hand, yielding encourages the opponent to adopt a tough bargaining strategy. In the face of this dilemma most bargainers refrain from adopting tough strategies.

Instead of trying to disguise one's utility schedule, it might be asked why one should not be honest and straightforward and simply tell the other person what is acceptable or "fair" and then hold onto that position? This apparently reasonable strategy was found to be ineffective by Komorita and Brenner (1968). In addition, they found that regular or predictable noncontingent concessions encouraged the adversary to adopt a tough strategy. Pruitt and Johnson (1970) have found that irregular and unpredictable concessions give the appearance of toughness and elicit reciprocal concessions from the opponent.

Bargainers may engage in bluffing tactics or deceitful statements to prevent the opponent from discovering their utility schedules. While these tactics may be successful in the short run and in a one-shot bargaining sequence, they are likely to backfire in the long run and across a series of bargaining sessions because of the distrust that is generated. Once one learns that a player continually bluffs and misrepresents his or her hand in a poker game, these tactics lose their effectiveness.

Bargainers may try to convince their adversaries that they have made their final concession by demonstrating their commitment to it. According to Schelling (1960:37), this strategy can be characterised in the following way:

> In bargaining, the commitment is a device to leave the last clear chance to decide the outcome with the other party, in a manner that he fully appreciates: it is to relinquish further initiative, having rigged the incentives so that the other party must choose in one's favor.

When bargainers make a commitment, they burn their bridges behind them. The commitment tactic communicates to the adversary that the bargainer has reached his or her resistance point and cannot make further concessions. This leaves the committed bargainer in an inflexible position, since he or she now must hold to the commitment whatever the consequences. The actor must not make commitments lightly. Suppose the commitment is made outside the bargaining range? Then no agreement can be reached unless the commitment is withdrawn. However, the loss of credibility associated with withdrawing a commitment makes it more difficult to reach an agreement with the opponent.

Bargainers who commit themselves to a particular offer must make it clear to their opponents that they would incur some unacceptable cost should they make any further concession. That is, it must be clear that it would cost more to take the last offer than an agreement would be worth. Management might tell labor negotiators that if their last offer is not accepted, they will close the plant in a lockout by a certain date. This commitment to a lockout communicates to the union that management would prefer the costs of not operating to those associated with an agreement that would give the union more than was last offered.

As we have seen, commitment tactics not only disguise one's own utility schedule but they also have the function of manipulating the adversary's bargaining position.

MANIPULATING THE ADVERSARY'S BARGAINING POSITION

The various modes of influence that we use as communications in everyday life can be and typically are used in the bargaining process. Bargainers may be concerned with presenting a particular image of themselves to their adversaries, may try to arrange the situation in which the bargaining will take place, may try to invoke various symbols of patriotism or morality to change adversaries bargaining position, and employ more direct types of influence, such as threats, promises, and persuasion.

TYPES OF INFLUENCE

Tedeschi and Lindskold (1976) classified direct modes of influence into those that involve control over reinforcement and those that rely upon control over information. Threats and promises and unannounced uses of rewards and punishments are modes of influence involving reinforcement control. Threats are communications from a source that that person may punish a target, whereas promises offer the prospect of rewards. Threats and promises may be contingent or noncontingent. That is, the punishment or reward threatened or promised may be based on some future behavior (or the withholding of response) by the target, or they may be indicated by the source as deliverable no matter what the target does.

Among the types of persuasion are warnings and mendations. These forms of information control inform a target about contingencies in the natural or social environment. A warning tells the target about forth-coming punishments which the source does not control but knows about, whereas a mendation predicts positive consequences. Warnings and menda-tions may be contingent or noncontingent. That is, the source may inform the target that punishment or reward may occur as a function of perform-ing some action or that these reinforcement outcomes will occur no matter what the target does. Warnings and mendations are not always different, since telling a target not to do something because of the negative conse-quences may at the same time point to an alternative behavior that would have positive consequences (for example, warning that failure to brush teeth will lead to cavities also communicates that proper dental hygiene will prevent cavities).

CREDIBILITY AND BELIEVABILITY OF INFLUENCE COMMUNICATIONS

In understanding when an influence communication is effective in changing the behavior of a target in any situation, including a bargaining one, it is important to distinguish between the concepts of credibility and believability. *Credibility* refers to the truthfulness of the source over the occasions when his or her communications can be checked for their accuracy. For example, sources who always back up their threats and fulfill their promises have high credibility, but sources who seldom do as they say have low credibility. *Believability* is the target's assessment of how likely it is that the source's present communication is true. Although the source's credibility is one factor that affects believability by the target in a current influence communication, source and target characteristics also have been shown to have important effects (Tedeschi, et al., 1973).

It is not known whether persons maintain a balance sheet of credibil-ities for each form of influence or whether they calculate an overall credibility for all the influence communications of others. However, com-mon sense and scientific research agree that sources who establish high credibility for their communications are more likely to get their way with targets than would sources with low credibility. For example, some offi-cials in the pentagon suggest that if a source establishes high credibility for his threats a target will subsequently believe his promises. It is sometimes asked, for example, that if the United States does not back up its threats (as in Vietnam) then how can its allies believe its promises? An interesting study by Schlenker et al. (1973) examined this hypothesis in a laboratory situation. They found that no matter what level of credibility was estab-lished by a source for a series of threats, a target's cooperative responses to subsequent promises were dependent only on the credibility of the promises. However, contrary to what might be expected, sources who established high credibility for their promises gained more compliance to subsequent threats whatever the credibility of the threats than did sources whose initial promises were not fulfilled. These results support the old adage that honey attracts more than vinegar. Generally, the more believable an influence communication is to targets, the more likely they are to give in to the requests, demands, or advice of the sources. Of course, the greater the amount of costs or gains associated with these communications, the more likely are targets to acquiesce to the sources' influence attempts. Thus, both the amount of reinforcement and the perceived probability that it will occur affect the target's decision regarding how to react to the source's threats, promises, warnings, or mendations.

It is not difficult to find examples of these forms of influence in bargaining situations. We often hear our national leaders state that we should never enter discussions with other nations unless we can bargain from a position of strength. This statement usually refers to the strength of our military forces. The possession of resources that can impose costs may tempt a bargainer into threatening the adversary. For example, when the North Vietnamese would not agree to American demands at the Paris Peace Talks several years ago, the United States threatened and then carried out a week-long intensive bombing campaign of that Asian nation.

The use of threats has the potential to change the utility schedules of both parties to bargaining. We have already seen that the target of a threat may perceive his or her status quo point as changed, since the failure to reach agreement may bring some magnitude of punishment from the threatener. Thus, from the target's point of view, if no agreement is reached he or she will be worse off than before interaction with the threatener began.

FACTORS AFFECTING THE USE OF COERCION

The source is not unaffected by using threats. There are three types of costs that can accrue to the source for using threats. *Fixed costs* are voluntary costs that the source knows will be incurred and which are considered acceptable, such as the amount of money it may cost to transmit a threat by cablegram. *Opportunity* costs are those which can be foreseen, but whether or not they will be incurred depends on what the target does (Harsanyi, 1962). For example, the threatener should punish the target only if the latter fails to comply to the threatner's demands. However, delivering contingent punishments is seldom possible without costs to the one who is doing the punishing. For example, it is not possible for a labor union to call for a strike without bringing costs to both sides in the negotiations. *Target-imposed costs* are those which may be delivered by the target. The target may issue counterthreats, become concerned about saving face, form coalitions or alliances for purposes of self-defense or to change the balance of power, or otherwise withdraw from the bargaining process.

In the context of a laboratory bargaining game, Tedeschi et al. (1969) found that players tend to take costs into account prior to sending threats. The greater the potential opportunity costs for sending threats, the less likely it was that a player would send them. In a similar research setting, Tedeschi et al. (1970) found that, holding the amount of costs constant, subjects were more deterred from sending threats by anticipation of target-imposed costs than by opportunity costs. Apparently, concern about escalation of conflict based on exchange of punishments is an additional factor that each party takes into account when deciding about whether or not to send threats.

Among the factors that lead bargainers to use threats is the degree of conflict between them. The intensity of conflict between two persons is proportional to how interdependent, incompatible, and vital are the goals of each. It should be noted that when one is in an intense conflict with someone else it is not likely that the adversary's persuasive communications will be believed or that one would rely on that person's promises to provide future rewards or that moral suasion would be effective. Conflict breeds distrust and suspicion about motives; hence, it undermines the use of positive modes of influence. Threats are easier to believe under these circumstances, and each party finds it easier to believe that his or her own use of threats is justified. Laboratory research supports the generalization that the greater the size of conflict between parties to bargaining, the more likely they are to use threats and punishment (Deutsch et al., 1971).

An escalation of conflict often occurs when bargainers resort to threats and punishments. A party may appear to be weak and compliant and as a consequence may invite further attacks against himself or herself if he or she does not retaliate when threatened. Although the person may privately be willing to give in to the threatener's demands, he or she may nevertheless defy the threatener because of the fear of encouraging even greater future demands. The first threatener then must either carry out the punishment or back down in the face of a counterthreat. Punishment and retaliation may then occur and each side may then issue threats of even greater magnitude. This process can continue until one side or the other exhausts the resources necessary to back up its threats or the costs of continuing become prohibitive.

Noncompliance, resistance, and retaliation may not only momentarily deter an aggressor but also serve to prevent future coercive influence attempts by other parties. Even a more powerful opponent may be deterred from attacking a determined person who can threaten sufficient costs to detract from and thus render worthless whatever gain could be acquired.

JUSTIFICATION FOR COERCION

Typically, bargainers try to justify any use of coercion. The reason for this is that unjustified uses of coercion are usually labeled as aggression, can anger the target, and encourage reciprocal uses of coercion. When considering the topic of aggression it is important to differentiate between the use of coercion by the source, which constitutes the action at issue, and the perception or labeling of that action by observers (Tedeschi et al., 1974). Research has shown that doing harm of any kind provokes anger and retaliation when it is perceived as unjustified, but that these volatile responses do not occur when the source can justify the use of coercion (Pastore, 1952; Mallick and McCandless, 1966). Of course, the way each party perceives the other will affect the likelihood that a justification will be accepted. Persons with a reputation for being aggressive, tough, and exploitative will have difficulty in justifying the use of coercion, while those who are respected for their intelligence, patience, and reasonableness will be more successful in rationalizing their actions to others.

A bargainer can justify the use of coercion by reference to various norms of conduct, such as self-defense and the norm of negative reciprocity. These norms can serve as justifications of coercion only when it seems clear or reasonable for the source to believe that a vital interest is endangered by the action of the adversary or that the latter used unjustified coercion against him or her. History, science, and common sense all agree that actors often take great pains to justify their use of coercion as legitimate, defensive, and necessary.

A concern to avoid a damaging escalatory process may inhibit bargainers from using threats and punishments against one another. However, they may instead engage in a series of covert operations that cannot unequivocably be attributed to them, including dirty tricks, espionage, and so on. For example, during negotiations between a railroad workers' union and management, groups of men may blow up railroad tracks or hinder movement of cargo. The union may deny any responsibility for these actions, but the costs to the railroad companies would continue until an agreement is made.

OTHER MODES OF INFLUENCE

An influence tactic that is closely related to threats is the *blocking of outcomes*. This tactic attempts to block the adversary's access to value outcomes. For example, the United States Congress has removed nations from favorite-nation status in international trade because of their failure to agree to some demand by our country. Presumably, an agreement to negotiations will not only resolve the issues in dispute but also restore favorite-nation status to the adversary nation. Thus, the promise to remove blocks to outcomes can become part of the incentive to reach an agreement favorable to the actor who initially introduced those blocks.

Promises have the effect of linking a bargainer's offer with some other gain not a direct part of the bargaining process. These side payoffs may reduce the adversary's level of aspiration or perhaps his or her resistance point. For example, negotiators for a labor union might accept somewhat less of a financial gain in the form of wages for strengthened grievance procedures offered by management.

Persuasion is used in bargaining to change the goals or attitudes of the adversary through the use of argument, propaganda, and special knowledge. The actor might attempt to directly affect the utility schedule of an opponent by communicating persuasive arguments. The adversary's level of aspiration may be shown to be associated with unforeseen costs, as when a government agency associates higher wages with a higher rate of inflation and an ultimate reduction in purchasing power. Other alternatives may be recommended to a preferred choice, or a nonpreferred alternative may be shown to have positive outcomes not considered by the target.

An important persuasion tactic is *demand creation* (Michener and Suchner, 1971). This tactic consists of building up the value of the commodities being offered in the bargaining process. For example, the Arab merchant of the earlier example may play up the finer points of the backgammon set he is selling by indicating the reputation of the artist who made the set, the fine quality of the African ivory, and the scarcity of similar sets. This spiel is directed toward enhancing the value of the backgammon set in the eyes of the American tourist. If this tactic works the tourist will presumably shift his level of aspiration and be willing to pay the Arab merchant more money for the set than before.

The opposite process may also occur. The tourist may devalue the backgammon set by saying that he has seen dozens just like it in other shops and that other merchants were willing to sell for less. These tactics may be referred to as *motivational withdrawal* (Emerson, 1962), since they indicate that the person using them has less interest in the commodity than might have earlier been thought. On New York City's Lower

East Side a good withdrawal tactic is to walk out of the shop after making a "last offer" and hope that the shopkeeper will come running after you with his acceptance.

Demand creation, blocking outcomes, and motivational withdrawal are all designed to affect the availability and/or the perceived value of the bargaining alternatives in the eyes of the adversary. Emerson (1962) views the possibility of forming coalitions or finding alternative sources to provide the value in question as *extending the power network* of the influencer which has the result of increasing the available resources to him. The aforementioned American tourist may actually find a similar set for a more affordable price in some other shop. Another example of extending the power network would be the increased bargaining strength of the OPEC nations. When each nation made its own price for oil, each received a much lower price, but now that the oil producing and exporting nations have formed an international cartel they can agree among themselves about what price to set. Of course, this tactic is usable only when there is sufficient demand for the product in question.

STRATEGIES FOR REDUCING TENSIONS AND
BREAKING IMPASSES IN BARGAINING

Sometimes it is difficult to break down hostilities or tension sufficiently to even undertake the bargaining process. When this is the case and one party wants to initiate the bargaining process, Osgood (1962) has suggested a strategy for the *graduated reduction in tension* (GRIT). This strategy consists of a set of preannounced, unilateral and noncontingent rewards which are provided the adversary with a request for some form of reciprocation. These unilateral initiatives may start with very small rewards and gradually increase in magnitude. However, parties adopting a GRIT strategy must be firm and not allow the opponent to take advantage of them or to give the appearance of appeasement. Thus, the initiatives are limited to those voluntary ones chosen by the active strategist, and demands or attempts by the opponent to take competitive advantage must be rebuffed. Of course, this strategy cannot be carried on indefinitely without reciprocation from the opponent. Fortunately, evidence reviewed by Lindskold (1978) indicates that GRIT strategies are effective in defusing hostilities and that it does facilitate compromise solutions to conflict situations.

Occasionally bargainers reach an impasse. Although they do not want to break off the bargaining process because each stands to benefit in some way from an agreement, neither party is willing to make a further concession. In this situation the impasse may be due to the fact that too large a package of issues is involved. A narrowing down of the issues of bargaining, referred to as *salami tactics,* may break the impasse and move the parties to an agreement. When the Soviet Union and the United States first began to explore the possibility of nuclear disarmament, Kremlin propanganda expressed the desire to negotiate total disarmament. It soon became evident that the technical, economic, and political problems associated with such a massive undertaking were too complex to resolve. An attempt to halt the nuclear arms race by zeroing in on limiting production and deployment of specific kinds of weapons has led to two Strategic Arms Limitations treaties (SALT) between the nations and the prospect for continuing negotiations on arms limitation. No one discusses disarmament any more except as a long-term and even utopian goal.

Alternatively, enlarging the number of values at issue may on occasion facilitate the bargaining process. During the Cuban missile crisis one suggestion (by Adlai Stevenson) was that the United States offer to dismantle its missiles forming a rim on the Turkish-Russian border in exchange for the removal of Soviet missiles from Cuba. Members of Congress are often quoted as attempting to increase the issues involved in the bargaining process, but often in a way likely to hinder progress toward an agreement. For example, it has been suggested that the sale of wheat to the Soviet Union or the Salt II agreement be conditional upon the release of all dissidents from that country.

TARGET CHARACTERISTICS AND REACTIONS TO INFLUENCE

The personality and past experience of the target may predispose him or her to be susceptible or resistant to the various manipulative tactics used by the bargaining opponent. A person's self-esteem represents a bias in his or her expectations of receiving benefits and punishments from others. Low self-esteem persons may generally believe they will be disliked and punished by others, while high self-esteem persons may expect that others will approve of and reward them. Research reported by Lindskold and Tedeschi (1971) indicated that high self-esteem subjects were more willing to respond cooperatively with a promisor than were low self-esteem subjects. Although low self-esteem persons are apt to be more self-destructive in their responses to threats, high self-esteem persons may be more compliant when it is in their best practical interests to do so.

A tendency to behave in a way that relies upon the good will and positive intentions of the other party displays the trust of a bargainer. Often the initial stages to bargaining may induce either trust or distrust that will affect the entire process(Deutsch, 1958; Rapoport and Chammah, 1965). As we saw earlier, Osgood's GRIT strategy was designed to initiate a bargaining process with a modicum of initial trust. However, Schlenker et al. (1973) have shown that positive initiatives can break a cycle of distrust and attempted exploitation can destroy trust. Although trust can ameliorate conflict and facilitate bargaining, it is not a necessary factor. The argument that one cannot make treaties with the Russians because they cannot be trusted ignores the fact that one can audit them or maintain surveillance over their actions and hence be assured that the terms are being kept. In much the same way, a bank does not trust its tellers; an auditor checks their records.

It can be disadvantageous to place adversaries in the position of protecting, defending, or reasserting an identity that is important to them. Most people want to maintain an image of competence, kindness, and strength. To embarrass them or to challenge that identity may bring about strong and negative reactions. A person will often endure great deprivation and sacrifice to restore face. Often negotiations take place in secret to eliminate the concern of the participants for their public images. Also, each bargainer would prefer that the other not make a public commitment to any particular position prior to the conclusion of an agreement, since it would make it more difficult for the other to make subsequent concessions.

Targets may be concerned with not appearing to appease the demands of their adversaries, since to do so would only encourage them to make even stronger demands. As Heywood Broun said, "appeasers believe that if you keep on throwing steaks to a tiger, the tiger will become a vegetarian" (cited by Yutang, 1942:268). A concern about appearing to be an appeaser, as conveying an image of weakness and lack of resolve, may bring swift retaliation and an unreasoning inflexibility in the bargaining posture of the embarrassed party.

As we have seen, there are a multitude of direct influence tactics available to the parties in bargaining and negotiations. The more subtle and less direct tactics may involve nonverbal communications, image management, and attempts to change the affective relationship between the parties.

INDIRECT MODES OF INFLUENCE IN BARGAINING

Less direct forms of influence include acquiring those resources or reputational attributes that make direct influence attempts more successful. Various forms of ingratiation and self-presentation contribute to the development of these power bases.

ACQUISITION OF BASES OF POWER

Influence may take the form of strengthening the bases of power that indirectly contribute to the success of influence attempts. Several source characteristics may be considered as bases of power (French and Raven, 1959), including possession of resources and the resolve to use them (prestige), the role position of authority the source has in relation to the target (status), special education, experience, or ability (esteem), and how much the target likes the source (attraction). By engaging in activities to bolster his or her prestige, status, esteem, or attractiveness, the source can indirectly enhance his or her power over the target.

Control over material resources in bargaining situations provides sources with the ability to back up their threats, keep their promises, and acquire knowledge and skills. Targets are unlikely to believe the sources' communications if the latter do not appear to possess or have access to the kinds of resources their threats and/or promises require, no matter how high the sources' credibility. Another effect of possessing the relevant resources is that targets may attribute a higher resolve to use them to the source. In general, the greater a source's prestige, the more likely it is the target will acquiesce to influence attempts. Because bargainers generally are aware of this relationship, each may engage in activities to convince the other than he or she possesses great resources. Thus, a salesperson picks up a client in a large and expensive automobile, is dressed in expensive clothes, and wears large and conspicuous jewelry. The appearance that one presents to others conveys an identity, which has important consequences for subsequent interaction.

Status requires deference from others. Bargainers are typically concerned not to allow apparent status differences to emerge in their relationship. Nevertheless, bargainers may attempt to claim status either directly or implicitly through the appearance or demeanor they adopt. Distinctive modes of dress or association with various symbols may convey status. For example, in the military the hierarchy of authority is associated with modes of dress and insignias. Bargainers may be polite to one another but they will usually refrain from any appearance of deference to one another. During World War II Stalin, Churchill, and Roosevelt negotiated in a room with three doors so they could all enter it at the same time—in this way each could avoid deciding who would enter the room first. In the same vein, the shape of the table to be used in negotiations between the North Vietnamese and the Americans in Paris was a matter of dispute because seating at the usual rectangular conference table might confer status to a particular delegation (Rosenfeld and Riess, 1979). The compromise solution was to use a round table.

It is well established that the expertise of a source of persuasion renders advice more believable. One would be at a serious disadvantage in bargaining that involved technical issues or problems on which the adversary was more expert. For example, an uneducated layman might be vulnerable to the sales pitch of an expert in art who is trying to sell a painting. In most negotiations, however, each side will usually include among their number delegates who possess whatever relevant expertise is needed to evaluate the issues.

Presumably it would be easier to be tough toward someone you dislike than someone you like. If so, it would be beneficial to cultivate a positive relationship with potential bargaining partners. Research has established that attractiveness of the source makes it more probable that a target will succumb to influence attempts. People who like one another are more likely to be cooperative and trusting, as well as less likely to use coercion against one another (Tedeschi et al., 1973). It should not be surprising, therefore, that persons who expect to interact with one another in situations where exchanges of rewards occur will attempt to establish at least a cordial and friendly relationship.

INGRATIATION

When persons deliberately foster liking for themselves in order to benefit through successful manipulation of others we speak of *ingratiation*. Among the tactics of ingratiation are flattery or enhancement of the other, self-enhancing statements, and conformity ingratiation (Jones, 1964). Each of these tactics is meant to transmit an image of the source as a kind, friendly, and intelligent person. Complimenting others tends to produce the intended effect because of a general and perhaps universal norm of reciprocity which stipulates that one ought to return positive acts of others (Gouldner, 1960). Other enhancing communications can have the effect of bringing about undeserved rewards and possibly better outcomes to the ingratiator (Kipnis and Vanderveer, 1971).

When sources publicize their own positive traits, they attempt to create an impression of worthiness. By associating self-enhancing communications with deprecation of others, they may indicate that they are more desirable bargaining "partners" than more undesirable others. Also, if targets are positively impressed by the sources, they may be led to respect sources opinions and be more susceptible to their influence attempts.

A well-known principle in the study of interpersonal attraction is that similarity of attitudes and values is associated with liking (Newcomb, 1961; Byrne, 1969). An ingratiator who is intuitively aware of this relationship may try to reap the indirect influence benefits from being liked by expressing attitudes similar to those of another person. Of course, it is necessary not to be too obvious about opinion conformity. The ingratiator may reflect back an opinion that supports an attitude expressed by the other person without directly repeating what has already been said. There are times when a bargainer may want to appear tough and strong rather than likeable and kind. Earlier we saw that if a tough strategy of initial bids and few concessions works, the bargainer stands to gain more, although the probability of reaching an agreement is reduced. There are actions that can be taken outside the bargaining relationship to establish a reputation for toughness. The history of individuals' behavior in past bargaining situations, how they have reacted to crises and coercion, the kinds of commitments they have made, and their record as credible influencers all contribute to an image of no-nonsense, tough bargainers. This image can, of course, backfire, in that it also encourages adversaries to take a tough stance to offset what is expected to be a difficult bargaining process. Diplomats view negotiations for the Soviet Union as very tough and hence almost always expect that discussions on any issues will be protracted and difficult.

SELF-PRESENTATION

Concerns for face are not reserved for citizens of the Orient. According to Ikle (1964), the role of reputation, firmness, bluff, and other "face" considerations are important factors in international negotiations. He noted that "bargaining strength depends not so much on what these [reputational] attributes really are as on what other believe them to be" (1964:76). To back down from a test of strength when it is appropriate or to allow one's bluffs to be called without acting is to admit strategic inferiority. An essential characteristic of face-saving behavior, according to Brown (1977), is that it is "future-oriented and offensive" and directed toward preventing any appearance of vulnerability.

Specific actions that may be taken to protect, increase, and/or demonstrate one's strength include allocating, mobilizing, or deploying resources and thus increasing one's prestige. In addition, staging of demonstrations, such as military parades, or other public displays of military strength constitute large-scale actions that can be taken to project an image of strength and determination.

Bargainers are not only concerned with how each perceives the other, but constituencies and other audiences may be observing their conduct. Significant audiences may control important reinforcements for bargainers and hence they may be more concerned with the audience's image of them than with the consequences of the bargaining process. It might be

suggested that negotiators for totalitarian nations are freer of face concerns regarding their publics than are negotiators from democratic nations.
The reason for this difference is that the latter are subject to recall or
reelection and the former are not.

THIRD PARTY INTERVENTION

An impartial third party may help bargainers reach a settlement after an
impasse has been reached and neither believes further concessions are
likely to be made. According to Tedeschi and Lindskold (1976), a mediator may have the following effects on the bargaining process:

> (1) he modifies the perceived meaning of concessions; (2) he causes
> both parties to shift their levels of aspiration; (3) he allows one or
> both parties to save face; and (4) he introduces norms of equity,
> fairness, and justice into the bargaining process [1976:389].

When a concession is made at the suggestion of a mediator, it is not
likely to be perceived as a sign of weakness, nor is it made necessarily with
an expectation of a reciprocal concession. Instead, the concessions made
under the auspices of a mediator may be perceived as bringing about a fair
solution to the bargaining problem. The mediator is not only perceived as
impartial but as having the information available to both sides in the
dispute. For these reasons his or her suggestions about compromises may
be perceived by both bargainers as fair. Thus, levels of aspiration may be
revised accordingly and an agreement reached.

Standards of morality or abstract concepts of justice may be used by a
mediator to convince bargainers or constituencies of negotiators' reasonableness in a particular agreement. The effectiveness of such exhortations
and moral suasion depend on the values of the bargainers and the degree to
which they share cultural norms. One of the problems associated with
moral suasion is that for every norm there is a competing norm and that
bargainers may have competing interpretations of the same norm. Under
these conditions a mediator may help the bargainers reach a split-the-
difference solution and break an impasse in bargaining.

CONCLUSION

Social psychological theories of bargaining have focused upon the
structure of bargaining situations, limited strategies, and norms in situations of restricted communications. However, as we have seen, communi-

cations serve critical functions in bargaining. Of paramount concern to the bargainers is the identity or image they present to the adversary. It is important to appear tough but flexible and fair. The bargainer may attempt to be conciliatory without transmitting the image of an appeaser. While bargainers are tempted to bluff or use decit or coercion to gain their objectives, they are frequently deterred from such tactics by a concern for losing credibility and a fear of retaliation and subsequent escalation of mutually costly actions.

It is our belief that influence communications and strategies in the bargaining process, along with self-presentation or impression management concerns, have been relatively ignored by social scientists. While structural factors are undoubtedly important to understanding the course of bargaining and the eventual agreement that is reached, dynamic factors of power and influence are probably just as important. It can be expected that future research will further expand the laboratory paradigms for studying bargaining to include all forms of communications.

REFERENCES

BARTOS, O.J. (1974). Process and outcome of negotiations. New York: Columbia University Press.
BROWN, B.R. (1977). "Face-saving and face-restoration in negotiation." In D. Druckman, (ed.), Negotiations: Social-psychological perspectives. Beverly Hills, CA: Sage.
BYRNE, D. (1969). "Attitudes and attraction." In L. Berkowitz (ed.), Advances in Experimental social psychology. New York: Academic Press.
CUMMINGS, L.L., and HARNETT, D.L. (1969). "Bargaining behavior in a symmetric bargaining triad." Review of Economic Studies, 36:485-501.
DEUTSCH, M. (1958). "Trust and suspicion." Journal of Conflict Resolution, 2:265-279.
––– CANAVAN, D., and RUBIN, J. (1971). "The effects of size of conflict and sex of experimenter upon interpersonal bargaining." Journal of Experimental Social Psychology, 7:258-267.
DRUCKMAN, D. (1977). Negotiations. Beverly Hills, CA: Sage.
EMERSON, R.M. (1962). "Power-dependence relations." American Sociological Review, 27:31-41.
FRENCH, J.R.P., JR., and RAVEN, B. (1959). "The bases of social power." In D. Cartwright (ed.), Studies in social power. Ann Arbor: Institute for Social Research.
GOULDNER, A.W. (1960). "The norm of reciprocity: A preliminary statement." American Sociological Review, 25:161-179.
HARNETT, D.L., and CUMMINGS, L.I. (1968). "Bargaining behavior in an asymmetric triad: The role of information, communication, and risk-taking propensity." (unpublished)
HARSANYI, J.C. (1962). "Measurement of social power, opportunity costs, and the theory of two-person bargaining games." Behavioral Science, 7:67-80.

HORAI, J., LINDSKOLD, S., GAHAGAN, J., and TEDESCHI, J. (1969). "The effects of conflict intensity and promisor credibility on a target's behavior." Psychonomic Science, 14:73-74, 76.

IKLE, F.D. (1964). How nations negotiate. New York: Praeger.

JONES, E.E. (1964). Ingratiation: A social psychological analysis. New York: Appleton-Century-Crofts.

KIPNIS, D., and VANDERVEER, R. (1971). "Ingratiation and the use of power." Journal of Personality and Social Psychology, 17:280-286.

KOMORITA, S.S., and BRENNER, A.R. (1968). "Bargaining and concession-making under bilateral monopoly." Journal of Personality and Social Psychology, 9:15-20.

KOMORITA, S.S., and CHERTKOFF, J.M. (1973). "A bargaining theory of coalition formation." Psychological Review, 80:149-162.

LINDSKOLD, S. (1978). "Trust development, the GRIT proposal, and the effects of conciliatory costs on conflict and cooperation." Psychological Bulletin, 85:772-793.

—— and TEDESCHI, J.T. (1971). "Self-esteem and sex as factors affecting influenceability." British Journal of Social and Clinical Psychology, 10:114-122.

MALLICK, S.K., and McCANDLESS, B.R. (1966). "A study of catharsis of aggression." Journal of Personality and Social Psychology, 4:591-596.

MICHENER, H.A., and SUCHNER, R.W. (1971). "The tactical use of social power." In J.T. Tedeschi (ed.), The social influence processes. Chicago: AVC.

NEWCOMB, J.M. (1961). The acquaintance process. New York: Holt, Rinehart & Winston.

NIEBURG, H.L. (1969). Political violence: The behavioral process. New York: St. Martin's Press.

OSGOOD, C.D. (1962). An alternative to war or surrender. Urbana: University of Illinois Press.

PASTORE, N. (1952). "The role of arbitrariness in the frustration-aggression hypothesis." Journal of Abnormal and Social Psychology, 47:728-731.

PRUITT, D.L., and JOHNSON, D.F. (1970). "Mediation as an aid to face saving in negotiation." Journal of Personality and Social Psychology, 14:239-246.

RAPOPORT, A., and CHAMMAH, M. (1965). Prisoner's dilemma. Ann Arbor: University of Michigan Press.

ROSENFELD, P., and RIESS, M. (1979) "Seating arrangements as strategic self-presentations." Presented at the 50th Annual Meeting of the Eastern Psychological Association, Philadelphia.

RUBIN, J., and BROWN, B. (1975) The social psychology of bargaining and negotiation. New York: Academic Press.

SCHELLING, T.C. (1960). The strategy of conflict. New York: Oxford University Press.

SCHLENKER, B.R., HELM, B., and TEDESCHI, J.T. (1973). "The effects of personality and situational variables on behavioral trust." Journal of Personality and Social Psychology, 32:664-670.

SCHLENKER, B.R., NACCI, P., HELM, B., and TEDESCHI, J.T. (1976). "Reactions to coercive and reward power: The effects of switching influence modes on target compliance." Sociometry, 39:316-323.

SCOTT, M.B., and LYMAN, S.M. (1968) "Accounts." American Sociological Review, 33:46-62.

SIEGEL, S., and FOURAKER, L.E. (1960). Bargaining and group decision making. New York: McGraw-Hill.

SMITH, W.P. (1968). "Reward structure and information in the development of cooperation." Journal of Experimental Social Psychology, 4:199-223.

TEDESCHI, J.T., and LINDSKOLD, S. (1976). Social psychology: Interdependence, interaction and influence. New York: John Wiley.

––– BONOMA, T.V., and NOVINSON, N. (1970). "Behavior of a threatener: Relation vs. fixed opportunity costs." Journal of Conflict Resolution, 14:69-76.

TEDESCHI, J.T., HORAI, J., LINDSKOLD, S., and FALEY, T. (1970) "The effects of opportunity costs and target compliance on the behavior of a threatening source." Journal of Experimental Social Psychology, 6:205-213.

TEDESCHI, J.T., SCHLENKER, B.R., and BONOMA, T.V. (1973). Conflict, power, and games: The experimental study of interpersonal relations. Chicago: AVC.

TEDESCHI, J.T., LINDSKOLD, S., HORAI, J., and GAHAGAN, J. (1969). "Social power and the credibility of promises." Journal of Personality and Social Psychology, 13:253-261.

TEDESCHI, J.T., SMITH, R.B. III, and BROWN, R.C., JR. (1974). "A reinterpretation of research on aggression." Psychological Bulletin, 81:540-563.

VON NEUMANN, J., and MORGENSTERN, O. (1944). Theory of games and economic behavior. New York: John Wiley.

WALTON, R.E., and McKERSIE, R.B. (1965). A behavioral theory of labor negotiations. New York: McGraw-Hill.

YUTANG, L. (1942). The wisdom of China and India. New York: Random House.

Chapter 9

PERSUASION DURING THE TRIAL PROCESS

Norman E. Fontes and Robert W. Bundens

THE LEGAL SYSTEM, like a ship's anchor, never touches bottom to stop social evolution, but thumps and drags along tempering change so it proceeds in an orderly fashion. The system has been forced to assume a diverse, peculiar array of conflict-resolution responsibilities which far exceed the problems it was initially intended to resolve. Moreover, from the layperson's perspective, the legal system is a mysterious entity shrouded in complexity whose tentacles seem to permeate all aspects of our lives.

Clearly, our society needs a legal system to ensure that conflict is resolved in a civilized manner. It must be a democratic system that facilitates participation by all segments of society in the jurisprudence process. It must guarantee societal members fair, just, moral, and humane treatment under the law and ensure that when basic human rights are violated, a civilized means of recourse is available to rectify social inequities. The legal system must symbolize to the masses that justice is possible in a complex society composed of competing forces seeking equality.

Unfortunately, the jurisprudence process—particularly the court system—has been unable to process the increasing number of disputes submitted for resolution. Legal experts have been aware of this problem for some time and have attempted to develop alternative conflict-resolution forums for settling disputes normally adjudicated in the courtroom (Johnson et al., 1977). Even though these alternative forums for conflict resolution promise heightened administrative efficiency and perhaps even better deliverance of justice, they also further illuminate the inability of the courts to process the number of cases requiring formal settlement. Although it is tempting to invoke one of the less meaningful diagnostic clichés available to communication scholars, namely *information overload,* as the primary reason for this problem, it would constitute a gross oversimplification of the problem.

The courts are indeed a complex, overworked component of the legal system. The scope of what the courts have been directed to address is so broad that their effectiveness has been jeopardized. They have been forced to process the products of poverty and misery without being equipped with the resources to eliminate the social inequities that produce most crime. For example, it is not within the professional province of the courts to deal with alcoholism, drug addiction, or compulsive gamblers; yet, because of the crimes that are frequently committed by individuals with these physical and psychological problems, the courts are forced to become involved.

Crimes against property contribute substantially to the case overload of courts. People seek equality, and the motivational level to achieve social and economic parity with others is positively correlated with the perceived deprivation experienced: the more severe the deprivation, the greater the motivation to achieve social and economic equality. This assertion is partially substantiated by the widespread rioting and looting in major metropolitan areas during periods of racial unrest or electrical blackouts. Until the social problems contributing to poverty are eradicated, we can expect crimes against property to dominate court caseloads. More stringent enforcement of laws governing the protection of property will only add to the number of cases that must be processed.

Civil disputes also contribute heavily to the number of cases that must be processed. A prime example can be found in the negligence issue associated with automobile accident litigation. Tragically, the victims of these accidents may have to wait years to realize social and economic compensation for losses sustained as a result of accidents. Fortunately, the adoption of no-fault insurance by many states has removed most of these cases from the courts, providing more immediate relief to the victims and relieving some of the caseload pressure.

Unfortunately, these types of cases are quickly being replaced by others. For example, the number of medical malpractice suits submitted to the courts for resolution has grown astronomically in recent years.

Undoubtedly, some medical practitioners do commit serious errors; either through ignorance, carelessness, or both, and their victims deserve immediate relief. Typically, however, time involved in formal litigation does not permit immediate relief to those who most need help. Moreover, the threat of legal action has dramatically added to the cost of medical malpractice insurance, adversely affecting the health delivery system by increasing the costs of medical care. Not only are physicians charging more for their services, the number of diagnostic tests administered to patients has soared in response to the threat of malpractice suits. The continually increasing number and ever-changing types of cases undoubtedly have contributed to the diminished effectiveness of the court system.

There may be another yet factor that militates against the information-processing efficiency of the court system. Former Supreme Court Justice Tom Clark made the following observation to one of the authors during a personal conversation in January 1975:

> Most trial attorneys are knowledgeable of the law. Many, however, don't communicate well in the courtroom. They don't know how to construct persuasive oral arguments and don't know what kinds of techniques influence a judge or jury, so they try all sorts of things and take up a lot of time sometimes getting both themselves and their clients in trouble.

Justice Clark suggested that communication scholars could help improve the quality of justice and the efficiency of the court system by providing legal practitioners with knowledge that would improve their ability to adequately represent their clients and reduce the amount of trial time consumed by a "shotgun" approach to influencing the trier(s)-of-fact in a trial.

The purpose of the following discussion is to provide a general overview of a significant information-processing problem confronting the court system that communication scholars can help resolve. Although communication scientists can do little to influence the number and types of cases submitted to the courts for adjudication, they are especially qualified to assess the effectiveness of the various persuasive techniques used by legal practitioners within the context of the trial process. This knowledge would be extremely useful in the education of law students as well as practicing attorneys. The use of ineffective persuasive strategies could be reduced, producing a savings in trial time while enhancing the ability of attorneys to competently represent their clients.

From the legal perspective, the trial process has been characterized in many different ways by numerous individuals. Sigler (1968:119) defined a trial in the following manner:

The trial is a formal event prescribed by law, as an official, socially sanctioned manner of determining facts, applying law to the facts, and pronouncing an official conclusion, called a *verdict*. In the simplest, and most common situation, the verdict as an output terminates the dispute for all official purposes.

From a communication perspective, a trial can be considered a dynamic, rule-governed, persuasive proceeding in which information is the primary commodity processed. Once a trial commences, it becomes a *theoretically* closed system because no information capable of biasing jurors which emanates from external sources such as the mass media is allowed to enter the system. In principle, all of the information exchanged is generated by participants within the trial process.

Generally, a judge, two or more attorneys, one or more plaintiffs, one or more defendants, witnesses, and jurors constitute the interactants in the system. The role of the trial judge as it is currently conceived may be impossible to fulfill. The judge is supposed to be both a neutral umpire, ensuring that the rules of the adversary process are not violated, and an active seeker of the truth. These conflicting demands almost require a trial judge to play active and passive trial roles simultaneously. The problematic nature of the judge's role during a trial is exacerbated by a reasonable concern among judges that the remarks they make during the course of a trial and/or the questions they ask of witnesses or litigants may have a disproportionate impact upon jurors. Frankel (1975:1042-1043) argues that it is unusual for a trial judge

> to present or meaningfully to "comment upon" the evidence. As a result, his interruptions are just that—interruptions; occasional, unexpected, sporadic, unprogrammed, and unduly dramatic because they are dissonant and out of character. The result—to focus upon the jury trial, the model for our system, including, of course, its rules of evidence—is that the judge's participation, whether in the form of questions or comments, is likely to have a disproportionate and distorting impact. The jury is likely to discern limits, a point of view, a suggested direction, even if none is intended and quite without regard to the judge's efforts to modulate and minimize his role. Whether the jury follows the seeming lead or recoils from it is not critical. The point is that there has been a deviant influence, justified neither in adversary principles nor in the rational competence of the trial judge to exert it.

The persuasive impact of the communicative behaviors of a trial judge upon the jury during the trial process remains an empirical question—one communication scholars are qualified to answer.

Of course, the role of the judge is intimately related to the behavior of the attorneys during a given trial. The goal of advocates in the adversary process "is to win if possible without violating the law" (Frankel, 1975:1037). The net result is that attorneys employ all of the legal persuasive means to win their cases. This persuasive effort to influence jurors may commence with the *voir dire* proceedings, continue during the trial, and reach fruition during deliberation proceedings.

A model has been developed for the purpose of clarifying what is meant by the term *trial process* (see Figure 1). Obviously, any static model of a dynamic process runs the risk of distortion resulting from oversimplification of the phenomenon being modeled. The trial is indeed a complex process, and our attempt to present a clear "picture" of the process has necessitated some simplifications. It is hoped that the degree of distortion introduced by these simplifications has been minimal. Some of the persuasive techniques used by attorneys during *voir dire* proceedings and trials will be discussed. In addition, some issues concerning persuasion during deliberation proceedings will be explored.

PERSUASION DURING THE *VOIR DIRE*

The *voir dire* is a concept central to the issue of trial by jury. The purported objective of the *voir dire* is to impanel a fair and impartial jury to function as triers-of-fact in a trial. In some jurisdictions, the trial judge conducts the examination of the prospective jurors, which allows attorneys only limited participation, while in other court jurisdictions attorneys have the primary responsibility for screening jurors. There is disagreement among legal practitioners concerning the value of the *voir dire*. According to F. Lee Bailey (cited by Kahn, 1974:1), jury selection is a very subjective enterprise: "Frankly, it's random guessing. Like spinning a roulette wheel. It is the most unscientific part of any trial." Some jurists subscribe to the position that it is impossible to identify biased jurors by questioning them. Consequently, these practitioners are willing to accept any 12 reasonable venirepersons and assume they will be impartial and fair.

Morrill (1972:1) believes the *voir dire* is an essential element of the trial process and is critical of attorneys who downplay its importance:

There are only two reasons for a lawyer to take such a position: either he is lacking in aptitude for jury trial work or he has had little or no trial experience. . . . Successful trial lawyers who have learned and applied the subtleties of proven techniques in the battle of jury persuasion give this phase of the lawsuit first priority.

Figure 1   A Three-Stage Model of the Trial Process

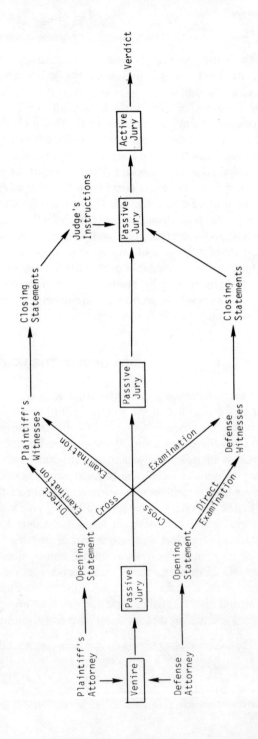

The purpose of the *voir dire,* for attorneys who agree with Morrill's position, is to impanel jurors who will be favorably biased toward their clients' cases; and when this objective cannot be realized, to impanel jurors who will not be biased against their cases.

Many different persuasion techniques are utilized by attorneys during the *voir dire* process; however, our discussion will be restricted to ingratiation and immunization strategies. Attorneys sometimes decline the opportunity to question venirepersons in a manner intended to ingratiate themselves with prospective jurors (Blunk and Sales, 1977). In doing so, they emphasize that they are confident the jurors will arrive at a fair and just verdict decision. The rhetorical ploy lurking behind this grand gesture, of course, is an attempt by attorneys to make themselves more attractive to the prospective jurors and bias them toward their cases.

Jones (1964) has conducted considerable research concerning the use of ingratiation. Essentially, the use of this strategy entails conferring esteem on another individual for the purpose of securing a desired benefit from the targeted individual. This strategy can backfire if it is obvious to a message recipient that manipulation is associated with the act of conferring esteem. Jones and Wortman (1973) labeled this phenomenon the "ingratiator's dilemma." While some attorneys believe this strategy is an effective method of influencing prospective jurors during *voir dire* proceedings, we are unaware of any research evaluating its effects in a legal setting.

Immunization strategies, including anchoring and commitment techniques, are also used during the questioning of prospective jurors. Both are techniques for inducing resistance to persuasion. Their effectiveness is based upon a cognitive consistency assumption that individuals have a need to maintain consistency among internal beliefs, verbal statements, and observable behavior. By manipulating the relationships among these three factors, a persuader can render a persuadee resistant to persuasive appeals originating from other persuaders. Within the legal setting specifically, an attorney may utilize one or more of these techniques to immunize jurors against persuasive arguments that will be articulated by the opponent during a trial.

Morrill (1972) discusses a number of different types of commitments that attorneys might seek from prospective jurors during the *voir dire,* including commitment to follow the law, commitment to duty, and commitment to set aside prejudice. A considerable amount of attention has been devoted to commitment techniques (Cronkhite, 1969; Kiesler, 1968, 1971; Kiesler and Sakumura, 1966; McGuire, 1969). In their discussion of commitment techniques, Miller and Burgoon (1973) conclude that "the evidence clearly demonstrates that forcing a person to publicly commit himself to a belief is an effective way to increasing resistance to subsequent persuasive appeals" (p. 28).

A public commitment to follow the law is solicited from jurors in cases where preconceived notions and attitudes concerning applicable law may influence juror information-processing and decision-making behaviors. Given certain types of cases, jurors may feel the law governing the offense in question is not fair or just. An example provided by Morrill (1972:7) illustrates this point. A defendant accused of hitting a child who ran out from between parked cars might be at a decided disadvantage during a trial. Assuming the defendant indeed hit the child, jurors might ignore that element of the law concerning the degree of control parents must exercise over a child and find an innocent defendant guilty. The defense attorney utilizing a commitment technique under these circumstances would obtain a public commitment from prospective jurors to apply the relevant law in accordance with instructions from the trial judge. During his or her closing arguments, the attorney would then remind the jurors of the commitment each made during the *voir dire* proceedings.

Commitment to duty is an appeal generally used with jurors who have already served in other trials during their tour of duty. Morrill (1972:8) makes the following observation:

> Most people enter the jury box with a strong desire to discharge their function as jurors honorably and with fairness to both sides. With this noble attitude coupled with the austerity of the courtroom, these people are psychologically prepared to enter a verdict in spite of their natural prejudices or sympathies. This is especially true in the beginning days of their tour of duty. After they have decided a few cases, they become more accustomed to their surroundings, lose some of their laudable principles, and are less apt to be held in line because of their natural feelings to the contrary.

This analysis suggests that as jurors serve in repeated trials, they may become more susceptible to the persuasive manipulations of contesting attorneys who rely upon the use of emotional appeals rather than the facts in the case. Unfortunately, no data bearing upon this issue are available. However, attorneys who believe such increased susceptibility to be the case may counter this effect by evoking a public commitment from jurors to execute their roles with fairness to both sides. This strategy purportedly will reduce the impact of emotional appeals made by the opposing attorney. The effectiveness of this strategy within the legal context has not been empirically assessed.

The final commitment strategy to be examined is commitment to set aside prejudices. Attorneys normally have some knowledge concerning the verbal and nonverbal communicative skills of their clients and sometimes those of witnesses they will summon to testify during the trial. If a client possesses any potentially biasing characteristics "such as an irritating speaking voice, a speech impediment, a nervous twitch, facial disfigurement, or any other obvious problem, it should be commented upon to meet the needs" (Morrill, 1972:8). If a defendant is black, for example, racially biased jurors may decide he or she is not a credible person and dismiss the testimony provided by that defendant. Research by Sunnafrank and Fontes (1979) suggests this is a possibility since individuals possess crime-specific ethnic stereotypes. Blacks are perceived as more likely than whites to engage in soliciting, assault-mugging, grand theft auto, and assault on a police officer. Embezzlement, child molestation, counterfeiting, fraud, and rape are perceived as crimes more likely to be committed by whites than blacks. The extent to which the influence of racial bias can be counteracted by obtaining public commitments from jurors has not been tested in a legal setting.

Anchoring techniques (Abelson and Rosenberg, 1958; Bennett, 1955; Carlson, 1956; McGuire, 1969) are also employed by attorneys during *voir dire* proceedings. These techniques, like commitment strategies, are employed by an attorney to induce resistance to persuasive appeals that may be made by the opposing attorney during the course of the trial. The use of anchoring techniques involves the linking of beliefs to other beliefs already held by a persuadee; the persuadee's values and goals; or other salient individuals or groups (McGuire, 1969). The primary distinction between these techniques and commitment strategies is that no public verbal statement is solicited from persuadees. A few examples will illustrate how these techniques can be employed.

Assume an attorney is defending a teenage client charged with reckless driving and the attorney subscribes to Morrill's (1972) belief that older jurors may be biased against teenage drivers. Anticipating arguments from the prosecuting attorney during the trial that draw attention to the age of the defendant, the defense attorney may attempt to immunize jurors against these arguments by appealing to a widely held belief that any American citizen accused of a crime is innocent until proven guilty and is entitled to a fair trial. The defendant, while an adolescent, is a citizen and is entitled to the same constitutionally guaranteed safeguards afforded adults in our society.

Another approach which could be used by the defense attorney is linking a venireperson's goal of satisfying a segment of his or her civic responsibility through jury duty to the belief that all defendants deserve a fair trial. Continuing with the teenage driver example, the defense attorney might argue that fulfillment of civic responsibility as a juror is determined by the degree of fairness exhibited while serving in a trial. Jurors biased by the defendant's age obviously could not render a fair and just verdict and consequently would not satisfy the civic responsibility entrusted to them.

The last anchoring approach to be discussed for use during the *voir dire* is an appeal focusing upon relationships with valued others. There are many types of relationships that can be used in an appeal of this nature, including those with family members, friends, or coworkers. The defense attorney in our example might appeal to the jurors' desire to be respected by their own adolescents and those of their friends. The attorney might argue this respect would be jeopardized by any unfair treatment afforded his or her teenage client by the jurors. Many adolescents have a negative impression of the "establishment" and individuals perceived to be part of it, which might be reinforced by jurors' biased treatment of teenage defendants.

The courtroom effectiveness of this persuasion strategy, as well as the others discussed, should be empirically evaluated. The knowledge generated would prove useful in the education of law students and legal practitioners. Moreover, it is possible that time could be saved during the trial process if it is demonstrated that the use of these strategies does not influence jurors. Specifically, attorneys might spend less time attempting to manipulate jurors at this stage of the trial process.

PERSUASION DURING THE TRIAL

A complex, interrelated set of variables undoubtedly operates during the course of a trial influencing jurors' evaluations of trial participants and the veracity of testimony presented. Rather than presenting a comprehensive overview of the research conducted to date, our attention will be restricted to two variables which have received limited attention within the legal context: the influence of *communicator style* and *language intensity* upon juror information-processing and decision-making behaviors.

The communicator style of attorney and trial participants may contribute to or detract from the persuasive impact of arguments and testimony presented during a trial. As Miller and Burgoon (1978) have observed, this potentially significant construct has received limited attention from persuasion researchers and little is known about its role in the persuasion process. Norton (1977) defined communicator style in terms of 12 variables or components: dominant, dramatic, contentious, animated, impression-leaving, relaxed, attentive, open, friendly, precise, voice, and communicator image. These dimensions were used by Norton (1977) to identify communicative style characteristics of effective teachers. Those teachers who were attentive, impression-leaving, relaxed, friendly, and precise were seen as being more effective than teachers not exhibiting these characteristics. In the courtroom setting, the communicative style that an attorney or witness should exhibit to maximize his or her persuasive ability remains to be determined. It seems entirely plausible that the framework developed by Norton may be extremely useful in determining what that style might be.

Giles and Powesland (1975:111) raised a number of specific unanswered questions concerning the role of communicator style within the legal setting:

> Is evidence by standard speakers generally regarded by courts as more reliable and substantial than evidence given by nonstandard speaking witnesses? Are juries prejudiced by the speech style of accused persons? How does the speech style of a lawyer affect his advocacy?

The importance of the potential influence of the communicator style variable has been recognized by social psychologists and communication scholars, as evidenced by the care given to control this variable in much of the research completed thus far concerning the trial process.

Research which has examined the influence of dimensions of communicator style in contexts other than a legal setting has produced some rather intriguing results. A study completed by Harms (1961) demonstrates that listeners are able to identify the status of speakers after hearing 10 to 15 seconds of speech. Moreover, listeners' perceptions of the credibility of speakers was influenced by the inferred status, with high-status sources being evaluated as more credible than low-status sources. Hopper and Williams (1973) demonstrated that employers' hiring decisions are influenced by the speech characteristics of job seekers.

O'Barr et al. (1974) identified four different linguistic components of communicator style used in courtroom settings: (1) formal legal language, (2) formal standard English, (3) colloquial or casual English, and (4) subcultural varieties of English. The researchers provided the following conceptual descriptions for these styles. Formal legal language encompasses standardized terminology used in the jurisprudence process. It is normally used when the judge is reading the charge against the defendant, giving jury instructions, pronouncing judgments, and so forth. Formal standard English is grammatically and lexically correct language usage. Casual English is a simplified form of formal English characterized by the use of relatively simple syntax and a more restricted vocabulary. Subcultural varieties of English include ethnic dialects and dialects spoken by poorly educated individuals. O'Barr et al. determined that while lawyers use formal legal language and casual English, they most frequently use formal standard English. Many witnesses employ or attempt to employ formal standard English when testifying in court. Some witnesses lack the ability to use standard English because of educational limitations or because they speak a dialect. While the researchers indicate that phonological differences exist among the latter three styles, they did not specify what the nature of these differences were, nor did they discuss possible differences in the persuasive impact of these phonological variations.

Some legal practitioners believe their ability to influence jurors is enhanced by adapting their style to that used by witnesses being questioned. These attorneys are convinced that stylistic adaptations result in questions being phrased in a manner easily understood by witnesses, who do a more adequate job of providing the information solicited, which thereby increases the probability of achieving the desired persuasive impact upon jurors. It is also conceivable that the influence of a witness' testimony can be diminished by deliberately using a style that is difficult for the witness to comprehend. A witness struggling to respond to questions not totally understood may contradict himself or herself or provide erroneous information that reduces jurors' consideration of the testimony provided. These are empirical issues meriting the attention of persuasion researchers.

Another potentially influential factor operating in the courtroom is the language intensity associated with the communicative behaviors of attorneys and witnesses. The construct of language intensity has received considerable attention from persuasion researchers. Bowers (1963:345) conceptually defined it as "the quality of language which indicates the degree to which the speaker's attitude toward the concept deviates from neutrality." Television presentations of courtroom drama typically involve intense verbal exchanges between attorneys and witnesses. These dramatizations are significant departures from the mundane nature of most trials. Observations of juror deliberation proceedings included in research by Miller and Fontes (1978, in press) clearly indicated many jurors' expectations concerning attorney and witness behavior during trials were influenced by televised legal dramatizations. Specifically, the performance of witnesses and attorneys were compared with the communicative behaviors of actors in dramatized trial proceedings.

This observation has some interesting implications for persuasion research. It may be the case that attorneys who fail to behave in a dramatic manner which includes the use of intense language during opening statements, interrogation of witnesses, and closing arguments compromise their persuasive impact by violating juror expectations. Even though the findings from prior research examining the relationship between language intensity and persuasion have been generally consistent, we can only speculate about the level of language intensity employed by an attorney and the influence exerted upon jurors.

McEwen and Greenberg (1970) demonstrated that a communicator's perceived credibility, at least on a dynamism dimension, can be enhanced through the use of intense language. Moreover, the communicator's message will be evaluated as being clearer and more intelligent than less intense messages. Bowers' (1963) findings indicate that highly intense language can precipitate a "boomerang effect" producing attitude change in a direction opposite that advocated by the message source. Burgoon and King (1974) produced similar results, and concluded that messages containing highly intense language will produce boomerang effects in *passive* message recipients.

Burgoon et al. (1975) suggest that the effects of language intensity upon attitude change are influenced by the expectations message recipients have of communication sources. If the level of language intensity employed by a persuader violates a persuadee's expectations in a positive manner, attitude change in the direction advocated by the source will occur. For example, used car salespersons are stereotypically expected to use language of high intensity when attempting to sell automobiles. Their ability to influence customers might be enhanced by reducing the pressure of the sales appeal through the use of language of low intensity. In a similar vein, attorneys might increase their persuasive impact upon jurors by utilizing moderately intense language, assuming that this would constitute a positive violation of jurors' expectations.

Knowledge concerning the influence of varying levels of language intensity upon juror information processing would be extremely useful to trial attorneys. This information would allow attorneys to make more enlightened decisions concerning the choice of language used in constructing arguments during a trial.

PERSUASION DURING DELIBERATION PROCEEDINGS

The potential effects of the numerous variables discussed thus far converge when jurors assemble to deliberate and decide upon a group verdict. Although legal practitioners are interested in what transpires during deliberation proceedings, the processes involved in verdict determination remain shrouded in mystery. The controversy associated with Kalven and Zeisel's (1966) recording of live jury deliberations produced both American Bar Association sanctions and a federal law precluding this type of research activity. These restrictions have forced researchers to rely upon simulated jury deliberations for data. Because of this development and perhaps the financial and time resources required to investigate deliberation processes, a limited amount of research has been completed in this area. More specifically, little attention has been given to the persuasive roles jurors themselves might assume during deliberation proceedings.

The need for research focusing upon deliberation processes has been discussed by numerous researchers (Kalvan and Zeisel, 1966; Erlander, 1970; Walbert, 1971; Zeisel, 1973; Kessler, 1975). Our discussion of some of the research completed thus far will include studies concerning the selection of the jury foreperson and his or her influence during deliberations, by the influence of the trial judge, and the types of information considered by jurors during their discussions.

Upon entering the deliberation room, jurors select a foreperson who assumes the leadership responsibility for the group and is the spokesperson for the jurors to the court. The foreperson is responsible for polling the jurors to assess individual juror verdicts. If any additional information is required from the court, the jury's request is directed through the foreperson to the judge.

The potential persuasive impact of the foreperson upon other jurors is significant in view of the central role he or she occupies. Research by Hawkins (1960, cited in Kessler, 1975) suggests that little consideration is given to the selection of the jury foreperson. Jurors who participated in Hawkins' research rarely sought the position and occasionally the individual who initiated discussion of the need to select a foreperson was chosen. At other times, when a juror was nominated, he or she was elected without controversy. In the initial stages of the deliberation proceedings, the forepersons dominated communicative transactions among jurors. As time progressed, however, the contributions made more closely approximated those of other jurors. Consequently, the amount of influence exerted by the jury forepersons was not a major determinant of the final verdict reached.

Research reported by Strodtbeck et al. (1957) and Miller and Fontes (1978, in press) produced findings suggesting that jury forepersons do exert a significant persuasive influence during deliberation proceedings. Strodtbeck et al.'s study indicates that jury forepersons are indeed selected in a casual manner with a predominant number coming from higher status socioeconomic groups. Among those juries having higher status forepersons, a strong, significant relationship was found between forepersons' predeliberation verdicts and the final jury verdicts. These individuals were quite dominant during the deliberations, as evidenced by the number of communication acts engaged in by jury forepersons. Approximately 25 percent of the total communication during deliberations involving higher status forepersons were attributable to these forepersons.

Findings from a study reported by Miller and Fontes (1978, in press) are consistent with those of Strodtbeck et al. Their research indicates that jury forepersons exert a significant impact upon the final decision reached during jury deliberations. Jurors in their study participated in a trial concerning an automobile accident case in which the defendant was admittedly at fault. The plaintiff was suing for damages to her back allegedly sustained as a result of the accident. The defense argued that the back condition resulted from a previous back injury, inadequate medical treatment, the plaintiff's failure to follow her physician's instructions, and the plaintiff's obesity. The strongest predictors of the award made by jurors were individual predeliberation awards and the influence of the jury foreperson during deliberations.

We are not suggesting that jurors are not influenced by other factors during deliberations. O'Mara (1972) determined through the use of post-deliberation questionnaires that jurors could be influenced by the trial judge's demeanor and attempt to return a verdict that would satisfy him or her. Broeder (1959) discovered that jurors disregard the judge's deliberation instructions and develop their own legal criteria for adjudicating cases. While studies of this nature shed some light on the persuasive influences operating during deliberation proceedings, they fall short of providing insight into the types of information focused upon during deliberation discussions.

More research such as that executed by James (1959) and Hawkins (1960, cited in Kessler, 1975) is needed to gain a better understanding of persuasion which transpires during deliberation proceedings. James recorded the deliberations of 10 juries and content analyzed them. She found that jurors devoted approximately 50 percent of their discussion to personal experiences and opinions tangentially or indirectly related to issues raised during the trial. Twenty-five percent of their communication concerned procedural matters while 15 percent of the deliberation transactions focused upon factual evidence. Discussions of the deliberation instructions accounted for 8 percent of juror communication (James, 1959:565).

Hawkins (1960, cited in Kessler, 1975) determined that the kinds of decisions required of jurors influence the types of persuasion employed during deliberations. Verdict judgments are generally dichotomous decisions leaving little room for negotiation and compromise. Consequently, jurors are inclined to employ very direct persuasive messages to garner support for their judgments. Damage award decisions normally encompass some monetary range and produce a different types of persuasive exchange among jurors, an exchange characterized by a greater willingness to negotiate and compromise. While these findings may not be earthshaking, they do draw attention to yet another variable capable of influencing juror communicative behaviors during deliberation proceedings. Of particular import from a persuasion perspective is the impact of speculative information offered by jurors during deliberations on verdict outcomes. The preliminary results of research by Miller and Fontes (1978, in press) focusing upon the persuasive activities of jurors during deliberations suggest that the influence of speculative information can have a significant impact upon verdict outcomes. Jurors participating in this study viewed a videotaped reenactment of an actual trial of a defendant charged with conversion of bank funds. Jurors deliberated after viewing the trial and these proceedings were videotaped without their knowledge. An initial review of these tapes suggested that speculative information is utilized in persuasive appeals when disagreement among jurors precludes a group verdict.

Some examples of this type of information introduced during the juror discussion should prove helpful in assessing the potential persuasive appeal of this type of information. The charge of conversion of bank funds resulted from a check deposit transaction between a female bank teller, the plaintiff, and a male customer, the defendant. The defendant allegedly took in cash a portion of a check he was supposed to deposit for the firm that employed him. The defense argued that the plaintiff was not responsible for the disappearance of the funds. During a number of the deadlocked deliberations, jurors speculated that the plaintiff and defendant were having an affair which was terminated by the defendant. In an effort to "get even," the plaintiff took the money and blamed the defendant. Shortly after this information had been introduced, these juries found in favor of the defendant.

Other juries having difficulties gaining verdict consensus were also apparently influenced by information of this type. Jurors considered other individuals who could have collaborated with the plaintiff and stolen the funds. A number of juries considered a possible relationships between the bank teller and the employer's son. They concluded it was possible that these two individuals maintained some type of relationship, conspired to steal the funds in question, and then blamed the act on the defendant. Once again, shortly after this information had been introduced into the proceedings, the juries found in favor of the defendant.

While these observations at best support only tentative statements about the persuasive role of speculative information posited during deliberation proceedings, they point to an area of research that scholars interested in persuasion might explore. Our discussion of persuasion during the *voir dire,* the trial, and jury deliberations has focused upon areas of persuasion research that have not been fully explored in trial settings. We have attempted to identify research avenues of interest to both communication scholars and members of the legal community. The knowledge generated from studies focusing upon the relationships among these variables holds forth the promise of increasing our knowledge of persuasion and improving the communicative effectiveness of trial lawyers during trial proceedings.

REFERENCES

ABELSON, R.P., and ROSENBERG, M.J. (1958). "Symbolic psychologic: A model of attitudinal cognition." Behavioral Science, 3:1-13.
BENNETT, E. (1955). "Discussion, decision, commitment and consensus in group decisions." Human Relations, 8:251-274.
BLUNK, R.A., and SALES, B.D. (1977). "Persuasion during the voir dire." In B.D. Sales (ed.), Psychology in the legal process. Jamaica, NY: Spectrum Publications.
BOWERS, J.W. (1963). "Language intensity, social introversion and attitude change." Speech Monographs, 30:345-352.
BROEDER, D.W. (1959). "The University of Chicago jury project." Nebraska Law Review, 38:744-760.
BURGOON, M., and KING, L.B. (1974). "The mediation of resistance to persuasion strategies by language variables and active-passive participation." Human Communication Research, 1:30-41.
BURGOON, M., JONES, S.B., and STEWART, D. (1975). "Toward a message-centered theory of persuasion: Three empirical investigations of language intensity." Human Communication Research, 1:240-256.
CARLSON, E.R. (1956). "Attitude change through modification of attitude structure." Journal of Abnormal and Social Psychology, 52:256-261.
CRONKHITE, G. (1969). Persuasion: Speech and behavioral change. New York: Bobbs-Merrill.
ERLANDER, H.S. (1970). "Jury research in America: Its past and future." Law and Society Review, 4:345-370.
FRANKEL, M.E. (1975). "The search for truth: An umpireal view." University of Pennsylvania Law Review, 5:1031-1059.
GILES, H., and POWESLAND, P.F. (1975). Speech style and social evaluation. New York: Academic Press.
HARMS, L.S. (1961). "Listener judgments of status cues in speech." Quarterly Journal of Speech, 47:164-168.
HAWKINS, C. (1960). "Interaction and coalition realignments in consensus-seeking groups: A study of experimental jury deliberation." Ph.D. dissertation, University of Chicago.
HOPPER, R., and WILLIAMS, F. (1973). "Speech characteristics and employability." Speech Monographs, 40:296-302.
JAMES, R. (1959). "Status and competence of jurors." American Journal of Sociology, 69:563-570.
JOHNSON, E., KANTOR, V., and SCHWARTZ, E. (1977). Outside the courts: A survey of diversion alternatives in civil cases. Denver, CO: National Center for State Courts.

JONES, E.E. (1964). Ingratiation: A social psychological analysis. New York: Appleton-Century-Crofts.

――― and WORTMAN, C. (1973). Ingratiation: An attributional approach. Morristown, PA: General Learning Press.

KAHN, J. (1974). "Social scientist's role in selection of juries sparks legal debate." Wall Street Journal, 184:1.

KALVEN, H., and ZEISEL, H. (1966). The American jury. Boston: Little, Brown.

KESSLER, J.B. (1975). "The social psychology of jury deliberations." In R.J. Simon (ed.), The jury system in America: A critical overview. Beverly Hills, CA: Sage.

KIESLER, C.A. (1968). "Commitment." In R.P. Abelson et al. (eds.), Theories of cognitive consistency: A sourcebook. Chicago: Rand McNally.

――― (1971). The psychology of commitment: Experiments linking behavior to belief. New York: Academic Press.

――― and SAKUMURA, J. (1966). "A test of a model for commitment." Journal of Personality and Social Psychology, 3:458-467.

McEWEN, W.J., and GREENBERG, B.S. (1970). "The effects of message intensity on receiver evaluations of source, message and topic." The Journal of Communication, 20:340-350.

McGUIRE, W.J. (1969). "The nature of attitudes and attitude change." In G. Lindzey and E. Aronson (eds.), The handbook of social psychology, 3. Reading, MA: Addison-Wesley.

MILLER, G.R., and BURGOON, M. (1973). New techniques of persuasion. New York: Harper & Row.

――― (1978). "Persuasion research: Review and commentary." In B.D. Ruben (ed.), Communication yearbook 2. New Brunswick, NJ: Tranaction Books.

MILLER, G.R., and FONTES, N.E. (1978). Real versus reel: What's the verdict? The effects of videotaped court materials on juror response (Final Report, NSF-RANN Grant APR75-15815).

――― (in press). Trial by videotape: A view from the jury box. Beverly Hills, CA: Sage.

MORRILL, A.E. (1972). Trial diplomacy. Chicago: Court Practice Institute.

NORTON, R.W. (1977). "Teacher effectiveness as a function of communicator style." In B.D. Ruben (ed.), Communication yearbook 1. New Brunswick, NJ: Transaction Books.

O'BARR, W.M., WALKER, L., and CONLEY, J. (1974). "Language variables in trial communication." Presented at the 60th Annual Meeting of the American Speech Communication Association, Chicago, December 28.

O'MARA, J.J. (1972). "The courts, standard jury charges-findings of pilot project." Pennsylvania Bar Journal, 120:166-175.

SIGLER, J.A. (1968). An introduction to the legal system. Homewood, IL: Dorsey.

STRODTBECK, F., JAMES, R., and HAWKINS, C. (1957). "Social status in jury deliberations." American Sociological Review, 22:713-719.

SUNNAFRANK, M.J., and FONTES, N.E. (1979). "The effects of ethnic affiliation on juror responses: General and crime specific ethnic stereotypes." Presented at the annual meeting of the Western Speech Communication Association, Los Angeles, February 17-21.

WALBERT, D.F. (1971). "The effect of jury size on the probability of conviction: An evaluation of Williams v. Florida." Case Western Reserve Law Review, 22:529-554.

ZEISEL, H. (1973). "Reflections on experimental techniques in the law." Journal of Legal Studies, 2:107-124.

Chapter 10

PERSUASIVE EFFECTS IN MARKETING
Consumer Information Processing Research

Robert W. Chestnut

THE CONCEPT OF PERSUASION has a clear and important focus in marketing. McGuire (1973:216) states it simply as "changing people's attitudes and behavior through the spoken and written word." One broad question is raised: How do commercial messages influence consumers' brand-related attitudes and, presumably through these attitudes, their purchasing behavior?

Practitioners have long recognized and pursued the answer to this question, particularly those involved in promotional stragegy and its use of mass media. As Alderson (1957:277) observes, "Advertising experts are inveterate theorists . . . practically all of the theories hold that advertising does not merely inform the consumer but motivates him by transforming his attitudes."

Academics have been equally, if not more, committed to this question. Models of consumer attitudes dominate basic science developments. Again, this is most apparent in the area of advertising effectiveness. Persuasion is the basis of a variety of experimental hypotheses relating communication to attitude change. Findings relevant to these hypotheses appear with predictable frequency in major reviews of consumer psychology (Jacoby, 1976). The first of these summaries notes in passing that "what might be considered a basic research area for much of consumer analysis is the social psychology of attitudes and their measurement" (Guest, 1962:335).

Acceptance of the centrality of this question is virtually unanimous. For many, persuasion *is* the cause-effect bond between a given communication and the observed attitude change. It is only with some difficulty, then, that a new paradigm for persuasion research has emerged and begun to influence this focus. The paradigm can be labeled "consumer information processing" (CIP). It directs investigators to a qualitatively different assessment and understanding of persuasive effects in marketing. Challenging the traditional emphasis on attitudes, it confronts practitioner and academic alike with a more general question: How is information (be it an advertisement, a sales presentation, or the product itself) processed within the framework of consumer problem-solving behavior?

Business has reacted to this question with scepticism, if not a degree of confusion. The constructs of "information" and "processing" are not yet clearly defined in a nonacademic vocabulary. Although initial applications have been made in the areas of pricing (Jacoby and Olson, 1977), promotion (Olson, 1977), and public policy (Bettman, 1975), the CIP paradigm has found a mixed reception. It often appears promising, but leads to few immediate actions.

Even the academic community has its doubts. Most accept the perspective, but still raise questions over the "new" or "unique" merits of CIP. After all, are not attitudes a form of information? Is not their change a form of processing?

> The information-processing approach provides the point of departure for more persuasion research than all other . . . (models) combined, though like Monsieur Jourdain speaking prose, many of the researchers whose work utilizes this prosaic approach have been doing it all their lives without knowing it [McGuire, 1977:157].

This reaction toward CIP and its general focus is noteworthy, for it points to a problem beyond that of the inertia or controversy one might normally associate with conceptual change. It appears that CIP has not provided an explicit or detailed alternative for research. Its potential for the understanding of persuasion has been left open. As the above quotation indicates, it is not enough to talk of persuasive effects as the processing of information. Theorists are likely to view such dialogue as a mere restatement of traditional assumptions.

CIP is quite different from the traditional focus on attitudes. Unfortunately, the concepts surrounding these differences are not firmly drawn. Although research and theory is accumulating, progress toward a more sophisticated modeling remains tentative (Chestnut and Jacoby, 1977,

1978). Major position statements are either being developed (Jacoby and Chestnut, forthcoming) or are just now appearing in the literature (Bettman, 1979).

To make what is known explicit, this chapter addresses the relationship between CIP and recent advances in persuasion research. It proceeds in three parts: the first contrasts CIP with the traditional focus on attitude; the second elaborates on this contrast by examining the nature and assumptions of a CIP system; and the third uses this system to organize and present selected findings. The emphasis throughout is on the potential for future research in marketing, given a more complex understanding of the context (that is, the cognitive system) in which persuasion takes place.

EXPERIMENTATION VERSUS PSYCHOPHYSICS

The advent of CIP involves a change in the assumptions underlying research. Simon (1974) describes this change by contrasting two scientific methods; these methods are referred to by their formal labels in psychology: experimentation and psychophysics.

Experimentation is designed to *establish* causality. It posits an independent variable (that is, cause) and a dependent variable (effect). The logic is deceptively simple: Specific independent variables are manipulated, while all others are controlled. If a change in the dependent variable is observed, this proves the existence of a cause-effect relationship.

Two developments are associated with this method. First, attention is devoted to creating theories which name variables and their potential relationships. Second, data are collected and the cause-effect predictions of theory are tested. Experimentation produces new information via "hypothesis-testing"; that is, its results are one-bit increments which either affirm or reject a statement of causality.

The traditional focus of persuasion research is a striking example of experimental interests. The objective is to relate communication variables (the cause) to attitude/behavior change (the effect). Theory development has been intensive. Communication, for example, is detailed as a process involving numerous considerations in each of its source-message-channel-receiver-destination components. Attitudes are seen to imply many effects. Hierarchical and nonhierarchical models are proposed, and different patterns of effect are considered. The number of variables steadily mounts, and the grounds for testing hypotheses becomes rich and varied.

The response in terms of data collection is impressive.

Literally thousands of studies . . . have focused on the manipulation of a plethora of independent variables. . . . [T]he major purpose of these studies has been to identify consistent patterns of response to the various independent variables, with the eventual goal of stating generalizable "principles" of communication [Lutz and Swasy, 1977:363].

For advertising alone, McGuire and Lipstein (1978) catalogue 7,000 selected references

The ability of these data to converge on principles of communication is still a matter of debate. One thing, however, is clear. Experimental method structures our understanding of persuasion. McGuire (1977:168) illustrates this in his attempt to integrate the literature. A "communication/ persuasion matrix" is used. On inspection, this is in one-to-one correspondence with the elements of method. Persuasion is conceptualized as an independent variable, a dependent variable, and an established cause-effect relationship.

This is not the approach of psychophysics; psychophysics is designed to *explore* (rather than establish) causality. It begins by positing a system which intervenes between cause and effect. Its objective is to measure that system and the process of its intervention.

In brief, a psychophysical theory is a set of statements (assumptions) that describe how an organism processes stimulus information under carefully specified conditions. The assumptions usually concern hypothetical processes that are difficult or impossible to observe directly. Once these assumptions are made explicit, however, formal models can be derived. The validity of the theory can be tested by comparing observations against the predictions of the model [Baird and Noma, 1978:2].

Method again has two developments: First, assumptions are made about system activities. These emphasize the operation rather than the existence of activity. As Calder (1978:630) observes, research begins to "examine the nature of cognitive mediation as well as the fact of it." Second, process measures (Jacoby, 1978) are implemented to capture more than the static outcome of "effect." New information is gained in complex, multibit results (via parameter-estimation; see Simon, 1974) which are then fed back into a better understanding of the system.

CIP is a reflection of the interests, if not the method, of psychophysics. In asking how persuasive communications in marketing are processed, it seeks to explore the consumer's role in mediating established cause-effect relationships. Its influence stems from the fact that "despite the seemingly powerful conceptualizations of the communications process available to researchers, very little empirical work has moved beyond the black box model" (Lutz and Swasy, 1977:363).

THE CIP SYSTEM

What assumptions can be made about the CIP system? To answer this question, a recent model by Chestnut and Jacoby (1977) is reviewed. The treatment is necessarily brief; for a full elaboration of these and other assumptions, the reader is referred to Bettman (1979).

The model begins with two observations. The first simplifies matters. Cognitive activity is classified into one of three sets: stimulus coding/perception, conscious evaluation, and long-term memory. The second complicates this picture. Each of these sets is assumed to interact (that is, combine the nature of their processing) and define a unique "sector" of the CIP system.

A Venn-diagramm (see Figure 1) depicts the resulting model. Three general sets overlap to produce seven distinct sectors of interest. The model proceeds by naming the sectors and describing their qualities.

Sector 1 (preconscious encoding) includes those activities surrounding the reception of information. The primary assumption is one of change.

Figure 1   A Consumer Information Processing System

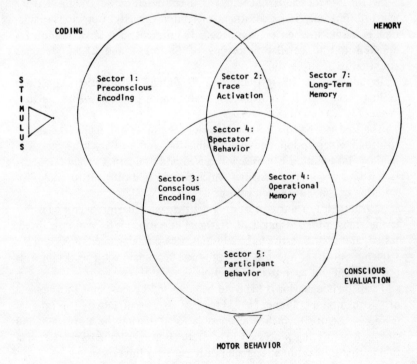

Information is restructured on input. This occurs automatically—that is, without conscious awareness or control structures.

Reading is a good example. Johnson (1977) describes some of the complexity underlying what appears to be an immediate awareness of word. Word units are identified in a sequencing of 16 stages of preconscious activity. In several of these stages, an interaction with memory is implied.

Sector 2 (trace activation) notes this interaction in our tendency to define the stimulus in light of past experience. "Studies of encoding show that input information quickly contacts memory units (i.e., activates trace structures) that serve to identify and provide a meaning or name for it" (Posner and Warren, 1972:26).

Taken together, Sectors 1 and 2 constitute an important part of the system. "The limited evidence from the experimental studies as well as from informed theory points to extensive preconscious processing." (Mandler, 1975:234). Rather than being "hardwired" or fixed by the system itself, preconscious activity is often programmed; it is trained through high degrees of practice or overlearning (LaBerge, 1974).

Sector 3 (conscious encoding) is a continuation of coding activity which differs only in its constraint of limited capacity. Conscious evaluation is easily strained or overloaded. It proceeds in a serial fashion (as opposed to the parallel processing of Sectors 1 and 2) and requires attention to be successful.

In addition to its restructuring of stimulus information, conscious evaluation engages the individual in reasoning or problem-solving activity, Posner (1973) describes two types.

The first is labeled spectator behavior (Sector 4) and implies the ability to combine perception, conscious evaluation, and memory in a synergistic manner. Information is passively received and evaluation, when it occurs, is the final product of activities which people find difficult to relate. An intuition or general reaction is formed.

Contrast this to active processing (participant behavior, Sector 5) which is that most often assumed of "rational" decision. Information is listed, tested, and used to arrive at conclusions. Reasoning proceeds in a complex sequence which, although it may produce the same results as Sector 4, is both explicit and open to introspection.

Participant behavior is likely to be governed by programs or schemata of information use. Posner (1973) suggests a sector of activity (operational memory, Sector 6) which is responsible for retrieving these programs and storing them during processing. The sector is atypical of conscious evaluation in that it does not appear subject to capacity limitations.

Finally, there are the structures of past experience, Sector 7 or long-term storage. Theory (Olson, 1977) highlights two assumptions: Information is not simply rehearsed and then written into memory. Instead, it is comprehended and, in the process, substantially altered to fit preexisting structures of knowledge. A second change occurs at the time of retrieval. Rather than a free-flow access to experience, conscious evaluation must generate a strategy for recall. These strategies are not always successful and may indeed alter the nature of information recalled.

In summary, a number of assumptions can be made about system activity. This section has referred to these assumptions at a general level. To show their relevance to an understanding of persuasive effects in marketing, the remainder of this chapter reviews research specific to this issue. Studies are categorized and their results presented in terms of each sector.

ADVANCES IN CIP RESEARCH

SECTOR 1: PRECONSCIOUS ENCODING

Investigators have become increasingly interested in this activity and its role in mediating marketing communications. The reasons for this heightened concern are a more realistic appraisal of the consumer's reception environment (Wright, 1977a) and an acknowledgement of the motivation underlying consumer behavior (Krugman, 1977, Robertson, 1976; Kassarjian, 1978).

Ray (1977) sets the following standard: "Consumer information processing (CIP) *research* relates to consumer information *processing* if the situation in research is the same as the situation in processing" (372). In most cases, the "real-life" situation is one of low-involvement, high degrees of practice, and capacity-strained or "overloaded" processing.

This is precisely the case where conscious encoding transfers to Sector 1 and becomes an automatic response. Consider the consumer's reaction to commercial breaks in programming (Ray and Webb, 1976). Data point to the existence of a skill at predicting the presence of commercials and allocating attention to other activities in advance of the message itself. "Consumers were amazingly well-schooled as to the pattern of commercial breaks on their favorite programs" (Ray 1977:374). It is unlikely that this would reflect a conscious attempt at tracking patterns, timing intervals, and managing distractions. Practice long ago turned these behaviors into a routine part of watching the program.

Unfortunately, research has not identified many of the processes at this level. The problem lies in measurement limitations. Psychophysical techniques (for example, reaction time; see Gardner et al., 1978) are still new to consumer research. In lieu of these techniques, research has proceeded with an almost total reliance on verbal response. At best, this approach only confounds the existence of coding activity in Sectors 1 and 3.

There are, however, exceptions. LaBarbera and MacLachlan (1979) isolate a phenomenon involving the rate or speed of information in the auditory channel. Faster or "speech-compressed" messages are found to elicit greater consumer interest and recall. This outcome occurs at low rates of increase (30 percent) and without awareness. The implication is that time may be an important parameter of preconscious encoding.

Lutz and Lutz (1977, 1978) examine the content rather than the speed of information; they point to the impact of imagery or visual coding on brand name recall. Interactive images (that is, those involving the brand name in the logo) increase recall. Visual information facilititates the memorability of verbal information to the extent that encoding associates the two (perhaps via a retrieval process) in long-term memory. "The use of interactive imagery is clearly implied for effectively promoting the association of a brand name with its product or service" (Lutz and Lutz, 1977:498).

It is likely that some of this association occurs automatically. Subjects in the Lutz and Lutz experiment were told to study the images for later recall, but were not aware of the mnemonic either at time of exposure or response. Conscious instructions might have enhanced recall even further by engaging mechanisms in Sector 3. Further research is needed to detail the nature of the activity which links visual and verbal coding.

These first few studies suggest the diversity and influence of activities in Sector 1. Preconscious encoding is undoubtedly complex and will require significant advances in concept and method before a coherent picture emerges.

SECTOR 2: TRACE ACTIVATION

Although research has faced similar problems in studying this sector, matters are somewhat more advanced. Namely, a theoretical position exists. "[T]o some small but measurable degree, one must note, perceive, or identify what one will not attend to. . . . I suggest that this 'pre-attentive process' leaves some trace of the rejected material" (Krugman, 1977:11).

Krugman's low-involvement hypothesis—that is, the influence of rejected or unattended information on memory—agrees with a general observation about the system. Preconscious encoding does more than contact memory in order to recognize, code, and screen incoming signals. In the process of comprehension, it actively changes and/or adds to the traces available. This process occurs gradually over time and is different from the conscious rehearsal usually thought of as learning.

What kinds of traces or memories are likely to be stored in this manner? Krugman (1977) talks of the objective characteristics of the stimulus. Traces are acquired which allow a familiarity with or recognition of brands in the purchasing environment.

Although recognition is important (for example, in generating an evoked set; see Howard, 1977), there is a second and potentially more powerful process. Affective reactions (in other words, encoding of the stimulus in terms of its reinforcement value) occur and are stored via trace activation (Posner and Snyder, 1975). These reactions have the ability to direct choice in an approach/avoidance manner and to enter it as subjective feelings in a conscious evaluation of attitude.

Rossiter and Percy (1978a, 1978b) investigate a model which emphasizes the role of reinforcement value or affect. Their findings support the existence of two independent mechanisms, verbal and visual affect. Whereas verbal information is likely to require conscious encoding, visual information fits well with the notion of low-involvement and preconscious activity.

SECTOR 3: CONSCIOUS ENCODING

To this point, information is processed in parallel and with little strain on cognitive processes. Multiple channel inputs are received, restructured, and used in interaction with memory. How are these activities changed by the attentional mechanisms which give us awareness?

Warshaw (1978) sees encoding reduced to a single channel. The extreme case is tested. Television commercials are manipulated to provide "single-channel copy." Results show that

when audio (video) information was presented without background video (audio), more material was recalled (and inferentially, attended) than when the audio (video) appeared simultaneously with relevant video (audio), regardless of the level of information content in the secondary channel [1978:371].

An earlier experiment by Hollander and Jacoby (1973) converges on this result. A different manipulation was employed. Instead of eliminating the competing channel at select points in the commercial, they make it irrelevant. Commercials are "split" by pairing the audio (video) of one with the video (audio) of a second, unrelated commercial. Besides imparting a certain degree of novelty, this effectively separates channel meaning. The consumer's task is no longer one of rapidly shifting attention in an attempt to integrate related messages because such shifts would be futile. When compelled in this manner to receive two separate inputs, consumers again demonstrate improved recall.

These studies suggest an important parameter of attention. Encoding is sequentially organized by channel. Depending on how the multichannel message is structured, the system is forced to interrupt processing and switch channels. The pattern of this switching behavior and its ability to match the development of key copy points in first one channel and then another may well be crucial to interpretation of the message.

The quantity of information within channel is also limited. There is a 7 ± 2 (Miller, 1956) upper boundary on the "chunks" of conscious storage. Furthermore, if these chunks are not then rehearsed to maintain awareness, they fade over time. Calder (1978) reviews the implications for persuasive effects.

Without positing an upper bound on storage capacity, one might expect a linear function between attitude and the number of advertising arguments. This is not the case. Persuasion reaches a plateau, beginning with the presence of seven independent arguments. The frequency of cognitive response (that is, the codings or thoughts elicited by these arguments) is found to parallel and, perhaps, mediate this result.

The timing of arguments is also important. Given the assumption of information decay over time, a primacy-recency phenomenon is expected. Information in the first and last parts of a commercial has the greatest impact. Calder (1978:632) concludes that "more cognitive responses stimulated by the beginning and the end of the message than by the middle must have been represented in short-term memory."

In raising the issue of cognitive response, we advance beyond the encoding of information to include general processing activities. "The new idea of cognitive response is simply the old idea of cognitive mediation updated to a view of the person as an active information processor" (Calder, 1978:630; Perloff and Brock, this volume). Emphasis should be placed on the word *active*. The system itself (not just the stimulus input) governs the degree and process of mediation.

SECTOR 4: SPECTATOR BEHAVIOR

Gardner et al. (1978) extend the concept of low-involvement learning in this direction of system control. They recognize two parameters in the system: attention and strategy. Attention limitations produce the effects noted earlier in Sectors 1 through 3. Strategy limitations are conscious and reflect a deliberate choice of processing routine. The system openly selects a passive or low involvement role vis-à-vis the message. "Low involvement learning can also occur in situations of full attention, if that attention is not devoted to an evaluative processing of the advertising message" (Gardner et al., 1978:584).

What might initiate this strategy? Wright (1975) points to an individual difference characteristic. Consumers are thought to vary in the confidence they attach to their own processing activities. A measure is operationalized and examined in terms of its relationship to counterarguing behavior. Those low in information processing confidence (IPC) are found to engage in less counterarguing and, consequently, exhibit greater acceptance of the message.

A second determinant is the problem-solving "set" (that is, involvement or motivation) with which the message is approached. The CIP system receives information in a specific context, namely, purchasing. The task is not to prove or disprove the truth of advertising, but to use advertising in a heuristic sense to manage choice behavior.

Wright (1977a) discusses one low involvement set by which the system might respond. "[I]n a world of information overload and overchoice, populated by advocates of all types hawking their wares, getting ideas about how to frame one's choice problems is of greater concern to most audience members than decoding or evaluating what an advocate thinks about the option he discusses" (1977a:26). Effortful evaluation is avoided by attending to and storing the attributes of purchase rather than the attributes of brand.

Consider the example of cigarette advertising. What takes place in a consumer's switch to a specific low-tar brand? Is this the result of a series of detailed brand claim evaluations? A simpler model is suggested. The cumulative effect of all advertising in this area (not just the brand's own advertising) is to "frame" the purchase task increasingly in terms of low tar. Separate from this problem-oriented learning, advertising creates traces in Sector 2 which lend themselves to a recognition of brand. When it comes time to purchase, these two effects act jointly to produce a brand-specific choice. Advertising is effective, but not along the conscious and deliberate lines that we usually attribute to "rational" decision.

SECTOR 5: PARTICIPANT BEHAVIOR

The preceding analysis is not meant to suggest, however, that the consumer is unable to evaluate messages. Consumers are persuaded in a detailed process of reasoning; they participate in understanding the communication, arriving at their own conclusions along the way. Research has addressed these conclusions from the standpoint of cognitive response (Wright, 1977a, 1977b).

Cognitive response is both a method and a concept. At the method level, it refers to relatively simple "thought-listing" procedures. An advertisement is exposed and verbal descriptions or statements of thought are collected. The assumption is made that these are the thoughts or impressions actually present in reaction to the advertisement.

At the concept level, matters are more complicated. Here, interest is not directed at the statements of thought per se, but in the processing activities implied. Although not always defined, these activities are what mediate the presence or absence of persuasive effect.

One activity is that of responding to the message in order to form brand attitudes. Olson et al. (1978) examine this process by relating cognitive response measures to the traditional elements of cognitive structure. "Informational" messages are exposed and categories of counter, support, and neutral response are monitored. "Both counterarguments and support arguments were found to be related to a wide range of cognitive variables including beliefs, attitudes, and purchase intentions" (1978:76).

A second activity is that of responding to the message in order to form judgments about the communication environment. Consumers engage in attribution processes. In particular, they evaluate advertising with an eye toward its selling purpose, often making inferences about the credibility of source or brand claim.

Mizerski (1978) investigates this process in terms of individual differences. Consumers are thought to vary in the "causal complexity" with which they approach messages. Results indicate that "simple" processors (those inferring few causes) are more persuaded by messages and develop extreme brand attitudes.

Smith and Hunt (1978) examine attributions in the form of cognitive response measures. In reaction to a single exposure of print advertising, they find over one-third (37.3 percent) of their sample exhibiting attributions.

This attributional level is hypothesized to increase under conditions of "varied" advertising. The assumption is that consumers are more likely to make attributions about a source who presents the unusual or unexpected. Varied advertising is the unexpected case of a source who both claims (on some features) and disclaims (on others) product superiority. "Here, analysis showed that varied product claims are indeed a potent elicitor (62.9 percent cognitive response) of attributions" (Smith and Hunt, 1978:156). Further, these attributions appear to work on behalf of advertising by increasing credibility.

Finally, a third activity is that of responding to information external to the message in a complex process of brand attitude formation. "The cognitive response approach postulates that when a person receives a persuasive communication, he will attempt to relate the new information to his existing repertoire of cognitions." (Petty, 1977:357)

One variety of cognition concerns our own past behavior. Dholakia and Sternthal (1977) illustrate the power of past behavior on source credibility and persuasion. They study experimental subjects who comply with a message presented by either a high or low credibility source. Counter to the traditional finding, the low credibility source achieves greater persuasion.

The explanation of this finding is found in processing activity. Subjects with low credibility sources face a dissonance-like situation in which information regarding their own behavior must be reconciled with information about the source. It is interesting to note that this conflict appears to exert its greatest impact on the affective component of attitude.

Sternthal et al. (1978) consider a different cognition. This time, source credibility is viewed in an interaction with positive versus negative initial opinion. High credibility is found more persuasive in the condition of a negative position, while moderate credibility is found more persuasive in the condition of a positive position.

The explanation offered, again, involves processing. Cognitive response measures are taken to validate this explanation.

> In cognitive response terms, the moderate credibility source induced greater positive attitude and support argumentation when identified at the outset of communication, presumably because message recipients felt a need to bolster support for a position they favored when the communicator was of questionable credibility [Sternthal et al., 1978:259].

All of these activities are deliberate and effortful. They can (but not necessarily do) surround marketing communications. Research must proceed with an eye toward Ray's standard of realism and with a continued interest in detailing the nature of processing activities. Developments in theory (Lutz and Swasy, 1977) and method (Gardner et al., 1978) hold promise for this objective.

SECTORS 6 & 7:
OPERATIONAL AND LONG-TERM STORAGE

These last two sectors are combined out of necessity. Little about these sectors is truly known; this lack of knowledge is ironic since their existence is the cornerstone on which advertising rests.

Part of the problem is that our interests in memory have widened considerably. As seen in the discussion of previous sectors, memory is implicated in a number of different processes. It is no longer just a storage location for past experience. Cognitive response is but one example "[T]he role of initial opinion in current cognitive response theory may be equated with retrieval from long-term memory" (Tybout et al. 1978:721). In order to raise a counterargument, the consumer must first go back and generate information from memory. What governs the retrieval processes involved? How may the advertisement itself provide the basis for retrieval?

A second area of currently unanswered questions concerns memory's role in directing cognition. Both Olson (1978) and Calder (1978) have emphasized this role. "[I]t may be useful to view cognitive response as scripts. The usual concept of cognitive response may be far too abstract.... As scripts, cognitive responses would be firmly anchored in the stored experience of the individual" (Calder, 1978:633). Data are not yet available on the formation or actual use of consumer scripts or schemata.

SUMMARY

Persuasion, as a concept, has begun to focus on a new paradigm, CIP. The research generated by this paradigm (with its psychophysical rather than experimental interests) has adopted a variety of assumptions about system activity and provided some idea of how information processing mediates persuasive effects in marketing. The attempt here has been to review the most recent of these advances with an emphasis on the potential for future research.

REFERENCES

ALDERSON, W. (1957). Marketing behavior and executive action. Homewood, IL: Richard D. Irwin.

BAIRD, J.C., and NOMA, E. (1978). Fundamentals of scaling and psychophysics. New York: John Wiley.

BETTMAN, J.R. (1975). "Issues in designing consumer information environments." Journal of Consumer Research, 2:169-177.

––– (1979). An information processing theory of consumer choice. Reading, MA: Addison-Wesley.

CALDER, B.J. (1978). "Cognitive responses, imagery, and scripts: What is the cognitive basis of attitude?" Advances in Consumer Research, 5:630-634.

CHESTNUT, R.W., and JACOBY, J. (1977). "Consumer information processing:

Emerging theory and findings." In A.G. Woodside, J.N. Sheth, and P.D. Bennett (eds.), Consumer and industrial buyer behavior. New York: North-Holland.

—— (1978). "Methods and concepts in consumer information processing: Toward an integrated framework." Research Paper No. 141A. New York: Graduate School of Business, Columbia University.

DHOLAKIA, R.R., and STERNTHAL, B. (1977). "Highly credible sources: Persuasive facilitators or persuasive liabilities?" Journal of Consumer Research, 3:223-232.

GARDNER, M.P., MITCHELL, A.A., and RUSSO, J.E. (1978). "Chronometric analysis: An introduction and an application to low involvement perception of advertisments." Advances in Consumer Research, 5:581-589.

GUEST, L. (1962). "Consumer analysis." Annual Review of Psychology, 13:315-344.

HOLLANDER, S.W., and JACOBY, J. (1973). "Recall of crazy, mixed-up TV commercials." Journal of Advertising Research, 13:39-42.

HOWARD, J.A. (1977). Consumer behavior: Application of theory. New York: McGraw-Hill.

JACOBY, J. (1976). "Consumer psychology: An octennium." Annual Review of Psychology, 27:331-358.

—— (1978). "Consumer research: A state of the art review." Journal of Marketing, 42:87-96.

—— and CHESTNUT, R.W. (forthcoming). Information acquisition in human problem solving: A behavioral process approach.

JACOBY, J., and OLSON, J.C. (1977). "Consumer response to price: An attitudinal information processing perspective." In Y. Wind and M. Greenberg (eds.), Moving ahead with attitude research. Chicago: American Marketing Association.

JOHNSON, N.F. (1977). "A pattern-unit model of word identification." In D. LaBerge and S.J. Samuels (eds.), Basic processes in reading: Perception and comprehension. Hillsdale, NJ: Lawrence Erlbaum.

KASSARJIAN, H.H. (1978). "Presidential address, 1977: Anthropomorphism and parsimony." Advances in Consumer Research, 5:xiii-xiv.

KRUGMAN, H.E. (1977). "Memory without recall, exposure without perception." Journal of Advertising Research, 17:7-12.

LaBARBERA, P., and MacLACHLAN, J. (1979). "Time-compressed speech in radio advertising." Journal of Marketing, 43:30-36.

LaBERGE, D. (1974). "Acquisition of automatic processing in perceptual and associative learning." In P.M.A. Rabbitt and S. Dornic (eds.), Attention and performance. London: Academic Press.

LUTZ, K.A., and LUTZ, R.J. (1977). "Effects of imagery on learning: Application to advertising." Journal of Applied Psychology, 62:493-498.

—— (1978). "Imagery eliciting strategies: Review and implications of research." Advances in Consumer Research, 5:611-620.

LUTZ, R.J., and SWASY, J.L. (1977). "Integrating cognitive structure and cognitive response approaches to monitoring communications effects." Advances in Consumer Research, 4:363-371.

MANDLER, G. (1975). "Consciousness: Respectable, useful, and probably necessary." In R.L. Solso (ed.), Information processing and cognition: The Loyola symposium. Hillsdale, NJ: Lawrence Erlbaum.

McGUIRE, W.J. (1973). "Persuasion, persistence, and attitude change." In I. DeSola

Pool, F.W. Frey, W. Schramm, N. Maccoby, and E.B. Parker (eds.), Handbook of communication. Chicago: Rand McNally.
——— (1977). "An information-processing model of advertising effectiveness." In H.L. Davis and A.J. Silk (eds.), Behavioral and management science in marketing. New York: John Wiley.
——— and LIPSTEIN, B. (1978). Evaluating advertising: A bibliography of the communication process. New York: Advertising Research Foundation.
MILLER, G.A. (1956). "The magic number seven, plus or minus two." Psychological Review, 63:81-97.
MIZERSKI, R.W. (1978). "Causal complexity: A measure of consumer causal attribution." Journal of Marketing Research, 15:220-228.
OLSON, J.C. (1977). "Theories of information encoding and storage: Implications for consumer research." Working Paper Series No. 65. College Park: College of Business Administration, Pennsylvania State University.
——— (1978). "Inferential belief formation in the cue utilization process." Advances in Consumer Research, 5:706, 713.
——— TOY, D.R., and DOVER, P.A. (1978). "Mediating effects of cognitive responses to advertising on cognitive structure." Advances in Consumer Research, 5:72-78.
PETTY, R.E. (1977). "The importance of cognitive responses in persuasion." Advances in Consumer Research, 4:357-362.
POSNER, M.I. (1973). Cognition: An introduction. Glenview, IL: Scott, Foresman.
——— and SNYDER, C.R.R. (1975). "Attention and cognitive control." In R.L. Solso (ed.), Information processing and cognition: The Loyola symposium. Hillsdale, NJ: Lawrence Erlbaum.
POSNER, M.I., and WARREN, R.E. (1972). "Traces, concepts, and conscious constructions." In A.W. Melton and E. Martin (eds.), Coding processes in human memory. New York: John Wiley.
RAY, M.L. (1977). "When does consumer information processing research actually have anything to do with consumer information processing?" Advances in Consumer Research, 4:372-375.
——— and WEBB, P. (1976). "Experimental research on the effects of TV clutter: Dealing with the difficult media environment." Report No. 76-102. Cambridge, MA: Marketing Science Institute.
ROBERTSON, T.S. (1976). "Low-commitment consumer behavior." Journal of Advertising Research, 16:19-24.
ROSSITER, J.R., and PERCY, L. (1978a). "Visual imaging ability as a mediator of advertising response." Advances in Consumer Research, 5:621-629.
——— (1978b). "A visual and verbal loop theory of the classical conditioning effect of advertising on product attribute." (unpublished)
SIMON, H.A. (1974). "How big is a chunk?" Science, 183:482-488.
SMITH, R.E., and HUNT, S.D. (1978). "Attributional processes and effects in promotional situations." Journal of Consumer Research, 5:149-158.
STERNTHAL, B., DHOLAKIA, R.R., and LEAVITT, C. (1978). "The persuasive effect of source credibility: Tests of cognitive response." Journal of Consumer Research, 4:252-260.
TYBOUT, A.M., STERNTHAL, B., and CALDER, B.J. (1978). "A two-stage theory of information processing in persuasion: An integrative view of cognitive response and self-perception theory." Advances in Consumer Research, 5:721-723.
WARSHAW, P.R. (1978). "Application of selective attention theory to television advertising displays." Journal of Applied Psychology, 63:366-372.

WRIGHT, P. (1975). "Factors affecting cognitive resistance to advertising." Journal of Consumer Research, 2:1-9.

——— (1977a). "Cognitive responses to mass media advocacy and cognitive choice processes." Research Paper No. 356. Stanford: Graduate School of Business, Stanford University.

——— (1977b). "Research on ad-stimulated thought processes." (unpublished)

Chapter 11

POLITICAL CAMPAIGNS
Mass Communication and Persuasion

Charles K. Atkin

IN MAJOR ELECTION CAMPAIGNS, the mass media offer voters an enormous array of informational and persuasive messages about political candidates and issues. Daily newspapers carry numerous campaign news articles and provide editorial endorsements of selected candidates and ballot propositions. The television and radio airwaves are filled with political commercials, candidate speeches, interview programs, and newscast glimpses of campaign events (and psuedo-events). Campaigns for minor offices may also generate considerable media content, although on a much more limited scale. Indeed, the amount of mediated stimuli becomes a defining characteristic of election campaigns, which can range from high definition contests for the presidency down to obscure races for the state legislature.

Since this chapter deals with *persuasive* messages, it will exclude media content that is manifestly intended to inform rather than convince voters. Campaign news reports will not be considered; the important political effects of these messages have been described elsewhere.[1]

Persuasive campaign messages are those which explicitly or implicitly advocate a candidate or issue position in order to influence the attitudinal preferences or turnout decisions of voters. The most pervasive type of message is political *advertising* which is increasingly used by campaigners at all levels. The *endorsement* recommendations of newspapers are another significant form of persuasion at election time. Televised candidate *debates* at the presidential level, although rare, generate great interest and excitement. These three categories of advocacy messages will be reviewed in this chapter. Little research attention has been given to infrequent or exotic types of persuasion, such as telethons, documentaries, broadcast speeches, and columnist commentaries. Before discussing the specific effects of campaign persuasion, some general theoretical perspectives will be summarized.

MODELS OF VOTER RESPONSE TO PERSUASIVE POLITICAL MESSAGES

Over the past few decades, a number of distinct research perspectives have evolved in the field of political communication. Mass media researchers have drawn heavily upon the dominant theories and paradigms of the traditional social science disciplines, particularly social psychology, political science, and sociology. Many of these approaches have been reviewed recently by Sears and Whitney(1973), Kraus and Davis (1976), and Nimmo (1977, 1978).

The pioneering work in this area focused on the role of propaganda in forming public opinion. Scholars and observers who examined the activities of skilled mass persuaders such as Roosevelt and Hitler were concerned about manipulative influence on a gullible public. The apparent persuasive success of political leaders, demagogues, and news commentators lead to the formulation of the "hypodermic" or "bullet" model of powerful direct impact on a passive audience. This conception was not subjected to adequate behavioral testing, however, since most researchers of that era relied solely on content analysis techniques.

Two classic survey studies conducted during elections in the 1940s attempted to measure the extent of mass media influence on voters (Lazarsfeld et al., 1948; Berelson et al., 1954). Contrary to earlier conceptions, these sociologists concluded that few voters were converted and that social influences outweighed any media impact. Despite critical limitations of this pair of investigations (there was no television persuasion available, the elections involved highly familiar presidential incumbents, and the criterion for effect was major change in voting intention), the "null effects" perspective was born.[2] The conclusion of minimal mass communication persuasiveness was perpetuated by sociologically oriented scholars such as Klapper (1960).

This reactionary position discouraged further attempts to measure mass media impact, especially among the political scientists who dominated voting research in the 1950s (Campbell et al., 1960, 1966). These investigators had far more interest in party attachments than communication variables, and their neglect of persuasive messages served to reinforce the limited effects conclusion.

Social psychologists who began to examine political communication in the 1950s and 1960s have relied on consistency theory approaches which minimize direct persuasive influence from mediated messages. These researchers emphasize the partisan nature of information processing (especially selective exposure to congruent messages), the resistance to attitudinal change, and the importance of reinforcement of predispositions (Sears and Freedman, 1967; McGuire, 1969; Weiss, 1969; Sears and Whitney, 1973).

Communication researchers have only recently become centrally involved in political persuasion studies. These scholars have tended to take revisionist perspectives that assign a more influential role to the mass media while acknowledging the active responses of the voters. Both learning and functional theories have guided contemporary research. In particular, the "uses and gratifications" approach has gained prominence in the past decade (Blumler and McQuail, 1969; Mendelsohn and O'Keefe, 1976). This framework proposes that various voter needs can be satisfied by mass media content, such as reinforcement of weak predispositions, guidance for decision-making, excitement from following the political "game," or surveillance of significant events. The uses and gratifications approach differs from the limited effects approach in that substantial influence may occur; it differs from mechanistic learning paradigms in that the receiver of the message primarily determines the nature of the influence. The motives of the voter become intervening variables that modify the direction and extent of response to political stimuli.

The more central role accorded the receiver in the learning process is reflected in approaches that focus on the level of involvement of the voter. In political advertising experiments, Rothschild and Ray (1974) have adapted Krugman's (1965) passive learning theory. A person who is highly involved will actively work through the "response hierarchy" of receiving, recalling, evaluating, forming attitudes, and acting. A low involvement receiver will passively gain awareness of certain stimuli after repeated exposure, but will not bother to critically evaluate the content in forming an affective disposition. Nevertheless, when objects are subsequently encountered in a decisional context, the more recognized one will be selected. In some respects, this is similar to Zajonc's (1968) mere exposure theory positing positive response to objects made familiar through repeated contact.

Expectancy-value approaches patterned after Fishbein's multiattribute attitude model (Fishbein and Ajzen, 1975) are also applicable to the analysis of political persuasion. The recent studies by Patterson and McClure demonstrate the utility of focusing on attribute belief changes that combine with existing values to produce attitude change toward candidates (Patterson and McClure, 1976; McClure and Patterson, 1974). This perspective assumes that stable affective dispositions toward political issues and leader traits provide a basis for responding to a candidate. The media images provide the cognitive connections between the candidate and issue positions or personal qualities. To the extent that those attributes associated with the candidate are positively valued by the voter, a favorable attitude will be formed. By contrast, negative movement will occur if the image projected by the candidate is discrepant from the voter's ideal attributes. The "agenda-setting" model of McCombs and Shaw (McCombs and Shaw, 1972; Shaw and McCombs, 1977), although primarily applied to news messages, offers a complementary feature concerning weights attached to attribute components. Agenda-setting researchers have found that audiences give greater salience to those topics, issues, and attributes that are emphasized by the mass media, as agenda orderings are adopted as personal priorities.

The applicability of various theoretical processes is contingent on specification of the context in which candidates and voters are operating. Three situational factors seem particularly pertinent to consider: degree of campaign definition, level of voter involvement, and stage of voter decision-making. These vary from one contest to another, among different voters responding to the same campaign, and at different points of time before the election.

Definition involves the degree to which discriminating attributes are available to distinguish between competing candidates. Differentiation depends on the existence of actual or projected distinctions, and on the communication of this information to the voter. A high definition situation involves differences in candidates' party affiliations, demographic characteristics, personal qualities, or ideologies. Thus, general elections are more clearly defined than primaries, and campaigns offering a choice between an incumbent versus a familiar challenger, black versus white candidates, or liberal versus conservative candidates allow for higher definition. Campaign communication provides a means for learning attributes beyond the bare party label that is identified on the ballot. Since party identification is becoming a less critical predictor of decision-making as personality or issue attributes rise in importance, the role of the mass media is now more central in political campaigns.

Involvement pertains to the level of voter engagement in the specific electoral contest. Although races for major offices tend to attract greater involvement than contests lower on the ballot, there is considerable variation from one voter to the next. Some voters may be far more concerned about a local mayoral race than a statewide gubernatorial race. Some may not care about any of the contests in the campaign, while others are psychologically involved in a number of races.

Decisional stage refers to the voter's level of certainty in intention. In the predecisional stage, no preference has been formed between the competing candidates and the voter is likely to be seeking guidance. After a decision has been made, messages may be selectively sought to provide reinforcement.

These three factors can be combined to produce several prototype voting contexts. The high definition, high involvement, predecisional situation is most appropriate for the multiattribute model with extensive exposure to mediated persuasion. The direct impact should be primarily cognitive as beliefs are formed; indirect effects on preferences will be limited by the role played by other definitional inputs. If the high involvement predecisional stage occurs in a low definition context, the influence of media persuasion will be stronger.

Predecisional uncertainty may also coincide with low voter involvement and low to moderate campaign definition. In this circumstance, the mere exposure model is most suitable; direct affective impact of persuasive messages is likely to be quite pronounced. Finally, the prototype post-decisional high involvement context should result in reinforcement-seeking whereby media persuasion bolsters the voter's intention.

In the next three sections of this chapter, the role of political advertising, debates, and editorial endorsements will be examined within this framework. For each topic, key processes will be identified, followed by a review of research dealing with message content, voter exposure patterns, and learning and preference effects.

POLITICAL ADVERTISING

In the past 15 years, candidates for major offices have increasingly relied on television advertising as the primary means of influencing the electorate.[3] For more localized campaigns, candidates find radio and newspaper advertising more practical. Advertising typically offers candidates their best opportunity to communicate directly with the majority of voters, bypassing the news gatekeepers and outreaching the other types of direct persuasion such as speeches and documentaries.

The persuasive outcome of political advertising is jointly determined by the qualitative and quantitative nature of the messages interacting with the affective predispositions of the receivers. Message content is designed to convey candidate name identification and establish linkages between the candidate and those personal qualities and ideological positions favored by a majority of the target audience. Structurally, the messages tend to be brief, simple, repetitive, and scheduled late in the campaign.

In higher involvement situations where voters are attempting to form a preferential ranking consistent with their predispositions, attitude toward each candidate can be conceived as a multiplicative function of three voter variables: (1) values regarding ideal personal qualities of an officeholder (for example, competence, trustworthiness, age, marital status) and ideological orientations toward relevant political objects (such as party, issues, leaders); (2) the agenda salience priorities among these attributes and objects in the campaign context (for example, sincerity or experience may be the overriding consideration for some voters, while inflation or abortion may be most important for others); and (3) the knowledge and beliefs linking the candidate to the attributes and objects (for example, the voter knows that the candidate is a Southerner, or believes that the candidate favors tax reduction). Since these components are multiplied and summed, all three must have non-zero values before attitudinal consequences are produced.

Personal values and ideology are developed slowly over a period of years as the individual is exposed to social, cultural, and media influences. Since most of these predispositions are firmly established and stable, political advertising is not likely to change them significantly; the direct impact of ads occurs primarily at the cognitive level. Advertising can be effective in creating or changing various belief linkages and in altering the relative salience of the attribute criteria for judging the candidate. These altered cognitions then combine with the affective predispositions to trigger indirect change in candidate attitude.

Since the affective change is mediated by the receiver, a given advertisement can produce both positive and negative movement depending on who evaluates the message. To minimize boomerang effects, candidates try to emphasize linkages to universally valued attributes and objects (for example, pro-honesty, anti-inflation). Nevertheless, most issue positions and many personal image attributes promoted in ads will be met with divergent reactions by different voters, resulting in counterproductive outcomes (perhaps an aging candidate or one who favors abortion will inevitably turn off a substantial segment of the electorate who do not appreciate those features). It should be noted that potency of advertising impact will vary according to the amount of other influences operating; in high definition-high involvement presidential races, the role of advertising may be outweighed by interpersonal persuasion or minimized by prior familiarity with the candidates.

For less involved voters seeking to form preferences with minimum effort, ads may have a more direct impact by producing name awareness and positive affect through familiarity. Repeated presentation of name, face, and vague imagery should produce generally favorable results with this uncritical and unconcerned segment of the electorate. The impact may be quite potent, since other inputs are likely to be absent in this context.

For voters who have already developed a tentative preference, ads may serve to intensify or erode the predisposition. To the extent that involvement is high and preferences are strongly felt, voters will attempt to use ads from both candidates for reinforcement. Those who are doubtful about their initial decision may react in either a positive or negative fashion.

Unfortunately, the research literature on political advertising has tended to examine only the end result rather than the specific processes of persuasion. There is little evidence specifying under which conditions advertising is influential and the extent to which boomerang effects occur.

Before describing the effects research, it is important to examine the nature of the content and the amount of exposure. Contrary to conventional wisdom, television advertising is surprisingly substantive in content. According to Patterson and McClure (1976), considerable issue information was presented in more than two-thirds of the commercials during the 1972 presidential campaign. The 12 issues dealt with in the ads received five times as much air time as in the network evening newscasts. Patterson and McClure's content analysis showed that the ads tended to blend soft imagery with hard issue material; of course, the candidates were careful to emphasize only those issue positions that they felt would win votes, since broadly educating the public about the most significant issues was not their goal. In an analysis of newspaper advertisements, Bowers (1972) found that issue assertions constituted the most frequent type of content in campaigns for governor and senator; candidates who were less familiar to the voters tended to stress name and personality characteristics. Regarding scheduling, Mullen's (1968) analysis of newspaper advertising during the 1964 presidential campaign showed that more than half of the expenditures occured during the final three days before the election.

Exposure data come primarily from a set of surveys conducted by Atkin during campaigns for governor in Wisconsin and Colorado and for

Congress in Michigan (Atkin et al., 1973; Atkin and Heald, 1976). Averaging across the six candidates studied, 90 percent of the voters reported seeing televised political advertising. This rate of penetration is higher than for any other form of political stimuli in the mass media. The frequency of exposure, in terms of number of ads noticed, is primarily influenced by accessibility factors: heavy TV viewers see more political ads than light viewers, and the candidate presenting relatively more commercials than his or her opponent achieves a higher amount of exposure.

Aside from raw exposure, voters were also asked how much attention they paid to ads. Averaging across the six candidates, one-fourth of the viewers said they devote "close attention," two-fifths reported giving "some attention," and one-third replied "little attention." Attentiveness is mainly a function of the entertainment quality of the messages and the partisan predispositions of the receivers. Those who feel that a candidate's ads are entertaining pay more attention, particularly uncommitted voters. Although most predisposed voters are equally attentive (or inattentive) to each contestant's TV ads, those partisans with unbalanced attention patterns display a strong tendency to attend selectively to ads for their preferred candidate. Attention is also higher for those with greater political interest, and for voters who are actively seeking information from ads rather than watching just because the messages are prominently available. Demographic variables are only weakly related to attentiveness.

Active avoidance of candidate advertising was reported by one-tenth of the voters; most avoiders are motivated more by boredom than by partisan defensiveness. However, a presidential campaign survey by O'Keefe and Sheinkopf (1974) showed a higher avoidance rate, with one-fourth of the partisans trying to escape the nonpreferred candidate's commercials.

How do voters evaluate political ads? There are indications that the selective perception principle operates, as partisans misperceive content according to their predispositions (Patterson and McClure, 1976). Voters who are favorably disposed tend to project their own beliefs into the statements made by candidates they admire by reading in favorable information and distorting inconsistent content; they are much more critical in interpreting ads for nonpreferred candidates (Donohue, 1973; Donohue a..d Meyer, 1973).

According to Patterson and McClure (1976), voters react to message content rather than style in evaluating political commercials. A study of TV versus radio ads by Cohen (1976) found that voters' evaluation of some candidates' performance was higher for televised messages, while other candidates were rated higher on radio. Finally, candidate ads employing a strategy of attacking the opponent are evaluated favorably by many voters, particularly those from lower socioeconomic backgrounds (Surlin and Gordon, 1977).

Research analyzing actual effects can be divided along cognitive and affective domains. In measuring cognitive impact on knowledge and beliefs, investigators have used both self-report and correlational techniques. In two gubernatorial surveys by Atkin et al. (1973), two-thirds of the voters reported that they learned something about candidate qualifications for office; one-half said they gained understanding about candidate positions on issues. Less learning occurs on the personality dimension, as two-fifths said they became better acquainted with each candidate as a person. In a survey by O'Keefe and Sheinkopf (1974), one-fourth of the voters reported that they learned "a lot" about Nixon and McGovern from their 1972 campaign TV ads. Kaid (1976) asked voters in a state legislature campaign how they became aware of each candidate's major issue theme; two-fifths said they learned from ads in the local newspaper rather than from news stories or interpersonal sources.

Among the correlational studies, McClure and Patterson (1974) compared voters who were heavy versus light viewers of television during the Nixon-McGovern campaign. They found that heavily exposed voters became more informed about candidate stands on issues. Across several advertised issues such as military spending, an average of 36 percent of the heavy viewers versus 25 percent of light viewers gained a more accurate belief about candidate positions during the course of the campaign. Ads were especially helpful to the less interested voters and those who seldom read newspaper news about the candidates. Atkin and Heald (1976) discovered a correlation of +.42 between exposure to broadcast ads and awareness of congressional candidate names and issue positions; advertising exposure was a stronger predictor than news exposure and interpersonal communication.

Another cognitive variable is the agenda salience of campaign issues and candidate traits. Atkin and Heald (1976) found a +.18 association between broadcast advertising exposure and the importance attached to points stressed in ads. For example, open-ended responses to a question about the most important issue showed that 23 percent of the highly exposed voters mentioned balancing the federal budget compared with 15 percent of the less exposed. Kaid (1976) content analyzed the issue agenda in newspaper ads and measured voter perceptions of the more emphasized issues; the rank-order of each listing showed close correspondence. In another content analysis of newspaper advertising in statewide campaigns, the top nine issues featured most prominently were the same nine problems felt to be most important to voters (Bowers, 1973). Of course, the corresponding priorities of candidate ads and voter perceptions in the latter pair of studies may be partially attributed to candidate sensitivity to prevailing public concerns rather than to an agenda-setting effect. Behavioral research on affective impact has focused on the role of message repetition. In laboratory experiments using mock races for state legislature and president, preferences increased monotonically as frequency of exposure was raised from zero to six advertising messages (Rothschild and Ray, 1974). In another experimental study, subjects were exposed to brief name-oriented radio ads either two, five, or ten times (Becker and Doolittle, 1975). Affective evaluations were highest in the moderate exposure condition; satiation may have set in by the tenth repetition.

Field surveys show modest evidence of impact on preferences. Small positive correlations between exposure frequency and affect toward advertised candidates was found for radio and newspaper ads in a legislative campaign (Kaid, 1976) and for radio and TV ads in a congressional campaign (Atkin and Heald, 1976).

Self-report data were obtained during two gubernatorial campaigns examined by Atkin et al. (1973). Among early deciders, one-third felt that ads for their preferred candidates "strengthened your intention to vote for him"; just one-tenth said that the nonpreferred candidate's commercials increased their preference for him, while one-fourth reported a boomerang effect as ads stiffened their opposition to him. Among the minority who made up their minds during the advertising campaign period, three-fifths indicated that their chosen candidate's commercials "helped you in making your decision to vote for him." Half of these late-deciders also reported that the unchosen candidate's ads contributed to their decision to reject him. Thus, many voters appear to be influenced by ads, although not necessarily in a manner intended by the candidates.

A final set of evidence comes from three aggregate analyses of advertising spending and electoral success. Examining congressional races in 1970, Dawson and Zinser (1971) found that the percentage of the vote is significantly predicted by the share of broadcast expenditures when other factors are controlled. Even stronger findings were reported for primary election campaigns (Wanat, 1974). Prisuta (1972) analyzed state legislature campaigns, and discovered that the candidate who spent the most on broadcast ads won 60 percent of the time. Of course, these associations may be somewhat spurious, since the stronger candidate tends to have more money available for advertising.

Although a number of advertising studies are now available, much of the research lacks theoretical grounding, external validity, or causal precision. Despite these shortcomings, there are indications that ads have a strong cognitive impact and that substantial attitude creation and change can be traced to ads. Since voters differ in values and ideological orientations, some of the affective response runs counter to the goals of the persuader. Thus, the absolute attitudinal movement is much more widespread than the net change across the overall electorate.

NEWSPAPER EDITORIAL ENDORSEMENTS

Most major daily newspapers editorially recommend candidates during the final week or two of the campaign. Typically, the newspaper identifies the chosen candidate in a prominent headline on the editorial page, provides a rationale for the choice, and then repeats the recommendation in a summary box on later occasions. Thus, the persuasive message takes the form of a classic logical argument with an explicit conclusion, with the basic theme readily accessible to the casual reader. These endorsements are usually confined to newspapers, as broadcast stations and new magazines have traditionally hesitated to appear partisan.

At the presidential level, a large majority of the dailies endorse the Republican candidate; even Barry Goldwater attained the support of two-thirds of the papers in 1964 (Emery, 1964; Robinson, 1974; Stemel, 1969). This conservative bias is generally traced to the tendency for publishers (who are characteristically Republican in outlook) to exercise control over endorsements in highly significant campaigns. For less crucial races, the more liberal editorial staff has freer rein over routine recommendations.

How do voters use this persuasive message? The most likely situation is when undecided or vacillating voters feel a need for authoritative guidance in arriving at a final decision. They desire to obtain a clear, concise, direct bit of advice from a trusted source, their favorite newspaper. Since many of these voters are not interested in receiving added factual material or detailed rationale, a simple instruction telling how to vote is sufficient to cut through the confusion. Thus, the headline and subsequent reinstatement of the bottom-line recommendation is the most crucial aspect of the overall endorsement message.

There are three basic conditions that may produce the situational uncertainty that generates reliance on newspaper endorsements to resolve decisional conflict. First, uncertainty may result from low definition election contests where informational and persuasive messages are minimal and partisan guideposts are obscure. Many newspapers are very thorough in making endorsements for minor offices (such as district court judgeships or county commissioners) and in primary or nonpartisan elections. In this type of situation, the editorial advice may be the only input available, or may be the most simple decisional input for voters seeking an efficient method of choosing among candidates.

Second, low involvement situations where the voter does not particularly care about certain races also breed uncertainty. Rather than exerting the effort to process and weigh news and advertising messages, the uninvolved voter may merely refer to the editorial advice as an efficient and helpful guide to decision-making.

Third, uncertainty is generated by a combination of high involvement and inability to discriminate between competing candidates. In contests that the voter feels are important, the net impact of all influences may produce fairly equivalent levels of affect toward each candidate. This may occur toward the end of a campaign when conflicting cross-pressures are felt from interpersonal sources, or when mediated stimuli about each candidate are equally impressive (or unimpressive). In such situations, a clear preference cannot be achieved and the voter relies on the endorsement to "break the tie." The persuasiveness of the rationale provided in the body of the editorial statement may be more significant for this type of voter.

A qualitatively distinct context for using editorial guidance occurs when the highly involved voter actively seeks out the endorsement message as a major input that is weighed along with other decisional influences. Rather than relying on the endorsement only to tip the balance in uncertain situations, the voter systematically incorporates the recommendation as one of the favorable or unfavorable attributes attached to the candidates.

Given a need for decisional advice, the primary factor that determines endorsement utilization is the credibility of the newspaper. Surveys indicate that readers typically ascribe moderate to high trust in their newspaper, probably because of shared sociopolitical perspectives. For instance, Vinyard and Sigel (1971) reported that two-fifths of Detroit voters sampled had "complete confidence" in their local paper's editorial recommendations, and another one-third had "some confidence."

The empirical evidence on persuasive impact of editorials is based on a variety of methodological techniques. Most of the investigations have examined low definition elections, although one key series of studies focuses on presidential campaigns.

Robinson (1972, 1974) performed secondary analyses on national sample findings from each presidential election between 1956 and 1972. He related candidate choice to the editorial stance of each voter's local newspaper. Averaging across the five elections, 55 percent of those reading a newspaper endorsing the Democratic candidate voted for the Democrat, compared with a 37 percent Democratic vote among readers of Republican newspapers. If the paper endorsed neither candidate, the rate of Democratic support was 44 percent.

Since these raw differences may be accounted for by a number of demographic, social, and political factors, Robinson performed multivariate analyses to control for spurious influences. After adjustments for 12 predictor variables such as party identification, political interest, education, opinion leadership, and preelection vote intention, the strength of the endorsement-preference relationship declined substantially. For example, the 25 percent raw difference between readers of Republican and Democratic papers in 1972 was adjusted to 7 percent. There was an adjusted 6 percent edge for the endorsed candidate in the Nixon-Humphrey campaign of 1968. Robinson also sought to identify which subgroups of voters were apparently influenced the most. In close elections of 1960 and 1968, the independents showed the largest differences according to newspaper readership. Both independents and identifiers of the losing party showed large differences in the landslide years of 1956, 1964, and 1972.

In a pair of studies with young voters attending a Michigan university, Atkin et al. (1974) found differential impact for high versus low definition campaign situations. In a relatively trivial nonpartisan city council election, the editorial endorsement of the campus newspaper had considerable impact, according to both self-report and correlational findings. Students exposed to the editorial were significantly more likely to vote for the endorsed candidates, and most felt that the recommendation had an influence over their decision. Since few voters followed campaign news and most had no opinion until the closing days of the campaign, this was clearly a high-uncertainty election requiring guidance from the trusted newspaper.

By contrast, Atkin et al.'s examination of the presidential primary election the following year showed no impact. Student preferences among the prominent candidates were well formed by the time the endorsement appeared. A quasi-field experiment was designed to test impact by interviewing a randomly assigned half of the sample the day before the endorsement, and the other half the day of the endorsement (to the extent that no other events occur during the Time 1-Time 2 period, then any significant differences between the subsamples should be attributable to the intervening message). No difference was obtained between those interviewed before and after the recommendation stimulus.

McCombs (1967) assessed the relationship between voting preference and endorsement exposure across several levels of California offices on the same ballot. He concluded that a substantial minority of the voters were influenced, especially for the more obscure contests where few other inputs were available to voters.

The rest of the investigations have focused on low definition elections, mostly at the local level. Two aggregate analysis studies measured the association between local newspaper endorsement patterns and electoral outcomes in a variety of elections in California (Gregg, 1965) and Texas (McCleghan, 1973). More than 70 percent of the recommended candidates were elected. Four researchers examined the role of endorsements in long ballot situations where voters faced great uncertainty due to unfamiliarity with numerous candidates who were running for office. McDowell (1965) and Hooper (1969) analyzed aggregate data from the Illinois at-large election for state legislature; voters had to choose from more than 100 candidates. Those who were endorsed by the Chicago newspapers were far more successful than unendorsed candidates, especially in areas served by the newspaper. Mueller (1970) reported similar results in another long-ballot situation. Finally, a survey by Hain (1975) compared the level of support for one of 33 mayoral candidates before and after he received editorial support from the local newspapers. Voter preferences improved substantially after the endorsement appeared, and a minority of voters reported that the message influenced their vote.

A final set of evidence comes from three surveys that describe voters' responses to hypothetical election decisions, rather than actual influence. Vinyard and Sigel (1971) asked Detroit voters how much they depended on the newspapers in deciding how to vote in city council and presidential elections; more than half indicated heavy reliance. Almost half of the Oregon voters sampled by Rarick (1970) responded affirmatively to similar questions about local offices. A much smaller proportion of Ohio voters said that their local paper's endorsements were a major determinant of their vote preferences (Blume and Lyons, 1968).

Although almost all of these studies indicate that editorial endorsements are persuasive, there are a number of alternative explanations that limit inferences of causality. Correlations between endorsement exposure and vote preference may be due to either reverse causality or spurious association produced by other contaminating variables. The reverse causal sequence occurs when voters who already prefer a candidate choose to selectively expose themselves to the editorial message. Since selective exposure is well demonstrated in political communication (Atkin, 1973), this explanation cannot be discounted. De facto selective exposure may contribute to spurious relationships (Sears and Freedman, 1967). For instance, Republican voters tend to have higher education levels than Democrats, and persons with high education tend to read newspapers and editorials more than the less educated. Since most newspapers endorse Republican candidates for major offices, the correlation between candidate preference and endorsement exposure is likely to be positive—not so much because Republican voters are seeking reinforcement, but because the third variable of education is related to both preference and exposure. Robinson's (1974) efforts to control statistically for such contaminating variables resulted in a sharp drop in the relationship between newspaper reading and candidate choice.

Even when voter characteristics are controlled, the correlation between endorsement exposure and preference cannot necessarily be attributed to the editorial itself. Instead, the partisan bias in presentation of news content in the newspaper may account for the apparent affect. Numerous content analyses have shown that newspapers which endorse a candidate tend to give that candidate relatively more news space and more prominent placement of stories (Stempel, 1969; Lee, 1972; McClenghan, 1973; Repass and Chaffee, 1968; Klein and Maccoby, 1954). Thus, editorial readers will also see more news coverage of the endorsed candidates; the contribution of this informational content must be separated from the influence of the endorsement before causal inferences can be drawn. Not even the multivariate Robinson analyses considered this factor.

Finally, researchers who related newspapers' endorsements to election voting statistics must be wary of several threats to validity of causal inferences. The fact that endorsed candidates tend to win may be due to the newspaper reflecting (rather than leading) community opinion; the editorial board may not want to offend readers by supporting an unpopular candidate. Another explanation for the electoral success of endorsed candidates is the likelihood that a strong candidate will independently impress both the voters and the editorial writers; this may be the case when one candidate is clearly superior to an opponent, or when a powerful incumbent is running for reelection.

Despite these challenges to definitive causal inference from each type of endorsement study, the array of evidence based on diverse methodological approaches still suggests that significant persuasive influence occurs. The impact appears to be particularly important in low definition election situations; even in highly defined presidential contests, surprisingly strong effects have been detected. A unique feature of this influence is that it originates with mass media institutions. Unlike media transmission of advertising and debates, which merely serves to extend the candidate's reach into the electorate, contribution of endorsements is beyond the control of the candidate.

PRESIDENTIAL DEBATES

Campaign debating originated long before the advent of broadcasting, yet only in recent elections have the masses had access to debaters via television. TV has carried debates for all levels of office, but most attract very little attention or interest. When candidates for Congress or mayor debate on TV, the most likely viewers are those faithful supporters of each contestant who are seldom open to influence. Thus, debates below the presidential level tend to be inconsequential, and few researchers have conducted investigations.

While candidates for some lower offices routinely debate each campaign, the major candidates for president have met just twice: Kennedy versus Nixon in 1960, and Carter versus Ford in 1976. Although rare, these two series of "Great Debates" attracted great public attention and generated an extensive body of research.

What outcomes should be expected from the presidential debate broadcasts? Clearly, these are high definition elections that stimulate high involvement among most voters. Numerous other sources of political messages are available; indeed, voters in nondebate years readily arrive at their presidential choice without benefit of a debate confrontation. Nevertheless, Great Debates have played an important role for voters in both 1960 and 1976.

The uses and gratifications paradigm seems well suited for interpreting the influence of the Great Debates. Disparate subgroups of voters approach the broadcasts with diverse motives: waverers are looking for decisional guidance while partisans seek reinforcement; some watch out of a sense of citizen duty, while others want to experience the excitement of the confrontation. Therefore, voter response to the debates may be partially dependent on prior motivations. According to Sears and Chaffee (1979), voters interviewed before the 1976 debates expressed high hopes for learning each candidate's issue stands, comparing them as personalities and using the events as a basis for making up their minds. Although fewer voters would admit it, the desire to root for one's favorite candidate and to find weaknesses in the opponent was also a major factor.

The multiattribute model also has implications for the way voters are influenced by debates, although the impact may be weaker than for political advertising. The debaters can project appealing images, but only on the narrow range of personality dimensions that can be conveyed in the debate setting. They can attempt to present issue positions, but the steady stream of subtle arguments, complex details, and dry facts does not allow as much basic learning as the repetitive hammering of clever yet simple ads. Thus, the belief formation component of the expectancy-value model may not show major change, restricting the degree of subsequent alterations in preference. On the other hand, the direct contrasts in candidate images and positions afforded by the head-to-head feature of the debate may aid in discrimination on key attributes for which other sources provide no comparative information.

There is considerable evidence concerning both sets of debates. Rather than cite the numerous individual studies, much of this review will discuss the integrative conclusions drawn by Katz and Feldman (1962) and Sears and Chaffee (1979).

Exposure to the broadcasts was widespread, but degree of attention was rather modest. In both years, about two-thirds of all voters viewed each separate debate, with almost 90 percent watching at one time or another. Attention was intermittent, as only one-fourth of the voters sat through the entire length of the typical broadcast and only two-fifths saw parts of all three presidential debates in 1976. It should be noted that the debates were carried simultaneously on the three major networks, so alternative programming options were minimal.   Voters' perceptions of the 1960 debates were biased in the direction of their predispositions. Democrats or Kennedy-supporters were far more likely to feel that their man had won the debates, while Republicans declared Nixon the winner. For example, the Gallup Poll found that 71 percent of the pro-Kennedy voters said Kennedy did a "better job" in the initial debate, while only 3 percent rated Nixon better. Similarly, individuals tended to remember those statements of their favorite candidate with which they agreed and to recall disagreeable points made by the opposing candidate (Sebald, 1962). Supporters were also more likely to see their candidate as better informed and more sincere than the opponent.

The 1976 research also showed that political predispositions strongly shaped the judgement of which candidate won. Less than one-third of the partisans would admit that the other candidate was the winner on a particular debate, even when expert observers thought otherwise.

The evidence on cognitive effects shows some gains. According to objective and self-report data in 1960, considerable learning of candidate positions occurred (Katz and Feldman, 1962). For instance, almost half of the voters in one sample said they learned "a great deal . . . about the candidates and what they stand for." In 1976, the debates produced clarification of positions on such issues as employment policies, government reorganization, defense spending, and draft-evader amnesty. One survey found a correlation of +.44 between number of debates viewed and knowledge of issue stands (Bishop et al., 1978). According to Sears and Chaffee (1979), "It seems safe to conclude that there was substantial political learning as a consequence of holding the debates." Thus, the voters obtained a clearer picture of the differences between candidates, which should enable more accurate application of their values in evaluating each man.

On the other hand, the research indicates very little change in the agenda priorities due to the 1976 debates. Debater emphases on certain issues or traits do not seem to change the weighting voters attach to those dimensions. Agenda-setting concepts were not examined in the 1960 campaign.

In terms of image changes, there are contrasting findings between the two elections. For example, Kennedy's image improved on evaluative characteristics such as experience and strength. The 1976 investigations indicated that few voters changed on individual image scales after seeing the debates.

Summary evaluative ratings, however, did show some movement in both years. The overall image of Kennedy improved far more than Nixon's, especially after the first debate. Kennedy's performance served primarily to rally wavering Democrats by dispelling doubts about his ability. Many voters reported becoming more positive toward Nixon, but the margin of favorable to unfavorable change was narrower in his case. Again, selective processes were in high gear, as more Republicans increased affect toward Nixon than toward Kennedy, and the opposite occurred for Democrats. While few voters altered their perceptions of specific traits or issue proximities in 1976, overall evaluations of Ford did become more positive after both the first and second debate, and Carter's rating gained slightly after the second broadcast.

The changes in actual preference between the candidates suggest that crystallization was the primary outcome. In both campaigns, the first debate helped voters become more confident that their initial leanings were toward the right man. Conversion from one candidate to the other was negligible. Studies in both years show that amount of exposure was associated with change rather than stability of prior preference, indicating that the broadcasts did have some impact. The net effect was to Kennedy's advantage in 1960 (perhaps a jump of three or four percentage points), while neither man had a relative gain in support in 1976. It should be noted that few voters reported that the debates directly influenced their voting intentions. A 1960 poll found that 6 percent felt that the debates "made them decide" who they would vote for. In 1976, 3 percent said they had changed their votes because of the debates.

In conclusion, the impact of the debates is subtle and complex. Although it is difficult to trace the degree of influence on voting preferences, dramatic change does not appear to occur. Affective response is clearly colored by selective perception processes, but evidence on image change is not definitive. Despite the detailed and lengthy issue expositions by debaters, voters seem to extract only vague impressions and learn little factual information from viewing. Thus, the popular conception that Great Debates play a pivotal role in campaigns may be somewhat overstated.

DIRECTIONS FOR FUTURE RESEARCH

Despite the sizable number of recent research studies on the persuasive effects of political media content, the field remains at a primitive stage of development. Few investigations have been guided by explicit theoretical paradigms; research in this area seldom rises much above raw empiricism. Thus, future researchers should give more attention to theory in devising campaign studies. Several approaches appear to be promising.

(1) Expectancy-value models should be applied to the study of campaign persuasion. The work of McClure and Patterson (1974) provides an elemental example of this approach. More elaborate equations that include a wide array of values, cognitions, and salience weightings can be developed to provide a sophisticated assessment of mass media impact. Investigators must first identify the relevant attributes that voters are using to evaluate candidates in order to assess the role played by mediated messages.

(2) Agenda-setting concepts should be utilized in studies of persuasive as well as informational learning processes. In particular, advertising that emphasizes certain attributes may enhance the salience of those criteria to the candidate's advantage. When incorporated in a multiattribute model, the reweighted attributes may produce changes in preference without requiring value or belief change.

(3) The uses and gratifications perspective should be explored in greater detail. This approach can provide a more precise examination of the determinants of exposure to persuasive messages, which is a critical prerequisite for responses to the stimuli. In addition, work is needed to find out if receiver motives serve as intervening variables in shaping the outcomes of exposure to persuasion.

(4) Conventional learning and consistency theories from the persuasion literature should be applied to political campaign messages, to determine the optimum strategies for selecting and structuring message appeals presented in the mass media. Very little attention has been given to the impact of content variables in ads or editorials.

(5) The contextual framework outlined in this chapter (definition, involvement, and decisional stage) should be considered when identifying which processes are operating in a given campaign situation.

(6) The response variables selected for study should be drawn from the more subtle corners of the cognitive domain as well as the more obvious affective reactions. In addition, the diverse nature of indirect influences on attitudes deserves close attention, since the same content may produce contrasting changes in affect depending on the values of different voters in the audience. Finally, researchers should go beyond preference effects to analyze overt voting behavior, since the real payoff of campaign persuasion requires turnout on election day.

Substantively, certain types of campaign messages deserve closer attention because of greater significance or lack of previous research. Political advertising on TV should continue to recieve top priority, and both newspaper and radio ads should be accorded a more central emphasis. Broadcast speech-making has attracted surprisingly little research; despite the limited audiences, these appearances may be quite influential at the presidential level. The persuasive impact of televised national conventions every four years also remains understudied. On the other hand, debates and other "critical events" such as the Watergate hearings are so rare and idiosyncratic that research conclusions have highly restricted applicability. Since intensive analyses of such events contribute little to the development of general political communication theory, fewer resources should be expended on them in the future.

While studying these mediated messages, researchers should also take into account the interpersonal influences operating during campaigns. The social context of the voter affects interpretation of media content, and the potency of mass communication effects depends on the relative magnitude of inputs from interpersonal sources. Furthermore, interpersonal channels may be important in extending or modifying mass media influences through multistep flows and opinion leadership.

Methodologically, field surveys appear to be most appropriate because situational factors are so crucial in political orientations. The panel method introduced by Lazarsfeld et al. (1948) should be revived; multiwave interviewing allows the researcher to trace the evolution of preferences and provides a sounder basis for causal analysis. For message strategy research, field experimentation can be useful; however, most types of campaign messages must be studied as they naturally occur. Laboratory experimentation appears to be distinctly unpromising because the artificial context is so different from actual campaign conditions; recent studies using this method have lacked external validity.

In conclusion, there are ample opportunities for researchers to make significant new contributions to the literature on mass communication and persuasion in election campaigns. In particular, theory-based investigations are needed to obtain a more sophisticated assessment of the role of mediated messages in voter decision-making in a variety of electoral contexts. It is hoped that the revival of research in this field will provide a basis for definitive conclusions in the near future.

NOTES

1. For reviews and research dealing with the impact of newspaper and television news, see Berelson et al. (1954), Blumler and McQuail (1969), Lazarsfeld et al. (1948), McCombs (1972), Mendelsohn and O'Keefe (1976), Nimmo (1970), Patterson and McClure (1976), Shaw and McCombs (1977), and Weiss (1969).

2. These classic studies have been critiqued by Katz (1971), Blumler (1959), Pool (1959), Swanson (1972), and Kraus and Davis (1976). A major point is that the Columbia studies really did not deal with media effects; the research was more concerned with sociological predictors of voting.

3. For reviews of the reliance of candidates on TV advertising, see Atkin et al. (1973), MacNeil (1968), Patterson and McClure (1976), and Dawson and Zinser (1971).

REFERENCES

ATKIN, C. (1973). "Instrumental utilities and information-seeking." In P. Clarke (ed.), New models for communication research. Beverly Hills, CA: Sage.

––– and HEALD, G. (1976). "Effects of political advertising." Public Opinion Quarterly, 40:216-228.

ATKIN, C., CROUCH, W., and TROLDAHL, V. (1974). "The role of the campus newspaper in the youth vote." College Press Review, 13:6-10.

ATKIN, C., BOWEN, L., NAYMAN, O., and SHEINKOPF, K. (1973). "Quality versus quantity in televised political ads." Public Opinion Quarterly, 37:209-224.

BECKER, L., and DOOLITTLE, J. (1975). "How repetition affects evaluations and information seeking about candidates." Journalism Quarterly, 52:611-617.

BERELSON, B., LAZARSFELD, P., and McPHEE, W. (1954). Voting: A study of opinion formation in a presidential campaign. Chicago: University of Chicago Press.

BISHOP, G., OLDENDICK, R., and TUCHFARBER, A. (1978). "Debate watching and the acquisiton of political knowledge." Journal of Communication, 28:4:99-113.

BLUME, N., and LYONS, S. (1968). "The monopoly newspaper in a local election: The Toledo Blade." Journalism Quarterly, 45:286-292.

BLUMER, H. (1959). "Suggestions for the study of mass media effects." In E. Burdick and A. Brodbeck (eds.), American voting behavior. New York: Free Press.

––– and McQUAIL, D. (1969). Television in politics: Its uses and gratifications. London: Faber and Faber.

BOWERS, T. (1972). "Issue and personality information in newspaper political advertising." Journalism Quarterly, 49:445-452.

––– (1973). "Newspaper political advertising and the agenda-setting function." Journalism Quarterly, 50:552-556.

CAMPBELL, A., CONVERSE, P., MILLER, W., and STOKES, D. (1960). The American voter. New York: John Wiley.

––– (1966). Elections and the political order. New York: John Wiley.

COHEN, A. (1976). "Radio vs. TV: The effect of the medium." Journal of Communication, 26:29-35.

DAWSON, P.A., and ZINSER, J.E. (1971). "Broadcast expenditures and electoral outcomes in the 1970 congressional elections." Public Opinion Quarterly, 35:398-402.

DONOHUE, T. (1973). "Impact of viewer predispositions on political TV commercials." Journal of Broadcasting, 18:3-15.

––– and MEYER, T. (1973). "Perceptions and misperceptions of political advertising." Journal of Business Communication, 10:29-40.

EMERY, E. (1964). "Press support for Johnson and Goldwater." Journalism Quarterly, 41:485-488.

FISHBEIN, M., and AZJEN, I. (1975). Belief, attitude, intention and behavior: An introduction to theory and research. Reading, MA: Addison-Wesley.

GREGG, J. (1965). "Newspaper editorial endorsements and California elections, 1948-1962." Journalism Quarterly, 42:532-538.

HAIN, P. (1975). "How an endorsement affected a non-artisan mayoral vote." Journalism Quarterly, 52:337-340.

HOOPER, M. (1969). "Party and newspaper endorsement as predictors of voter choice." Journalism Quarterly, 46:302-305.

KAID, L. (1976). "Measures of political advertising." Journal of Advertising Research, 16:49-53.

–––, and FELDMAN, J. (1962). "The debates in the light of research: A survey paigns." Journalism Quarterly, 48:304-314.

KATZ, E., and FELDMAN, J. (1962). "The debates in the light of research: A survey of surveys." In S. Kraus (ed.), The great debates. Bloomington: Indiana University Press.

KLAPPER, J. (1960). The effects of mass communication. New York: Free Press.

KLEIN, M., and MACCOBY, N. (1954). "Newspaper objectivity in the 1952 campaign." Journalism Quarterly, 31:285-296.

KRAUS, S., and DAVIS, D. (1976). The effects of mass communication on political behavior. University Park: Pennsylvania State University Press.

KRUGMAN, H. (1965). "The impact of television advertising: Learning without involvement." Public Opinion Quarterly, 29:349-356.

LAZARSFELD, P., BERELSON, B., and GAUDET, H. (1948). The people's choice. New York: Duell, Sloan and Pearce.

LEE, J. (1972). "Editorial support and campaign news: Content analysis by Q-methodology." Journalism Quarterly, 49:710-716.

MASON, G. (1973). "The impact of endorsements on voting." Sociological Methods and Research, 1:463-495.

McCLENGHAN, J. (1973). "Effect of endorsements in Texas local elections." Journalism Quarterly, 50:363-366.

McCLURE, R., and PATTERSON, T. (1974). "Television news and political advertising." Communication Research, 1:3-31.

McCOMBS, M. (1967). "Editorial endorsements: A study of influence." Journalism Quarterly, 44:545-548.

——— (1972). "Mass communication in political campaigns: Information, gratification, and persuasion." In F.G. Kline and P. Tichenor (eds.), Current perspectives in mass communication research. Beverly Hills, CA: Sage.

——— and SHAW, D. (1972). "The agenda-setting function of the media." Public Opinion Quarterly, 36:176-187.

McDOWELL, J. (1965). "The role of newspapers in Illinois' at-large election." Journalism Quarterly, 42:281-294.

McGUIRE, W. (1969). "The nature of attitudes and attitude change." In G. Lindzey and E. Aronson (eds.), Handbook of social psychology. Reading, MA: Addison-Wesley.

MacNEIL, R. (1968). The people machine. New York: Harper & Row.

MENDELSOHN, H., and O'KEEFE, G. (1976). The people choose a president: Influences on voter decision making." New York: Praeger.

MUELLER, J. (1970). "Choosing among 133 candidates." Public Opinion Quarterly, 34:395-402.

MULLEN, J. (1968). "Newspaper advertising in the Johnson-Goldwater campaign." Journalism Quarterly, 45:219-225.

NIMMO, D. (1970). The political persuaders. Englewood Cliffs, NJ: Prentice-Hall.

——— (1977) "Political communication theory and research: An overview." In B. Ruben (ed.), Communication yearbook 1. New Brunswick, NJ: Transaction Books.

——— (1978). Political communication and public opinion in America. Santa Monica, CA: Goodyear.

O'KEEFE, M.T., and SHEINKOPF, K. (1974). "The voter decides: Candidate image or campaign issue?" Journal of Broadcasting, 18:403-412.

PATTERSON, T., and McCLURE, R. (1976). The unseeing eye. New York: Putnam.

POOL, I. (1959). "TV: A new dimension in politics." In E. Burdick and A. Brodbeck (eds.), American voting behavior. New York: Free Press.

PRISUTA, R. (1972). "Broadcast advertising by candidates for the Michigan legislature." Journal of Broadcasting, 16:453-459.

RARICK, G. (1970). "Political persuasion: The newspaper and the sexes." Journalism Quarterly, 47:360-364.

REPASS, D., and CHAFFEE, S. (1968). "Administrative vs. campaign coverage of two presidents in eight partisan dailies." Journalism Quarterly, 45:528-531.

ROBINSON, J. (1972). "Perceived media bias and the 1968 vote: Can the media affect behavior after all?" Journalism Quarterly, 45:239-246.

——— (1974). "The press as king-maker: What surveys from last five campaigns show." Journalism Quarterly, 51:587-594.

ROTHSCHILD, M., and RAY, M. (1974). "Involvement and political advertising effect." Communication Research, 1:264-285.

SEARS, D. (1969). "Political behavior." In G. Lindzey and E. Aronson (eds.), Handbook of social psychology. Reading, MA: Addison-Wesley.

——— and CHAFFEE, S. (1979). "Uses and effects of the 1976 debates: An overview of empirical studies." In S. Kraus (ed.), The great debates 1976: Ford vs. Carter, Bloomington: Indiana University Press.

SEARS, D., and FREEDMAN, J. (1967). "Selective exposure to information: A critical review." Public Opinion Quarterly, 31:194-213.

SEARS, D., and WHITNEY, R. (1973). "Political persuasion." In I. Pool (ed.), Handbook of communication. Chicago: Rand-McNally.

SEBALD, H. (1962). "Recall of debate content." In S. Kraus (ed.), The great debates. Bloomington: Indiana University Press.

SHAW, D., and McCOMBS, M. (1977). The emergence of American political issues: The agenda-setting function of the press. St. Paul, MN: West Publishing.

STEMPEL, G. (1969). "The prestige press meets the third party challenge." Journalism Quarterly, 46:699-706.

SWANSON, D. (1972). "The new politics meets the old rhetoric: New directions in campaign communication research." Quarterly Journal of Speech, 58:30-40.

SURLIN, S., and GORDON, T. (1977). "How values affect attitudes toward direct reference political advertising." Journalism Quarterly, 54:89-98.

VINYARD, D., and SIGEL, R. (1971). "Newspapers and urban voters." Journalism Quarterly, 48:486-493.

WANAT, J. (1974). "Political broadcast advertising and primary election voting." Journal of Broadcasting, 18:413-422.

WEISS, W. (1969). "Effects of the mass media of communication." In G. Lindzey and E. Aronson (eds.), Handbook of social psychology. Reading, MA: Addison-Wesley.

ZAJONC, R. (1968). "The attitudinal effects of mere exposure." Journal of Personality and Social Psychology, 9:1-27.

ABOUT THE CONTRIBUTORS

CHARLES K. ATKIN is Professor of Communication at Michigan State University, where he teaches courses in mass communication effects. He received his Ph.D. from the University of Wisconsin. His research interests include the impact of television on children and voter responses to campaign media.

CHARLES R. BERGER is Professor of Communication Studies and Director of the Communication Research Center at Northwestern University. He received his Ph.D. in communication from Michigan State University. His areas of research interest are the development and disintegration of interpersonal relationships, attribution processes in interpersonal relationships, and interpersonal knowledge processes.

ERWIN P. BETTINGHAUS received his Ph.D. from the University of Illinois. He is presently Professor of Communication and Dean of the College of Communication Arts and Sciences at Michigan State University. His research interests include persuasion and language behavior. Among his publications is *Persuasive Communication* (Holt, Rinehart & Winston, 1973), which is in its second edition.

ROBERT N. BOSTROM is Professor of Communication at the University of Kentucky. He received his Ph.D. from the University of Iowa. His interests are attitude change and theory development in communication.

TIMOTHY C. BROCK received his Ph.D. from Yale University under Carl Hovland. Currently Professor of Psychology at Ohio State University, he has contributed extensively to social psychology journals and books. His research interests include persuasion, corrective advertising, and evaluation.

ROBERT W. BUNDENS is a graduate student in the Department of Communication at Michigan State University. His research interests are in interpersonal processes and communication in the legal system.

MICHAEL BURGOON received his Ph.D. from Michigan State University where he is now Associate Professor of Communication. His major areas of research include language, social influence, and resistance to persuasion.

ROBERT W. CHESTNUT is Assistant Professor of Business at the Graduate School of Business, Columbia University, New York City. His teaching and research activities focus on marketing strategy advertising and consumer decision-making behavior. He holds the M.S. and Ph.D. in social/ consumer psychology and is former National Science Foundation graduate fellow of the Department of Psychological Sciences, Purdue University. His publications include a text on brand loyalty and articles in the *Journal of Marketing Research, Journal of Consumer Research,* and *Advances in Consumer Research.*

GARY CRONKHITE is Professor of Rhetoric at the University of California at Davis. He received his Ph.D. from the University of Iowa, and is interested in attitude change and person perception. His publications include *Persuasion: Speech and Behavioral Change* (Bobbs-Merrill, 1969).

NORMAN E. FONTES received his Ph.D. from the Department of Communication at Michigan State University, and is currently an assistant professor in that department. He has authored and coauthored numerous journal articles and book chapters focusing on communication in the legal setting.

JO R. LISKA is lecturer of Rhetoric at the University of California at Davis. She received her Ph.D. from the University of Colorado. Her interests include attitude change and factors influencing the perception of communication sources.

GERALD R. MILLER, who received his Ph.D. from the University of Iowa, is Professor of Communication at Michigan State University. His major research interests are in the areas of interpersonal communication, persuasion, and communication in legal settings. The author of numerous books and journal articles, he has previously edited a Sage Annual Reviews of Communication Research volume titled *Explorations in Interpersonal Communication,* and has coauthored with Norman Fontes a forthcoming Sage volume titled *Videotape on Trial: A View from the Jury Box.* Dr. Miller is past editor of the journal *Human Communication Research,* and is presently President of the International Communication Association.

RICHARD M. PERLOFF is an Ohio State University postdoctoral fellow in social psychology, journalism and communication. He received his Ph.D. in mass communications from the University of Wisconsin. His research interests include cognitive responses to persuasion and the implication of the self and sex roles for communication behavior.

MICHAEL E. ROLOFF is Assistant Professor of Communication Studies at Northwestern University. He received his Ph.D. in communication from Michigan State University, and has published articles, books, and book chapters concerning interpersonal conflict resolution and compliance-gaining.

PAUL ROSENFELD is a third-year doctoral student in the Social Psychology Program at the State University of New York at Albany. His interest areas include attitude change and aggression.

JAMES T. TEDESCHI is Professor and Director of the Social Psychology Program at the State University of New York at Albany. He received his Ph.D. in Experimental Psychology from the University of Michigan (1960). He has published extensively in professional journals and is the editor of *Perspective on Social Power* (Aldine, 1974) and *The Social Influence Processes* (Aldine, 1972).